D1279049

URBAN LAND USE PLANNING

UNIVERSITY OF ILLINOIS PRESS, Urbana, 1963

URBAN LAND USE PLANNING

BY F. STUART CHAPIN, JR.

Professor of Planning, University of North Carolina

THIS EDITION FIRST PUBLISHED IN 1957
BY HARPER & BROTHERS, NEW YORK

© 1957 by Harper & Brothers. Copyright assigned 1963 to the
Board of Trustees of the University of Illinois. Manufactured in
the United States of America. Library of Congress Catalog Card
No. 57-8061.

contents

tables

figures

foreword

What has come to be known as city planning in contemporary municipal administration has assumed the stature and earned the recognition of being a distinct professional field. No longer is it an offshoot of architecture, engineering, law, public administration, or the other social sciences. It is a union of them all, a new discipline which is both a science and an art. Its roots go back into the earliest known civilizations, as far back as settlements existed as urban entities. The Egyptian pyramid builders planned cities as early as 3000 B.C., long before the time of Hippodamus of ancient Greece, the first known city planner. From these earliest known beginnings down to the twentieth century, city planning existed essentially as civic design. But in the past fifty years, other fields have become concerned with problems of cities—engineering, law, public administration, the social sciences—and emerging from the melting pot is a twentieth century development: the science and art of city planning.

How this union took place in America is a phenomenon of the times. It is an outgrowth of the rise of industrialism and the accompanying urbanization of the North American continent. With the mechanization of agriculture and the phenomenal development of transportation and communications, populations of entire regions have become redistributed with large proportions clustering in the new centers of commerce and industry. Even as these changes have been realized, progress in science and technology has set new forces into motion. While centralization of population continues, but at a slackening rate, countermovements within metropolitan centers have been touched off, notably decentralization movements to the urban fringe. With recent developments in atomic energy and a new emphasis on the dispersal of industry, there are potentially greater, more far-reaching urban changes in prospect.

Such a complex of forces and counterforces produces many problems in cities, problems which become compounded by long neglect and complicated by piecemeal improvisations. So, it is little wonder that the increasing complexity of urban society has created myriads of problems and the need for adjustment and modification in the physical form of the urban environment. Thus there are very deeply rooted bases for the genesis of contemporary emphases toward improved city planning methods, techniques, and controls.

What, then, does contemporary city planning encompass? From the foregoing it is apparent that many and diverse forces are continually reacting upon urban society, creating pressures for growth and renewal in the physical form of the urban environment. City planning may be regarded as a means for systematically anticipating and achieving adjustment in the physical environment of a city consistent with social and economic trends and sound principles of civic design. It involves a continuing process of deriving, organizing, and presenting a broad and comprehensive program for urban development and renewal. It is designed to fulfill local objectives of social, economic, and physical well-being, considering both immediate needs and those of the foreseeable future. It examines the economic basis for an urban center existing in the first place; it investigates its cultural, political, economic, and physical characteristics both as an independent entity and as a component of a whole cluster of urban centers in a given region; and it attempts to design a physical environment which brings these elements into the soundest and most harmonious plan for the development and renewal of the urban area as a whole.*

Land use planning is a part of this larger process of city planning. While taking into account its interrelatedness with transportation and utility planning, land use planning is basically concerned with the location, intensity, and amount of land development required for the various space-using functions of city life—industry, wholesaling, business, housing, recreation, education, and the religious and cultural activities of the people. Fundamentally, the land use plan as a part of an overall plan embodies a proposal as to how land should be used as expansion and how renewal should proceed in the future.

Besides being limited to one element of comprehensive planning, this book treats only limited aspects of the land use planning process. It is primarily focused on theory and methods, with special attention given to the techniques required in making analyses of land use, in measuring trends, and in estimating present and future requirements for the uses of land. In short, in the pages which follow, an attempt is made to bring together in one book the theoretical background for land use planning and to summarize techniques the city planner employs in diagnosing the ills and needs of land

* Adapted from the author's definition of city planning used in "City Planning: Adjusting People to Place," in Rupert B. Vance and Nicholas J. Demerath (eds.), *The Urban South,* University of North Carolina Press, 1954.

development. Those aspects concerned with the legal basis of planning, its legislative controls, and its administrative organization are specifically excluded from detailed treatment.

In so defining the scope of this book, the author is fully cognizant of the difficulty and the temerity of outlining the theoretical basis of land use planning and of setting down techniques in a field which is changing so swiftly from year to year. He is cognizant of the incomplete, and in some respects, tentative character of the theory he attempts to introduce. Moreover, he is fully aware of the imbalance in the degree to which techniques are developed and the imbalance in the relative utility of the different methods described herein. Some will be found to be too crude and others too refined for the purposes for which they are used. Many of the techniques will be found to be too recent in development to have been tested for reliability, accuracy, and general adaptability for any extensive use. These are all inherent difficulties in a field so young and one which is changing so rapidly. Yet the author is firmly convinced that, if nothing more is accomplished, a useful purpose is served simply by bringing this material together where it can be subject to more critical examination and provide a stimulus for research and experimentation so sorely needed.

One further word of interpretation is perhaps warranted. While much of the material here presented applies to most cities, the techniques are slanted primarily toward the small to medium-size urban centers, with metropolitan populations ranging from 100,000 to 500,000.

The material in this book is organized in three parts. Part I brings together theoretical work which has relevance to land use planning. Part II is concerned with "tooling-up" studies which, though basic to all city planning inquiries, are treated with special attention to the needs of land use planning. Finally, Part III covers the land use planning process itself, presenting in sequence techniques for the development of the land use plan.

This introduction would be incomplete without acknowledgement of the encouragement and critical suggestions from a number of colleagues. In this connection, the thoughtful comments on Part I of Professor Louis B. Wetmore, Professor George H. Esser, and Dr. Rupert B. Vance are warmly acknowledged. Grateful note is made of suggestions on early versions of the chapter on the urban economy received from Dr. Walter Isard, Dr. Richard B. Andrews, and Dr. Ralph W. Pfouts. A special note of acknowledgement is due Professor John A. Parker for his encouragement throughout the period this book was in preparation.

F. STUART CHAPIN, JR.

Chapel Hill, N.C.
February, 1957

PART I

land

use

determinants

URBAN LAND USE is a term commonly used to refer to the spatial distribution of city functions—its residential communities or living areas, its industrial, commercial, and retail business districts or major work areas, and its institutional and leisure time functions. The broad geographical pattern of these functional areas, their characteristics, how they developed and how they change, have been the subject of research and writing from a variety of city planning-related fields such as architecture, land economics, geography, human ecology, sociology, and others. Depending upon the interests and background of the writer and the research traditions of his field, some of this work is subjective and speculative, some of it is documentary and descriptive, and some of it is experimental, adhering closely to the maxims of the scientific method.

Perhaps the most systematic attempts at a theoretical explanation of land use arrangements come out of the work of such people as Burgess, Hoyt, McKenzie, Harris and Ullman, and Firey.[1] Yet even within this scientifically oriented segment of the writings on the subject there are some important differentiations in emphasis. For example, in the work of Hoyt there is a predisposition to seek explanations of city structure and its land use configuration primarily in terms of universal economic forces which tend to govern the make-up and change in this configuration. On the other hand, in Firey's work, land use arrangements are interpreted

[1] Ernest W. Burgess, "The Growth of the City," R. E. Park *et al.* (eds.), *The City,* University of Chicago Press, 1925; Homer Hoyt, *The Structure and Growth of Residential Neighborhoods in American Cities,* Federal Housing Administration, 1939; Arthur M. Weimer and Homer Hoyt, *Principles of Real Estate,* The Ronald Press Company, 1954; R. D. McKenzie, *The Metropolitan Community,* McGraw-Hill Book Company, Inc., 1933; Chauncy D. Harris and Edward L. Ullman, "The Nature of Cities," *The Annals of the American Academy of Political and Social Science,* November, 1945; and Walter Firey, *Land Use in Central Boston,* Harvard University Press, 1947.

in terms of values and attitudes held by city residents and the resultant actions in the selection of locations to satisfy these values and attitudes. Both in Burgess' concentric zone concept and in Hoyt's sector theory and to a less extent in the Harris-Ullman extension of McKenzie's multiple nuclei concept, heavy emphasis is placed on economic determinism of land use, with the implication that human value systems and group action are self-regulating and contained by dominant economic forces. In contrast, Firey sees these elements of human behavior as key variables in the make-up and change of urban land use patterns, with spatial use locations determined to an important degree by social values and conscious social action in the city.

As these explanations of land use have developed, each in a theoretical system of its own, city planning, in slowly maturing as a professional field, has been more directly concerned with the applied aspects of land use arrangements. Due perhaps in part to this practical orientation, in part to the great variety of fields it draws upon, and in part to the process of "coming of age," it has had little occasion until recently to engage in fundamental research, particularly of a kind aimed at defining a theoretical frame of reference for urban planning. Such a theoretical framework is urgently needed, and work of the above order in related fields has much to contribute toward accomplishing this objective. While such work has been largely unidisciplinary in orientation with understandable emphasis on the concepts which predominate within these respective fields, obviously city planning as a field cutting across many different disciplines cannot very well overlook this significant work. Indeed, the task of developing a theoretical orientation for ur-

4

ban planning might well begin by linking up available work and by relating concepts from the "pure" disciplines relevant to city planning.

This needed theoretical underpinning will probably emerge not as a product of city planning research per se, but as a collaborative effort of people from all these fields. Such a "team" approach is implied in the very nature of the problem. Thus theoretical research should not search exclusively for "universals," i.e., generalizations built upon observed "trends" or "forces," implied in a theory of urbanism. It must also be oriented toward economic and social behavior of urbanites which produces these trends and forces. In other words, it must also be concerned with a theory of urban behavior.

The chapters of Part I endeavor to summarize some of the conceptual bases of urban land use planning methods and techniques set forth in Parts II and III. As fundamental research begins to supply systematic foundation theory to guide the planning practitioner in land use planning, the concepts presented in these chapters may be altered and will certainly become considerably more refined and less fragmentary in the future. Directed as it is toward the city planning practitioner, this summary aims to bring together only those concepts which have direct present or potential application to the land use planning procedure.

Part I deals with three basic determinants of the urban land use pattern. Chapter 1 is concerned with economic determinants, and Chapter 2 with socially rooted explanations of land use. Chapter 3 takes up the public interest as it becomes a basis for influencing the location and arrangement of land uses in the urban area. The seemingly disproportionate balance in the scope and detail presented in these three *chapters in many ways is a reflection of the relative attention in research and writing accorded these three ways of viewing the urban land use configuration.*

In Chapter 4, an attempt is made to relate these somewhat compartmentalized explanations of land use as a means of assisting the city planner in charting a balanced approach to his land use planning task. In suggesting the interrelationships among all three ways of viewing land use, no attempt is made at this time to knit together these three conceptual approaches into one integrated system of theory on urban land use. This is a task for the future.

economic determinants of land use

The economic explanations of the urban land use pattern begin with forces extending far beyond the immediate environs of any particular urban center of interest, and involve considerations of the structure and functioning of the urban economy as it fits into the larger economy of the region and the nation. Implicit in this way of approaching the economic basis of land use is a rationale that both regional and localized forces interact to shape the urban land use pattern, or more specifically, that external forces affecting the make-up and vitality of the economy act upon internally focused processes of the urban land market to determine the location of urban functions on the land. To an important degree these regional forces influence how much and at what rate land goes into development.

While we acknowledge at the outset the role that these external forces play in determining land use in a given urban center, discussion of regional considerations is postponed until Chapter 5 in which the urban economy in the context of the region is examined in fuller detail. The present chapter will concern itself primarily with the intraurban workings of the land market, maintaining a rough parallelism in approach followed in Chapters 2 and 3. Considered here are first the factors influencing the use of the individual parcel of land, then an examination of the total configuration of land uses in the urban center, and finally a discussion of the application of land economics theory to land use planning.

USE OF THE INDIVIDUAL LAND PARCEL

The land economist views land use in terms of equilibrium theory, with the use of each land parcel determined in what he calls "the urban land market." He looks upon land (real estate in the generic sense) as a commodity traded in this market subject to the forces of supply and demand. According to classical equilibrium theory, price then becomes both a function of the costs of making land productive (in the sense of providing valuable services) and a function of the net income or return realizable by the development of that land. All land is viewed as being in the market competing for the consumer's money, and decisions to buy or sell are prompted by the opportunities for maximizing return from a transaction in the market. It is beyond the scope of this discussion to go into the intricacies of the operation of forces of supply and demand, except to note that in the process of interacting in the market, these forces are viewed as the final determinants of the uses to which urban land is put.

Urban land is considered to have value because of its potential to produce income in the future. This value is based on what developers would be economically justified in paying for it according to an assumed plan for its use and development. As considered in this assumed plan, "the value of land is the sum of all the net land incomes that will accrue in perpetuity discounted for the period of time that will elapse before they are received. Since incomes due one hundred years in the future have only a negligible value today, the valuation of land involves a prophecy as to the net income of the land for the next thirty or forty years."[1]

Economic value of land approaches the selling price under conditions of perfect competition in the market. "It may deviate from price and often does, especially since value is often identified with specific purposes, such as value for mortgage-lending purposes, for tax purposes, for insurance purposes, for estate settlement, for condemnation, for quick sale in a current market, and for many others."[2] Since the developer is seeking the most favorable return, the market value to him or the price he is willing to pay is the net worth that his development would have based on his anticipated profits. "If he assumes that so many dollars must be invested in the buildings and land improvements, then the calculated net worth less this sum will represent what he would be justified in paying for the land. But if he assumes an acquisition cost for the land, then the balance of the net worth after deducting land cost will represent what he would be justified in paying for building and improvements. His decision to proceed with the investment in the enterprise will depend upon the relationship of the hypothetical initial net worth of the proposed land development and the necessary or actual total capital cost of acquiring the land and erecting the buildings."[3]

[1] Homer Hoyt, *One Hundred Years of Land Values in Chicago*, University of Chicago Press, 1933, p. 449.
[2] Arthur M. Weimer and Homer Hoyt, *Principles of Real Estate*, The Ronald Press Company, 1954, p. 28.
[3] Richard U. Ratcliff, *Urban Land Economics*, McGraw-Hill Book Company, Inc., 1949, p. 356.

The market value of land varies, among other things, according to the functional type of area in which it is located in the overall pattern of land uses and with respect to other sites within one particular type of use area. "Each parcel of land occupies a unique physical relationship with every other parcel of land. Because in every community there exists a variety of land uses, each parcel is the focus of a complex but singular set of space relationships with the social and economic activities that are centered on all other parcels. To each combination of space relationships, the market attaches a special evaluation, which largely determines the amount of the bid for that site which is the focus of the combination. Thus certain locations are more highly valued for residential use than other sites because of the greater convenience to shops, schools, centers of employment, and recreational facilities. Corner locations command a higher price for certain types of retail use because of greater convenience to streams of pedestrian traffic."[4]

Thus to the economist, land is pressed into use by the existence of a value as established by the alternatives of land development, and the use of a particular parcel is finally determined in the operations of market forces by the price paid and the decision as to what alternative will yield the highest return.

THE TOTAL LAND USE PATTERN

Once having explained how the use of specific parcels is determined in the market, the land economist then views the total pattern of urban uses in a city as the aggregate of individual decisions of land owners and developers with respect to the development of all such parcels. "Thus the land use structure of the city is fashioned, plot by plot, parcel by parcel as a product of the urban land market. It is the competition of land uses in the market that distributes the use types in an arrangement that approaches the most efficient pattern."[5] The land economist acknowledges that as cities grow and mature, they exhibit similarities in the basic arrangement of their land use patterns, and he ascribes the repetitive natural order in these patterns to economic forces. "If it can be assumed that urbanism is basically an economic phenomenon, it is logical deduction that the internal organization of cities has evolved as a mechanism to facilitate the functioning of

[4] *Ibid.*, pp. 283–284.
[5] *Ibid.*, p. 289.

1. Central Business District
2. Zone of Transition
3. Zone of Workingmen's Homes
4. Zone of Better Residences
5. Commuters' Zone

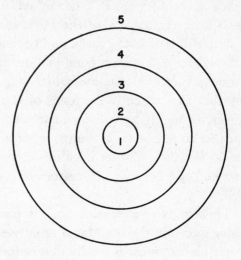

FIGURE 1. Generalized Explanations of the Land Use Patterns of Cities. (*Source:* Chauncy D. Harris and Edward L. Ullman, "The Nature of Cities," *The Annals of the American Academy of Political and Social Science,* November, 1945.)

CONCENTRIC ZONE THEORY

economic activities and that the apparently haphazard arrangement of use areas does have an essential order."[6]

Three different explanations of this order have been advanced: one known as the concentric zone theory, a second referred to as the sector theory, and the third, the multiple nuclei concept (see Figure 1). The first and last descriptions deal with the entire pattern of use areas, whereas the sector system of explanation was developed primarily to explain the structure of residential areas. The zonal and sector theories are used to describe changes in the basic arrangements of land use patterns, whereas the multiple nuclei approach is primarily an observation of the structural form of the urban land use pattern at a particular point in time.

Concentric Zone Theory

Early land economists frequently used Ernest W. Burgess' conventionalized diagram to explain the composite effect of market forces upon

[6] *Ibid.,* p. 368.

1. Central Business District
2. Wholesale Light Manufacturing
3. Low-Class Residential
4. Medium-Class Residential
5. High-Class Residential

6. Heavy Manufacturing
7. Outlying Business District
8. Residential Suburb
9. Industrial Suburb

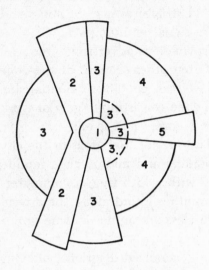

SECTOR THEORY

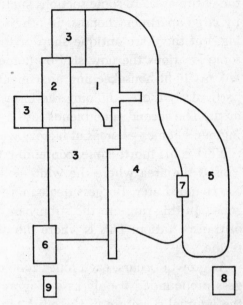

MULTIPLE NUCLEI CONCEPT

land use arrangements.[7] Developed in the early twenties to explain eco-logical processes in the city, Burgess conceived the city as a series of five concentric zones. At the core is his "loop" district with its shopping areas, its theater districts, its hotels, its office buildings, its banking houses, and the other businesses which seek a central location. In small communities these business functions intermingle; in large cities they form more or less distinct subdistricts.

Adjoining the "loop" and fanning out into the next zone are the city's com-mercial functions. Here the market districts and the older wholesale dis-tricts and warehouse areas are located. When the city is situated on the edge of a body of water, its port functions in most cases are interspersed with these functions. Usually industries which do not require much ground area also locate here. Cutting across this and the remaining outer zones along railroad rights of way and forming long wedgelike areas are the larger industrial sections of the city.

His second zone is the area which has been termed "the zone of transi-

[7] Ernest W. Burgess, "The Growth of the City," in R. E. Park *et al.* (eds.), *The City,* University of Chicago Press, 1925.

tion." It is easily identified by the variety and changing character of uses. Here the residential areas commence. In one portion of the zone, there may be an islandlike cluster of "first citizen" homes persisting behind brick walls and iron fences, clinging tenaciously to the respectability that once marked the entire area. In some sections such structures may have been supplanted by large apartment houses. In others the old structures may be still standing, but there are antique shop or tearoom signs signifying a new use. In some locations the now shabby homes display signs advertising "rooms to let" or "light-housekeeping apartments." Often other sections of the zone, particularly those adjoining the industrial wedges, contain residential slum areas. The second zone blends into a third zone consisting largely of workingmen's homes—homes of factory workers, laborers, and so on.

Next is his fourth zone, containing the large residential areas of the city. This is the area where the white-collar workers and middle class families are found. Later, Burgess dealt more fully with a fifth ring, a commuters' zone.[8] In this ring are the suburban communities found along the arteries of transportation. This is where the middle class and upper income groups reside.

As growth occurs, each inner zone of the generalized diagram (and Burgess propounded it only as a diagram to explain observable tendencies in the internal structure of the city) tends to invade the next outer zone following what the human ecologist refers to as a sequence of "invasion-succession" (see Chapter 2). The rate of progression of this rippling tendency depends on economic expansion in the city and rate of population growth. In contrast, when urban areas are decreasing in population, the outer zones tend to remain stationary, but the inner fringe of the transitional zone tends to recede into the commercial district. In this connection the accompanying contraction of the commercial district and a consequent expansion of the transitional area (which in reality is no longer transitional), is frequently interpreted to mean the creation of "permanent" commercial as well as residential slums.

As a theoretical explanation of the positioning of the major functional areas of land use in a city and how they change over the years, the elemental simplicity of this approach has had considerable appeal. While it is a useful and pictorial way of describing broad and general tendencies at work in the patterning of urban land uses, in many respects it is an oversimplification. More recent work relating to the sector and multiple nuclei approaches, as described below, seeks theoretical explanations of

[8] Ernest W. Burgess, "Urban Areas," in T. V. Smith and L. D. White (eds.), *Chicago: An Experiment in Social Science Research,* University of Chicago Press, 1929.

land use patterns which take into account irregularities that tend to develop in use patterns.

Following Burgess' work about a decade later, Homer Hoyt's well-known study of residential areas in the United States provided some new insights into the patterning of land uses and led to a theoretical explanation of residential land uses in terms of wedge-shaped sectors radial to the city's center along established lines of transportation. This theory holds that the different income group classes of a city tend to be found in distinct areas describable in terms of sectors of a circle centered on the central business district. The high-rent or high-price residential areas can be identified in particular sectors, and "there is a gradation of rentals downward from these high rental areas in all directions. Intermediate rental areas, or those ranking next to the highest rental areas, adjoin the high-rent area on one or more sides, and tend to be located in the same sectors as the high rental areas. Low-rent areas occupy other entire sectors of the city from the center to the periphery."[9]

Viewed in the context of change, the theory holds that similar types of use originating near the center of the city tend to migrate within the same sector and away from the center. High-rent areas (and high-price areas) are conceived as having a dominant influence on the direction of residential area growth, and exhibit the following growth characteristics:

1. High-grade residential growth tends to proceed from the given point of origin, along established lines of travel or toward another existing nucleus of buildings or trading centers.
2. The zone of high-rent areas tends to progress toward high ground which is free from the risk of floods and to spread along lake, bay, river, and ocean fronts, where such waterfronts are not used for industry.
3. High-rent residential districts tend to grow toward the section of the city which has free, open country beyond the edges and away from "dead end" sections which are limited by natural or artificial barriers to expansion.
4. The higher-priced residential neighborhood tends to grow toward the homes of the leaders of the community.
5. Trends of movement of office buildings, banks, and stores pull the higher-priced residential neighborhoods in the same general direction.

[9] Homer Hoyt, *The Structure and Growth of Residential Neighborhoods in American Cities*, Federal Housing Administration, 1939, p. 76.

6. High-grade residential areas tend to develop along the fastest existing transportation lines.

7. The growth of high-rent neighborhoods continues in the same direction for a long period of time.

8. De luxe high-rent apartment areas tend to be established near the business center in old residential areas.

9. Real estate promoters may bend the direction of high-grade residential growth.[10]

The operations of these characteristics are observable in the way in which old fashionable close-in boulevard developments have been left for the more recent exclusive outlying subdivisions—a move attributed to the modern automobile. With some exceptions, these moves have been found to occur in the same sectors. The abandoned homes, often too expensive to maintain for succeeding groups of lower income level, become areas of small housekeeping apartments, with a few institutions taking over properties here and there. Parts of these areas may be cleared later to make way for the exclusive high-rent apartment developments.

In the same way that the high-rent or high-price residential areas move radially outward, it is noted that where, "a certain sector develops originally as a low-rent or low-price area, the balance of that sector is likely to be occupied by low-rent or low-price residences as expansion proceeds outward. The same tendency is typical of intermediate-rent or -price sectors."[11]

The sector theory thus provides a more detailed explanation of residential patterns of land use than that set forth in the concentric zone formulation, particularly in the more discriminating way in which it deals with the dynamics of growth processes. It has received criticisms, but these and the stream of commentary that have followed the publication of Hoyt's study clearly indicate the profound effect the sector theory has had in stimulating awareness of the need for a theory of urban land use to which all fields can subscribe.[12]

[10] *Ibid.*, pp. 117–119.
[11] Weimer and Hoyt, *op. cit.*, pp. 335–336.
[12] See Walter Firey, *Land Use in Central Boston*, Harvard University Press, 1947, pp. 41–86. In a critique of the exceptions Firey has taken to the theory that relate largely to what Firey considers to be errors of omission with respect to the determinism of group values and social action in land use, Lloyd Rodwin gives the theory a clean bill of health on these grounds, but goes on to discuss what he considers to be other defects which he summarizes as follows: (a) the ambiguous formulation and use of the sector concept; (b) its oversimplified version of class structure; (c) its distorted dependence on upper class "attractions" as a basis for interpreting shifts in residential location; (d) the inaccuracy of some of the empirical generalizations; (e) its potentially misleading reliance on nineteenth century free market residential trends; and (f) the narrow perspectives resulting from the essential purpose of the inquiry. For this critique, see Lloyd Rodwin, "The Theory of Residential Growth and Structure," *The Appraisal Journal*, July, 1950, pp. 295–317, and for rejoinders by Hoyt and Firey, see *The Appraisal Journal*, October, 1950.

Multiple Nuclei Concept

First suggested by R. D. McKenzie, the multiple nuclei hypothesis is built around the observation that frequently there are a series of nuclei in the patterning of the urban land uses rather than the single central core used in the other two theories.[13] In expanding on this concept in an essay on the nature of cities, Chauncy D. Harris and Edward L. Ullman observed that sometimes these were distinct centers in the origins of the metropolitan area, persisting as centers as growth has filled in the areas between them, and sometimes they have emerged as new centers as urbanization has proceeded.[14]

Harris and Ullman note that the number and the function of each nucleus vary from one metropolitan area to another. The central business district clearly serves as one nucleus. Others may appear in the form of industrial or wholesaling centers where specialized economic activities of similar or complementing character have gravitated together. Still others may emerge in the guise of a major outlying retail center or a university center. Finally, the suburban center and the more distant satellite community for commuters are mentioned as nuclei to be recognized in this conception of the urban land use configuration.

In discussing the multiple nuclei hypothesis, Harris and Ullman identify four factors that tend to account for the emergence of separate nuclei in urban land use patterns. One is the interdependency of certain types of activities and their need for close physical proximity to one another. A second is a natural clustering tendency among certain types of activities which find it mutually profitable to congregate together, as evidenced in retail centers, medical centers to some extent, and outlying office building centers. A third is the converse of the last—the appearance of centers to accommodate activities that may have no particular affinity for one another, but which are inimical to other uses by virtue of the traffic they generate, the extensive railroad or truck-loading facilities they require, and so on. Finally, there is the related factor of high rents or high land costs which have the effect of attracting or repelling uses in the process of nucleation.

As a hypothesis, the multiple nuclei concept appears to recognize many

[13] R. D. McKenzie, *The Metropolitan Community*, McGraw-Hill Book Company, Inc., 1933, pp. 197–198.
[14] Chauncy D. Harris and Edward L. Ullman, "The Nature of Cities," *The Annals of the American Academy of Political and Social Sciences*, November, 1945.

realities of contemporary metropolitan area land use patterns. At
e time, it needs elaboration, and probably modification, on the basis
ical investigations of the kind undertaken by Hoyt before it can
n operationally useful theory of urban land use, and it requires
differentiation between factors explaining the structure and dynamics of change. For example, some nuclei recognized in the concept
probably find their explanation primarily in terms of "natural" market
forces; others in terms of overcoming the "friction of space" made possible
by the automobile, the development of electric power, and other technological advances; and still others in terms of community values and legalistic controls such as zoning. Some may be sluggish, and some may be
volatile in their response to forces of change. Some may affect surrounding
patterns of land use in one way, and some may affect them in quite another
way.

LAND ECONOMICS THEORY AND LAND USE PLANNING

The above theoretical explanations of the patterning of urban land uses
serve a useful purpose in securing a picture of the effects of the economic
forces which the land economist tells us are fundamental in shaping these
patterns. If his view is accepted, and if land use patterns, by whatever
structure theory they are described, are the aggregate result of the interplay of the forces of supply and demand acting on the sum total of all land
parcels in the urban area, then some nexus, some intermediate set of operational generalizations that recognize these forces is needed to serve as
guides in making the transition from economic theory to land use planning
principles. Such generalizations do exist, and consciously or unconsciously,
have been long recognized in land use planning practice. Two of many
are mentioned here: (1) land values operate to determine land use patterns; and (2) land values influence the intensity of land use. As opposed
to assessed values for taxing purposes, "land values" are used here in the
sense of economic value.

As Homer Hoyt's classic study of land values in Chicago indicates, the
relationship between land values and land uses is a two-way street and
involves a complex of factors which function as both cause and effect influences. Thus while the first operational generalization above is taken as
primary in the formulation of land use planning principles, the corollary

premise, that land values at the same time are influenced by land use patterns, is also of interest.

Let us first examine the variations in the spatial pattern of values in the static context:

> If the land values in Chicago were shown in the form of a relief map, in which the elevations represented high land value, a picture of startling contrasts would be disclosed. In the center would be the Himalaya Mountain peaks of the Loop, but on all sides except along a high ridge running north along the lake there would be a descent into the deep valleys of the blighted areas. Gradually, as one went farther from the center, the elevation would begin to rise. Along the lake, both north and south, would be a high ridge which slopes down sharply as ones goes west. Beginning 5 or 6 miles from the center of the city, there would be a plateau several miles wide encircling the city that is uptilted toward the lake, on top of which would be high ridges a mile apart that culminated in towering pinnacles at each intersection.[15]

While such spatial variations in land values have long been recognized and accepted, Hoyt's work provided the first systematic empirical demonstration that these variations and the "topography" of the entire pattern bear a close relationship to the land use configuration of the city. His study confirmed another long-accepted relationship, namely, that as the patterns of values change in time, use patterns change, and conversely, as the patterns of uses change, the patterns of values change in time.

His work indicates that these changes are bound up in the social and economic history of the community, and suggests that the behavior of one in relation to the other involves a complex of factors, the effects of which defy clear-cut differentiation. For example, viewing population shifts as a factor associated with changes in land values, and recognizing the existence of a kind of human "pecking order" among ethnic and racial groups, then it can be said that movements into an area by lower-order groups result in lowered land values (noting, too, that lowered land values in turn may induce further movement of one group out and the other group into the area). But at the same time the lowered values may be traced back to a great variety of other factors, such as the economics of convenience, tax policies in the vacated area, shifting tastes of the vacating group, the disruptive effect of a new superhighway, the intrusion of industry in adjoining areas, and so on. Thus woven into this pattern of land values, there are threads of population change made up of strands related to changes in convenience, taxes, physical deterioration, and other factors, but at the same time there are the other related threads fitting into the fabric, for example, the attitudes and tastes, each with a set of strands made up of

[15] Homer Hoyt, *One Hundred Years of Land Values in Chicago, op. cit.,* p. 297.

the human values behind these attitudes and tastes. To sort out each influence and assess its role in the determination of land values and uses thus becomes extremely elusive. It is difficult enough to view these relationships in the contemporary scene, but in a historical context, they present an even greater problem. The complexity of the back and forth relationships, and the almost unlimited combinations of the way in which factors could interact in the future, make it even more difficult if not impossible to estimate *future* trends in land values.

Intensity of land use is a related consideration that enters into "the equation" and is associated with the pattern of land values. Intensity of land use is measured in various ways. It may be in terms of *density* or population per unit of land area, e.g., persons per acre, families per residential acre of land, peak daytime population per acre of business area, manufacturing workers per acre of industrially used land, and so on. It is sometimes used in terms of *coverage* of the land, e.g., such and such percentage of ground area covered by buildings. Finally, it is sometimes used in terms of *floor area ratios,* i.e., the ratio of total floor area for all stories of the buildings to the area of site. Generally, land use planning is concerned with density measures, with other measures being employed primarily in supplemental detailed studies involved in the later site planning extensions of land use planning.

Here again there is a reciprocal relationship, and it may be said that the intensity of use has a feedback relation to land values just as the intensity of use also derives from land values. Economic factors affecting intensity of use also involve a complex of other related factors covering a similar and, in some respects, an identical range of considerations as are involved in the determination of the use itself.

While there are thus a host of factors to explain value-use relationships, for land use planning purposes it would appear that the economics of use location can be given crude recognition by reference to the broad pattern of land values and the trends of change in this pattern. Once use locations in generalized patterns are determined, site selections of a more detailed character can be made. Land economics theory tells us that in the urban land market certain sites have value for certain specific purposes, and that this value is established by a web of relationships with other surrounding uses and their value structure. Thus operational applications of land economics theory at the detailed site-selection stage of land use planning similarly can give crude recognition to the great complexity of factors present in the more localized setting by a sharply focused examination of the present gradation of values and their trends in a particular neighborhood or district area of interest.

The purpose of the foregoing summary has been to sketch out economic explanations of urban land use with relevance for the land use planning process. Although presented separately, the economic are constantly interacting with the social determinants which are taken up in the next chapter. Broadly, the economic explanation of land use has its roots in the structure and functioning of the urban economy and in the forces of external origin reacting on this economy. Studies of the urban economy presented in a later chapter give us a clue as to how much land is going into development for various purposes, the amount being a function of economic expansion and resultant population growth. In turn, the vitality of the local economy, also discussed later, provides an indication of the rate at which land goes into development. Finally, supply and demand forces of the urban land market activated by these primary considerations operate to determine the location of various functional use areas and the siting of specific land uses in the urban area.

socially rooted determinants of land use

Another series of influences affecting the location and arrangement of land use are those with social origins—what are referred to here as socially rooted determinants of urban land use. These are less understood and frequently confused with the economic determinants discussed in the previous chapter. Most research in this aspect of urban development lacks an operational slant and has not progressed sufficiently so that it is possible to make an entirely satisfactory differentiation between social and economic determinants. Probably for this reason, there is a strong predisposition in much of the writing on the subject to equate social influences with the economic, and social motivations of people and groups with economic motivations. While unquestionably both kinds of influences are constantly in interaction and complexly interrelated so as to make differentiation and measurement of the separate effects extremely difficult, social scientists are increasingly directing attention to the slighted role that social values and ideals play in the determination of land use patterns in cities.

The sociologist usually views the city partly in the context of urban ecology with its concern for the physical, spatial, and material aspects of urban life, and partly in the context of social structure in the city with its concern for human values, behavior, and interaction as reflected in such social institutions as the family, the church, government, business, and so on. Socially rooted factors of land use thus can be explained in terms of "ecological processes" with their physical context and "organizational processes" with their social structural context. While in the classical traditions of the field, sociologists have tended to view these aspects of city life in separate compartments, in more recent approaches to the study of the city, ecological processes are more closely associated with social behavior of people and groups and related considerations of human values and social action processes.

In recognition of the need for a fully rounded perspective, one that takes into account social as well as economic factors influencing land use patterns, this chapter attempts to briefly summarize what the sociologist identifies as the socially rooted processes exerting an influence on the location and arrangement of urban land uses. What the sociologist has termed "the basic ecological processes" are taken up first, followed by some very sketchy observations as to the ways in which the social behavior of people and groups influence land development.

SOCIAL PROCESSES AFFECTING LAND USE

Urban ecology is a term the sociologist has adapted from the biological sciences to describe the physical change processes in the city. In the natural science usage, ecology is concerned with the interrelations of living things and their environment. Plants and animals are classified into communities of living things with varying but distinct patterns of community development according to such interacting factors as the migration of species, climate and vegetation, topography and drainage, soils, and so on. Community patterns of development occur in a sequence of phases, what are referred to as processes of succession, converging in the most advanced sequence on a *climax condition.* This condition is reached when the community is stable and self-perpetuating, with all factors in appropriate equilibrium.[1]

The application of this biological concept to human life and the human habitat is not difficult to follow. The urban community and its successive patterns and phases of community development, even the notions of populations in optimum adjustment to one another and their environment, have found their way into writings on urban ecology. In the natural science concept of ecology, there is a strong emphasis upon processes by which living things adapt to their environment, and so it is not surprising to find urban ecologists centering their attention on processes by which man adapts to his urban environment. As might be expected, economic forces figure prominently in explanations of these ecological processes. However, since our concern in this chapter is with man's social behavior, the discussion here will concern itself primarily with the socially rooted rather than the economic forces extant in these processes.

[1] For a fuller discussion of ecology in the natural science context, see Wilbur C. Hallenbeck, *American Urban Communities,* Harper & Brothers, 1951, pp. 93–96.

The primary and broadest basic process identified by urban ecologists —the one that describes the evolution and development of urban communities in time and space—is called *aggregation.* As typified in studies of dominance and subdominance of urban centers, it can be regional in its scope, but at the same time it has a localized frame of reference involving the sequences of change which occur within a particular locale. E. Gordon Ericksen has identified the most important localized subprocesses of aggregation as: (1) concentration and dispersion of services and populations, (2) centralization and decentralization, (3) segregation of populations into various distinctive areas, (4) dominance and the gradient of receding dominance in the successively more peripheral subareas of the community, and (5) invasion of areas by groups, giving rise to succession of one group by another.[2]

While all bear a relation to one another, subprocesses reviewed here will be grouped as follows: (1) dominance, gradient, and segregation, (2) centralization and decentralization, and (3) invasion and succession. Inasmuch as there appears to be implicit acceptance among urban ecologists that economic forces are controlling in the functioning of ecological processes in a regional framework, we will dispense with the intermetropolitan context and concentrate on subprocesses as they function internally within a single metropolitan center. Within this context, all "these subprocesses of aggregation are made possible through *mobility,* referring to in-and-out migration, residential, commercial, and industrial sifting and sorting, plus daily movements within the city and metropolitan area in a more or less routine manner."[3]

Dominance, Gradient, and Segregation

Viewed as a group, these three ecological processes offer a means of understanding the social aspects of the patterning of the city. Although most often used in a static context, these processes can also be used to describe change in the patterning. *Dominance* is used in the sense of one area in the city bearing a controlling social or economic position in relation to other areas. Usually dominance is considered in a vertical sense as applying to like use areas, although obviously there are patterns of dominance in a horizontal sense involving multiple use areas. *Gradient* is a term

[2] E. Gordon Ericksen, *Urban Behavior,* The Macmillan Company, 1954, p. 155.
[3] *Ibid.,* p. 155.

the sociologist has developed to indicate the receding degrees of dominance from some selected dominant center to the more distant locations relative to that center. *Segregation* is a related process of clustering. It is a "selective process which reveals the tendency of like units to form clusters, these units tending to be quite similar in economic strength and in terms of likes and dislikes."[4] Taken as a series of processes, the ecologist employs them to describe the way in which natural social areas develop.

These processes were first identified in a systematic fashion as part of the concentric zone conceptualization of the city (see Chapter 1). Thus the central business district is obviously one center of dominance, and the gradient of its influence over other business centers or even over other use areas can be described in each successive concentric zone. The clustering or segregative process as manifest, for example, in the way used-car and automotive service centers, wholesale districts, or light-housekeeping apartment areas for single persons or working couples develop in one or more of these concentric zones, is also explained in this concept of the city. In the more conventional usage of the term segregation, the various Little Sicilys, Gold Coasts, Negro districts, and so on are used as illustrations of the workings of the segregative process.

The sector theory explaining the distribution of high-value residential areas is also adaptable to describing these processes. For example, such processes are seen in the presumed controlling position of high-value areas, in the downward gradients noted in adjoining sectors, and in the clustering of uses of like character and intensity of development within certain segments of the pattern. The multiple nuclei concept is particularly graphic for describing dominance and subdominance within the urban center and is adaptable to explain each of the other related processes.

Taking up these processes separately, dominance is a term most frequently used to describe the economic positioning of cities in a whole constellation of communities, as discussed in Chapter 5. In a more localized and socially oriented context and with particular reference to land use, the process is most readily illustrated in studies of residential areas. Assuming some physical basis for delineating residential neighborhoods in a metropolitan area, they can be ordered into a system of dominant and subdominant neighborhoods, positioned according to prestige factors. Although these factors are closely related to land values or rental levels as employed by Hoyt in the development of his sector theory, prestige is a more socially rooted determinant of dominance. The actual measurements of prestige employed in identifying dominance and subdominance of course

[4] *Ibid.*, p. 187.

must recognize and allow for differentials in the values of people residing in the various neighborhoods. The foregoing application of the concept of dominance is but one of many that might be used. In place of studying the prestige status of various residential neighborhoods, one might examine these areas for patterns in the spatial distribution of poverty, disease, and so on, identifying dominant and subdominant areas of an entirely different order.

Gradient is directly related to the concept of dominance. The degree of increasing or decreasing intensity in prestige, poverty, disease, or whatever phenomenon is being observed, establishes the gradient or gradation from full dominance to total subdominance. "To study the gradient of a function we begin with the point of greatest dominance, the area marked by the highest proportionate incidence of the phenomenon to be measured. As we move away from the central and generally unstable point [with reference to poverty, disease, delinquency, etc.] we are made aware of increasing stability or balance, the gradual alteration of the function denoted in the central area. Thus gradient is to imply a measure of receding dominance."[5]

Associated with the processes by which use areas are positioned, displaying a hierarchy and gradient, is the segregating process that results in the identification of distinct prestige areas, islands of slums, areas of high incidence of disease, and so on. "This sifting, segregating process is constant, retarded here and accelerated there by sentiments and human policies as reflected in ordinances, restrictive covenants, and land speculation, among other things. . . . Segregation is not simply forced clustering of people as commonly held; it has voluntary aspects often developing unwittingly or according to a plan. Jewish ghettos in large foreign cities were voluntarily created long before they were compulsory."[6]

The implications of these processes for land use planning have never been fully explored. The urban ecologist has identified them in a descriptive "what is" or "what has been" context, but their research has yet to be directly oriented toward the operating needs of the city planner. To what extent can city planning recognize these social considerations and preserve desired natural areas? How are the social to be reconciled with economic considerations, and how are conflicts with broad social goals to be dealt with? Further empirical research is needed to establish what forms of the natural ordering of use areas described by the ecologist are important to recognize and provide for in land use planning and land development practices.

[5] *Ibid.*, p. 186.
[6] *Ibid.*, pp. 188–189.

Centralization and Decentralization

Two pairs of reciprocal terms need to be distinguished at this juncture. One pair relate to the massing and spreading out of population in a regional setting. Sociologists have given these processes the terms *concentration* and *dispersion*. Since they generally apply to large territorial regions consisting of several scattered urban centers such as Bogue's 67 metropolitan regions (see Chapter 5) in which processes tend to be controlled by economic forces, these are not included in the present discussion. Centralization and decentralization, on the other hand, apply to a particular metropolitan area where socially rooted forces, though complexly related to the economic, are potentially distinguishable from them. *Centralization* usually refers to the congregation of people and urban functions in a particular urban center or its functional use areas in the pursuit of certain economic, cultural, or social satisfactions. *Decentralization* generally refers to the breaking down of the urban center with the accompanying ebb movements of people and urban functions to fringe areas or to new satellite centers.

Our concern here is not with the individualistic and philosophical concepts and proposals toward the creation of a wholeness of life as set forth in Ebenezer Howard's work on garden cities at the turn of the century or in the varying notions advanced in recent time by Wright, Saarinen, Gropius, Neutra, Le Corbusier, Sert, and other architects. Rather we are presently concerned with the broad attracting and repelling processes as they stem from the basic values and ideals of people and groups.

Viewed in terms of the social institutions of the community, e.g., business, industry, recreation, education, religion, etc., centralization involves the settlement of people and the related development of places of work, entertainment, education, and worship in a more or less compact relationship in a single center. Conversely, decentralization involves settlement patterns of a polynucleated order with the appearance of outlying centers of work, entertainment, education, and so on. One involves migration of people and economic activity into the central city, and one involves migration outward to fringe areas or nearby subcenters.

The establishment of social institutions in the course of centralization-decentralization processes occurs in response to both economically and socially rooted needs and wants. At one time, basic factors of convenience to raw materials, labor, and markets dictated central locations for economic institutions. Today modern technological developments in power, transportation, and communications permit the development of places of business and industry in outlying areas. While the location of workplaces tends to become a dominant influence affecting centralization and decentralization processes, social forces can function sympathetically with economic forces or they can run counter to them. Thus values concerning quality, convenience, and variety in the choice of stores, entertainment, and schools may be a deterring force in the decentralization process. On the other hand, fashion, ethnic conflict, the desire for an open-order pattern of living without the noise, confusion, hazards, and dirt of the densely developed areas of the central city may become motivational social forces working in unison with economic considerations to facilitate decentralization.

The degree and rate of suburbanization are sometimes used as measures of decentralization. In an exploratory study of factors involved in the growth and suburbanization of Standard Metropolitan Areas (SMA's) between 1940 and 1950, Donald J. Bogue and Dorothy L. Harris examined both the degree and rate of suburbanization. They suggest that the degree of overall suburbanization of an SMA can be expressed as the percent of total SMA population found in what they call the *metropolitan ring* (the area within the SMA but outside the central city).[7] In order to differentiate between satellite city forms and the more diffuse rural forms of suburbanization, they used the ring population living in unincorporated areas and places of less than 2500 as a percentage of total ring population to establish the extent that suburbanization is diffused. Their analysis of 125 principal SMA's indicated that the highly suburbanized situations were those with large suburban city populations rather than those with a large diffused rural population surrounding them.

The Bogue and Harris analysis indicated that of several ways of measuring the rate of suburbanization, the difference between the percent of total SMA population living in the ring at the end and beginning of the decade appeared to be the best measure of rate. By statistical analysis they isolated the influence of a variety of factors considered to have an effect on the rate of suburbanization and concluded that:

1. A rapid SMA growth rate during the 1940–50 decade was conducive to rapid suburbanization.
2. A densely inhabited central city in 1950 was conducive to rapid suburbanization.
3. SMA's with small 1940 populations were suburbanizing more rapidly than large ones.
4. The more industrialized SMA's in 1940 were suburbanizing faster than the less industrialized ones.

[7] Donald J. Bogue and Dorothy L. Harris, *Comparative Population and Urban Research Via Multiple Regression and Covariance Analysis,* Scripps Foundation for Research in Population Problems and University of Chicago's Population Research and Training Center, 1954.

5. The older SMA's were suburbanizing more rapidly than the younger ones.
6. Metropolitan rings that were predominantly urban were suburbanizing more rapidly than the predominantly rural rings.
7. SMA's that previously were highly centralized suburbanized more rapidly than areas that had already achieved a substantial degree of suburbanization.[8]

In investigating decentralization trends, Bogue and Harris also examined centralization tendencies in the same SMA's. They observed that the more dense, older, and more industrialized areas tended to grow at slower rates, while places that were undergoing rapid industrialization tended to have greater central city growth. The highest rates of growth in the city were observed either in newly developing SMA's where suburbanization had not advanced appreciably and where there was still a high proportion of rural population in the ring, or where the ring was experiencing rapid growth.

Invasion and Succession

Associated with both of the foregoing sets of processes is a third set which the sociologist calls invasion and succession. These two processes are usually linked in sequence. *Invasion* is the interpenetration of one population group or use area by another, the difference between the new and old being economic, social, or cultural. *Succession* occurs when the new population group or use types finally displace the former occupants or uses of the area. Of course, it is possible for an area to experience invasion, but through concerted action of local groups, never reach the succession stage.

Invasion of one population group by another is usually a spatial manifestation of the change processes at work in the social structure of the city. Spatial mobility is associated with social mobility, and as the term implies, social mobility involves changes in social status or position. Thus vertical shifts from one social stratum to another usually involve spatial shifts, whereas horizontal social mobility within the same stratum has no special significance in the invasion-succession processes. Population group invasion is usually associated with residential areas, with one income, racial, or ethnic group penetrating an area occupied by another. The term is also used to describe shifts in land use as, for example, when business penetrates into residential areas or apartment districts take over areas of single-family homes. (In these examples, under the old "nuisance" approach to

[8] *Ibid.*, pp. 51–52.

classification of land uses, residential areas are considered a "higher" order of use than business areas, and single-family areas a "higher" use than apartment areas.) Usually these displacements occur by an upper-status social group or a higher use giving away to a lower-status group or lower use, although the reverse may happen, as evinced in restoration projects (for example, the reclaiming by whites of the old aristocratic areas of Charleston, South Carolina, from former Negro occupants) or in the more formal procedures of urban redevelopment where local government assisted by federal funds can alter the whole complexion of an area and the functioning of ecological processes.

The principal consequence of invasion is a breakup of the existing population and land use make-up of an area. Succession is the culmination of this breakup, with the new achieving complete displacement of the old. Viewed in a land use context, business and industrial uses tend to follow transportation routes, creating ribbon developments along major thoroughfares or islands along railroads, sometimes jumping from one area to another. The process is less visible when changes occur within an area of the same land use, with upper-order shifts being less discernible than lower-order shifts. At the lower-order extreme where areas have gone through a series of general invasion-succession cycles, occupancy turnover, vacancy, slippage in the maintenance of structures, increasing intensity of use, and rising density of occupancy are some of the indicators of these processes.

The cycle is most graphically illustrated in residential areas. As invasion begins, families sensing the implications of these changes begin a quiet withdrawal in the interests of minimizing economic losses anticipated in lower-order succession to the area. As these withdrawals become evident, other families take the cue and the exodus of the old group accelerates until the new group for the most part is in possession of the area, thus completing the cycle. Ericksen describes this cycle of change in a sequence of six steps:

Step A. Equilibrium in the district, marked by lack of awareness on the part of the inhabitants of any invasion by an alien group.

Step B. Disequilibrium arising from the flight of several upper-strata members of the community. This flight is in response to rumors of invasion. . . .

Step C. The creation of new restrictive covenants or reinforcement of dormant covenants following from these rumors. . . .

Step D. The rush invasion by the in-migrants to exploit the outposts established earlier. . . .

Step E. Reintegration of the area as the alien group acquires cumulative power. Mass exodus of the old occupants takes place at this level. . . .

Step F. Change of community status. The new occupants organize and dominate the area. Thus orderly succession and a new equilibrium has taken place.[9]

In their broad gross effects, the processes of invasion and succession tie directly into the concentric zone theory of describing physical structure and change in the city. Indeed, these processes were first identified in a systematic way in terms of this conceptual scheme. In describing growth of the city in terms of expanding concentric rings, the theory anticipates the operation of these processes and the "filtering down" process of residential occupancy, with the invasion-succession processes being most in evidence in the "zone of transition." It also gives recognition to the overall directional orientation of residential invasion processes. While short-run shifts can occur in any direction, the long-term orientation of invasion-succession shifts tends to be in the direction that the rings expand. However, assuming a positive and effective broad-gauge, long-range program of urban renewal is being vigorously pursued, it is probable that these ecological observations as to direction, and possibly the very nature of the invasion-succession processes, would be altered. The notion of control, of course, is inseparably bound up in city planning, and when applied in the pursuit of a program for a better physical living environment, all ecological processes may be influenced in the way they function.

As in the other ecological processes, the invasion-succession concept is a descriptive device which portrays mass tendencies resulting from individual and group decisions and actions in the community. The foregoing conceptual explanations imply that invasion and succession have the quality of a self-regulating law. They imply something of a universal rationale that guides people and groups into certain predictable courses of action. If there are certain universals of human behavior involving certain predictable patterns of social action, these notions have great importance for land use planning. These considerations bring us to a discussion of the elements and dynamics of social behavior as a factor in land use planning.

SOCIAL BEHAVIOR AS A DETERMINANT OF LAND USE

It would be both presumptuous and beyond the scope of this discussion to attempt to review all the complex and great variety of factors involved

[9] Ericksen, *op. cit.*, pp. 215–216.

in understanding the behavior of the urbanite. This is a task for the social psychologist and the sociologist. Yet it is essential to recognize the role of human values and ideals in the framework of group action if we are to develop an understanding of social behavior as it influences land use patterns in cities. In examining this aspect of land use determinants, it would also be well to recognize that there are a great many more questions in the minds of land planners than there are answers. Indeed, except for a few benchmarks such as Walter Firey's work on land use in central Boston, this is largely an uncharted and undeveloped area.[10]

We shall first sketch out a conceptual framework to describe some of the major elements and the dynamics of human behavior as they relate to land use.[11] This will be followed by a discussion of social values and land use.

Human Behavior and Land Use

Expressed crudely, human behavior refers to the way in which people and groups conduct themselves, how they act in the context of the values and ideals they possess. These values and ideals, whether latent or manifest, are the product of human experience in a specific cultural, economic, and physical setting, and consist of a kind of superstructure built around the basic drives of human life (survival, procreation, etc.). Human behavior is two-directional. It conditions and is conditioned by this setting, and in turn, actions in relation to the setting motivate and are motivated by values, both the unexpressed subconscious ones and the expressed conscious values.

Looking at urban land use patterns as the aggregate product of many individual and group actions in occupying and improving the land, we may view these actions as a form of human behavior activated by certain human needs and wants. In an oversimplified way, we may identify human *needs* with values relating to the necessities of urban living, and we may identify *wants* with values concerning economic and social desires which supplement the necessities of urban living. The economic behavior of people and groups in seeking to satisfy needs and wants in the urban land market is taken up in Chapter 1. Here we are concerned with their be-

[10] Walter Firey, *Land Use in Central Boston*, Harvard University Press, 1947.

[11] Although representing an extension of it, this material draws upon the work of the Urban Studies Committee, a cross-disciplinary group from the staff of the Institute for Research in Social Science of the University of North Carolina. Since 1953, it has been concerned with the study of "Processes of Control and Patterns of Urban Living, An Integrated Social Science Approach to the Analysis of Urban Development."

havior and their antecedent values as they seek to influence land use in pursuit of their social desires.

As shown in Figure 2, certain individual or group values concerning, let us say, the renewal of a particular blighted area in an urban center produce a cycle of behavior. This cycle involves four phases: (1) experiencing of needs and wants, (2) defining goals, (3) planning alternative courses of action, and (4) deciding and acting. First, the values with economic and/or social ends in view result in the experiencing of a need or want for action to change this pattern of land use. Second, this need or want becomes crystallized into a resolution, e.g., the philanthropist may simply conclude in his own mind that the slums must go and be replaced by safe and sanitary housing, the mortgage holders or an enterprising businessman may see a more profitable reuse, or the Renewal Agency may formally define and adopt a set of goals concerning the needed or wanted action. Third, in pursuit of these goals, the various alternatives for planning the area are established, e.g., the possibility of undertaking rehabilitation measures combined with "spot" demolition of structures here and there *versus* complete area clearance and redevelopment of the area in new structures, streets, and uses. Finally, having examined the alternatives, the philanthropist, mortgage holders, entrepreneur, or Renewal Agency reaches a decision. A plan is selected and set in motion to achieve the goals. The final result is change in the urban land use pattern. This change may produce new values which set in motion a new series of actions that may

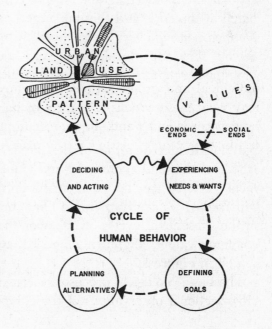

FIGURE 2. The Sequence of Action and the Influence of Values in Bringing About a Change in the Urban Land Use Pattern. Certain individual- or group-held values concerning the use of a particular parcel or area set in motion a four-phase cycle of behavior which culminates in the parcel or area being put to a particular use. This action sequence may bring into play new values or involve the values of other persons or groups, setting in motion new action sequences.

further influence the pattern of land use in the area. The cycle thus follows a circular sequence, actually more nearly taking the form of a spiral rather than a circle, since no two cycles produce exactly duplicate results.

Now let us view urban land use patterns as influenced by the behavior of many individuals and groups. Figure 3 is a schematic representation of this complex, with the mass values held in common identified at the rim and the urban land use pattern appearing as the end product at the hub. The behavior of individuals or groups (1, 2, 3, 4, '. . ., *n*), the sum total of which forms the universe of all behavior with respect to a particular land use, is shown in a complex of action patterns similar to the prototype illustration (Figure 2). Obviously there are many combinations of action patterns not shown in the diagram. For example, two or more individuals or groups, each with their own value system and behavior pattern, might act or even plan and act coöperatively in the satisfaction of entirely different sets of values. Moreover, Figure 3 pictures actions relating only to a single change in the land use pattern. If all concurrent actions influencing the total pattern of uses were diagramed, the result would be a much more complex chart involving whole clusters of the Figure 3 type behavior patterns.

Viewing these series of individual and group actions occurring in a situation without guidance of an urban land development plan and its implementing regulatory and other planning controls, the resulting land use pattern develops or changes by a multitude of related and unrelated actions. These actions or behaviors have certain planned and unplanned consequences (in the diagram the planned consequences are indicated by a hatch at the core, and the unplanned consequences by white space). The *planned consequences* are planned in the sense that the group which conceived the land development or change anticipated and consciously brought about the intended end result. The *unplanned consequences* of human behavior are the resulting relationships, or more correctly the lack of relationships, between several independent actions such as to produce an unexpected end result. This may be an inconsistent, or even an incompatible product in terms of the larger setting. Even assuming a guiding land use plan and conforming individual and group action, land development patterns can be expected to produce new responses and new and superseding values involving a changing alignment of people and groups in the subsequent cycles of behavior that develop. The dynamics of these changing values, alignments, and behaviors involve a dimension not presented in Figure 3.

The basic ecological processes discussed earlier in the chapter represent cross-sectional observations of the composite effects of mass behavior. Al-

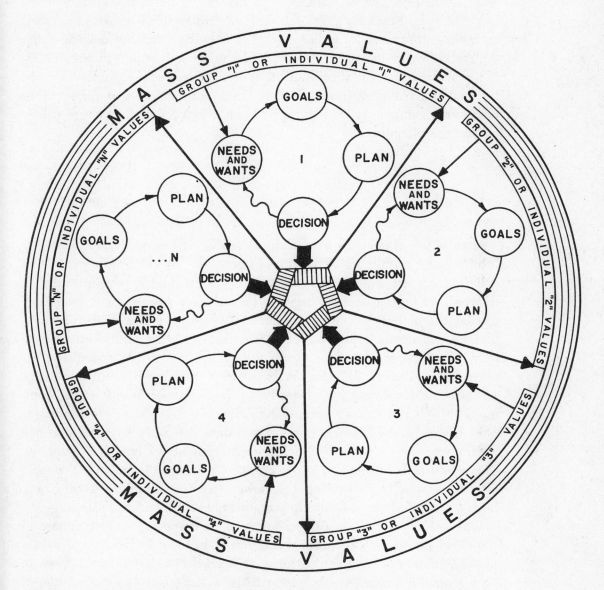

FIGURE 3. Abstract Representation of a Behavior Pattern Consisting of Several Independent Cycles of Human Behavior. This diagram shows that without conformance to a general land development plan, each of 1, 2, 3, 4, . . . , n groups or individuals, motivated by mass values held in common and by distinct group or individual values, follows a sequence of distinct actions which in the aggregate tend to have rational and irrational consequences for urban land use. The rational consequences (shaded portions at the hub) are the intended changes in land use, and the irrational consequences (unshaded portion) are the unanticipated, often inconsistent relationships between two or more new or changed uses.

though there are many other effects of this behavior which are of interest in other fields, land use is the end product of particular interest here. The land use planner has an interest in observing these composite effects of behavior in so far as his proposals seek to modify them or are predicated on their continuance. In either case, it is important that he develop some understanding of the values which set behavior cycles into operation, for in the final analysis the success of his efforts is dependent upon how closely his land use planning proposals harmonize with group and mass values held in the community. This brings us to a discussion of the role of values in land use planning.

Social Values and Land Use

In the crude framework above, values are viewed as motivating behavior resulting in a certain organized form of action by people or groups. In this sense, values are logical constructs of the individual or the group with reference to desired ends. They can be latent or subconscious, and they can be articulated or conscious values. They may be classified as to content, e.g., economic, social, political, religious, aesthetic, and so on, or they may be categorized by other means, e.g., positive-negative, specificity, explicitness, and so on. The term *mass values* is used here to indicate a consensus of values shared by a majority of the people or groups in the community. Mass values have particular significance for urban-wide considerations of land use planning, but group values generally have significance for the more particularized and localized segments of land use planning. The most notable exception is the instance in which the influential people of the community composing the power structure function as a group. Such a group has very obvious importance to overall land use planning.

Walter Firey's work in Boston involved an empirical investigation and the development of a theoretical framework to identify the role of values in the evolution of land use patterns. Disturbed by what he considered to be a general acceptance of a "rationalistic" approach to the explanation of land use with a strong explicit or implicit emphasis on self-regulating economic forces that distribute people and uses in the urban area, he studied sections of Boston to determine how values and ideals functioned with respect to past and existing land use patterns. In his own words, these rationalists (and he identifies several groups) "readily acknowledge the reality and effectiveness of social values in spatial adaptation; but they make no attempt to incorporate the empirical concession into their theoretical system. . . . All factual departures from the kind of spatial order called for by the theory are lumped together into a loose category of 'limiting' or 'complicating' factors. This category embraces 'custom,' 'moral attitudes and taboos,' 'political and administrative measures,' 'cultural biases,' 'traditional patterns,' and the like. These are supposed to limit or complicate the natural competitive process, but they are not regarded as ultimate causative factors."[12]

Firey set out to test two general propositions: (1) socially rooted values exert a causative influence on urban land use patterns, and (2) rationally functioning interests (what we have identified in Chapter 1 as market-governed forces), in exerting a causative influence on land use patterns, stem indirectly from larger cultural systems and cannot be viewed as self-given ends in themselves. Studying locational trends in Boston's Beacon Hill, central area, and North End, he concludes with respect to the first proposition that space may be not only a productive agent, but also a symbol, and that people and groups choose locations not only in relation to market considerations but also in response to values. In the Beacon Hill section, he identifies three kinds of influences which values exert on land use—what he terms the "retentive," the "recuperative," and the "resistive" —and on the basis of his tests concludes that "values are indeed self-sufficient ecological forces and that they have a very real causative influence upon land use."[13] In highlighting the origins and the preservation of historic sites in central Boston, he uses them as examples where symbolic attributes attached to an area become embedded in the social values of the people to the extent that "it appears that space has been divested of its role as a productive agent and . . . has been put to wholly uneconomic uses. . . ."[14]

With respect to the North End, the one distinctive Italian community in Boston, he points out that in this instance social values were not a result of fetishism where space is a conscious object of veneration as in the preceding two areas, but rather a result of processes of social organization where residence in the area to persons of Italian origin is a means of becoming identified with the Italian community and its distinctive values relating to occupation, family, choice of friends, group membership, and so on. On the basis of evidence presented on patterns of association and interaction, population movements and turnover, property ownership, and so on, he concludes that the North End is a symbol of "social solidarity" and that residence there is a token of identification with Italian groups

[12] Walter Firey, *op. cit.*, pp. 20–21.
[13] *Ibid.*, p. 130.
[14] *Ibid.*, p. 168.

and with Italian values. "Those persons who most fully identify themselves with Italian patterns tend to remain in the North End, in spite of the deteriorated, congested conditions which prevail there. Apparently the affect which attaches to 'one's own kind' outweighs awareness of the slum's undesirability as a place in which to live. Social values thus have an influence upon land use which is not at all limited to areas with congenial physical and architectural characteristics."[15]

The second purpose of his Boston study was to discover whether locational processes can be wholly separated from a cultural context. Here he concludes from his study of the retail center of Boston, the Back Bay, and the South End that "rational" determinants of land use are indeed themselves contingent upon a particular culture-bound value system and the cultural component is central to locational processes. The failure to recognize the cultural component in spatial adaptation he finds to be a major omission in existing formal theories which seek to explain land use. "All of them invest physical space with a 'non-cultural givenness,' and all of them consider social systems as passive, compliant and disparate adapters."[16]

Firey concludes his study with a theoretical construct suggesting the use of a "principle of proportionality" as a means of giving proper recognition to the role of values in the allocation of space to functional uses in the city. He discusses values in terms of a multiplicity of ends to be achieved in the location of land uses, with these ends requiring a certain balance, a degree of proportionality, in order that every component end of the community will in some measure be attained. He illustrates his theory of proportionality graphically in the form of a U-shaped curve (see Figure 4).

> Let us imagine a city that is made up of certain ends defined for it by the value system of the society in which that city exists. We can postulate that there will be an hypothetical point [the lowest point in the U-shaped curve] at which the amount and "kind" [in terms of accessibility and applicability to the end in question] of space devoted to a particular end or function balances off with the spatial requirements of each other end or function comprising the city. At this point the total deprivation of all the ends comprising the system is at a minimum. It is important to recognize that this "end-deprivation" is not synonymous with "cost" in the economic sense of the word, since it refers not only to the dearth of scarce goods but also to thwarting of intangible and non-empirical ends which are just as real functional requirements of a city. All of these ends and functional requirements must be attained, yet no one of them can be pursued to an unlimited degree lest others be unduly deprived. That point along the "deprivation continuum" of a particular end, at which point the degree of deprivation comports with a minimal deprivation of all other ends comprising the com-

[15] *Ibid.*, p. 220.
[16] *Ibid.*, p. 324.

munity, may be called point *x*. Now, by definition, any deviation away from *x* will entail increased deprivation to one or more of the other ends comprising the community as a system. Thus an allocation of too much space to park and recreational facilities will obstruct certain other requirements of the city as a functioning social system, such as commerce or manufacturing. Likewise the allocation of too little space to park and recreational facilities will obstruct the "best" functioning of the community as a system. Reasoning deductively, then, it may be suggested that departure from point *x* in either direction as to degree of deprivation of a particular end is accompanied by a *progressive* increase in deprivation to the system as a whole —more specifically, to one or more of the other ends comprising the system.[17]

In this statement of his theory, Firey appears to assume that there are limitations in the land area available for various uses—a built-in quantitative balance, as it were. If his principle of proportionality is applied to central city situations alone where the subject city is completely surrounded by independent and incorporated towns as in the case of Boston, the assumed limitation on space can be construed to apply. In most cities, particularly in the medium-size and small ones, the automobile has made larger land areas accessible to urban populations, suggesting that there are changing quantitative relationships rather than fixed limits on the availability of space. Of course, it might be argued that the time people

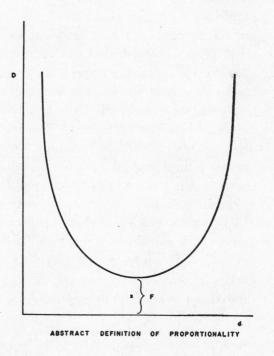

FIGURE 4. Graphic Representation of Firey's Theory of Proportionality. "In the figure, *d* indicates deprivation of a particular spatially contingent end; *D* indicates deprivation of all other ends comprising the system. At *x* along the *d* continuum the overall functioning of the system is being least obstructed, or, to put the same thing positively, the overall functioning is being most fully attained. Just enough space in terms of area, and just the right distribution of space in terms of suitability (accessibility . . .) to the respective ends, has been allocated to the several ends comprising the system as to comport with the 'best'—i.e., least thwarted—functioning of the system." (*Source:* Walter Firey, *Land Use in Central Boston,* Harvard University Press, 1947, p. 327. Copyright, 1947, by The President and Fellows of Harvard College.)

ABSTRACT DEFINITION OF PROPORTIONALITY

[17] *Ibid.,* pp. 326–327.

are willing to spend in "the journey to work" may ultimately provide fixed limits to an urban area, but even here new developments in technology and changing attitudes as to the time people are willing to spend in commuting suggest that there is a changing quantitative balance.

Socially Rooted Values and Land Use Planning

The importance of viewing land use as having socially rooted explanations has been stressed throughout this chapter. Social values and the behavior of people and groups activated by these values have significant implications for land use planning analyses of city planners. As a practical expediency at this stage of research development in the field, probably the points at which most attention should be focused are (1) the identification of mass and group values so that they may be taken into account in planning proposals, and (2) the design of a land use plan so that the locations, arrangements, and amount of land allocated for each functional use so far as possible are made consonant with these values.

With respect to the first purpose, it is well to recognize that values are difficult to identify and measure. This is particularly true of the hidden unarticulated values. Social psychologists have developed indirect techniques for identifying and measuring some forms of these hidden values, but comparatively little is known as to the validity of results. For example, it has been suggested that the very attempt at identification may in itself alter the values that are sought to be measured. In the case of the articulated values held by individuals and groups, techniques of attitude surveys and public opinion polls have reached a high degree of refinement and development. The continuing "Detroit Area Study" of the University of Michigan employs these techniques with considerable success and cumulatively is building up a source of information on explicit mass values of people in the Detroit area.[18] More will be said of the utility of these surveys in later chapters.

To give recognition to these values in the design of the land use plan at present is a subjective procedure. This is true partly because of the impossibility of subjecting the synthesizing and aesthetic aspects of the design process to a rigid mechanical approach, and partly because of the limited operational knowledge and experience we have had in classifying

[18] Detroit Area Study, *A Social Profile of Detroit 1954*, Survey Research Center of the Institute for Social Research, University of Michigan, 1954. Also see others in this series from previous years.

values, in identifying dominant and critical ones, and in making the transition from values to desired patterns of land use. While there is thus much research needed to assist the planning practitioner in giving weight to socially rooted determinants of land use, undoubtedly he in turn needs to give greater attention to emerging developments in the social sciences, even though at the outset it involves him in somewhat subjective interpretations covering this aspect of land use analysis.

the public interest

as a determinant of land use

This introductory orientation to land use planning has been one of singling out the more important considerations which set the emphases and condition the manner in which the land use planning task is approached. In the first two chapters, basic economic and social determinants of land use have been sketched out as they affect this task. The underlying significance to urban land use patterns of regional spheres of influence has been stressed, particularly in the way regional economic forces influence local economic growth. Through the eyeglasses of the economist, it was seen that the urban land use configuration is explainable in terms of the economic motivations of individuals and firms functioning in the urban land market. It was also seen that to the sociologist, urban land use has a direct relation to social processes and can be explained as the product of individual and group behavior in response to certain purely social as well as economic values. Though taken up separately, both ways of looking at land use have been presented as complementary, each complexly related to the other.

There is still another consideration to round out this introductory picture. While guided by these tenets of man's economic and social behavior in the community, the city planner must also view land use in the context of "the health, safety, and general welfare"—what is termed here "the public interest." The scope of the public interest is broad, the health, safety, and general welfare encompassing many things about the conduct of people in urban society. Our concern is with the public interest in land development, more particularly with public action that seeks to assure livability and sound development in the city as land is put to urban use. Not by any means dissociated from the other determinants of land use we

40

have been considering, the public interest involves another dimension, another way of viewing land use. It involves the notion of control for public ends as they may be distinguished from private economic or social ends. These public ends are associated with "public interest values" which compose one segment of the larger system of mass values discussed in the last chapter. These public interest values come into play in the legalistic actions of formal governmental organizations—what we refer to as "actions taken in the public interest." In place of focusing on economic and socially rooted actions discussed in Chapters 1 and 2, here we are primarily concerned with governmental actions to achieve livability in the urban setting and unity and efficiency in the overall land use pattern. The task of the city planner, then, is not only to develop a land use scheme fitted to the needs and sensitive to the wants of the urbanite, both economic and social, but also to harmonize these considerations with the public interest in a plan that maximizes livability in the city and insures sound development for the community as a whole.

Livability is used here to refer broadly to those qualities in the physical environment of the urban area which tend to induce in citizens a feeling of mental, physical, and social well-being according to the extent to which their fundamental day-to-day living needs and wants are satisfied. Thus defined, livability is both an individual matter and a community-wide concern—that is to say, actions of individuals or families in search of more satisfying living conditions have a random but cumulative effect of altering the land use pattern just as these same urbanites seeking satisfaction of their needs and wants through formal community action have an organized effect of altering the pattern of land development. In the first instance, actions are based on individual or family notions of livability; and in the second instance, they are based on shared notions of livability, these urbanites having discovered that they have a certain common interest in livability. Thus livability in the city becomes a matter of public interest when there is consensus among city residents about the fundamental living needs and wants to be recognized as the urban area expands and develops.

In this chapter we are concerned with the public interest rather than the individual interest as a determinant of land use. In such a context, the public interest connotes the notion of control. It involves control not only in the conventional action sense of imposing regulatory measures, passing on street and utility locations, renewing the outworn blighted areas of the city, and so on, but also in the preaction sense which is involved in the city planning process itself. Earlier we defined city planning as a means for systematically anticipating and achieving adjustment in the physical environment of an urban area consistent with social and economic forces and sound principles of land planning. This chapter is concerned with livability derivatives of these principles that have come to be accepted as sound in the public interest. In addition and more generally associated with what is sound, this chapter also deals with livability-related considerations involved in achieving an efficient unity and harmony in the way in which the physical environment develops.

It is not necessary to establish that the public interest is, in fact, a determinant of land use. This is inherent in the notion of control as it is coupled with the public interest. Of more direct concern here are: What basic elements of the public interest prompt the use of controls, and what practical considerations affect the use of controls? Material presented in this chapter is organized in terms of these two questions.

ELEMENTS OF THE PUBLIC INTEREST PROMPTING THE USE OF CONTROLS

The public interest is frequently used in law to refer to what the courts will sanction as a public purpose, whether under the police power, the power of eminent domain, or the power of taxation. For example, health, welfare, morals, and safety have become generally recognized tests of the public interest in American jurisprudence. Convenience, comfort, and prosperity are sometimes cited, but are less frequently allowed by the courts and usually only in combination with the other four tests. In a restricted sense, the courts thus provide a barometer of what are generally held to be the limits of the public interest. As indicated in the history of court actions, the public interest concept in a legal sense is an evolving one, tending to broaden in time as new elements become more generally sanctioned in a cultural context, but also tending to lag behind their social acceptance.

For planning purposes, a more advanced concept of the public interest is warranted, one which builds on the legal tests but which seeks forward-looking guideposts taken directly from the social currents of the times. In land use planning, the purposes usually identified with the public interest are five: health, safety, convenience, economy, and amenity. Morals come into play in some aspects of land use planning but play a relatively less important role. "Economy" may be identified with prosperity, and perhaps, by a stretch of the imagination, "amenity" may be associated with comfort in the legal definitions of the public interest. In all cases, it will become apparent that in the context of land use planning each of the five public purposes has broader meaning than that ascribed to it by the courts alone.

Health and Safety

Though they may be considered as separate public purposes, health and safety are frequently involved in combination and thus are customarily linked together. As might be expected, regulatory measures such as health, sanitation, housing, and building codes provide the principal operating definitions of the public interest. Such usages place a strong emphasis on constraints to prevent (or directives to ameliorate) conditions injurious or hazardous to the physical well-being of the people of the community.

In recent time there have been two notable developments toward a broader, more positive definition of health and safety in the public interest. First, in addition to a concern for physical health and safety, there is an emphasis on mental and emotional well-being. Secondly, there is not only the necessary emphasis on constraints in the interest of public health and safety, but stress is also being given to improved health and safety by planning and building it into the physical environment. In other words, contemporary thinking centers more on what is optimum or desirable, than what is minimum or adequate in the interest of health and safety.

This trend has been given impetus by the pioneering work of the Hygiene of Housing Committee of the American Public Health Association. As seen in the following list of criteria considered by the Committee to be a test of an *adequate* environment, many of the formerly optimal features of planning have advanced to the status of being regarded as minimal features:

1. Protection against accident hazards.
2. Protection against contagion and provisions for maintenance of cleanliness.
3. Provision of adequate daylight, sunshine, and ventilation.
4. Protection against excessive noise.
5. Protection against atmospheric pollution.
6. Protection from fatigue and provision of adequate privacy.
7. Provision of opportunities for normal family and community life, and protection against moral hazards.
8. Provision of possibilities for reasonable aesthetic satisfaction.[1]

Seen here are not only the "protection against" criteria invoked to safeguard the public from injurious and hazardous conditions, but also the more positive planning and design types of criteria proposing an environment developed for more optimal living conditions.

[1] Committee on the Hygiene of Housing, American Public Health Association, *Planning the Neighborhood*, Public Administration Service, 1948, p. vii.

Many of the regulatory controls commonly associated with health and safety usually apply to individual structures or relate to specific practices or services carried on in the community. Illustrative of these are the requirement of a flush toilet and bath with hot and cold running water for each dwelling unit, the requirement of fire exits and fire escapes in hotels and places of public assembly, control over food handling, rodent and insect control, and so on.

Focusing attention more directly on land use planning, there are other forms of control exercised in the public interest. These are the controls which relate to the broad patterns of land use as opposed to the individual structure or a particular activity carried on inside the structure. The following are illustrative of public purposes to be served through proper planning of the location and internal arrangement of land uses:

1. Control of daytime and nighttime population densities.
2. Control over use and development of hazardous areas.
3. Control of exposure to accidents, noise, and atmospheric pollution.

Controls may take the form of *developmental measures* as involved in the programming and carrying out of public works or urban renewal proposals. They may involve the public acquisition of certain built-up or open areas in the community and the planning or replanning of these areas for specific uses. Such areas may be retained in public ownership and developed for such uses as recreation, low-rent housing, and so on, or they may be sold for private development in accordance with plans determined to be in the public interest. More generally recognized land use controls in the interest of health and safety take the form of *regulatory measures* involved in zoning, subdivision regulation, and the reservation of lands for public uses through official map procedures.

DENSITY CONTROLS

In a land use planning connotation and a control context, *density* is a measure of the designed population capacity of urban land. While density

FIGURE 5. Distribution of Population for Selected Times During the Day and Night, June, 1950, Flint, Michigan. The low point in the daily activities of this population occurs at 4 A.M. when most people are in their homes. During the daytime hours the population redistributes itself, until in Flint the largest concentrations occur at 3 P.M. at the time of shift changes at the five large industrial plants. (*Source:* Special tabulations prepared by the Industrial Areas Study, Institute for Research in Social Science, University of North Carolina, from the Flint Metropolitan Area Traffic Study, conducted by the Michigan State Highway Department in coöperation with the U.S. Bureau of Public Roads.)

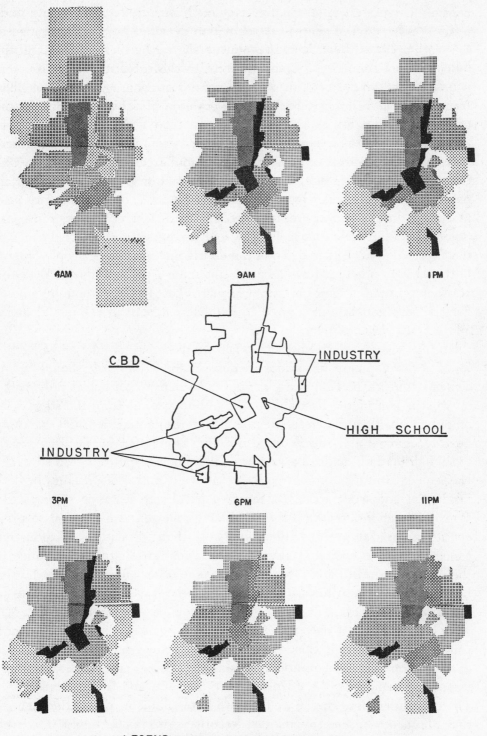

4AM   9AM   1 PM

CBD   INDUSTRY

HIGH SCHOOL

INDUSTRY

3PM   6PM   11PM

LEGEND (PERSONS/MILLION SQUARE FEET)

☐ 0-99	▦ 200-299	▨ 400-499
▨ 100-199	▦ 300-399	▨ 500-599

■ 600-699   ■ 800-899   ■ 1000-1249
■ 700-799   ■ 900-999   ■ 1250-1499

controls have been traditionally associated with residential areas, more recently the notion of controlled population densities has been extended to the work areas of the community—to the central business district and the industrial and commercial concentrations. In this extension of the concept, people present in an area during peak periods of congregation, rather than place of official residence, becomes the criterion of density. Obviously, the peak nighttime densities of residential areas tend to correspond with conventional measures of density as determined from U.S. Census enumerations. Thus, while tests of density in residential areas can be based on U.S. Census data, tests for work areas must be based on peak congregations of population, usually occurring during daylight hours. The extreme variations in density that can occur are indicated in Figure 5, which shows the variations in population density in Flint, Michigan, for various selected times of the day and night. Figure 6 shows the hourly fluctuations of people present in the various functional use areas of this same city. In Figure 5 densities are shown in population per million square feet. In most planning studies densities are generally measured in families per acre in residential areas, and persons per acre in work areas.

The establishment of densities—what the designed population capacities for land development in various sections of the urban area should be—is a major concern of land use planning. The densities are generally based on what is considered desirable in the public interest from the standpoint of public health and safety. Regulation of residential densities has long been recognized as a means for controlling contagion, for insuring access to sunlight and air, and for a variety of the other purposes identified in the Hygiene of Housing Committee listing above. Control of densities in both residential and work areas has received particular attention since World War II as a civil defense measure.[2] Although viewed as a national security consideration to reduce the vulnerability of urban population and industrial concentrations to enemy attack, it is also a matter of great importance to the peacetime health and safety of the people of urban areas. Indeed, even before the war, steps toward the control of the huge daytime densities in the heart of Manhattan and in the work centers of other metropolitan areas were being viewed as necessary in the interest of public health, safety, and convenience. Control in this instance would be concerned with the hazards of contagion and conflagration, mental well-being and physical fatigue from congestion, and the adverse effects of noise and fumes from traffic. These considerations might well dictate lower limits of population density than those established by military security criteria. Certainly it is well

[2] See National Security Resources Board, *National Security Factors in Industrial Location*, U.S. Government Printing Office, 1951.

within the realm of possibility that density ceilings will be designed into work areas in the public interest in the same way that they are now established for residential areas.

As basic as the planning for certain designed population capacities is to the whole notion of control in the public interest, such measures must nevertheless be reinforced by regulatory devices controlling the intensity

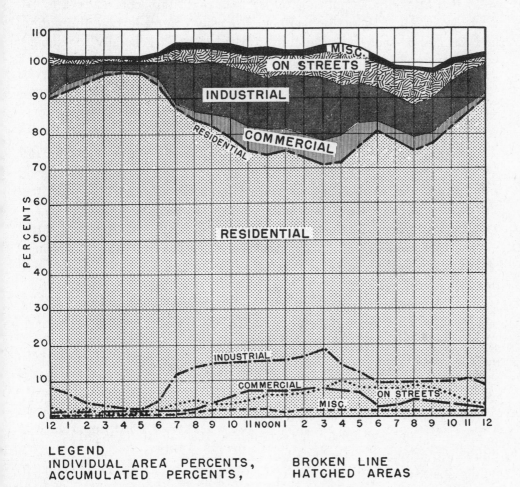

LEGEND
INDIVIDUAL AREA PERCENTS,   BROKEN LINE
ACCUMULATED PERCENTS,   HATCHED AREAS

FIGURE 6.   Population Present in Various Functional Use Areas for Each Hour of the Day and Night During an Average Summer Weekday, June, 1950, Flint, Michigan. Figures are expressed in percentages of the total population resident inside the "cordon area" (approximately equivalent to urbanized area). The hatched background in the chart shows the distribution of population among use areas by accumulated percentages, and the broken lines superimposed over the hatched areas provide a direct measure of percentages. (*Source:* Special tabulations prepared by the Industrial Areas Study, Institute for Research in Social Science, University of North Carolina, from the Flint Metropolitan Area Traffic Study, conducted by the Michigan State Highway Department in cooperation with the U.S. Bureau of Public Roads.)

of land use and the occupancy of structures in order to insure that the designed capacity of the land is not exceeded. In this connection, zoning and subdivision control are fundamental effectuation devices. Moreover, in residential areas regulatory controls over the crowding of dwelling units and the doubling up of families are widely used (these are usually found in housing codes). By the same token, designed daytime densities in work areas will also require policing by suitable regulatory controls yet to be worked out. All of these applications of density control involve the public interest, and as such, whether fully worked out and generally sanctioned by the courts or not, figure prominently in the land use planning task.

CONTROLS OVER HAZARDOUS AREAS

Depending upon physiographic conditions prevailing in a particular urban area, there are conditions and circumstances that warrant the use of control measures to protect man from himself, as it were. These are the situations in urban areas where land is subject to flood or difficult to drain. The danger of flood would seem to represent a control in itself and serve to keep such land free of development, yet there are countless illustrations of families resettling in areas even after being flooded out of home and property on several occasions in their lifetime. Less dramatic, but nevertheless troublesome and a concern to the public health, is the situation where marshy places or areas difficult to drain are pressed into development. Where there is a polluted ground water supply, a condition that is common in most urban areas, the public health is especially affected where this water stands or tends to pond at the earth's surface. Typhoid fever can be a public concern anywhere, and malaria can become a major problem in the southern parts of our country.

The most effective means for controlling the use of these areas is by public acquisition, developing them as an integral part of the permanent public open space system of the community. However, the costs involved in public acquisition of all such areas or in carrying out corrective flood control or drainage projects may be prohibitive. Where this is the case and where there is no provision for federal or state participation in the costs, regulatory controls alone or in combination with the above alternatives may provide the only practicable solution. Although still in the process of experimental development, flood plain zoning is an example of a regulatory device employed in the public interest in these situations.[3] The experience of Rhode Island with several hurricane disasters in recent years has be-

[3] See Robert W. Siler, Jr., *Flood Problems and Their Solution Through Urban Planning Programs*, Tennessee State Planning Commission, 1955.

come a matter of such great public concern in this state that the principle of flood plain zoning has been applied to regulate the settlement patterns of both summer and permanent residential areas. This regulatory measure has been used to supplement the more direct forms of control involved in state acquisition of certain shore lands and the construction of protective structures along the coast.[4]

Thus, in much the same way that land use planning serves as a means for achieving a rational solution to the control of densities, it also provides a rational approach to the channeling of development into the good areas and discouraging development in areas unsafe or unhealthy for settlement. However, here also land use planning must be reinforced by the proper regulatory and public works measures to implement the planning solutions.

CONTROL OF EXPOSURE TO ADVERSE ENVIRONMENTAL INFLUENCES

The third major public health and safety purpose to be served by land use planning relates to hazards developing out of (1) the heavy movements of automobile traffic and other forms of transportation and the adverse effect of their noise, fumes, or smoke on adjacent areas, and (2) the operations of industrial establishments with uncontrolled atmospheric or stream pollution or the noise they may create. While objectionableness has traditionally been measured in terms of the way that transportation routes and the lower-order uses (industrial and business) affect the higher-order uses (residential and public uses), there is a growing tendency to view these relationships not so much by functional use characteristics as by the standard of performance they achieve or the degree to which adverse influences are brought under control. Thus, in the same way that variations in density can be prescribed in the public interest in the different sections of the urban area, so can standards of performance be established for various areas in the community in the interest of public health and safety.

The effects of noise on fatigue are well known, and the adverse physiological effects on the respiratory system of smoke, dust, and gasoline fumes have recently received much attention in medical circles. These considerations and the hazards of heavy streams of traffic along major transportation routes and at employment centers are frequently cited as evils of the city. While the adverse effects can be abated, obviously these arteries and centers can never be eliminated, for they involve the very life and existence of urban areas.

[4] See Rhode Island Development Council, *Hurricane Rehabilitation Study*, October, 1954. Other types of control measures are suggested in a more recent report: North Carolina Council of Civil Defense, *North Carolina Hurricane Project*, December, 1955.

These transportation and industrial hazards to public health and safety are perhaps most directly controlled by various technological abatement measures. However, land use planning offers a means of controlling *exposure* to adverse influences involved in these activities. Space, orientation, and internal design are all elements of land use planning which can be utilized to minimize exposure. Separation of inimical uses by space—by open space or by areas developed in uses that are mutually compatible—can be used as an alleviating factor. The selection of locations so that prevailing winds can serve to reduce rather than accentuate exposure to smokestack industries is another control mechanism of land use planning that can be used to advantage. The internal design of use areas can also assist in minimizing exposure—for example, a layout that discourages through traffic from moving through residential areas, the routing of transport along channels specifically designed for these facilities, the introduction of buffer or insulation strips of planted open space all serve to moderate the effects of adverse environmental influences.

Convenience

In the foregoing discussion of control, health and safety have been the prime elements of the public interest at stake. Though frequently viewed as a lower-order consideration of the public welfare, convenience is nevertheless closely associated with the public interest and constitutes a third major basis for the exercise of control. The courts have recognized public convenience to be an element of the public interest in upholding the construction of streets and highways as a public purpose, and viewed in combination with health and safety, convenience has been given judicial sanction as a basis for regulating the traffic using these streets and highways.

However, public convenience is not a function of the circulatory systems of the community alone. More basically it is a derivative of the locational arrangements of land use and the relationship that each functional use area bears to every other one. Thus convenience can be judged in terms of home-to-work, work-to-recreation, home-to-shopping, shopping-to-work, and a variety of other area relationships intrinsic to the urban land use pattern. It may also be judged in terms of relationships between wholesale and retail areas, retail and industrial areas, or other use combinations where the movement of goods rather than of people is the basis of judgment. According to the reasons for movement in the urban area, convenience is measured in miles or blocks of walking distance, or more normally and in the modern day sense, in minutes of transportation time. In transportation planning, convenience is viewed in terms of movement systems and the ease of moving large volumes of people or goods from one destination to another over these systems. Land use planning is concerned with the locations of these destinations which obviously play an important role in maximizing the ease of movement.

In addition to the location factor, convenience is affected by the intensity of land development, i.e., the degree to which land is occupied and the density at which it is developed. Intensity of development in an urban area is influenced by such interrelated considerations as the character of the terrain and its drainage features, the pattern of land values, the whims of original land owners in the subdivision of property, the amenities of the area, the marketability of land titles, and so on. Now obviously, a spread-out pattern of development and the presence of low population densities (individually or in combination) tend to increase time-distance relationships between outlying sections of the built-up area and the center and between the various functional use areas. Further, the larger the metropolitan area, the more extreme these time-distance relationships tend to become. Thus intensity of development along with location is basic to the concept of public convenience.

It should be noted that while health and safety criteria dictate an emphasis toward low-order densities, convenience requirements favor an emphasis toward high-order densities. However, these seemingly disparate public purposes are in reality considerations of degree and do not need to be in conflict. In practice, a balance can be achieved in the land use planning process. For example, within the same development area it is possible to design for high *net* densities in the interests of convenience and for low *gross* densities in the interests of health, safety, and amenity.

In the light of the foregoing observations, convenience is obviously a public purpose that goes to the very heart of the land use planning task. Indeed, the land use plan may be viewed as a developmental control device aimed at achieving maximum convenience in the location and arrangement of land uses. Regulatory controls such as zoning and subdivision regulations then become the means for building convenience into the pattern of land development.

Economy

As the fourth major element of the public interest warranting control of land development, "economy" is a term associated with efficiency in the land use pattern and its public cost implications, whether in terms of municipal expenditures or cost to the urbanite in general. In a broader sense the public economy may be coupled with the general vitality of the urban economy as a whole and its implications for the revenue structure of an urban center. Since the urban economy is taken up later, we shall confine our discussion here to governmental and citizen costs of land development. In this usage, it has to do with land development from the viewpoint of the community as a whole as opposed to the viewpoint of the entrepreneur or the collective actions of many people functioning in the urban land market as discussed in the first chapter. What land use arrangement is most efficient and least costly to the municipality and to the citizen is the basic concern here in the exercise of control.

As an element of the public interest, economy is closely associated with convenience. Indeed, economy and convenience are frequently involved in tandem, just as health and safety are linked together. A land use scheme in which residential areas have easy access to schools and recreation areas also permits a more efficient and economical school plant or recreation program in terms of persons served and *per capita* costs. Convenient proximity of places of residence to places of work also makes for the most efficient and least expensive circulatory system in terms of public works expenditures or citizen outlay for gasoline or transit fares. In this sense, convenience has to do with expenditure of time and effort, whereas economy relates to the cost of this time and effort to the urbanite and to the city as an institution.

As in the case of public convenience, both the location of use areas and their intensity of development are key considerations of economy. The location of use areas affects public costs in a variety of ways. For example, it makes an obvious difference in public costs if industrial areas are located in relation to existing or proposed utility lines capable of supplying large amounts of water and handling heavy industrial waste requirements, than if these considerations are ignored. Similarly, it is a matter of public economy that the location of new commercial and industrial development occur where it can be efficiently served by existing fire protection facilities and by what would constitute an economical expansion of them. In still another example, it is important to give preference to areas where residential development can be located in relation to existing utility or school capacities or to areas where these facilities can be economically and efficiently extended. What is economical to provide in the form of streets, recreation areas, and other community facilities in relation to existing facilities also enter into the picture and also become, in effect, control factors in the patterning of urban land uses.

In addition to location considerations, the intensity in the way land is put to use also affects the public cost aspects of land development. A spread-out pattern of development involves a greater mileage of streets and more lineal feet of water and sewer lines than more compact and densely developed settlement patterns. These considerations of the public interest of course must be balanced against the dictates of health and amenity where the emphasis is toward an open-order pattern of urban development. They must also be viewed in terms of community values, attitudes, and preferences and the taxes and other costs people are willing to assume in order to satisfy their wants. Again these considerations are intimately bound up in the land use planning process, and controls exercised in the public interest to achieve maximum economy are relative to other controls and the economic and social considerations at stake. Here too, land use planning may be viewed, then, as a kind of master control, but at the same time reinforced by effectuating regulatory controls such as zoning, subdivision regulations, and the establishment of major street locations and sometimes school and recreation sites through official map procedures.

Amenity

This is a term in more general usage in the United Kingdom than in the United States, and refers to the pleasantness of the urban environment as a place in which to live, work, and spend one's leisure time. It relates to the perceptual aspects of urban surroundings—their aesthetic appearances to the eye and the comfort and enjoyment offered to the other senses. Viewing all five elements of the public interest in the continuum of judicial acceptance, amenity is situated at the lower end of the scale. It is not specifically excluded as an element of public interest in court decisions generally, but is most frequently accepted in combination with one or more of the other four elements. Yet in the array of public purposes to be served by land use planning, from a social point of view it is of no less importance than the other four as a basis for the exercise of control. While in judicial tenets it may be viewed as an optimal rather than a minimal element of the public interest, the increased importance being attached to amenity as a dimension of public health and mental well-being may well result in a more positive recognition of aesthetics as a basis for the exercise of regulatory controls in the future.[5]

[5] Indications of the changing judicial climate toward the use of the police power to regulate aesthetics in the public interest appear in the U.S. Supreme Court decision of November 22, 1954, *Berman v. Parker* (23 LW 4012). "The concept of the public welfare is broad and in-

Perhaps the major deterrent to a wider use of regulatory controls in the interest of amenity is the range of variation inherent in public tastes. What is attractive and pleasant in the living environment tends to vary with every person. According to the values, whims, and beliefs of people, one thing may be pleasing to some persons, and it may yield an entirely negative response in others. It is this aspect of amenity that sets it off from other elements of the public interest. Thus the difficulty of subjecting tastes to a test of consensus may explain why amenity has not been accorded the same recognition that health, safety, convenience, and economy have been given in the courts. Nevertheless, there are extremes in the visual appearances of a city that evoke some degree of unanimity in response, either of a positive or negative kind. For example, there tends to exist a general consensus that highway entrances to one's city that are flanked by automobile graveyards are unsightly and should be regulated in the public interest. Other similar examples, perhaps of a more localized character could be cited in almost any community. But as we proceed upward on a scale of from "bad" to "good," there may be less unanimity. Thus some people would favor large open spaces in the townscape as a welcome relief to the monotony of "urban sprawl." Some would place the emphasis on planted green areas to relieve the drabness of concrete and steel. Some would feel that the miles of structures and streets create variety and choice to match every desire of the urbanite—from total anonymity to any amount of neighboring that might be desired. As we proceed up the scale, we enter an area approaching unanimity again—this time of a positive form. Thus there are generally favorable reactions concerning tree-shaded streets that alleviate the heat of pavements and general approval of landscaped freeways that make driving pleasant and easy.

With recent advances in survey research methods and sampling techniques in the social sciences, the identification of these attitudes poses no major problems.[6] However, there are problems in interpreting responses obtained in such surveys. In the course of identifying negative and positive extremes of reaction, the displeasing or distasteful must somehow be connected with forms of physical development that elicit general approval. Where negative and positive responses are reciprocal with respect to par-

---

clusive. . . . The values it represents are spiritual as well as physical, aesthetic as well as monetary. It is within the power of the legislature to determine that the community should be beautiful as well as healthy, spacious as well as clean, well-balanced as well as carefully patrolled." This interpretation had a direct influence on the subsequent Wisconsin Supreme Court decision upholding architectural control provisions in the zoning ordinance of Fox Point, Wisconsin (*State ex rel. Saveland Park Holding Corporation v. Wieland*, 69 NW 2d 217). For a more complete discussion of the problem, see J. J. Dukeminier, Jr., "Zoning for Aesthetic Objectives: A Reappraisal," *Law and Contemporary Problems*, Spring 1955.

[6] As noted in Chapter 2, the underlying values that influence attitudes and beliefs are more complex to identify and measure.

ticular features in the townscape, no problem exists. But where there is no positive counterpart to match up with an undesirable feature in the list of plus and minus aspects of amenity, difficulty is encountered. Corrective solutions which meet with general approval must be discovered by posing alternatives and singling out the solution which meets with the greatest approval.

Yet it can be expected that there will be a whole range of aesthetic considerations that are outside the experience of the people of a particular community. These may be advanced notions that heretofore have been given only experimental application in a few scattered localities. For example, this is true of the superblock principle in residential design.[7] The idea of residential areas with complete separation of pedestrian and traffic ways may be totally foreign to the people of a community. In other situations, the city may not have advanced in its growth sufficiently to experience certain conditions that produce a marked reaction. This is true of a community facing a period of rapid growth for the first time.[8] At the outset the local people have no particular convictions, but as urbanization accelerates, they form very articulate notions about developments they consider to be detrimental to the amenity of the community, the negative reactions tending to develop more rapidly than the positive ones.

The problem here is one of anticipating responses and matching up negative ones with solutions calculated to meet with favorable reaction. At this point and at the present stage of development in this aspect of survey research, there is no alternative open to the city planner but the application of judgment backed up by experience and observation in other communities. Thus against a background of experience from communities of similar make-up where alternative approaches have been tried, a judgment is made as to the transfer value of each solution to a given locale of interest, with the one judged to be most suited to local circumstances being eventually selected. Here there is a fine line of distinction to be noted between what is experience and unbiased observation and what constitutes the values of the city planner himself. It is not within the scope of the public interest for the city planner to plan for Le Corbusier tower apartments or Frank Lloyd Wright Broadacres communities where

[7] As pioneered by Henry Wright and Clarence Stein, town planners and architects of Radburn, N.J., the superblock, as the term implies, is an unusually large residential block which, in effect, is turned inside out, with pedestrian access provided by a system of internal walkways in a setting of landscaped open space, and with automobile access provided to individual houses from short dead-end streets or *cul-de-sacs* penetrating the block from the peripheral collector street. Superblocks are planned in clusters, with a system of interconnecting pedestrian ways that underpass or overpass the bounding collector streets. The superblock principle thus involves the element of safety as well as amenity.

[8] See F. Stuart Chapin, Jr., *et al., In the Shadow of a Defense Plant*, Institute for Research in Social Science, University of North Carolina, 1954.

the choice is made simply on the basis of his personal preference. This is quite different from the obverse situation where experience or knowledge of response in other similar situations is made the basis for his choice. The solution selected is made in the public interest, and this calls for an approach based on prevailing community concepts of amenity, not those of the planner.

In view of these problems of securing a consensus of tastes, control exercised to achieve attractive and pleasant civic growth and development is difficult to systematize into codes or laws. Present solutions rest with the land use plan reinforced by effectuation controls, both regulatory measures such as zoning, subdivision control and the official map, and developmental measures that are involved in public works programs and urban renewal programs. At the same time amenity must be balanced against the other four elements of the public interest. Thus the introduction of open space into a city to give it greater variety in visual appearance and to introduce pleasant green areas for relaxation and leisure time use also involves considerations of convenience and economy. The process of discovering this balance constitutes one of the basic tasks of land use planning.

FACTORS CONDITIONING THE USE OF CONTROLS

Having reviewed the five major elements of the public interest which prompt the use of controls in land development, we can now proceed to examine some of the practicalities that condition the application of such controls and thus establish the way in which the public interest ultimately functions as a determinant of land use. Stated another way, it is now possible to highlight the factors involved in bringing the public interest considerations into equilibrium with the economic and social considerations covered in Chapters 1 and 2. How convergence of the public interest with the economic and social determinants of land use is accomplished, and how the synthesis is expressed in physical form in a land development plan constitute the very essence of the land use planning process.

As indicated earlier, controls employed in the public interest may reflect a range of community consciousness varying from optimal to minimal points of view. Thus in general terms, control over the physical setting of the city may be viewed at one extreme as an opportunity to realize the full potentialities of a safe, healthful, convenient, efficient, and pleasant place in which to live, with gradations to the other extreme in which control is viewed more in the sense of a necessary constraint to protect the public interest. What the point of acceptance or tolerance is will vary with the community and local circumstances. In one community, for example, there may be general acceptance of public ownership of riverfront lands as a means of control, with development secured through leasing arrangements or public works. In another community, there may be limited constraints over the private use of riverfront lands with little or no tolerance of the notion of public ownership as a means of control. In still other communities, there may be variations from both extremes. Within the same community, there may be unequal emphasis among the five elements of the public interest, with perhaps an acceptance approaching an optimal emphasis on one or two and a minimal approach to the other three or four.

Why a community accepts one element of the public interest, tolerates another, and perhaps even rejects another, or why one community exhibits an advanced point of view in the degree of control exercised under one or more of the five elements and another shows a very low tolerance for control in the public interest are frequently matters of historical circumstance. The prevailing public temperament may have its origins in a public emergency caused by a San Francisco type fire, a Pittsburgh type flood, a Providence type hurricane, or an economic collapse such as is involved in some New England communities with the wholesale withdrawal of textile plants. It may have its origins in a symbolic phenomenon—for example, a group sentiment concerning the community's historical heritage, a long tradition of nurtured community values concerning the past with accompanying pressures to protect the historical parts of the city. In other cases it may stem from a distinctive natural resource and a general desire to maximize its economic potential—our Miamis, Ashevilles, Tucsons, etc. In still other cases, it may have evolved over a period of time from a vigorous, forward-looking civic leadership with an accompanying growth in civic pride and awareness of the essentials of community livability— the outgrowth of nameless devoted individuals or groups: the work of the Daniel Burnhams in communities across the country.

Whatever the community or circumstance, obviously the temperament of the community—its mass community values and the extent that they are articulated in behavior that comports acceptance of control in the public interest—will dictate how far land use planning can go in providing for health, safety, convenience, economy, and amenity in the physical environment. So the task of land use planning becomes one of gauging the public temperament, discovering and recognizing levels of acceptance and tolerance, and balancing these considerations with local practicalities. This final aspect of bringing all public interest determinants of land use into focus in one perspective is concerned with local practicalities: (1) physical characteristics, (2) fiscal capabilities, (3) jurisdictional considerations, and (4) the political climate. All affect the extent to which control is necessary or feasible in the face of economic and social realities, and together they include the more practical considerations which condition the use of controls in the public interest.

Physical Characteristics

Perhaps the most tangible series of factors dictating the way in which controls are applied are the local physical characteristics. These include both the physiographic factors associated with the site of the urban area and the settlement characteristics that have been superimposed on the site. They involve then, on the one hand, the terrain, its drainage features, and the way in which the winds, the sun, and the climate warrant the use of controls. On the other hand, they involve the practicalities of the way in which the land has been developed, and more particularly the extent to which this settlement pattern can be altered through planning as a form of control.

PHYSIOGRAPHIC FACTORS

It was noted above that controls are invoked to minimize the ravages of the rivers and the sea where they impinge on the public health and safety. It was also observed that controls may be employed to take advantage of orientation with respect to prevailing winds to minimize exposure to smoke and fumes and maximize summertime and wintertime comfort and well-being. Controls may also be employed to insure that natural features of the landscape may be wisely and pleasingly utilized, providing the amenities of a pleasant living environment. All these considerations stem from physiographic features in the urban landscape.

While modern-day engineering is able and has wrought many changes on the earth's surface, it is rarely feasible to change the townscape in the sweeping way undertaken in many resource use and development programs in open country. Mountains and major drainage courses cannot be moved or appreciably altered without involving a multiplicity of property ownership rights and a whole complex of economic and social values running with the land and its relationship to prevailing patterns of land development. Yet at times the public interest may be so compelling and critical as to involve stringent control measures. Hibbing, Minnesota, moved to an entirely new site to permit open-pit iron ore mining on its original site, and there are a number of instances where whole towns were moved to new sites to make way for flood control works. However, these were small communities and represent the exception rather than the rule.

Nevertheless the physiographic features of the city's site present some of the most obvious practicalities affecting acceptance of control in the public interest. In Pittsburgh, mountains and drainage courses represent very practical considerations, suggesting the probabilities of a higher tolerance toward certain developmental and regulatory forms of control than would be acceptable in Omaha in the plains area. To cope with local topographic problems, in Pittsburgh even the most minimal notions of public safety and economy can be expected to carry acceptance for costly public works programs (e.g., highway projects, drainage control, etc.) and stringent subdivision and zoning controls. It happens too that the heavy coal consumption in this area (industrial added to the domestic) in combination with the local physiographic characteristics has made smoke abatement a health matter of considerable public interest, permitting high public tolerance limits to smoke control measures. Indeed, it is probable that physiographic features have been major factors in the development of an advanced public awareness of planning control measures here.

LAND USE FACTORS

Closely related to the basic physiographic features of the urban locale, the character of existing land use is also a practical consideration that affects the extent to which controls are employed. In this connection, Charles Abrams identifies five public purposes for which land use controls are employed in the public interest:

1. Guide the *use* of land to promote the advantageous development of the community (e.g., protection of factory, residential, commercial, park, parking, and other sites under a master plan).
2. Curb the *misuse* of land so that it will not injuriously affect the interests of the community (e.g., prevention of slum construction or unnecessarily intense development).
3. Prevent the *abuse* of land (e.g., prevention of abortive subdivisions, cut-over land).
4. Regulate the *nonuse* or *disuse* of land (e.g., taxation to enforce development, clearing of unmarketable titles, keeping land from development,

or restraining owners of occupied dwellings from discontinuing their use).

5. Guide the *reuse* of land for more appropriate purposes (e.g., urban redevelopment, slum clearance, and rehousing).[9]

In the context of this discussion, the first and fifth represent developmental forms of control, and the other three involve regulatory forms of control. All are concerned with needs or problems of land use and are generically referred to as planning controls.

The degree of acceptance of these public purposes and thus of the control measures themselves may be prompted by *reaction* to the misuse, abuse, or disuse of land, or it may be prompted by *action* to achieve certain goals in the use or reuse of land. In general, reaction to adverse conditions results in a stronger, more prompt exercise of control measures than action that is positively oriented toward certain new patterns of land use. In cities where there are large blighted areas with the accompanying human misery and deprivation, public acceptance of such control measures as slum clearance and redevelopment, rehabilitation, and conservation tends to be stronger and faster than the acceptance of controls used to promote orderly and attractive industrial districts, open space systems, shopping centers, or residential communities in new developments. It is human nature to be more immediately stirred by corrective needs than by the need for preventive measures.

The misuse, abuse, or disuse of land as seen in the slums is a very tangible basis for the use of controls. To be sure, vigorous campaigns by the leaders of the community must often dramatize the facts if public action is to develop in a concerted manner. Perhaps it is shock or horror—such as the rat that bit the child in a Chicago slum—which provides a symbol and the drama needed to arouse public indignation and create a demand for control measures. Thus when dramatized in terms of human misery, Chicago's 22 square miles of blighted and near-blighted areas and 50 square miles threatened by blight become a staggering fact in the public eye.[10] The abstraction of a statistic then assumes a semblance of reality, and the prevailing slum conditions become the basis of a public issue, sometimes approaching the proportions involved in a fire, a hurricane, or other public emergency. Whether or not the newspaper campaign that ferreted out the rat incident in Chicago was a key element in the subsequent introduction of new control measures (e.g., the community conservation law—a national "first" in Chicago) is difficult to establish. Undoubtedly a

[9] Charles Abrams *et al., Urban Land Problems and Policies,* Housing and Town and Country Planning Bulletin 7, United Nations, 1953, p. 34.
[10] Jack M. Siegel and C. William Brooks, *Slum Prevention Through Conservation and Rehabilitation,* Housing and Home Finance Agency, November, 1953, p. 53.

variety of considerations were involved. Nevertheless, the extended scope of control measures employed for blight prevention and elimination was based on practicalities related to the character of land use. These conditions set in motion a chain of action patterns that served to alter tolerance limits toward controls used in the public interest.

Such other land use–related problems as the speculative subdivision of the land, traffic congestion, the shortage of parking space, fringe development overspilling the corporate limits of the central city, and so on, involve the use of other control devices. The exact kinds of control and the degree of acceptance of these control measures depend in each case on such factors as the acuteness of the problem, the public awareness of the needed corrective action, and other local practicalities.

Fiscal Capabilities

Fiscal considerations affecting the use of controls are so obvious as to require little amplification. Patently, the extent to which a community can acquire land in areas subject to flood, develop its public open space system, engage in urban renewal programs, or employ other forms of developmental control is directly related to its financial condition and its fiscal capabilities.[11] Even in the case of regulatory forms of control, the costs of administration may become a limiting factor. Few cities have a full complement of field investigators required for the enforcement of such regulatory measures as building, fire, housing, sanitation, and zoning ordinances. Accordingly budgetary appropriations affect the locality's ability to enforce regulatory measures and thus the extent of control exercised.

Granted that the fiscal capabilities of a municipality place limitations on the use of controls in the interest of public health, safety, convenience, efficiency, and amenity, it must also be recognized that these capabilities are a function of the taxes people are willing to pay balanced against their expectations for municipal facilities, services, and controls. All too often a control sanctioned by the majority of the people of the community is one thing and the capabilities for putting it into effect are another. Discounting the lag between the time that consensus is reached concerning the need for a new control and the time that may be involved in putting it into

[11] While the fiscal capabilities for the exercise of controls would appear to be self-evident, it is startling to note how many master plans are developed without reference to the locality's financial ability for carrying them out. Master plans that are not carefully scaled to long-range estimates of local revenues, expenditures, and the debt structure of the community have limited utility, and their land development proposals tend to become ineffectual control mechanisms.

effect, we cannot overlook the fact that few people connect their demands for governmental action with the costs involved. In a formal sense an improvement, a service, or a control can easily be voted in, yet, even where price tags are attached, for example in general obligation bond issues, few people associate the desired change with needed compensatory advances in the tax rate. What they demand as citizens is generally completely dissociated from their attitudes as taxpayers.

The foregoing observations indicate the inertia encountered in putting new controls into effect. However, there are variations among cities in the public sensitivity to the need for improving their fiscal capabilities. Attitudes in this respect involve economic and social values of civic leaders, influential civic groups, and the citizenry in general, and to assess these considerations requires not only a knowledge of patterns of citizen and group behavior as reflected in the history of past governmental reforms, but also an understanding of the present temperament of the community and its likely patterns of action in the face of present attitudes and their derivative values. Thus fiscal capabilities affect the extent to which controls are employed in a particular locality not only in terms of what is discernible on the surface in the existing municipal balance sheet, but also in terms of the underlying public temperament and what level of public support to progressive improvements in municipal government this temperament will sustain in the future.

Jurisdictional Considerations

Related to the physical and fiscal practicalities that affect the use of controls in the public interest, there are jurisdictional considerations which enter into the picture. These are the very real and practical problems associated with the multiplicity of political jurisdictions that have come into being in urban areas over the years. Most of these problems arise in connection with the financial plight faced by these separate jurisdictions, particularly the plight of central cities. As a consequence, control policies with respect to land development are being increasingly guided by considerations of the revenue-producing potentials of the various land uses.

Though artificial creations in the economic and social sense and inefficient and expensive to perpetuate in an administrative sense, jurisdictional factors continue to exert an influence on the way in which controls are applied. Indeed, they can be expected to remain a factor in the picture until metropolitan government becomes a reality. Thus, no matter how logical it may appear for a central city to hew to certain metropolitan-wide land use objectives or how compelling these objectives may seem in terms of the public interest of the metropolitan community as a whole, so long as separate jurisdictions exist within one urban area, the central city will tend to exercise controls in the best interests of its own limited constituency. The same observation, of course, applies to all other political jurisdictions in the urban area.

Examples of these political realities are not difficult to find. The central city's policies concerning sewer and water extensions beyond its boundaries to adjoining incorporated or unincorporated areas tend to be a function of what is in the best interests of the central city. These jurisdictional considerations can thus exert an influence on the direction and rate of development in the urban area. Schools and other public facilities and services will usually be provided in each of the several jurisdictions, according to the public interest dictates of each particular jurisdiction rather than according to the public interest of the total metropolitan area.

Political boundaries affect other elements in the land use pattern. Apart from the way in which jurisdictional-based decisions on public facilities and services will tend to influence residential, commercial, and industrial land use patterns, the central city (or any of the adjoining political jurisdictions) may take more direct steps and embody in a zoning ordinance land use concepts that are conceived entirely in terms of its own set of interests. Clearly what is determined to be sound in the interest of one segment of the whole may be in conflict with what is sound in the public interest of the other segments of the whole, and further, what is established to be sound for each of these political jurisdictions may be quite another thing from what is best in the interest of the overall metropolitan area. And so, along with physical and fiscal considerations, the way the political boundaries are drawn represent a practicality affecting the use of controls.

The Political Climate

Implicit in the discussion so far is the notion that what is physically, fiscally, and jurisdictionally feasible in the exercise of developmental and regulatory forms of control is closely associated with what is politically expedient. As used here "the political climate" refers to what is acceptable to those elements in the community who wield influence and make decisions. In one sense, it relates to what is acceptable to the citizenry in general, in another, to what is acceptable to influential individuals and organized groups in the community, and in still another and in the conventional sense, to what is acceptable to the formal governmental structure—the mayor and city council. All three elements may be in harmony or completely at odds with one another. Where there is full harmony, it is tantamount to effective acceptance of a control measure, but where there is disagreement, the effective degree of acceptance is at the mercy of the dominant element in the community.

Using the term "control" in its broadest sense, the forms of control and degree of control which are acceptable depend upon attitudes that prevail and their more deeply rooted antecedent values. Thus the political climate in relation to any particular control measure involves an exceedingly complex web of value relationships which determine a certain alignment of attitudes, which in turn suggest the likely actions that these attitudes would elicit. To sort out these values, attitudes, and expected action patterns, to relate them to the power structure in the community, and to determine the dominant ones that would prevail under any particular set of local circumstances is an extremely complex proposition that would tax the most advanced research tools of the social scientist.[12] This problem and all its technical ramifications, the substitution of judgment and empirical observation for scientifically based analyses of the political climate, and other similar methodological considerations are beyond the scope of this discussion.

It is sufficient for purposes here to recognize that the political climate, however complex in its origins and its functioning and in whatever way it is analyzed, is a basic practical consideration that affects the nature and extent of control exercised in the public interest. Physical practicalities may identify what is feasible from a technical or engineering viewpoint; fiscal capabilities and jurisdictional considerations may define these limits more narrowly; and political considerations may set still lower limits or entirely eliminate the use of particular control measures. Thus renewal of the blighted sections of a city may be clearly in the interests of public health and safety; a whole range of renewal measures may be technically and financially feasible; and an integrated series of redevelopment, rehabilitation, and conservation control measures may have wide support from civic groups and public agencies. Yet the kinds of measures and the degrees of control which are politically acceptable may be much more narrowly defined and limited in scope. According to values and attitudes they hold,

[12] The concept of community power structure and the pyramid form it appears to take in terms of the hierarchy of influence which key persons in the community exercise on public issues is described by Floyd Hunter, *Community Power Structure*, University of North Carolina Press, 1953.

influential individuals or special-interest groups may exert pressure in the state legislature to block legislation supplying the necessary legal powers for certain renewal measures, or if the legal authority already exists, they may seek to influence the forms of control sanctioned by the local governing body, and so on.

Though the political climate is a practical consideration which affects the control exercised over land development at a particular time, this is not to imply that land use planning is wholly governed by political expediency. The city planning agency aims toward what is consistent with economic and social forces and sound in the public interest. Its perspective includes the present, but its sights are set toward the future. Public objectives are patently concerned with things beyond the present, and plans for the fulfillment of these objectives are no more tied to what is presently politically feasible than to what the courts will allow today in the public interest. Thus in developing a land use plan, the planning agency is viewing land development against a backdrop of long-range considerations, among them the long-run political and legal eventualities. Yet at the same time the foundations are in the present, and progress in bringing plans into reality involves a day-to-day sorting and sifting process and the selection of the best move with reference to the prevailing political climate.

Our concern here has been related to the political climate as a factor affecting the use of controls rather than any detailed consideration of the dynamics of political action. More broadly, our concern has been to identify some of the more important practicalities which tend to condition the effectiveness of control measures utilized in the public interest. This concern in turn relates to a larger, more fundamental one of establishing how the public interest along with the economic and social factors affect the pattern of urban land uses. Let us now proceed to bring together these determinants of land use and examine their significance in relation to one another.

CHAPTER 4

relationships among

land use determinants

Although urban land use determinants have so far been somewhat arbitrarily grouped into three classes, it is the purpose of this concluding section to show that these separate explanations of land use have little practical meaning unless viewed in one interrelated matrix. Basic to a full understanding of this matrix of factors shaping the pattern of land uses in an urban area, of course, is the need for an inclusive theoretical frame of reference mentioned at the outset. Until this kind of foundation theory emerges to provide the guidelines for applied analyses of city planning, land use planning must somehow function as an open-ended process that seeks empirically the balance that is needed among the many factors summarized in the preceding pages.

Short of a rigorously tested theory of land development, it would seem to serve a useful purpose to bring together the concepts of the preceding chapters, array them side by side, and hypothesize some of the interrelationships involved. Such an organization of concepts at the very least should be helpful as a checkoff sheet to insure that all factors are considered in the technical studies undertaken in the land use planning process.

INTERRELATIONSHIPS AMONG DETERMINANTS

Let us first draw upon the behavioral concept set forth in Chapter 2. According to this concept, land goes into use as a consequence of a myriad of individual and group actions. Motivated by values, ideals, and resultant articulated attitudes held by the various organized and unorganized segments of the urban population, these actions follow a defined behavioral sequence that culminates in land use changes.

This concept appears to supply the common thread in all three ways of viewing the origins of land use patterns. In the first chapter, there is a clear indication that land use is a consequence of the economic behavior of the urbanite in the urban land market. In the second chapter, land use is explicitly seen as being influenced by the urbanite's behavior in response to such culture-bound phenomena as customs, traditions, and beliefs. Finally in the last chapter, the health, safety, convenience, economy, and amenity controls employed in the common public interest, can be viewed as the result of behavior consciously calculated to influence land use. In each of these approaches "forces" are sometimes spoken of as determinants. In the behavioral concept, various patterns of behavior are viewed as the ultimate determinants, with "forces" being used as intermediate abstractions to signify the interplay of factors in any particular phase of one or more behavioral cycles.[1]

Now by charting actions connected with each of the three major forms of urban behavior side by side (and there may well be more than three classes) and fitting them to a single sequence of the behavior cycle, interrelationships begin to suggest themselves (see Figure 7). Thus profit-making values concerning the use of the land result in a variety of behavior patterns in the urban land market which in the aggregate *tend* to produce purely economically motivated changes in the land use pattern. At the same time certain livability and culturally oriented values may have the effect of modifying these purely economic actions.[2] Such modifications may occur at the value-forming stage or they may occur in any phase of a behavioral sequence in one or more behavior patterns.

Each of the three forms of urban behavior *tends* to have pure consequences, but because of side effects the ultimate consequences to land use may be quite different from the originally anticipated results. In Figure 7 a crude generalization of this sequence of behavior is presented, with x being the point of equilibrium after all side effects have exerted their influence on a projected change in the land use. More particularly points x_1, x_2, . . . , x_n represent the points where all behavioral relationships involv-

[1] The *behavior cycle* has been previously identified as a recurring sequence of phases in the action process: (1) experiencing needs and wants, (2) setting goals, (3) planning alternative courses of action, and (4) reaching a decision for action (see Figure 2). A series of related cycles are considered to be a *behavior pattern* (see Figure 3).

[2] *Livability* values refer here to public interest considerations of health, safety, convenience, public economy, and amenity. Obviously this segment of the whole has traditionally been of particular concern to the city planner.

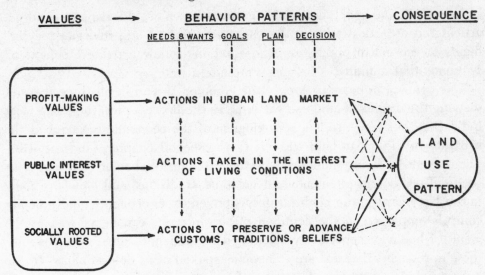

FIGURE 7. Interrelationships Among Land Use Determinants. Points x_1, x_2, . . . , x_n represent points where all side effects of actions seeking changes in land use reach equilibrium, with a consequence of 1, 2, . . . , n changes occurring in the land use pattern.

ing a series of *n* actions reach their equilibriums, resulting in 1, 2, . . . , *n* changes in the land use pattern. Walter Firey's theory of proportionality is a more formal statement of this general concept, and the point *x* on his U-curve representation of the theory (Figure 4) would correspond to point *x* in Figure 7.[3]

Broadly, many actions are evolving concurrently in the sequence suggested in Figure 7, with some in different stages of advancement in the behavior cycle than others. As suggested in Chapter 2, some have planned consequences in the sense that land use changes follow a conscious and rational course of evolution even though they may have undergone modification in the course of the behavior cycle in the manner described above. Some have unplanned consequences in the sense that there is a lack of relationship emerging from two or more planned actions, more particularly a lack of relationship among the one or more phases of each behavior cycle. The absence of such relationships results in unexpected, sometimes inconsistent, or possibly even incompatible uses of land.

Even with the consummation of one or more planned changes in land use and often with the emergence of unplanned consequences, new behavior cycles are set in motion with feedback effects upon human values in the community. Sometimes this feedback process starts before the consum-

[3] Walter Firey, *Land Use in Central Boston,* Harvard University Press, 1947, pp. 326–327. See Chapter 2 for a summary of the theory.

mation of the planned or unplanned changes in the land use patterns, and the final consequence is further modified by ensuing new behavior cycles.

A hypothetical illustration will make the dynamics of these behavioral concepts clearer. Let us say that a combine of builders motivated by profit values sets out to acquire at the outskirts of a city a sizable acreage of open land for development into a large-scale housing project including a regional shopping center. In one behavioral sequence they determine an income-producing need for this activity, define their objectives, cons'·ler the alternatives, and reach a decision to go ahead and acquire a site. The consequent purchase of a site involves a second sequence of behavior. They determine the extent of their profit needs, set their goals, consider alternatives, and again reach a decision. In this process they consider a variety of sites. With respect to Site No. 1, the developers' interpretation of public interest values indicates a possible stalemate that they can ill afford. First, they foresee difficulties in obtaining changes in zoning to permit the kind of development they have in mind, and second, they anticipate that prevailing public policies on extensions of sewer and water facilities will interfere with their plans.

In the case of Site No. 2, the public interest considerations are less important than the culture-bound values. Several members of the combine of developers are respected residents of the small estate community surrounding Site No. 2, and have been accepted into the colony only after prolonged social maneuvering. Not only can strong opposition from this area be expected, but these resident partners of the enterprise face social ostracism if they permit their profit-making values to prevail. Because of social symbols held by the developers themselves, this highly promising site is eliminated from consideration. Thus in this behavior cycle, purely profit-making values do not lead to pure consequences, but rather the subsequent decision on Site No. 3 represents a modified decision in consideration of other values.

With the public announcement of intent to build on Site No. 3, a whole new pattern of behaviors occurs. One group of nearby residents, motivated by livability values, suddenly becomes organized, and in a series of behavioral sequences, takes steps to thwart the new development. One element of the group opposes changes in zoning that would permit the development of a large shopping facility in the area, maintaining that the great traffic loads converging on the area would involve hazards to their children and noise and fumes to the general detriment of the area, that the flashing neon signs at night would have a disturbing effect, that the shopping center would deface the natural attractiveness of the area, and that all these considerations would have a cumulative effect of generally depressing property values for residential purposes in the entire surrounding area. Another element of the group, motivated by socially rooted values, opposes the proposed lower-order residential zoning on grounds of social disruptions. In effect, they maintain that the influx of lower-income groups alien to their symbols of social status will threaten the entity of the group presently resident in surrounding areas. Both elements of the group organized initially as separate groups, but in the subsequent behavioral sequence, finding they had similar goals, they merged in the action phase of their missions.

Other groups may align themselves with the developer according to other values: the social need for more housing, the industry-attracting significance of an adequate supply of housing, the prosperity symbolism of outward signs of growth, and so on. As the behavior cycles move from value stimulus to action, these groups too may merge and function as one. Other new cycles may be introduced. For example, the consolidated opposition may seek support of political groups, or the developers and their sympathizers may seek support of influential persons in the community, bringing the community power structure into the controversy.

Obviously a whole new complex of values quite different from the original profit-making values have been introduced affecting the final outcome of this struggle. The whole scheme may be abandoned, a modified scheme may be adopted as a compromise, or the original proposal may be carried out. What happens and how it affects the configuration of land uses is a consequence of a variety of behavior patterns stemming from a variety of value systems. Thus the land use pattern evolves. Sometimes parts of it are based on actions stemming from a pure system of values unmodified by other systems; and sometimes, as the foregoing illustration suggests, these actions derive from interacting values, not purely profit-making, nor purely public interest or culture-oriented values, but a combination of several values.

APPLICATIONS TO LAND USE PLANNING

What is the significance of this behavioral concept to the technical land use planning process? Now obviously the city planner cannot identify, much less keep tab on all the complex patterns of behavior that the average community sustains. Neither is it realistic to expect that his long-range land development plan will be shaped to accommodate all forms of land-use-oriented behaviors. At the present level of research development in this aspect of social science, the immediate significance of such a concept is the purpose it serves in focusing attention on slighted or overlooked considerations in the technical procedures and in indicating the potentialities of fitting plan effectuation activities more successfully and less blindly to action processes.

Our concern here is primarily with technical rather than effectuation considerations. Accordingly, the foregoing discussion indicates a need for a *balanced* consideration of economic, socially rooted, and public interest factors throughout the land use planning process. This means that land use planning analyses must go beyond the customary emphasis on such public interest considerations as health, safety, convenience, economy, and amenity, and give more focused attention to the way in which the urban land market factors tend to site and arrange land uses and to the way in which culture-bound considerations such as customs, traditions, and beliefs influence the pattern of land uses. This kind of broadened emphasis leads the city planner into a number of uncharted areas much in need of researching. For example, how can he identify dominant patterns in land market behavior? Does the shifting pattern of land values provide an adequate index of market behavior? Or in the matter of customs, traditions, and beliefs, how are these identified and set forth in terms usable to the land use planning technician? More specifically, how does the typology of social areas such as Shevky and Williams have undertaken in the Los Angeles area assist in this task?[4] Future research must come to grips with these questions. Meanwhile more systematic and conscious attention must be directed to the use of available measures of economic and social factors that impinge on the distribution and arrangement of land use to insure that the needed balance is achieved.

Beyond these considerations is the need for recognizing the role that attitudes can play in technical studies in fitting the land development plan to the realities of urban behavior. While the identification of behavior patterns may presently be an impractical appendage to the technical task of land use planning, sampling polls of attitudes may be expected to give perception into values held by strategic action groups and the community at large. Much has been written about "planning for people," but there is a strong possibility that some planning may reflect more of the values of the city planners themselves than those of the people of the community. A soundly conceived method of investigating attitudes in many respects provides information just as basic to the technical land use planning

---

[4] Eshref Shevky and Marilyn Williams, *The Social Areas of Los Angeles,* University of California Press, 1949.

process as the land use survey. Not only would attitude data assist in establishing fundamental needs and wants of the urbanite, but it can be expected to provide insight into both immediate and long-range actions that follow from point x in Figure 7. The task is not "intelligent coöperation with the inevitable" in the live-and-let-live sense of the words, but rather one of seeking rational land use guidelines consonant with dominant attitude trends about the use of space in the city. Thus realistic land use planning must not only take into account the physical practicalities of the land and existing uses it sustains, but it must also identify and interpolate from a changing base of the economic, cultural, and public interest values and project the kind of land development pattern that achieves a balance between all the relevant considerations.

tooling up

for

land use

planning

NARROWING OUR *focus from the general to the particular and shifting from a conceptual to an operational approach, we now enter upon a tooling-up phase in the discussion of urban land use planning. In making this shift, the emphasis will be increasingly directed toward methodological considerations. This is a phase concerned with data collection and data processing in preparation for land use planning analyses taken up in Part III. Involved here are studies of the urban economy, employment, population, and the physical setting of the urban area. While the same kinds of studies are required in analyses for other components of the comprehensive plan, such as thoroughfares and transportation facilities, public utilities, and community facilities of all kinds, the emphasis here is primarily upon the special needs of land use planning.*

Of first importance in tooling up for land use planning are studies of the structure and vitality of the urban economy as key considerations in gauging the amount and rate of land development that is likely to occur in a city. Accordingly, considerable attention is given to methods of studying the make-up and general health of the urban economy. Analyses of employment and population prospects are extensions of these foundation studies, and supply the actual yardsticks needed for estimating amounts and rates of future land development. But to apply these measurements of growth, it is necessary to have a basic description of the existing and past physical setting of the urban area. This is obtained from surveys and analyses of land use and vacant land in the urban area. Thus studies of the urban economy (Chapter 5), employment (Chapter 6), population (Chapter 7), and urban land (Chapter 8) are related prerequisites to the actual determina-

tion of land requirements and the subsequent development of a land use plan. However, along with these prerequisite studies, certain studies of a paralleling nature relate and contribute to the land use planning analyses. Transportation studies (Chapter 9) are of this category and particularly merit passing recognition, especially the relationship between traffic and land use.

The different methods presented in the following chapters have been selected for their general utility to land use planning analysis. Many of them have distinct shortcomings and may be open to question when used out of the accompanying context in forms of investigation or research where a higher level of accuracy may be required. Even within the present context some of the methods presented have limited utility, but these limitations are identified as the various methods are taken up below.

One common consideration in all types of studies taken up in the succeeding chapters is the early identification of a study area to represent what has heretofore been loosely termed "the urban area." As will be seen in Chapter 5 and will become evident again in Chapters 6 and 7, several systems of study areas are required and frequently used in background studies of planning. These are necessary and entirely proper so long as each system is internally consistent and serves a useful purpose within the framework for which it was intended. Nevertheless, ultimately cross comparisons at the urban level are useful and essential to land use planning, and it is in this connection that the question of the need for a common study area is introduced at this point. The urbanized area, the reporting unit new to the U.S. Census in 1950, might prove ideal for planning purposes if data for previous census years were summarized on the same basis, thus permitting trend analyses.[1] Since its area of coverage in a self-regulating way adjusts according to changes in the urban settlement patterns observed in each census, the need for a fixed study area, constant for studies of the urban area—past, present, and future—becomes less crucial in the statistical reporting of population, economic, and other similar characteristics of the urban area.

Since this more flexible approach is not at present feasible, it appears that the use of some suitable geographic area with constant boundaries is the next best solution. Ideally this area would correspond to what is later referred to as the planning area, an area of special concern to land use planning but often quite different from the standard statistical areas employed in census summaries. But since the extent of this area and the specification of its boundaries generally remains fluid until the land use plan is firmed up, some other form of study area must be settled upon at this tooling-up stage of the land use planning process.

The urban study area has two major requirements. First, it should be an area officially used for reporting census information. Second, it should be larger than the census-defined urbanized area, but not so large as to be out of scale with, and impractical to cover in land use and vacant land surveys. It

[1] An urbanized area is an area with at least one city of 50,000 population or more and the surrounding urban fringe which includes: (1) incorporated places of 2500 or more; (2) incorporated places of less than 2500 having at least 100 dwelling units with a density of at least 500 dwelling units per square mile; (3) unincorporated territory with a density of at least 500 dwelling units per square mile; and (4) territory devoted to commercial, industrial, transportation, recreational, and other purposes functionally related to the central city. Also included are noncontiguous areas with the specified dwelling unit density if they are within 1½ miles of the main contiguous urbanized area as measured along the shortest connecting highway. See Bureau of the Census, *U.S. Census of Population: 1950*, U.S. Government Printing Office, 1952.

*should be an area that may reasonably be expected
to contain the contiguous development functionally
related to the urban center of interest that will be
building up in the next 20 to 25 years. For the larger
metropolitan centers, the Standard Metropolitan
Area (SMA) generally is a logical choice as the urban study area for employment and population
analyses because of the availability of both standard
census information and special census tabulations
made for SMA's.*[2] *The limits of these areas also usually extend beyond the contiguous built-up area of
the central city. Where these areas involve impracticalities from a land use point of view, downward
adjustments of the area and the data obtained from
standard sources may be made to correspond to
fewer counties or fractional parts of counties. Where
parts of counties are employed, the limits are drawn
around smaller civil division areas, such as townships, towns, or boroughs. For a smaller urban area
not identified by the Federal Committee as an SMA,*

[2] As officially approved by the Federal Committee on Standard
Metropolitan Areas (an interagency committee with the Bureau of
the Budget serving as coördinator), SMA's are selected on the
basis of the following principles:
1. Each Standard Metropolitan Area must include at least one city
   of 50,000 population or more. Areas may cross state lines.
2. Where two cities of 50,000 population or over are within 20
   miles of each other, they will ordinarily be included in the same
   area.
3. Each county included in a Standard Metropolitan Area must
   have either 10,000 nonagricultural workers or 10 percent of the
   nonagricultural workers in the area, or more than one-half of the
   county's population must have been included in the "metropolitan district" as originally defined by the Bureau of the Census.
   In addition, nonagricultural workers must constitute at least
   two-thirds of the total employed labor force of the county.
4. Each county included in a Standard Metropolitan Area must be
   economically and socially integrated with the county containing
   the largest city in the area. A county has been regarded as integrated (a) if 15 percent of the workers living in the county work
   in the county containing the largest city in the area, or (b) if
   25 percent of those working in the county live in the county
   containing the largest city in the area, or (c) if telephone calls
   from the county to the county containing the largest city in the
   area average 4 or more calls per subscriber per month.
Taken from Bureau of the Budget, *Standard Metropolitan Area
Definitions,* a mimeographed bulletin dated July 28, 1950.

a simple county or fractional parts of one or more counties may be used as the urban study area. Here, too, the limits are drawn around a suitable combination of recognized minor civil divisions.

One other general observation on the tooling-up phase merits attention at the outset. It relates to data collection. To avoid needless dissipation of time and effort, each of the studies covered in the succeeding chapters requires careful planning and disciplined execution. A "broadside approach" to data collection simply because "we may need the information sometime" rarely proves to be justified. Selectivity is essential, and this is possible only if the exact needs of the study are worked out in advance. This is such an elemental and self-evident aspect of survey operations that its mention would appear to be superfluous, yet the "broadside approach" continues to be used with consequent waste of time and effort spent in processing data not tabbed for a specific use, summarizing it, puzzling over possible uses for it, storing it, and eventually scrapping it.

CHAPTER 5

the urban economy

A knowledge of the structure and functioning of the urban economy is fundamental to all land use planning analyses. The destiny of an urban center is controlled by the extent and character of its productive or income-producing activity and by its general vitality. Studies of the economic basis for this activity hold the key to why a city exists in the first place, and tell how it has developed to where it is today and what its future prospects are. Stated another way, most metropolitan areas exist because they serve as centers for the production and distribution of goods and services. Production and distribution functions create jobs, and employment opportunities attract people, who in turn symbolize the city.

Viewed in these terms, the urban economy thus conditions the amount of land development that occurs. For example, an expanding economy with the implications it holds for new businesses and industries and population growth means more land going into use. Similarly economic forces that are responsible for leveling off or declining trends in economic activity also exert influences on the pattern of urban land uses in the city. Apart from their significance in understanding the dynamics of land use changes, studies of the urban economy have very fundamental implications for land use planning analyses. With a knowledge of the trends of growth, leveling off, or decline in economic activity, the city planner is better able to develop yardsticks (see Chapters 6 and 7) which assist him in estimating the extent and character of changing land requirements (see Part III) that form the basis for a land development plan. For example, studies of employment are a key element in population forecasts, and population estimates are used in scaling land development needs. Estimates of future land requirements for industrial uses are based on manufacturing employment trends, and future space needs for commercial uses draw upon employment trends in whole-sale trade, and so on. Plans for central, regional, community, and neigh-

81

borhood shopping centers draw upon studies of population and purchasing power in and around the urban center.

The importance of economic studies and the fundamental role they play in land use planning will become apparent again and again in later chapters. This chapter considers first methods of analyzing the structure and functioning of the urban economy, and then takes up techniques for gauging its general vitality.

What is termed *the urban economy* is regarded here as a system of production, distribution, and consumption embracing the sum total productive activity within an urban center and that part of its hinterland which is dependent to a marked degree on facilities and services available in the city. Productive activity thus refers not only to manufacturing, agricultural, fishing, and extractive activity in which products are processed and/or marketed, utilizing facilities and services of the city, but also to trade, finance, transport, government, and other services using the city as a base of operations. Thus defined, productive activity in a localized economic area possesses the characteristics and dynamics of a miniature national economy.

Because of the specialized and complex character of the work involved, a full-fledged analysis of the economy of an urban area in all its manifold aspects requires the skills of an economist. He is the specialist who probes into all the facets of production and distribution activities, employment trends, family income and expenditure patterns, and other elements which explain the economic structure and functioning of a city and give a picture of its general economic health. While the economist may be employed in the role of a specialist in these studies, the city planner as the generalist must not only know something of the scope of such studies, but he must also be prepared to execute limited types of investigations, particularly those that tie directly into land use planning analyses.

There are two conceptual approaches to the study of the urban economy, one regionally oriented, and the other urban-oriented. It is an underlying premise of the first approach that economic activity in any urban center of interest is affected by other centers of activity in its immediate region and is ultimately linked to the national economy as a whole. To put it another way, an urban center's *present* economic position in relation to other urban areas is dependent on what share of the regional and ultimately the national total of goods and services it produces in each line of local economic activity. Its *future* position is dependent on its capacity to develop new productive resources and expand existing ones in relation to other cities capable of engaging in the same activities within the same regional framework.

The urban-centered approach to the analysis of the urban economy begins at home (a given urban center of interest), but at the same time is externally focused, in that it seeks to explain the city's economic structure in terms of the goods and services it produces that are consumed outside the localized area of study. It identifies as the "base" of the urban economy the goods and services which are consumed externally. Thus any industry is classified as basic if it produces or distributes goods and services for "export" outside the localized area of study, and any industry whose goods and services are marketed at home is classed as service or nonbasic.

In the immediately succeeding sections of this chapter both concepts are considered in greater detail, premised on the necessity of viewing the urban economy from both a regional and localized vantage point. To obtain a fully rounded understanding of the urban economy, it is necessary to look first at national economic forces and trends and successively examine how they are influenced or altered in the larger regions of the United States, in the subregions, and so on down to the locale of interest. At the same time it is necessary to look at local productive activity, particularly local resources—the productive and distributive resources, labor resources, and the capital resources for financing new economic activity or for expanding established activities—and gauge the capacity for expanding the locality's productive activity *in harmony with regional factors.*

REGIONALLY ORIENTED APPROACHES

A central consideration in the regionally oriented approach to the study of the urban economy is one of linkage—the interdependence of the locale with its region and a whole system of regions which make up the nation. In the American economy, differences in the distribution of natural resources and variations in the degree of economic organization, technological development, and labor specialization have the effect of increasing the interdependence of regions, and within them, their urban centers. If the economy of an urban area were self-sufficient, as is approached in the cultures of some parts of the world, there would be no need to relate the local economy to that of the region and the nation. However, in our mechanized and highly organized economy, where transportation and communication systems are developed to an advanced degree and where there is territorial division of labor, localized productive activity is conditioned by the interplay of forces in the region and nation.

The existence of spatial linkage is observed in a number of studies. Alfred

Weber's work in the early 1900's on the theory of industrial location gives implicit recognition to the economic interdependence of regions in his "agglomeration analysis."[1] More recent work of other economists working under different location theories, for example, Sargent Florence and his work on the spatial dependence between industries[2] and Walter Isard and his emphasis on space-economy analyses[3] also lend credence to the fundamental importance of linkage factors in the study of a particular economy, whether national, regional, or local.

The foregoing references further recognize that there are marked variations in the linkage between cities and between regions as reflected in industrial location patterns. In pursuing his interregional space-economy analyses, Isard points to the volume of commodity flows from region to region as an indication of the extent of their economic interdependence. "If these flows are regarded as bonds which link components of the system to one another, it can be seen that the greater the magnitude of the flows in any area, the more highly interrelated are the components in that area."[4] Indeed, Isard hints at a system of economic dominance and subdominance among regions (very much along the lines of Bogue's conclusions discussed later in the chapter), suggesting that through variations noted in interregional flows between aggregates of economic activity, hierarchal tendencies of varying order among regions may be identified.

From the foregoing, it should be evident that studies of the urban economy must recognize these elemental intra- and interregional relationships which profoundly affect the analysis and ultimate conclusions concerning the economic structure and functioning of any particular urban center. But having established the importance of a regional orientation to economic studies, how can regional influences be determined and made an integral part of studies of the urban economy, and how are regions identified for purposes of these analyses?

Two approaches to the study of regional spheres of influence are discussed below. The first, input-output analysis, is concerned with the dynamics of commodity flows between aggregates of industry. These aggregates or focal areas of economic activity can be single urban centers or a whole metropolitan complex of centers. Whatever study area is selected, the

[1] Alfred Weber, *Uber den Standort der Industrien*, 1909. See also C. J. Friedrich, *Alfred Weber's Theory of Location of Industries*, University of Chicago Press, 1929.

[2] P. Sargent Florence, *Investment, Location and Size of Plant*, Cambridge University Press, 1948.

[3] Walter Isard, "The General Theory of Location and Space-Economy," *Quarterly Journal of Economics*, November, 1949; see also his "Interregional and Regional Input-Output Analysis: A Model of Space-Economy," *The Review of Economics and Statistics*, November, 1951.

[4] Walter Isard, "Regional and National Product Projections and their Interrelations," *Long-Range Economic Projection*, Volume 16, Studies in Income and Wealth by the National Bureau of Economic Research, Princeton University Press, 1954, pp. 456–457.

structure and functioning of its economy is viewed and analyzed in the context of the web of flows in a larger region and whole systems of regions. The second approach, an approximation analysis, uses conventional divisions of the nation into regions, subregions, and so on, and by crude step-down procedures from a larger parent area, develops gross measures of how the parts of the whole are estimated to share in total national productive activity.

Input-Output Analysis

Some recent empirically based theoretical work by Leontief[5] and some experimental extensions of it by Isard and others have resulted in the development of what is termed the "input-output technique" for measuring interindustry relationships in a given spatial setting—localized, regional, or national. The technique postulates that any given line of economic activity bears a measurable relationship to every other industry in the economy, and that these relationships can be set forth in a series of equations readily solved by computing machines. These interindustry relationships can be expressed in terms of what Leontief has referred to as a huge revenue expenditure accounting system.[6] The revenue side of the balance sheet shows how the output for every industry is distributed, and the expenditure side records for each industry the distribution of inputs per unit of output from all industries.

Table 1, reproduced from some recent work of Isard, shows a simplified hypothetical table of basic coefficients for a single region, indicating input per dollar value of output. This table of coefficients is computed from a similar type of table giving actual total dollar values imputed to all transactions in economic activity in the region's economy.[7] It is read by columns. Column 1 shows the input per dollar value of output from each of all the other industries supplying goods or services to the agriculture and fisheries industry. The other columns show similar relationships for the other industrial groups.

[5] Wassily Leontief, *The Structure of the American Economy, 1919–1939*, Oxford University Press, 1951.

[6] *Ibid.*, p. 11.

[7] To obtain some idea as to the detail possible in presenting the interindustry flow of goods and services both as to actual dollar transactions and as to input-output coefficients, the reader is referred to the published 200-sector tables (actually abridged from 500-sector tables) of the Interindustry Relations Study of 1947 for the United States as a whole, prepared by the Division of Interindustry Economics, U.S. Department of Labor. For a review of this project see W. D. Evans and M. Hoffenberg, "The Interindustry Relations Study for 1947," *The Review of Economics and Statistics*, May, 1952.

TABLE 1.   Interindustry Transactions, Hypothetica˙ Region X, 19xx[a]
(Cents of Direct Inputs per Dollar of Output)

	Industry Purchasing									
Industry Producing	Agriculture and Fisheries (1)	Food and Kindred Products (2)	Textiles, Leather, and Allied Products (3)	Lumber, Paper, and Allied Products (4)	Chemicals, Nonmetallic Minerals, and Allied Products (5)	Primary Metals, Machinery, and Equipment (6)	Coal and Electric Power (7)	Transportation (8)	Trade, Services, including Government (9)	Households (10)
1. Agriculture and fisheries	25	40	8	1	5	0	0	0	0	30
2. Food and kindred products	5	11	0	0	3	0	0	0	2	17
3. Textiles, leather, and allied products	0	1	23	3	1	2	2	1	1	7
4. Lumber, paper, and allied products	0	1	1	14	3	2	1	0	3	2
5. Chemicals, nonmetallic minerals, and allied products	3	4	4	5	21	4	5	5	3	4
6. Primary metals, machinery, and equipment	1	1	2	3	2	38	3	4	4	3
7. Coal and electric power	0	1	2	2	3	2	15	5	4	0
8. Transportation	3	3	2	5	5	6	2	0	1	4
9. Trade, services, including government	14	11	13	13	15	12	13	17	20	33
10. Households	49	27	45	54	42	34	59	68	61	00

[a] Adapted from Walter Isard and Vincent Whitney, "Atomic Power and Regional Development," *Bulletin of Atomic Scientists*, April, 195 p. 121.

Table 2, taken from another work of Isard and using a slightly different industrial classification system, presents a hypothetical matrix of coefficients to illustrate how the input-output technique can be used in interregional analyses.[8] For purposes of illustration, Isard drew this table to differentiate between three kinds of regions according to the characteristic export industry of each, with Region I specializing in heavy manufacturing, Region II in light manufacturing, and Region III in agricultural and extractive activity. Reading by columns, any single column shows the cents' worth of input from each industrial class of activity in each region appearing in the stub of the table, per dollar's worth of output for the selected class of industry in a specified region at the head of the table.

The technique therefore establishes a basic relationship between the volume of output of any given industry in any given region and the volume of input required in the production process from all other industries in this

[8] Had the same classes of industry been used, for all purposes Table 1 might have been the equivalent of Metropolitan Region I in Table 2.

and all other regions. Thus, for a factory engaged in producing aluminum cooking ware in a specified region, there are so many cents of input per dollar value of saucepan output attributable to one or more alumina reduction plants of the aluminum industry located in this and other regions in the matrix, and so many cents of input attributable to other industries contributing to the final product from this and other regions. Moreover, in addition to the first set of relationships, there are secondary ones, tertiary ones, and so on. Thus the input equivalent from the alumina reduction works for each dollar value of saucepan output involves second-round input equivalents from the electric power industry drawn upon in reducing alumina to aluminum, and this in turn involves third-round input equivalents in coal, machinery, and transmission lines used in the generation and distribution of power, and so on.

To explain the round-by-round analysis in terms of the Table 2 matrix, Table 3 and the following explanation are taken from the work of Isard and Kavesh:

> To illustrate the usefulness of input structure information, suppose a resource development program calls for an increase of one million dollars in the output of heavy manufacturing in Region I.[9] How will this affect the output of each activity in each region?
>
> In column 1 of Table 2 are listed the coefficients which indicate the cents' worth of various inputs required per dollar output of heavy manufacturing. Multiplying these coefficients by one million gives us the direct inputs required to produce one million dollars' worth of heavy manufactures. These are called the first-round input requirements and are listed in column 1 of Table 3.
>
> But to produce the first-round requirement of $330,000 of heavy manufacturing (item 1 in column 1, Table 3) likewise requires a whole series of inputs. These can be obtained by multiplying column 1 of Table 2 by 330,000. And to produce the $20,000 of transportation (item 3, column 1, Table 3) requires inputs which can be obtained by multiplying column 3 of Table 2 by 20,000. Similarly, the inputs required to produce each of the other items listed in column 1 of Table 3 can be derived. . . .
>
> Adding together all these inputs . . . necessary for the production of the first round of requirements yields the second round of requirements which is recorded in column 2 of Table 3. In turn, the production of the second round of requirements necessitates a third round. . . . Furnishing a third round requires a fourth; a fourth round, a fifth; etc. Each of these rounds is recorded in Table 3. It should be noted that the totals of the rounds converge. After a point it becomes feasible to stop the round-by-round computation and to extrapolate the remaining requirements.[10]

[9] Isard has published with Robert E. Kuenne an actual case study of such a situation in "The Impact of Steel upon the Greater New York–Philadelphia Region: A Study in Agglomeration Projection," *The Review of Economics and Statistics,* November, 1953.

[10] Isard and Kavesh, *loc. cit.*, p. 155.

TABLE 2. Hypothetical Intermetropolitan Transactions Table, 19xx[a]
(Cents Worth of Inputs per Dollar of Output)

Industry Producing	Metropolitan Region I									Power and Com-muni-ca-tion		
	Heavy Man-ufac-turing (1)	Power and Com-muni-ca-tion (2)	Trans-por-ta-tion (3)	Trade (4)	Insur-ance and Rental (5)	Busi-ness and Pers. Serv. (6)	Edu-ca-tional and Other Serv. (7)	Con-struc-tion (8)	House-holds (9)	Light Manu-fac-turing (10)	Power and Com-muni-ca-tion (11)	Tr... po... t... ti... (1...
Metropolitan Region I:												
1. Heavy manufacturing	33	1	3	1	—	9	1	18	3	2	1	
2. Power and communication	1	11	3	2	8	4	2	—	1	—	—	-
3. Transportation	2	2	5	1	1	1	2	4	3	—	—	-
4. Trade	1	—	2	—	2	3	5	9	12	—	—	-
5. Insurance and rental activities	1	1	3	5	7	5	4	2	12	—	—	-
6. Business and personal services	1	1	2	7	1	4	2	3	3	—	—	-
7. Educational and other basic services	—	—	—	—	—	—	1	—	10	—	—	-
8. Construction	—	4	6	—	10	—	1	—	—	—	—	-
9. Households	34	58	58	63	53	46	50	40	1	—	—	-
Metropolitan Region II:												
10. Light manufacturing	4	1	2	2	1	14	15	4	20	28	1	
11. Power and communication	—	—	—	—	—	—	—	—	—	1	11	
12. Transportation	—	—	—	—	—	—	—	—	—	2	2	
13. Trade	—	—	—	—	—	—	—	—	—	2	—	
14. Insurance and rental activities	—	—	—	—	—	—	—	—	—	1	1	
15. Business and personal services	—	—	—	—	—	—	—	—	—	2	1	
16. Educational and other basic services	—	—	—	—	—	—	—	—	—	—	—	
17. Construction	—	—	—	—	—	—	—	—	—	—	4	
18. Households	—	—	—	—	—	—	—	—	—	25	58	5
Region III:												
19. Agriculture and extraction	6	5	4	1	2	—	4	18	6	21	5	
20. Power and communication	—	—	—	—	—	—	—	—	—	—	—	-
21. Transportation	—	—	—	—	—	—	—	—	—	—	—	-
22. Trade	—	—	—	—	—	—	—	—	—	—	—	-
23. Insurance and rental activities	—	—	—	—	—	—	—	—	—	—	—	-
24. Business and personal services	—	—	—	—	—	—	—	—	—	—	—	-
25. Educational and other basic services	—	—	—	—	—	—	—	—	—	—	—	-
26. Construction	—	—	—	—	—	—	—	—	—	—	—	-
27. Households	—	—	—	—	—	—	—	—	—	—	—	-

[a] Walter Isard and Robert Kavesh, "Economic Structural Interrelations of Metropolitan Regions," *The American Journal of Socio* The University of Chicago Press, September, 1954, p. 153. Copyright, 1954, by the University of Chicago.

	Metropolitan Region II					Region III								
	Insurance and Rental	Business and Pers. Serv.	Educational and Other Serv.	Construction	Households	Agriculture and Extraction	Power and Communication	Transportation	Trade	Insurance and Rental	Business and Pers. Serv.	Educational and Other Serv.	Construction	Households
de)	(14)	(15)	(16)	(17)	(18)	(19)	(20)	(21)	(22)	(23)	(24)	(25)	(26)	(27)
	—	9	1	18	3	1	1	3	1	—	9	1	18	3
-	—	—	—	—	—	—	—	—	—	—	—	—	—	—
-	—	—	—	—	—	—	—	—	—	—	—	—	—	—
-	—	—	—	—	—	—	—	—	—	—	—	—	—	—
	—	—	—	—	—	—	—	—	—	—	—	—	—	—
-	—	—	—	—	—	—	—	—	—	—	—	—	—	—
-	—	—	—	—	—	—	—	—	—	—	—	—	—	—
-	—	—	—	—	—	—	—	—	—	—	—	—	—	—
-	—	—	—	—	—	—	—	—	—	—	—	—	—	—
2	1	14	15	4	20	6	1	2	2	1	14	15	4	20
2	8	4	2	—	1	—	—	—	—	—	—	—	—	—
1	1	1	2	4	3	—	—	—	—	—	—	—	—	—
-	2	3	5	9	12	—	—	—	—	—	—	—	—	—
5	7	5	4	2	12	—	—	—	—	—	—	—	—	—
7	1	4	2	3	3	—	—	—	—	—	—	—	—	—
-	—	.	1	—	10	—	—	—	—	—	—	—	—	—
-	10	—	1	—	—	—	—	—	—	—	—	—	—	—
3	53	46	50	40	1	—	—	—	—	—	—	—	—	—
1	2	—	4	18	6	28	5	4	1	2	—	4	18	6
-	—	—	—	—	—	1	11	3	2	8	4	2	—	1
-	—	—	—	—	—	3	2	5	1	1	1	2	4	3
-	—	—	—	—	—	2	—	2	—	2	3	5	9	12
-	—	—	—	—	—	4	1	3	5	7	5	4	2	12
-	—	—	—	—	—	1	1	2	7	1	4	2	3	3
-	—	—	—	—	—	—	—	—	—	—	—	1	—	10
-	—	—	—	—	—	—	4	6	—	10	—	1	—	—
-	—	—	—	—	—	40	58	58	63	53	46	50	40	1

TABLE 3. Input Requirements (Hypothetical), by Round, for $1 Million Output of Heavy Manufacturing in Me[t]ropolitan Region I[a]

Industry Grouping	First-Round Input Requirements (1)	Second-Round Input Requirements (2)	Third-Round Input Requirements (3)	Fourth-Round Input Requirements (4)	Fifth-Round Input Requirements (5)	Sixth-Round Input Requirements (6)	Seventh-Round Input Requirements (7)	Sum of Rounds (8)
Metropolitan Region I:								
1. Heavy manufacturing	$330,000	$118,810	$ 47,793	$ 23,417	$ 13,407	$ 8,559	$ 5,884	$ 550,87
2. Power and communication	10,000	8,670	7,763	4,614	2,858	1,667	994	36,56
3. Transportation	20,000	14,910	7,417	4,508	2,516	1,475	871	51,69
4. Trade	10,000	31,440	15,687	11,021	6,042	3,573	2,060	79,82
5. Insurance and rental activities	10,000	32,940	18,965	12,612	7,135	4,155	2,430	88,23
6. Business and personal services	10,000	11,810	8,159	4,860	2,906	1,664	983	40,38
7. Educational and other basic services	—	22,700	10,077	7,463	3,945	2,359	1,344	47,88
8. Construction	—	2,600	4,759	2,731	1,789	1,031	622	13,53
9. Households	340,000	148,070	110,102	57,920	34,886	19,773	10,805	721,55
Metropolitan Region II:								
10. Light manufacturing	40,000	75,600	60,601	47,894	34,849	25,264	18,115	302,32
11. Power and communication	—	400	971	1,182	1,190	1,056	856	5,65
12. Transportation	—	800	1,781	1,821	1,601	1,309	1,016	8,32
13. Trade	—	800	2,364	3,044	2,858	2,470	1,963	13,49
14. Insurance and rental activities	—	400	1,696	2,689	2,706	2,490	1,972	11,95
15. Business and personal services	—	800	1,825	1,954	1,772	1,479	1,159	8,98
16. Educational and other basic services	—	—	670	1,387	1,394	1,275	1,033	5,75
17. Construction	—	—	104	325	446	455	391	1,72
18. Households	—	10,000	20,747	20,613	18,918	15,744	12,381	98,43
Region III:								
19. Agriculture and extraction	60,000	60,220	50,741	39,365	29,244	21,250	15,387	276,20
20. Power and communication	—	600	1,122	1,402	1,386	1,229	1,019	6,75
21. Transportation	—	1,800	2,430	2,360	2,085	1,673	1,310	11,65
22. Trade	—	1,200	3,226	3,541	3,481	2,922	2,385	16,75
23. Insurance and rental activities	—	2,400	4,646	4,962	4,701	3,917	3,156	23,78
24. Business and personal services	—	600	1,256	1,490	1,463	1,260	1,032	7,10
25. Educational and other basic services	—	—	1,600	1,876	1,969	1,680	1,397	8,52
26. Construction	—	—	372	664	719	682	581	3,01
27. Households	—	24,000	27,936	28,508	25,037	20,595	16,189	142,26
Total	$830,000	$571,570	$414,810	$284,253	$211,303	$151,006	$107,335	$2,583,27

[a] Walter Isard and Robert Kavesh, "Economic Structural Interrelations of Metropolitan Regions," *The American Journal of Sociology*, Th[e] University of Chicago Press, September, 1954, p. 156. Copyright, 1954, by the University of Chicago.

The input-output rationale thus involves (1) *an interindustry analysis* establishing in any given region the basic relationships existing between the volume of output for each industry and the volume of input required from all other industries in the production processes of each such industry, and (2) what Isard refers to as *a space-economy analysis* establishing relationships in the flow of commodities between regions which occur in fulfillment of input-output requirements in the interindustry analysis as given in Step 1 above. Step 1 derives a table of interindustry coefficients applicable to the region under study, and Step 2 derives a table of interregional-interindustry coefficients. Thus when these coefficients are applied to actual figures of output and results are summed up industry by industry, it is possible not only to have a measure of interindustry relationships but also to obtain a picture of the distribution of economic activity with respect to a given urban center of interest and with respect to the system of regions employed in the analysis.

The examples above illustrate in greatly simplified form the theoretical use of the input-output technique in analyzing existing productive activity within a localized, regional, or national economy. To estimate future productive levels, the technique assumes as "given" some reliable forecast of the effective demand for all the various economic lines for the system of regions involved in the study. Successively applying to the assumed future demand levels the input-output coefficients from the basic tables, the urban center's share of estimated future regional productive activity in all economic lines is determined.

This is not to imply that the set of values appearing in the basic tables of input-output coefficients will remain constant. These can change in time and will require adjustment. Over a period of time, changes in technology will necessitate adjustments in the basic tables, but these changes do not occur so rapidly that they cannot be anticipated and the appropriate adjustments made to the basic tables. Variations in price relationships also occur in time, but tests made by Leontief suggest that there is sufficient degree of stability in the pattern of price relationships that here too adjustments can be estimated with a fair degree of accuracy.[11]

The basic principles of the input-output technique are not new to economic theory, but go back a great many years.[12] However, their applications to the analysis of the structural make-up of an economy are relatively recent and offer much promise to a wide variety of studies, among them city plan-

---

[11] Leontief, *op. cit.*, pp. 201–202.

[12] Evans and Hoffenberg cite a French work published some 200 years ago, *Tableau Economique,* by Francois Quesnay, Adam Smith's classic work, and the work of Leon Walras, a French economist, 100 years later, as containing some of the ideas which Leontief first applied in the modern economic environment. See Evans and Hoffenberg, *loc. cit.*, p. 97.

ning analyses of the urban economy. Methodologically the technique not only offers an important means of evaluating interindustry and interregional relationships in all their complexities, but by examining these relationships in the context of aggregates of industry in particular urban settings, it also permits analysis of the economic functioning of one urban center in relation to other urban centers in its region and other regions of the nation.

However, there are obstacles to immediate general use of input-output analyses for these purposes. There is the mechanical problem of data availability in the detail and form needed to trace interindustry-interregional flows of goods and services. This situation can be remedied in time, but the complex character of the procedural and mathematical operations involved is another deterrent to general usage of the technique. However, if the technique can be simplified to permit general understanding and use by the nonexpert and if it can be geared to utilize standard sources of data (or, alternatively, if the presently required data can become a part of the regularly reported statistics of a governmental agency), it offers much promise of becoming a widely used instrument for analyzing the structure and dynamics of the urban economy.

Of course, where the technique is used in estimating future trends in the make-up of the economy, it faces a limitation common to all projective analyses, namely, the difficulties inherent in estimating future demand levels. Even in a context involving the use of highly qualified and carefully stated alternate assumptions, the input-output technique is no better off than other techniques. Here too, future demand levels must necessarily be presented by gross aggregate classes of industry and cannot extend to the same level of detail possible in analyses of current interindustry-interregional relationships.

One of the most promising uses of the technique in projective analyses is in experimental studies. These employ approaches closely paralleling those of the natural sciences. For example, using a hydraulic engineering prototype experiment, one can approach the study of an urban economy in this vein: If a certain series of flows are introduced into a given system of flows, what are the resultant rearrangements in this system of flows? Isard's interesting analysis of the impact of the new steel production and steel fabricating activity in the New York–Philadelphia industrial region triggered by U.S. Steel's Fairless Works furnishes a tangible illustration of the potentialities of such an approach.[13] The study found that chain reaction from the construction of plants with an estimated three million tons of new steel capacity would produce for this region in the period of a decade a minimum new employment in all forms of industry amounting to more than

[13] Walter Isard and Robert E. Kuenne, *loc. cit.*

180,000, with a resulting population equivalent estimated at 419,000 persons. Even though this study is concerned with expansion only in one sector of this region's economy, it illustrates the possibilities of this kind of projective analysis for city planning studies.

Approximation Analyses

In identifying the linkage between the localized urban economy and its region and the nation, what is the alternative to the foregoing types of analyses which trace out the industry-to-industry and region-to-region flows of goods and services? As suggested earlier, another much less meaningful approach sometimes used is a comparative analysis as to how regions, subregions, and other more localized economic areas successively share in national productive activity, using such standard measures as value added by manufacture, wholesale sales, retail sales, and receipts from services. By taking cross-sectional readings of productive activity for all component geographical areas in a given system of study areas and expressing them as a percentage of the larger parent area, and by taking them for different periods of time, comparisons are drawn as to the relative position of each study area in each line of activity in relation to all other areas in that system and whether that position is improving, remaining constant, or deteriorating in time.

Such analyses thus employ ratio techniques involving the computation of a series of interlocking ratios of productive activity for the particular system of study areas considered to exert an influence on the localized areas being studied. Table 4 illustrates the form in which results can be summarized. It shows that successively smaller geographic areas examined from the nation as a whole down to the Charlotte, North Carolina, primary trade area, for the most part, appear to be increasing their share in the economic activity of their respective parent areas, whereas the Charlotte Standard Metropolitan Area, viewed in relation to its larger primary trade area, appears to be gaining steadily in wholesale activity, falling off in its share of manufacturing activity and the services, and remaining more or less constant in retail activity.[14] Such a table can be expanded to show subcategories of manufacturing, wholesale, retail, and service lines, depending on the detail reported by the census for the particular urban center being studied.

[14] The Charlotte primary trade area is here assumed to correspond roughly with the composite of N.C. State Economic Areas 4b and 5 and S.C. State Economic Area 3. These area delineations are discussed in the next subsection of this chapter.

TABLE 4. Some Illustrative Indices Showing How Successively Smaller Geographical Areas Share in a Parent Area's Productive Activity

Geographic Areas Compared	Value Added by Manufacture 1929 1939 1947			Wholesale Sales 1929 1939 1948			Retail Sales 1929 1939 1948			Receipts from Services[a] 1939 1948	
South Atlantic states as a percent of U.S.	8.0	9.0	9.3	6.7	8.3	8.6	8.6	10.4	11.3	10.7	13.4
Charlotte area of metro. dominance as a percent of South Atlantic region[b]	32.6	30.4	32.8	18.9	20.0	21.8	18.5	18.8	19.6	1.3	6.2
State Economic Areas N.C. 4b and 5 and S.C. 3 as a percent of Charlotte area of metro. dominance[c]	18.3	25.0	29.0	31.0	31.9	36.9	22.4	21.7	22.1	21.6	24.8
Charlotte Standard Metro. Area as a percent of Economic Areas N.C. 4b and 5, and S.C. 3	19.5	15.5	12.2	68.0	71.8	75.6	29.8	28.6	28.8	38.1	36.1

[a] Personal, business, and repair services only.

[b] Charlotte area of metropolitan dominance adapted from Bogue's delineations; see Figure 8 and accompanying discussion.

[c] For map of State Economic Areas, see Figure 11 and accompanying discussion.

Where projective estimates are desired, this approach, as in the case of the input-output technique, requires a "given" forecast of national productive activity. Such a forecast, of course, must be available broken down into the standard measures being employed, viz., value added by manufacture, wholesale and retail sales, and receipts from services.

There are two variations on the ratio technique used in such projective analyses. The most common form expresses these standard measures of productive activity in terms of simple direct ratios of figures for a particular area to those of the larger parent area. Past values for these relationships are arranged in a time series and extrapolated by fitting a mathematical curve to the data. The projected region-to-nation ratio is then applied to the "given" absolute figures of the nation to obtain absolute values for the region; the projected subregion-to-region ratio is next applied to this resultant absolute regional estimate to obtain an estimate for the subregion in absolute terms; and so on. The other variation on the ratio technique employs the same procedure but introduces an element of control to the procedure by making tandem analyses of all subarea parts of the parent area and balancing the results with the total before proceeding to the next step-down. This is sometimes called the apportionment technique to distinguish it from the direct ratio step-down procedure first described.

Such an analysis reflects the combined effects of interindustry-interregional flows and indicates where gross changes are occurring in time, but it cannot trace flows between industries within and between regions. Thus it does not provide a direct measure of linkage, but only a crude cross-sectional view of the gross effects of commodity flows as they figure into the total transactions recorded for the selected system of study areas.

Delineating Regional Spheres of Economic Influence

As indicated above, regional concepts are introduced into economic analyses as a means of studying how small economic units—a particular industry or a grouping of economic activities that are represented by the urban center or complex of urban centers—are linked to one another, to the region, and to the national economy. However, there are certain practicalities that dictate the kinds of study areas employed in these analyses of linkage. At present the regionally oriented approaches to the study of the urban economy described above are dependent on the system of study areas for which U.S. Census data on productive activity are reported. As can be seen in Table 4, approximation analyses are undertaken entirely within the framework of conventional regional and political division delineations.

Input-output analyses also face limitations in the regions selected for study. In theory the term "region" is used in these studies in a fluid sense to denote a study area containing an observable series of commodity flows of specified internal consistency. This is generally one which possesses self-sufficiency with respect to a maximum number of like goods and services, or, stated another way, one which exhibits a marked internal interdependence of income as determined through flow phenomena.[15] If data requirements presented no problem, the system of regions thus employed would be derived in the course of the input-output analysis. But we know that there are restrictions involved in the form in which needed data are reported, and so, among those proficient in the use of the input-output technique, there is explicit recognition that regions employed in these studies also must be selected according to data availability.

Even though data availability places constraints on the selection of study areas, there is some latitude for choice. In the interests of providing

[15] See Isard, *Long-Range Economic Projection, op. cit.*, pp. 455–459, and "Interregional and Regional Input-Output Analysis: A Model of a Space Economy," *The Review of Economics and Statistics*, November, 1951, p. 319.

more flexibility in the use of standard sources of data, there has been some recent effort directed toward recombining census areas into more functional study areas, with the result that there are now at least three systems of study areas from which to make a choice. There is first a subdivision of the country into regions on the basis of "regions of metropolitan dominance."[16] More recently, some work has been undertaken looking toward the use of assemblages of counties in a system of economically homogeneous study areas. Finally, there are the long-standing conventional series of census reporting units consisting of regions, census divisions, and such political divisions as states and counties.

METROPOLITAN REGIONS

Metropolitan concepts of regionalism for the most part stem from urbanism studies of demographers and sociologists. In search of ways of describing metropolitan spheres of influence and the positioning of cities in a region according to their dependence on a single dominant metropolitan center, several such studies are suggestive of approaches which might be used in defining a region for economic analyses.

In the words of R. D. McKenzie, one of the first to emphasize the regional character of urban influences, "geographically the metropolitan region extends as far as the city exerts a dominant influence."[17] This region of influence is described in terms of "metropolitan dominance and subdominance." The concept likens a region to a system of magnetic fields, each surrounding a city and each, according to its relative economic strength, variable in its power to attract growth.

A city is defined as dominant when it occupies a controlling economic position in relation to all other communities in the surrounding region, particularly in such functions as services and wholesaling and in its capacity to attract industrial development. A dominant city exerts a strong influence over what types of economic activity develop in the immediate hinterland. A subdominant city, while being dependent on the larger center for one or more of its many specialized services and wholesale outlets, is a subservice and subwholesaling center for hinterland areas, with a more limited pulling power in the attraction of new industry. In order to survive, subdominant centers must specialize in the direction indicated by the dominant center,

---

[16] Not to be confused with "metropolitan regions" in a more limited sense as used by the city planner in referring to a particular urban center and its immediate built-up area.

[17] R. D. McKenzie, *The Metropolitan Community*, McGraw-Hill Book Company, Inc., 1933, p. 70.

particularly in the trade and service functions but to a less extent in manufacturing activity.

Building on the earlier work of McKenzie, Donald J. Bogue presents evidence that the cities of the nation group into regional patterns with definite and measurable ties with the major metropolitan centers of the country.[18] His study takes some 67 metropolitan centers with 1940 populations of 100,000 or more, and divides the country into regions tributary to these centers. Then, using as measures of dominance such census-reported indices as value added by manufacture, wholesale sales, retail sales, and receipts from services, it demonstrates how dominant and subdominant patterns in the economic positioning of cities can be identified within such regions, and clearly shows the interdependency and the interrelationships which exist among the cities of metropolitan regions.[19]

Figures 8 to 10 present three different metropolitan systems of regions in the nation. Figure 8 shows how the foregoing approach would break the country down into metropolitan regions. Figure 9 shows McKenzie's conception of metropolitan regions as defined by daily newspaper circulation. Figure 10 shows another early representation of the nation's regions of metropolitan influence as developed by the National Resources Committee.[20] In this study, regions were defined around 17 major metropolitan centers.

To be put to use in economic studies, the McKenzie and National Resources Committee delineations of regions would need adjustment to conform to assemblages of counties, probably in the manner employed by Bogue. Moreover, before being used as a basis for economic analyses, these regions, having been defined some years ago, would require boundary realignments as may be indicated by changes in the positioning of cities occurring in the interim. Accordingly, it would appear that, with some adjustments for known physiographic, economic, or other impracticalities, the

[18] Donald J. Bogue, *The Structure of the Metropolitan Community, A Study of Dominance and Subdominance*, University of Michigan, Horace H. Rackham School of Graduate Studies, 1949.

[19] In this study, metropolitan centers with 100,000 population or more were selected so as to exclude any such cities which were located next to, or very near, larger cities. The subdivision into regions was accomplished by connecting each center with adjoining centers by straight lines. These lines were bisected and the resulting mid-points were connected. The boundaries of each region were then defined by outlining the outer boundaries of all outlying counties the greater part of which fell within the geometric delineation. As might be expected, such a geometric approach to the subdivision of the country into metropolitan regions neglects such elements as physiographic features and transportation factors except in so far as these are reflected in the original siting of the urban center. While perhaps suitable for purposes of the original study, such an approach to defining regions would require adjustment if interregional comparisons are contemplated.

[20] National Resources Committee, *Regional Factors in Planning*, U.S. Government Printing Office, December, 1935.

Bogue delineation of regions offers the most immediately usable system of metropolitan regions of the three presented here.

HOMOGENEOUS ECONOMIC AREAS

As opposed to the essentially nodal concept of regionalism embodied in a metropolitan system of study areas, an approach based on economic homogeneity gives more direct recognition to the spatial distribution of economic activity. It takes into consideration the specialization of areas that occurs in selected economic activities, the interdependency among

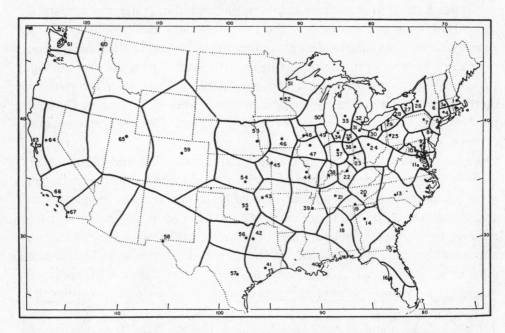

FIGURE 8.   Regions of Metropolitan Dominance in 1940, after Donald J. Bogue. *Key to numbered regions:* 1—Boston; 2—Providence; 3—Springfield; 4—Hartford; 5—New York City; 6—Albany; 7—Scranton; 8—Philadelphia; 9—Baltimore; 10—Washington, D.C.; 11—Richmond; 12—Norfolk; 13—Charlotte; 14—Atlanta; 15—Jacksonville; 16—Tampa; 17—Miami; 18—Birmingham; 19—Chattanooga; 20—Knoxville; 21—Nashville; 22—Louisville; 23—Cincinnati; 24—Columbus; 25—Pittsburgh; 26—Syracuse; 27—Rochester; 28—Buffalo; 29—Erie; 30—Cleveland; 31—Toledo; 32—Detroit; 33—Grand Rapids; 34—South Bend; 35—Fort Wayne; 36—Dayton; 37—Indianapolis; 38—Evansville; 39—Memphis; 40—New Orleans; 41—Houston; 42—Dallas; 43—Tulsa; 44—St. Louis; 45—Kansas City; 46—Des Moines; 47—Peoria; 48—Davenport-Moline-Rock Island; 49—Chicago; 50—Milwaukee; 51—Duluth; 52—Minneapolis-St. Paul; 53—Omaha; 54—Witchita; 55—Oklahoma City; 56—Fort Worth; 57—San Antonio; 58—El Paso; 59—Denver; 60—Spokane; 61—Seattle; 62—Portland, Ore.; 63—San Francisco; 64—Sacramento; 65—Salt Lake City; 66—Los Angeles; 67—San Diego.

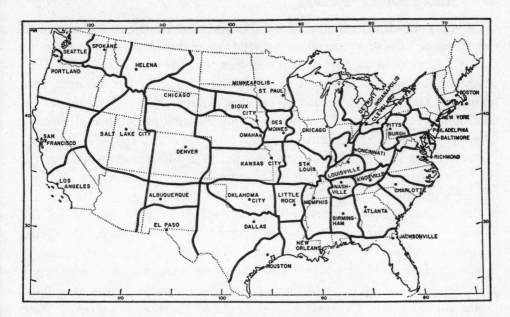

FIGURE 9. Metropolitan Regions as Defined by Daily Newspaper Circulation in 1929, after R. D. McKenzie. (*Source:* National Resources Committee, *Regional Factors in Planning,* U.S. Government Printing Office, December, 1935.)

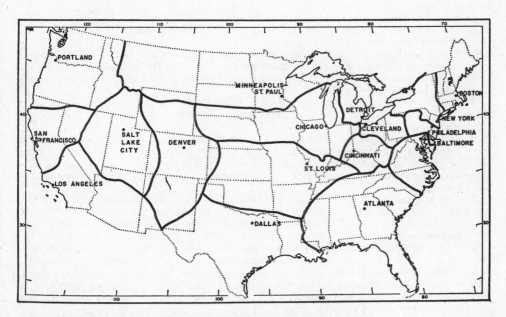

FIGURE 10. National Resources Committee's Delineation of Possible Planning Regions Based upon Composite Criteria of Metropolitan Influence, 1935. (*Source:* National Resources Committee, *Regional Factors in Planning,* U.S. Government Printing Office, December, 1935.)

these areas, and the exchange which goes on between them, and it reflects the influence of resources and raw materials on the location of productive activity. Thus such an approach recognizes that the nation can be broken down into geographic areas of specialization that take into account contemporary trends in the territorial division of labor, differences in the distribution of resources, and the necessity for the flow of goods and services between sections of the country.

Recognizing that these considerations led to a different order of regions, Bogue has more recently turned his attention to the development of a system of economically homogeneous study areas. Working with the Bureau of the Census and the Bureau of Agricultural Economics, he divided the 48 states into a system of 501 "State Economic Areas."[21] These consist of one or more counties with similar economic and social characteristics, including a special class of Metropolitan State Economic Areas which, with some exceptions,[22] are equivalent to the Standard Metropolitan Areas as defined by the Bureau of the Census.[23] Figure 11 shows the Bogue system of State

[21] Donald J. Bogue, *State Economic Areas,* a Bureau of the Census publication, U.S. Government Printing Office, 1951.

[22] Standard Metropolitan Areas in New England, which are delineated on a town basis, are shown on a county basis in this system of State Economic Areas, and Standard Metropolitan Areas with a 1940 population of less than 100,000 have not been made Metropolitan State Economic Areas.

[23] The general principles adhered to in defining these areas are set forth in *State Economic Areas* as follows:

1. The areas must follow county lines in all cases. . . .
2. The areas must permit the separation of the principal metropolitan centers and their environs from other areas.
3. Homogeneity with respect to economic and social conditions should be a principal criterion in judging the quality of the State Economic Areas delimitation.
4. The delimitation should be made on the basis of statistical and other objective evidence to the greatest extent possible. . . .
5. Counties within any one grouping shall be contiguous. Only minor deviations from this principle are permitted. Metropolitan counties or bodies of water may separate the counties of a group. . . .
6. Because agricultural and some other statistics require a more detailed area breakdown outside the metropolitan areas than do most statistics for population, industry, and commerce, the areas should be delimited on two levels: (a) a detailed level for use in publishing agricultural data and (b) a more generalized level for all other census tabulations. . . .
7. Most Metropolitan State Economic Areas contain an insufficient number of farms to permit a separate agricultural tabulation. Hence, for tabulations of agricultural statistics, it is permissible, if desired, to combine each metropolitan area with the surrounding State Economic Area. . . .
8. Each area intended for general tabulations shall contain at least 100,000 inhabitants. Areas intended for agricultural tabulations should contain at least 10,000 farms. . . .
9. All state boundaries shall also be State Economic Area boundaries. . . .
10. It must be possible to integrate State Economic Area boundaries across state lines in order to permit the summarization of data for the entire United States in terms of a few major economic and resource areas.

FIGURE 11. Economic Subregions and State Economic Areas, 1950. (*Source:* Donald J. Bogue and Calvin L. Beale, "Economic Subregions of the United States," *Farm Population,* Series Census-BAE No. 19, U.S. Government Printing Office, June, 1953.)

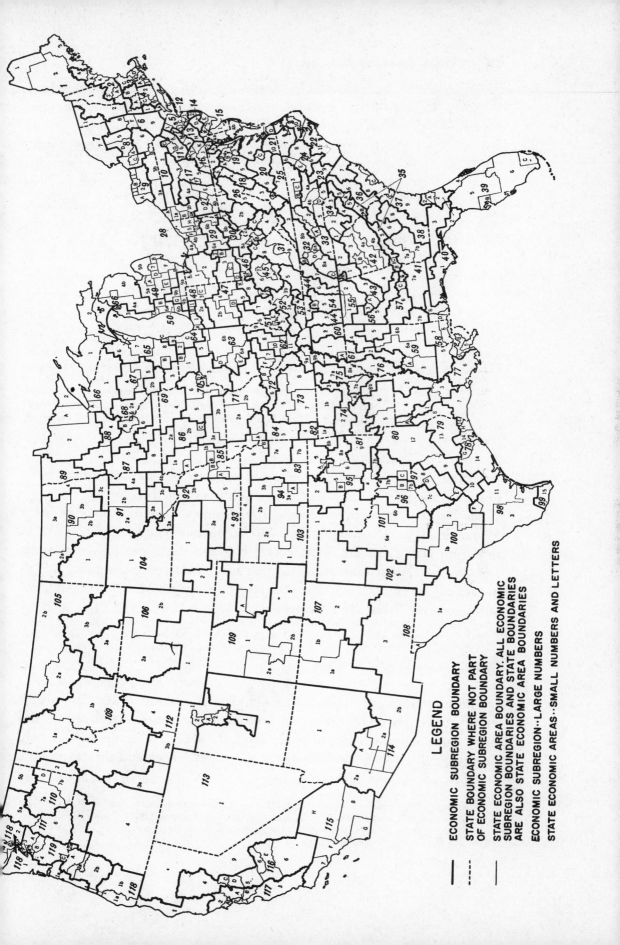

LEGEND

| ECONOMIC SUBREGION BOUNDARY

‖ STATE BOUNDARY WHERE NOT PART
OF ECONOMIC SUBREGION BOUNDARY

| STATE ECONOMIC AREA BOUNDARY. ALL ECONOMIC
SUBREGION BOUNDARIES AND STATE BOUNDARIES
ARE ALSO STATE ECONOMIC AREA BOUNDARIES

ECONOMIC SUBREGION··LARGE NUMBERS

STATE ECONOMIC AREAS··SMALL NUMBERS AND LETTERS

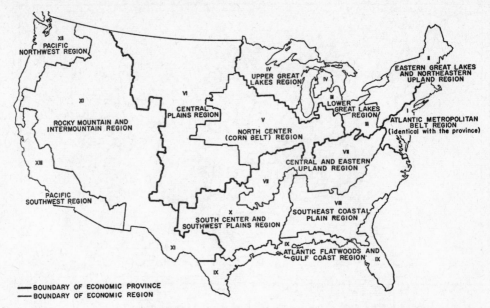

FIGURE 12. Economic Provinces and Economic Regions, 1950. (*Source:* Donald J. Bogue, "An Outline of the Complete System of Economic Areas," *The American Journal of Sociology,* The University of Chicago Press, September, 1954. Copyright, 1954, by the University of Chicago.)

Economic Areas. Selected economic and population data taken from census records from 1900 to 1950 have been published for these areas.[24]

For larger area analyses, Bogue has developed combinations of State Economic Areas consisting of some 119 "Economic Subregions," also shown in Figure 11.[25] These are intermediate between the State Economic Areas and the next larger divisions consisting of 13 "Economic Regions," which in turn can be combined to form the largest geographical delineations, consisting of five "Economic Provinces" (see Figure 12).[26]

CONVENTIONAL CENSUS AREAS

The systems of geographical areas employed in standard federal government summaries of population and economic statistics are obviously the most universally used sets of study areas for economic analyses. Not only do these sources provide data in the most convenient and directly usable

[24] Summaries for 1900 to 1940 appear in *State Economic Areas, op. cit.,* and data for 1950 appear in special census bulletins.

[25] Donald J. Bogue and Calvin L. Beale, "Economic Subregions of the United States," *Farm Population,* Series Census–BAE No. 19, U.S. Government Printing Office, June, 1953.

[26] Donald J. Bogue, "An Outline of the Complete System of Economic Areas," *The American Journal of Sociology,* September, 1954.

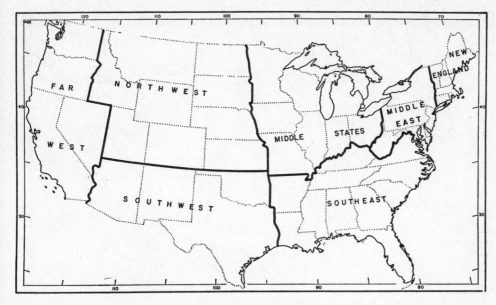

FIGURE 13.   Odum's Regions as Modified by the Office of Business Economics, U.S. Department of Commerce.

form, but summaries are published at periodic intervals and thus permit the construction of time series for trend analyses. The sheer labor of tabulation involved in recombining small area statistics to obtain summaries in terms of other areas becomes a deterrent to the use of new systems of study areas. Even more important, where new areas are created by aggregating small areas, there is the problem of missing detail in the publicly reported small area summaries because of gaps in data where operations of individual firms would be revealed.

There are two systems of regions used in U.S. Department of Commerce summaries. One is the seven-region subdivision of the nation employed by the Office of Business Economics in their national income series and a few other Department of Commerce summaries (see Figure 13).[27] Information using this system of regions is generally not reported for areas smaller than states. The other system is the nine-region breakdown (called census divisions) used by the Bureau of the Census (see Figure 14). Because the Censuses of Population, Manufactures, and Business are all summarized by states, counties, and cities as well as by census divisions, it is the most commonly used system of areas for economic studies.

Further empirical research in the identification of economic areas suit-

[27] These delineations are based on the cultural-economic regions of the nation as defined by Howard W. Odum, *Southern Regions of the United States,* University of North Carolina Press, 1936. The only difference is the breakdown of Odum's Northeast Region into a Middle East and a New England region.

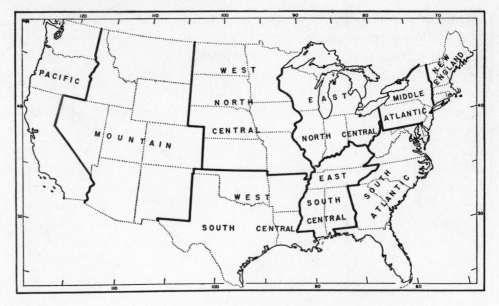

FIGURE 14.   Census Divisions as Used by the Bureau of the Census.

able for studies of economic linkage between the nation and its urban centers is clearly needed. While there are obvious obstacles to realizing completely the flexibility desired in input-output analyses, certainly a more functional system of regions and subareas—perhaps on the order of Bogue's homogeneous economic areas—would assist in these analyses. It would appear that some new basis for reporting data on productive activity along the lines of Bogue's economic areas is needed to supplement the conventional system of areas presently used. Meanwhile expediency dictates the use of the crude statistical regions and political divisions in general usage in census publications, namely, the nine-region breakdown in Figure 14, the states and the counties.

THE ECONOMIC BASE: AN URBAN-CENTERED APPROACH

In contrast to the rather limited and experimental uses which have been made of input-output theory in studying the structure and functioning of the urban economy, the "economic base" approach has received rather extensive applications in city planning analyses. This is perhaps explained partly by the fact that input-output techniques of analysis have been adapted to urban studies only fairly recently, partly by the complexities of its analytical procedures, and partly by the mechanical obstacles involved in obtaining data in the form and detail required. In contrast, base analyses employ much simpler analytical procedures and are geared directly to standard sources of data which are regularly reported.

Base theory conceives the structure of the urban economy as made up of two broad classes of productive effort—the basic activities which produce and distribute goods and services for export to firms and individuals outside a defined localized economic area, and the service or nonbasic activities whose goods and services are consumed at home within the confines of this localized economic area. It thus seeks to make a distinction between productive activity which brings new money into the community (basic activity), and productive activity which simply recirculates money which is already there (service activity). The concept holds that basic industry is the key to a city's economic strength, and expansion in basic lines usually means growth in service activities and thus growth in the total economy. In other words, base theory maintains that new money can bring expansion capacity in basic lines and provide the base for growth in service lines. Moreover, it can create new jobs and improve levels of living among those employed on existing jobs, hence providing increments for still further growth.

Some base theorists see the concept as having parallels in international trade theory. Though viewing it in a much simpler context, they direct attention to "export balances" and how these balances become a measure of the strength of the urban economy in much the same manner that export balances have an important influence on the position of the national economy within the framework of international trade. They point out, also, that the balance-of-trade concept holds important implications for understanding changes in the urban economy. Thus, according to base theory, a rising export balance, or more particularly a rising balance of payments, has positive implications for the local economy, but where the export balance falls off and an excess of payments for imports over exports develops and continues over a period of time, this change has negative repercussions and the local economy faces a decline.

Classification of Basic-Service Activity

Homer Hoyt, whose experimentation and work in economic base analysis has provided the contemporary operational model of the base concept now in general use, repeatedly emphasizes that it is the extent to which a city can command income from beyond its borders which is the key element in its growth.[28] He observes that any one or a combination of the following activities are important basic sources for outside income: manufacturing, extractive industry, wholesale and retail trade, finance and banking, and special sources of income such as political, educational, institutional, resort, or amusement activities.

Under such a classification, the service or nonbasic activities are usually represented by local-serving stores, doctors, lawyers, banks, schools, city government, and so on. Base theory recognizes that all categories of economic activity cannot be sharply defined, and there will be some such lines producing for or serving the outside as well as local markets. Thus a portion of the goods of a department store or a portion of the services of a doctor, lawyer, or a bank may be consumed beyond the metropolitan area and hence may be classified partly as basic and partly as service.

In dealing with this classification problem, Richard B. Andrews, who has made perhaps the most exhaustive analysis of the base concept, has introduced some new distinctions into the classification of basic activities.[29] He has suggested that basic industries be analyzed separately as to whether they involve (1) the movement of goods, services, and capital to the consumer or purchaser, or (2) the movement of consumers or purchasers to the goods, services, and capital. In other words, he is proposing a classification which recognizes the peculiar nature of the export activity—whether an export transaction involves the purchaser coming into the area to receive his goods, services, or capital, or whether the nature of the transaction is such that he receives delivery out of the area. Along with this dual classification of basic activities, he identifies two classes of service activities as meriting separate analysis: (1) that which imports goods, services, and capital for local processing and/or distribution, and (2) that whose goods, services, and capital are entirely locally consumed.

While possibly there are urban areas where a basic-service system of classification can be applied with little or no qualification—particularly in the smaller communities engaged in activities that are mutually independent of one another—the larger the urban center and the more interdependent the lines of activity within this center, the greater the difficulty

---

[28] See Arthur M. Weimer and Homer Hoyt, *Principles of Real Estate*, The Ronald Press Company, 1954; Homer Hoyt, *Economic Status of New York Metropolitan Region in 1944*, Regional Plan Association, Inc., 1944; Homer Hoyt, *The Economic Base of the Brockton, Massachusetts, Area*, Brockton, 1949; and other studies by Homer Hoyt.

[29] Richard B. Andrews, "Mechanics of the Urban Economic Base," *Land Economics*, November, 1953, pp. 344–349. This is one of a series of articles on economic base theory and methods of analysis appearing over a two-year period in *Land Economics*, beginning with May, 1953, issue.

encountered in applying this system of classification. For example, in a particular metropolitan area, the entire output of, let us say, a number of parts manufacturers may be absorbed in a local exporting fabricating plant. Under the base concept, these parts manufacturers are service activities—their goods are consumed at home. The question arises as to whether it is meaningful to classify them as service activities when functionally they are actually a contributing element in an export activity. Even if it were possible to sort out activities, grouping together the interdependent lines for basic-service analyses, the complex interregional-interindustry relationships in the flow of commodities are not reported in a manner that would readily permit differentiation between "exports" and "imports" of each such functional grouping of "basic" industries so as to obtain a measure of the balance of payments of export over import activity. Moreover, further difficulty is encountered in identifying imports of competitors and taking these into account in classifying what proportion of the output is basic and what is service. Too, it might be observed that in many instances, the existence of these service or ancillary industries are frequently a crucial factor in attracting the basic industry to the urban center in the first place, suggesting that service lines may be more important in some cases in achieving urban growth than the preëxistence of basic activity there. These problems will be discussed further in the concluding section below.

Delimiting the Base Area

Base theory recognizes that the determination of what activities are basic and what ones are service can be markedly influenced by where the lines of the base area are drawn. If the city limits are selected as the perimeter of the base area, an entirely different description of economic structure is obtained than if the Standard Metropolitan Area or the grouping of several counties had been selected. Indeed, it is pointed out that an entirely misleading picture of the make-up of the economy is obtained if the base area is taken to be the incorporated area alone. How, then, is an area defined for the purposes of economic base analyses, or for that matter, for any economic studies that the analyst desires to make?

As a point of departure, it is useful to examine the tests for defining a metropolitan area as advanced by N. S. B. Gras, whose work had a direct influence on concepts of metropolitan dominance and subdominance developed by McKenzie and Bogue as discussed earlier in the chapter. In 1922 Gras suggested the following criteria:

Where the systems of transportation begin to veer off toward other metropolitan centers.

The radius served by the metropolitan press and other advertising media.

The dependence of outlying financial institutions on the center for clearances and reserves.

Whether it is the center from which the retailers in a borderline town direct their supplies.

Whether the borderline town is independent or dependent upon the center for many of the following functions: (1) storage for the convenience of consumer, retailer, wholesaler, manufacturer, shipper; (2) whether the outlying producer markets directly to the local consumer or through the metropolitan machinery; (3) whether a borderline community communicates by rail, telephone, etc., through the center or independently of it; (4) where the borderline town sends its surplus products for disposal or storage; (5) whether a firm or industry which boasts its independence in some one respect, e.g., the marketing of its wares, is or is not dependent upon the center for its supplies and finances; and (6) whether the borderline town is too far away to avail itself of the central assemblage of museums, theaters, libraries, institutions of learning, and where it looks for guidance in fashions, tastes, and amusements.[30]

Obviously, even within the limits of these criteria, there is considerable latitude of choice for delineating the study area. In the absence of some systematic basis for indicating which of such criteria are most suitable to use as guides in defining a local economic area, the primary trade area is often selected as "the best fit."

Even accepting the expediency of using the primary or retail trade area as the local economic area, there is no universal agreement as to how the limits of this area are to be tied down finally. One approach identifies a "consensus area" of several available trade area delineations, using as the local economic area the grouping of counties which is most frequently included in these trade area delineations. The available trade area delineations may include ones defined for the local newspapers by the Audit Bureau of Circulation, those defined by local credit, merchant, and similar groups, the area defined as containing the bulk of the charge accounts of local department stores, and so on.

An empirical approach to the problem was developed by Reilly on the basis of observations made in some 132 American urban areas in the late twenties and early thirties. His *law of retail gravitation* states that "two cities attract retail trade from any intermediate city or town in the vicinity of the breaking point approximately in direct proportion to the populations of the two cities and in inverse proportion to the square of the distances

[30] Thomas Adams, Harold M. Lewis, and Theodore T. McCrosky, *Regional Survey of New York and Environs,* Volume II, "Population, Land Values and Government," Committee on Regional Plan of New York and Its Environs, 1929, p. 201.

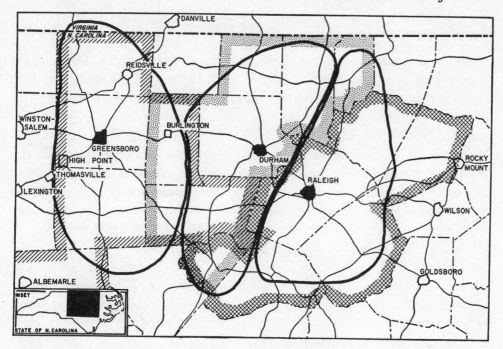

FIGURE 15. Retail Trade Areas in Three North Carolina Cities. Shaded
boundaries identify trade areas as defined in 1950 by the Audit Bureau of
Circulation for local newspapers, and the solid heavy lines identify the theoretical trade areas determined by applying Reilly's law of retail gravitation.

from these two cities to the intermediate town."[31] The breaking point is
"a point up to which one city exercises the dominating retail trade influence, and beyond which the other city dominates."[32] The distance is
measured along the most direct improved highway.

In addition to developing a formula to compute the location of breaking
points, Reilly also supplies tables for those interested only in approximating
these locations. He notes that in addition to population size and distance,
there are other factors which may introduce variations in the definition
of a retail trade area, for example, transportation facilities, lines of communication, business attractions such as delivery and credit services and
banking facilities, social and amusement attractions, parking facilities, business leadership in the city, and so on. A comparison of Reilly's trade areas
with those outlined by the Audit Bureau of Circulation for three North
Carolina cities is shown in Figure 15.

Another technique for delineating the retail trade area is through a
consumer survey. This may be done on a sampling basis by means of

[31] William J. Reilly, *The Law of Retail Gravitation,* G. P. Putnam Sons, 1931, p. 9.
[32] *Ibid.,* p. 8.

household interviews in which families indicate where they go for household goods and services. Because of the expense of conducting such a survey, it is rarely practicable to consider the use of this technique in local economic studies. Sometimes, however, such surveys can be combined with consumer expenditure surveys or similar field studies made for other purposes, and sometimes it may be practicable to undertake a limited survey confined to the peripheral areas, where the survey is used to sharpen delineations established by methods described above. Another approach, the reverse of the consumer type survey, namely, a sampling survey of retail and service establishments, is essentially the consensus approach described above. Still another approach, and usually combined with a parking survey, is the systematic recording of automobile license plate numbers of all cars parked in central or regional shopping centers. When these numbers are checked for home address on the license registration books, it is possible to estimate the extent of the retail trade area. Whatever approach or combination of approaches may be employed, usually the final result is translated into one or more counties, so that standard sources of data may be used in the economic analyses.

Measurement of Basic-Service Activity

Having briefly examined the rationale of the economic base concept, the generally accepted system for the classification of economic activity into basic and service components, and methods of delineating the local economic area, it is now possible to consider techniques of measurement. To apply the base theory to operational situations, some means of distinguishing and quantifying the basic and service components is necessary. According to the economic base concept, the measure employed must identify what lines of economic activity and how much of each line can be ascribed to one component or the other, and it must be capable of establishing the relative quantitative position of each basic line to every other one.

Andrews identifies six units of measure which are either in use or have been proposed for use at one time or another: employment, payrolls, value added, value of production, physical production, and dollar income and expenditure accounts for an entire urban area.[33] The last is the measure employed in input-output analyses. It provides the most comprehensive and complete measure of economic activity, including a measure not only

[33] Andrews, *loc. cit.*, February, 1954, pp. 52–60.

of goods and service transactions but also of capital. However, because of the complexity and difficulty of tracing monetary transactions, especially considering the form in which data are currently reported in standard sources, its use is distinctly restricted. The physical production, the value added, and the value of production approaches have advantages for analyses within particular sectors of the economy, but because they do not apply to some sectors of economic activity (even excluding capital transactions), the use of these measures is regarded as limited. Because of these difficulties, the two remaining measures are in most general usage, with employment commonly used as the primary measure and payroll data being used as a supplemental means of examining each basic line.

However, among those who have experimented with base techniques, it is generally recognized that, while offering certain obvious advantages in data availability, employment as a measuring unit for basic and service activity poses several problems. First of all, while providing a yardstick for production and distribution functions as basic activity, employment obviously has no meaning as a measure of capital export. Secondly, where historical studies or investigations of change are contemplated, raw employment data do not reflect important derivative considerations such as changing worker productivity (output per worker per unit of time). For example, if employment in a particular line is viewed as the quotient of the total annual output and the annual output per worker in that line, an increase in employment can be attributed to a variety of combinations of these two factors. Thus lower productivity at the same level of total output would yield an employment increase. Similarly, a constant value for worker productivity and an increase in output would have the same effect, or differential increases in both could result in rising employment. Moreover, if the analysis is extended to derivative considerations, let us say to those of worker productivity, it can readily be seen that output per worker can increase because of rising wage rates, overtime work, more efficient management practices, improved machinery, and so on. Thus it is evident that the use of employment data alone as a measure may obscure a variety of underlying trends of change in the structure of the urban economy.

With or without qualifying assumptions concerning these factors, employment is the universally used unit of measurement in applications of base theory. In such applications, it is customary to express the basic-service relationship as a ratio of the number of workers in service or secondary lines to every worker in basic lines. (In some quarters this ratio has been expressed in terms of service workers per 100 basic workers.) Among those who have experimented with the technique, it is now generally recognized that the numerical value of this ratio varies from one urban area to another. For estimating or comparative purposes, a norm ratio of 1.5 to 2 service workers to every basic worker has been suggested.[34] While such fixed norms have been the object of some experimentation in making approximations of basic and service employment in studies of completely new towns or of towns facing a sudden very large expansion in economic activity, locally derived ratios are favored in the more usual situation in established urban centers.

Adherents of base theory point out that there can be a relatively sizable range of variation in the value of this ratio. Although differences in methods of defining the base area and in techniques of analysis may explain some differences, in this connection it might be observed that Flint, Michigan, a one-type-industry manufacturing city, in 1951 had about 0.5 workers in service lines to every worker in basic lines;[35] in 1940 the New York metropolitan area had a ratio of 2.1;[36] for the same year, Cincinnati had a ratio of 1.7;[37] and Albuquerque in 1948 had a ratio of one to one.[38] Students of the base approach to the analysis of the urban economy also suggest these values do not necessarily remain constant for long periods of time, pointing out that the detailed study of one center alone can show change in the ratio over a period of time depending upon changes in the economy of the urban area and national economic conditions. In this connection, a test study of Rocky Mount, North Carolina, using approximation methods discussed below, showed changes from 1.46 in 1930 to 1.11 in 1940 to 1.48 in 1950.[39]

The preferred method of determining what proportion of current employment is engaged in activities which export, and what proportion is engaged in activities producing for local consumption, is through a local economic survey. Usually employing sampling techniques, such a survey establishes the percentage of sales during the preceding year which were local and nonlocal. Thus the survey determines the percentage of locally manufactured goods sold at home and in more distant places, the percentage allocation of wholesale and retail sales, the percentage allocation of receipts in places of amusement, hotels, tourist establishments, garages, gas stations, and other service industries, the percentage distribution of bank depositors and loans, and so on down the list. Once these percentages are

[34] See *Planning Community Facilities for Basic Employment Expansion,* Technical Bulletin No. 16, Urban Land Institute, September, 1951.

[35] Industrial Areas Study, a project of the Institute for Research in Social Science, University of North Carolina, 1951.

[36] New York Regional Plan Association, Inc., *op. cit.,* p. 6.

[37] Cincinnati City Planning Commission, *Economy of the Area,* City of Cincinnati, 1946, p. 23.

[38] Federal Reserve Bank of Kansas City and Bureau of Business Research, University of New Mexico, *The Economy of Albuquerque, New Mexico,* Federal Reserve Bank of Kansas City, 1949, p. 47.

[39] From some unpublished studies, Department of City and Regional Planning, University of North Carolina, 1953.

available, they are then applied to total employment figures (recorded in the survey) for each line of activity to obtain basic and service employment. This method is illustrated in the Albuquerque study.[40]

Even though such a survey yields primary data assembled especially for basic-service analyses, the method is not without its problems. For example, in some lines, particularly in manufacturing, results of such a survey obviously do not reflect figures for local consumption of goods from outside competitive manufacturers producing the same lines as the local establishments. Thus it may be necessary to adjust export percentages derived in the survey so that they represent a truer picture of the balance of exports over imports. In this connection, data sources for making these adjustments present a problem. But assuming these problems can be overcome, the survey itself can offer other difficulties. The survey method is just as accurate as the reliability of the responses received. Some interviewees may not want to reveal their markets. If the managements interviewed do not have their records ordered according to the delineation of the local economic area that has been selected to differentiate between local and outside markets, they are compelled to employ estimates. If it develops that estimates are required in a large number of cases, the possibilities of error are that much greater. Finally, there is the very compelling consideration of the time and expense involved in undertaking the sampling survey. Such surveys have been employed in several medium-size and small cities, but have never been undertaken in the large metropolitan centers. In these areas presumably the magnitude of the task and the cost have been deterring considerations.

An approximation technique, perfected by Homer Hoyt and employed in his study for the New York Regional Plan Association, is frequently used when time and cost do not permit use of the approach discussed above. It makes use of data available from such standard sources as the Census of Manufactures, the Census of Population, Sales Management, Inc., publications, and other sources. This technique assumes that the population of a particular urban area consumes its proportionate share of the national production of goods and services and that all production in excess of this amount may be considered basic. For lines of activity where consumption tends to vary with consumer income, the locality's share of the national purchasing power is used as a measure of local consumption, but in a few lines such as the manufacture of food staples where consumption tends to be independent of income, the locality's population as a percentage of the national population is used as a measure of local consumption.

Thus basic employment in manufacturing is estimated by first determin-

[40] Federal Reserve Bank of Kansas City *et al., op. cit.,* pp. 26–46.

ing, for each standard census classification of manufacturing activity, the percentage that the city's total number of workers in each line of activity is of the total number in each equivalent line in the country as a whole, and then comparing this figure with the city's share of the U.S. purchasing power or population.[41] For each line in which the city's showing in the employment ratio exceeds the city's showing in the purchasing power or population ratio, the increment in excess is attributed to basic activity. By converting these increments into employment figures and totaling them for all manufacturing lines, the technique arrives at a total basic employment in manufacturing.[42]

By similar analyses of wholesale and retail trade, finance, the professions, transportation, government, and other classes of economic activity, the technique estimates basic employment in each of these lines. Totaled, these estimates are used as an approximation of all basic employment in the urban area.

This technique is sometimes used in estimating future changes in the structure of the local economy. Where projective estimates are attempted, this approach, as in the case of the other approaches discussed above, requires a "given" forecast of national levels of demand in each line. In generalized form, the procedure used involves: (1) analysis of past trends in each line of the local area's basic activity relative to national trends in these lines, (2) projection of these local trends forward in time, considering the estimated future national demand levels in each such line, and (3) expansion of basic employment estimates for the locality thus derived to total employment by applying an assumed future ratio of service to basic employment. The above procedure assumes the use of direct local to national ratios.

Criticisms of Base Theory

The seeming simplicity of the base concept as a means for analyzing economic activity in an urban area is probably responsible for much of its present-day appeal. Indeed, it may have obscured some of its limitations, for if it is interpreted in an unqualified manner, it can unwittingly lead

[41] Estimates of a city's share of the total U.S. purchasing power for any year can be obtained from *Sales Management* magazine's "Survey of Buying Power" issue, published each year in the spring.

[42] A variation on this approach is used in the Cincinnati study which compares the total U.S. employment in each line of activity, expressed as a percent of the U.S. population, to the equivalent local percentage. In using this approach, the Cincinnati study made various adjustments to correct for differences between national and local consumption characteristics.

to some fallacious and contradictory results. For example, Ralph W. Pfouts has suggested that an extension of base theory that adheres too closely to mercantilist doctrines and a favorable balance of trade is open to serious question, pointing out that the precursor system of thought, bent on supporting the homeland to the detriment of colonies and foreign nations, has largely been discredited.[43] Closely related to this question, Pfouts asks: Can all cities reasonably try to develop by promoting basic industry? Assuming basic industry is actually identifiable, can it be demonstrated that a large proportion of basic industry will always result in community growth and stability? Are there not other variables to consider such as the value of wage payments in basic industry? Similarly, even if it can be shown that an appreciable proportion of basic industry is necessary for urban growth and development, does it follow that this alone is sufficient for growth and development?

In some preliminary but exhaustive statistical tests, Pfouts has found evidence to suggest that there is no significant relationship between basic activity as measured by the above-described approximation approach and population growth.[44] Indeed, his tests suggest that if the crude dual classification of economic activity involved in the base system of analysis has validity, the service component may be more important as an indicator of growth potential than the basic component.[45] Having thus raised serious questions concerning this system of analysis, Pfouts then turns his attention to an alternative approach to the study of the urban economy. Drawing on general economic theory and supporting it with illustrative mathematical formulations, he poses the possibility of community income analysis as a substitute approach worthy of exploration. "Why should such great emphasis be placed on exports? . . . Are exports of such overwhelming importance that such variables as imports, savings, value-added, etc. can be safely neglected? . . . Surely it can be argued that imports, since they represent money leaving the community, should be given a place in considering the income stream within the community. Similarly, the amounts that individuals within the community save represent money withdrawn from the income stream within the community. These observations suggest that simple income models similar to national income models can be drawn up for the individual community."

[43] From an outline of a study of *Economic Base Theory and Urban Development*, Institute for Research in Social Science, University of North Carolina, 1955.

[44] Ralph W. Pfouts, "An Empirical Testing of the Economic Base Theory," to be published in 1957 in *The Journal of the American Institute of Planners*.

[45] Relationships were examined in some 27 cities with an SMA population between 100,000 and 300,000. In dividing them into diversified and manufacturing groups, Pfouts found that in the latter group a fairly strong relationship existed but that it was the opposite that would be expected from interpretations of the base theory.

In a penetrating critique of the base concept as it has been used in recent years, Hans Blumenfeld identifies what he considers to be a number of misconceptions and contradictory interpretations of base theory.[46] Acknowledging that the concept has some value in learning about market areas of local economic activity and about the competitive advantages and disadvantages of an urban center, he questions its meaningfulness in predictive studies, especially in metropolitan areas, and raises questions concerning the traditional distinction between basic and nonbasic activity. ". . . If an area produces its normal share of, say, electrical machinery, it would be completely erroneous to assume that this is 'nonbasic' industry working exclusively for the local market. It is entirely possible, and indeed quite probable, that most locally produced machinery is exported, while at the same time most locally consumed electrical machinery is imported." He points out that by carrying the quantification of import-export relationships to their logical conclusion, they get into the intraurban ramifications of purchases and sales between local economic activities in the production process. The distinction between basic and nonbasic then becomes "a function of the inner organization of the industry: the higher the degree of specialization and differentiation . . . the higher is the 'nonbasic' share." Blumenfeld then goes on to observe that if the economy of an urban area is thus viewed as an integrated whole of mutually interdependent activities, "the distinction between 'basic' and 'nonbasic' seems to dissolve in thin air."[47]

Blumenfeld notes that the applicability of the basic-nonbasic concept tends to decrease with increasing size of an urban center, suggesting that the numerical value of the ratio tends to be highest in small, relatively new cities and lowest in large, mature ones. He also notes that applicability tends to increase with increasing specialization and division of labor between centers and tends to decrease the greater the amount of nonwage income flowing into or out of a center. He maintains that the large metropolitan areas exist, survive, and grow because their highly developed business and consumer services enable them to substitute new export industries for those that decline, that these nonbasic activities are the permanent and constant element, indeed, the truly "basic" element of the metropolitan area economy, while the export activities are variable, subject to continual change and replacement, and thus more truly the "service" elements.

On the basis of these and other observations he makes in his critique,

[46] Hans Blumenfeld, "The Economic Base of the Metropolis," *Journal of the American Institute of Planners*, Fall, 1955.
[47] *Ibid.*, pp. 120–121.

Blumenfeld urges an approach (especially in larger metropolitan area studies of the urban economy) which emphasizes in place of the basic-service dichotomy what he calls "criticality" and "balance of payments" studies. A criticality study would be concerned with the potential vulnerability of local economic activity from outside competition and the potential capacity of the local economic activity to expand into outside markets; and a balance of payments study would be concerned with actual sales—"all types of payments, and giving equal weight to both sides of the ledger [the import and the export sides]."[48]

In the foregoing sections of this chapter, two approaches to the analysis of the structure and functioning of the urban economy have been presented. In the case of one approach, input-output analysis, it was found that while conceptually a promising approach, the techniques it employs require data in detail not currently obtainable from standard sources, and involve extensive, highly specialized analyses presently outside the competence of the average city planner. In the case of the economic base approach, it was noted that while offering insights into the general make-up of the local economy, this approach has been found lacking in several respects as an entirely satisfactory system for the analysis of the urban economy. Clearly, this whole subject area needs much more attention in research, both in the development of theory and in the perfecting of suitable and workable techniques for applying theory to the realities of city planning analyses.

VITALITY OF THE ECONOMY

While the make-up of the urban economy, considered in terms of the extent of economic activity and population it supports, influences the amount of land which will go into use, the general health of the economy is an important determinant of the rate at which land will go into use. In short, the vitality of the local economy is a key consideration in whether land development is active or sluggish in the urban area and whether whole areas stagnate and become vulnerable to urban blight.

The general vitality of the economy is customarily described in terms of such factors as stability, balance, worker productivity, and quality of economic leadership. Stability refers to capacity of the economy both to weather the business cycle over the years and to absorb the seasonal business

[48] *Ibid.*, p. 122.

changes in any single year. Balance is usually expressed in terms of diversification in productive activity, and productivity refers to output per worker at prevailing wage levels for the prevailing standard work week.

In assessing the susceptibility of an urban center to fluctuations in national economic activity, Ernest and Robert Fisher have suggested that the character of local industry, the scope of its markets, and its relative diversification and concentration will be particularly important considerations.[49] With respect to the character of local economic activity, they note that industries least susceptible to fluctuations tend to be: (1) those whose products and services cater to a broad consuming base as measured by personal and corporate income, e.g., industries dealing in low- and medium-price lines as opposed to high-price lines; (2) those producing goods and services the purchase of which is least postponable by the consumer, e.g., nondurable as opposed to durable; (3) those that have the most favorable prospects for long-term growth of demand; (4) those in the extractive category that have substantial resource reserves on which to draw; and (5) those dealing in consumer goods and services as opposed to those dealing in producer goods and services (except where producer goods industries are producing for stable types of consumer goods industries).

With scope of the market measured in terms of population served and its purchasing power, the Fishers observe that the greater the scope, the more stable the urban economy tends to be. In the matter of diversification and concentration, they mention that a wide spread in the type of economic activity as between manufacturing, trade, construction, and so on, in addition to variety within the manufacturing category alone, is more conducive to a stable urban economy. Where these conditions exist and where there is spread of employment and payrolls among a variety of firms and no marked interdependence among these firms, more stable conditions are apt to exist.

> Probably the most favorable combination is represented by an economic base composed of numerous strong, independent firms (preferably dominated by industries, such as government, with relatively small income volatilities) with complementary labor requirements and high average wages and salaries, turning out a large variety of low-priced, nondurable consumers' goods and services distributed widely over separate markets, from a community whose operating statement and rate of savings are both positive and whose balance sheet reveals a great number of comparative advantages held by it over rival areas.[50]

Although not without their limitations, there have been some attempts to develop objective measures of the cyclical stability of various kinds of

[49] Ernest M. and Robert M. Fisher, *Urban Real Estate,* Henry Holt and Company, 1954, pp. 280–294.
[50] *Ibid.,* p. 301.

economic activity. One such measure has been suggested by Edward F. Denison of the U.S. Office of Business Economics.[51] It employs a technique of classifying private nonagricultural industries in the nation as a whole with respect to their sensitivity to cyclical changes in the level of national income. The Denison study first computed the percentage that the income of each private nonagricultural industry in the nation was of total private nonagricultural income for the years from 1929 to 1947, inclusive. Taking the span from 1929 to 1937 as containing the downward movement of the business cycle in the last great depression, for each industry, the study next used a straight-line interpolation between these years to obtain percentages for 1932 and 1933 which might have been expected had 1932 and 1933 been prosperous years and had the trend (assumed to be linear) been the only factor which affected the industrial distribution of income from 1929 to 1937. Next, for all industries the ratio of the actual percentage to the hypothetical percentage was computed separately for the two depression years 1932 and 1933 and then averaged to give a single ratio. The final ratio, termed the "stability ratio," was used as a measure of cyclical stability during the depression.

Those industries whose income trend was exactly like that of the aggregate of private nonagricultural industries had a stability ratio of 1.00. A higher ratio indicated that income originating in the industry fluctuated less during the depression than the income of the aggregate of industries. Those industries which had no cyclical variation maintained a ratio of 2.11. A ratio below 1.00 indicated that the particular industry's income was more affected by the depression cycle than the income for the private nonagricultural industries as a whole. The practical minimum ratio was zero, though theoretically it could be negative. Table 5 shows Denison's grouping of private nonagricultural industries by degree of sensitivity, with the range of the stability ratio shown beside each group.

This measure of the relative cyclical stability of various lines of private nonagricultural economic activity was developed primarily with the purpose in view of examining fluctuations in the national economy. It has certain limitations when applied to the economy of a particular urban center. The characteristics observed in the national scene should not be attributed to local industries without a careful analysis of the pattern of relationships among industries, within the local area and within the larger region. For example, while a durable goods industry, such as one producing furniture, may generally be regarded as sensitive to national fluctuations, it may have a long record of highly stable sales made largely to stable nondurable goods industries. In the final analysis, investigations

[51] Edward F. Denison, "Industrial Composition of National Income," *Survey of Current Business,* December, 1948, pp. 11–27.

into factors of this kind provide the surest means of assessing the susceptibility of the local economy to fluctuations.

In a study of the effects of diversification of manufacturing industry on
local economic development, Allan Rodgers developed a gross measure

TABLE 5.   Classification of Private Nonagricultural Industries by Stability Groups[a]

GROUP I (highly insensitive)—2.06 to 1.38

Tobacco manufactures	Insurance agents and combination offices
Air transportation (common carriers)	Local railways and bus lines
Religious organizations	Miscellaneous repair services and hand trades
Educational services, not elsewhere classified	Telephone, telegraph, and related services
	Medical and other health services
Nonprofit membership organization, not elsewhere classified	Highway freight transportation and warehousing
Legal services	Anthracite mining
Utilities: electric and gas	

GROUP II (markedly insensitive)—1.32 to 1.14

Insurance carriers	Food and kindred products
Personal services	Highway passenger transportation, not elsewhere classified
Local utilities and public services, not elsewhere classified	Printing, publishing, and allied industries
Pipe-line transportations	Business services, not elsewhere classified
Real estate	Engineering and other professional services, not elsewhere classified.

GROUP III (average cyclical sensitivity)—1.13 to 0.88

Chemicals and allied products	Retail trade and automobile services
Leather and leather products	Motion pictures
Water transportation	Apparel and other finished fabric products
Railroads	Services allied to transportation
Private households	Hotels and other lodging places
Paper and allied products	Radio broadcasting and television
Amusement and recreation, except motion pictures	Security and commodity brokers, dealers, and exchanges
Wholesale trade	Banking

GROUP IV (markedly sensitive)—0.87 to 0.64

Textile-mill products	Rubber products
Crude petroleum and natural gas production	Furniture and finished lumber products
Bituminous and other soft coal mining	Miscellaneous manufacturing industries
Commercial and trade schools and employment agencies	Contract construction

GROUP V (highly sensitive)—0.56 to —0.35

Electrical machinery	Machinery (except electrical)
Nonmetallic mining and quarrying	Iron and steel and their products, including ordnance
Transportation equipment except automobiles	Lumber and timber basic products
Nonferrous metals and their products	Products of petroleum and coal
Stone, clay, and glass products	Metal mining
Automobiles and automobile equipment	Finance, not elsewhere classified.

[a] Adapted from Edward F. Denison, "Industrial Composition of National Income," *Survey of Current Business,*
December, 1948, p. 15.

TABLE 6. Illustration of Method for Determining Index of Diversification as Applied to Indianapolis Industrial Area, 1950[a]

	Employment by Industrial Group	Percent	Ranked Percentage[b]	Cumulative Addition[b]
1. Lumber and wood	831	1.08	13.33	13.33
2. Furniture	1,085	1.41	12.47	25.80
3. Stone, clay, and glass	1,200	1.56	11.32	37.12
4. Primary metals	4,092	5.32	9.73	46.85
5. Fabricated metals	6,256	8.13	8.19	55.04
6. Machinery except electrical	9,596	12.47	8.13	63.17
7. Electrical machinery	10,256	13.33	6.63	69.80
8. Transportation equipment	4,444	5.78	5.78	75.58
9. Motor vehicles	7,488	9.73	5.32	80.90
10. Professional equipment	636	0.83	2.94	83.84
11. Miscellaneous durable	1,571	2.04	2.87	86.71
12. Food and kindred	8,712	11.32	2.59	89.30
13. Tobacco	43	0.06	2.04	91.34
14. Textiles	1,996	2.59	1.98	93.22
15. Apparel	1,524	1.98	1.56	94.88
16. Paper and allied	2,262	2.94	1.41	96.29
17. Printing and publishing	5,101	6.63	1.08	97.37
18. Chemical and allied	6,300	8.19	0.97	98.34
19. Petroleum and coal	424	0.55	0.83	99.17
20. Rubber	2,210	2.87	0.55	99.72
21. Leather	173	0.22	0.22	99.94
22. Not specified	745	0.97	0.06	100.00
Total	76,945	100.00	Crude Diversification Index	1,697.71

$$\text{Refined index} = \frac{\text{Actual crude index} - \text{Crude index for all industrial areas}}{\text{Crude index for least diversity} - \text{Crude index for all industrial areas}}$$

Example: Indianapolis

$$\text{Refined index} = \frac{1698 - 1553}{2200 - 1553} = \frac{145}{647}$$

Refined index = 0.224

[a] Allan Rodgers, "Some Aspects of Industrial Diversification in the United States," *Papers and Proceedings*, Volume One, Regional Science Association, 1955.
[b] Figures in these columns are rearrangements of percentage figures in second column, and thus do not correspond with industrial categories in the stub of the table.

of diversification and applied it to 93 Standard Metropolitan Areas (SMA's) with manufacturing employment exceeding 20,000.[52] Using 22 industrial groups appearing in the U.S. Census of Population, he developed indices of diversification for the 93 SMA's. Table 6 is Rodgers' illustration of the procedure for deriving his "refined index" as applied to Indianapolis. After ranking employment percentages from highest to lowest, he sums the cumulative percentage totals to obtain his "crude index of diversification." Where

[52] Allan Rodgers, "Some Aspects of Industrial Diversification in the United States," *Papers and Proceedings*, Volume One, Regional Science Association, 1955.

industries are absent, he uses totals of 100 percent. Thus in the extreme situation where a single industry contains all the recorded manufacturing employment, the crude index would be 2200, or the situation of least diversification. By applying this procedure to the totals for all 93 SMA's, he found that the crude index for all urban centers was 1553. The derivation of the refined index is indicated in Table 6.

These computations were made for all 93 SMA's and the refined indices divided into five broad groups: highly diversified (Group I), moderately diversified (Group II), average diversification (Group III), moderately specialized (Group IV), and highly specialized (Group V). Figure 16 shows the geographical distribution of the 93 SMA's and the regional variations in diversification based on 1950 census data with the legend showing the range of index values used for each of the five groups. The Flint SMA was the most specialized (index value of 934) and the Philadelphia SMA the most diversified (index value of 36). The reader is referred to Rodgers' paper for interpretations of the regional distribution patterns and to his supplemental studies of changes in diversification patterns in time. He observes that "any index of this nature tends to mask elements in the pattern of individual areas. Thus high indices can result from concentration on one or more industries. In addition, the index gives no indication of the composition of industry in an area, such as employment in the production of durable versus nondurable goods, which may be highly significant in an analysis of diversification."

In a very useful research monograph prepared by Columbia University's Institute for Urban Land Use and Housing Studies, Chester Rapkin has developed an index by which it is possible to measure some of the factors of diversification and concentration cited above from the work of the Fishers.[53] It utilizes two elements of economic diversification: the relative number of industries operating in a local area, and the distribution of employment among these industries. Applied to a particular locality, the index involves the statistical computation of the extent to which the number of workers in each industry deviates from the average number of workers

[53] Chester Rapkin, Louis Winnick, and David M. Blank, *Housing Market Analysis, A Study of Theory and Methods,* a Housing and Home Finance Agency research monograph, U.S. Government Printing Office, 1953, pp. 88–90.

FIGURE 16.   Industrial Diversification in 93 Standard Metropolitan Areas, 1950. This map shows the distribution of cities by the degree of diversification as determined by Rodgers' refined index. The range varies from highly diversified (Group I) to highly specialized (Group V). (*Source:* Allan Rodgers, "Some Aspects of Industrial Diversification in the United States," *Papers and Proceedings,* Volume One, Regional Science Association, 1955.)

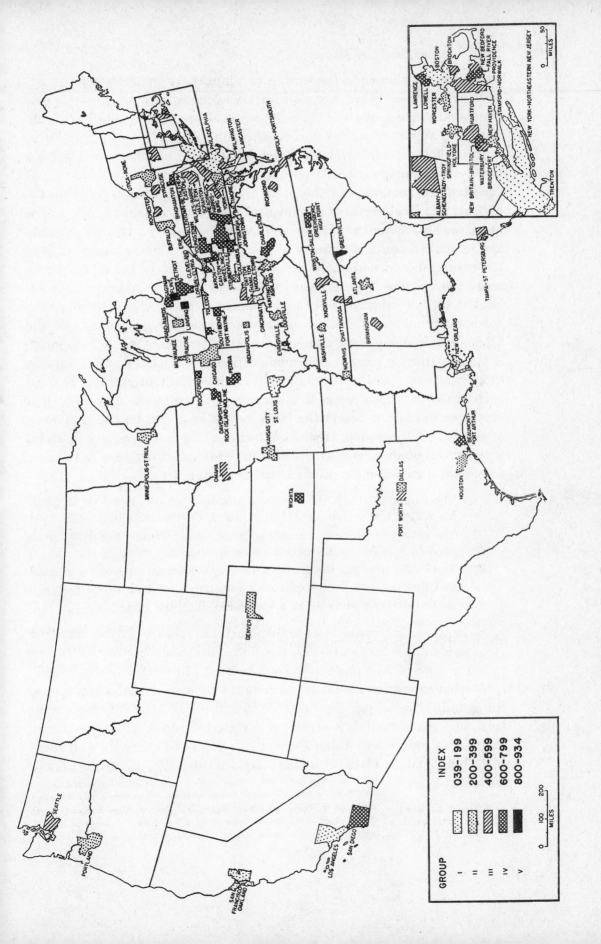

GROUP   INDEX
                         039-199
                         200-399
 I   400-599
 II   600-799
 III   800-934
 IV
 V

MILES
0   100   200

per industry to indicate the degree of diffusion or concentration of employment. While evaluation of all factors affecting diversification involves a more extensive analysis of the economy, such an index is useful in quantifying two important factors of diversification.

Most efforts toward evaluating the whole range of factors affecting the vitality of the economy are somewhat subjective extensions of the economic base type of analysis. For the most part, these approaches examine the national and local record of employment for the urban area's existing basic industries in relation to the business cycle and note which ones are subject to marked seasonal variations in employment. Then, considering local labor, capital, and natural resources, a tentative list of industries is prescribed as offering good prospects for diversifying the economy, matching local skills and other resources, and having high levels of productivity.

Some attempts at a more systematic evaluation of the strength of the urban area economy merit more detailed consideration. One such approach is Harriet Herring's work with southern industry.[54] This study is particularly significant because it ties into the framework of national-regional analyses set forth earlier in this chapter. Proceeding on a premise that "optimum production means the best: for the long run, for the well-being of regions and the nation, for the utilization of the resources and skills, for economy of production and distribution," Miss Herring sets forth three successive tests for optimum industrial development:

1. The extent to which the economy produces *for the nation* those goods for which the region is peculiarly fitted by resources and skills.
2. The extent to which the economy produces *for its own use* those goods for which it has sufficient resources and skills.
3. The extent to which the economy develops potential resources and skills, and produces, *at least for its own use,* goods in lines which give it a greater measure of balance, stability, and productivity.[55]

Applying these successive tests to manufacturing activity in the Southeast (region identified in Figure 13), the study ultimately derives for the region a picture of its strengths and weaknesses. More significantly, it indicates what industries should be encouraged by reason of the region's existing and potential resources and skills, and of the relatively high wage levels and general stability attributed to these industries. These are termed "high-index industries." Table 7 reproduces from this study the end result of such an analysis of the Southeast based on the 1937 Census of Manufactures.

[54] Harriet L. Herring, *Southern Industry and Regional Development,* University of North Carolina Press, 1940.
[55] *Ibid.,* p. 5.

TABLE 7.   Industrial Balance in the Southeast, 1937[a]

Industry	No. of Wage Earners	Wages per Wage Earner	Value of Product per Wage Earner	Value Added By Mfr. per Wage Earner	Percent Wage Earners in Southeast
High-Index Industries Southeast "Needs"					
Shortenings, vegetable	4,901	$1,150	$48,862	$ 7,160	*15 cir*
Flour, grain-mill products	26,390	1,144	32,448	5,063	14.5
Butter	19,437	1,009	30,342	4,110	4.8
Sugar refining	14,024	1,140	30,200	4,410	*27 cir*
Blast-furnace products	23,075	1,647	29,145	5,532	*10 cir*
Feeds, prepared, for animals	14,397	1,100	28,840	5,328	12.5
Milk, evaporated, condensed	8,967	1,110	23,600	4,930	*10 cir*
Meat packing	127,477	1,337	21,866	3,148	5.6
Soap	14,008	1,362	21,509	8,290	*2 cir*
Paints, pigments, varnishes	31,664	1,350	17,005	7,149	4.7
Drugs and medicines	24,095	1,084	14,356	10,255	5.5
Chemicals (industrial, etc.)	78,951	1,485	11,814	6,050	9.7
Malt liquors	47,037	1,685	11,419	7,126	5.8
Low-Index Industries Southeast Has					
Rayon woven goods	57,949	845	3,965	1,391	36.0
Furniture, household	130,765	947	3,614	1,855	22.7
Cast-iron pipe	17,613	1,027	3,470	2,026	*60 cir*
Boxes, wooden except cigar	25,981	752	3,323	1,574	39.6
Men's shirts, except work	55,570	629	3,149	1,298	*13 cir*
Cotton yarn and thread	86,206	659	3,023	1,224	78.5
Knitted underwear	39,923	715	2,950	1,361	33.3
Men's work clothing	69,502	594	2,941	1,029	35.3
Cotton goods, over 12 in.	336,104	761	2,877	1,313	74.0
Clay products, except pottery	59,585	971	2,740	1,884	18.9
Lumber and timber products	323,928	849	2,610	1,555	44.5
Hosiery	150,460	906	2,403	1,340	44.2

[a] Adapted from Harriet L. Herring, *Southern Industry and Regional Development*, University of North Carolina Press, 1940, p. 68.

The first two tests used in this approach draw upon analyses of basic and service industries in the regional economy. Using similar techniques as described in economic base analyses, the first test determines what industries in the region are manufacturing for national markets, and the second is concerned with those producing for local regional consumption. Each of these two classes of industry in the region is compared industry by industry with the same industry in the national economy. The degree to which each uses available regional resources and skills and their levels of productivity are noted. From these studies is derived a listing of industries which could be advantageously expanded in the region by reason of available resources and skills and general high levels of productivity. The final test results in a listing such as Table 7, indicating what industries are "needed," considering potential resources and skills, the general stabilizing and diversifying effect they would have on the economy, and the higher levels of productivity they would bring to the region.

Once such an analysis has been made of the region, it can be extended to a particular urban center in the region, yielding a similar evaluation of the urban area economy within the framework of the region's economy. Thus we may expect that a selection of high-index industries appropriate to a southeastern urban center could be drawn from Table 7 and listed as offering good prospects for balanced expansion in the local economy.

Such an approach offers one means of evaluating the vitality of an urban area's economy. In an effort to get at this problem with greater objectivity, the Cincinnati City Planning Commission developed a crude scoring technique using selected general criteria such as wage and salary levels, use of skilled workers and the degree of seasonal and cyclical stability.[56] Using 1940 census summaries for the country as a whole, each of 109 industries in the nation was scored in the following manner. The critical range of variation was determined for each criterion and broken down into four classes from I to IV as shown in Table 8. Each criterion was graded numerically, and assuming equal weighting for all criteria, these ratings were then combined to obtain a total score for each industry. The presence or absence of additional characteristics with special significance to the Cincinnati area such as the use of female, nonwhite, or older labor was also identified. Where an industry had a relatively high proportion of employment from these groups it was singled out with special letter designators F, N, or M, respectively.[57] Under this scoring technique, the total score of any industry can range from 0 to 15FNM. The authors of this study note that adjustments in data shown in Table 8 would probably be necessary from census to census.

Table 9 presents the 1940 scores of the 15 major census economic groups for the nation as a whole using the Cincinnati technique. The results indicate that in 1940 the Census categories including utilities, finance-insurance–real estate, communications, and government carried high ratings, whereas the manufacturing group, failing to receive the highest rating, (3), for any of the five general criteria, was considerably lower. The Cincinnati study

[56] Cincinnati City Planning Commission, *op. cit.*, pp. 98–99.
[57] F was used for all industries in which 30 percent or more of total employment in March 1940 was female, N when 10 percent or more of all employment was nonwhite, and M when 35 percent or more of all employment was at least 40 years of age.

TABLE 8.   General Criteria of Economic Well-Being and Scoring Factors[a]

| Class | Wages and Salaries | | Skill | Seasonal and Cyclical Stability | | Numerical Ratings |
	Median Yearly Wage or Salary in 1939	% of Total Workers Receiving $2500 or More, 1939	% of Total Workers Classed as Skilled, March 1940[b]	% of Total Workers Employed 12 Mos. 1939	% Drop in Mfg. Empl. 1929–1931–1933 (whichever is lower)	
I	$1500 and over	15 and over	50 and over	80 and over	Under 10	3
I	$1200–1499	10–14.9	30–49.9	70–79.9	10–19.9	2
II	$ 900–1199	5– 9.9	15–29.9	50–69.9	20–44.9	1
V	Under $900	Under 5	Under 15	Under 50	45 and over	0

[a] Adapted from Cincinnati City Planning Commission, *Economy of the Area*, City of Cincinnati, 1946, pp. 98–99.
[b] In manufacturing industries, percentage of craftsmen among employed craftsmen, operatives and laborers; in nonmanufacturing industries, percentage of professional, proprietors, and craftsmen among total employed workers.

should be consulted for the actual scores obtained for all 109 industries covered in the 1940 census.

The Cincinnati approach next calls for the use of this scoring technique applied to the urban area of interest. The results are evaluated in terms of maximum achievable scores and in terms of the national showing. This kind of analysis is thus used to identify from the U.S. listing those lines of economic activity which can be introduced into the local economy to offset areas of weakness, considering local advantages as to markets, raw materials, transportation, labor skills, and other resources available in the urban center.

Undoubtedly more experimentation is needed in the use of this tech-

TABLE 9.   Rating of 15 Major Industrial Groups Employing Cincinnati City Planning Commission Technique, 1940[a]

Major Industrial Group	Rating
Utilities	13M
Finance, insurance, and real estate	12FM
Communication	12F
Government	11M
Wholesale trade	9
Professional and related services	8F
Transportation	7M
Business and repair services	7
Amusement, recreation, and related services	7
Manufacturing	6
Retail trade	4
Construction	4
Personal service	3FN
Mining	3M
Agriculture, forestry, and fishing	3N

[a] Adapted from Cincinnati City Planning Commission, *Economy of the Area*, City of Cincinnati, 1946, p. 66.

nique. While offering an objective approach to diagnosing weaknesses in the structure of the economy, there is some arbitrariness to the scoring system. The use of equal weights for all factors employed in the scale may be open to some question. Moreover, there may be other factors, some perhaps not reported in census summaries, which should appear in the equation. Further research can be expected to remedy some of these problems. Meanwhile, until such time as techniques of this kind can be refined and given greater precision, they can be of considerable assistance in guiding subjective determinations and judgment as to how the economy can be strengthened and maintained in healthy balance as economic expansion proceeds.

CHAPTER 6

employment studies[1]

In the foregoing discussion of the structure and vitality of the urban economy, it was seen that employment is one of the most common units for measuring economic activity. Although imperfect as a measure of many qualitative aspects of economic growth, if allowances are made for these imperfections, it represents an extremely useful unit of measurement for scaling land development requirements. It is this kind of application of employment data that is of ultimate concern here. A review of the more broadly focused analyses in all their complex aspects that the economist might undertake for his needs is beyond the scope of this discussion. Moreover, to be consistent with our own admonishments above, the studies described in this chapter are morally bound to those which have specific application to land use planning analyses. In particular, these have to do with techniques of forecasting employment in the urban study area.

In the land use planning process, the employment forecast serves two specific purposes: (1) it provides information of concern to population studies which in turn are used in estimating space needs for residential areas and community facilities, and (2) it supplies a direct yardstick for use in scaling land requirements for industrial and commercial areas. As brought out in some detail in Chapter 7, perhaps the most important variable affecting the population growth of an urban area is the migration component. Since migration tends to be regulated by economic opportunity, i.e., employment prospects, the employment forecast provides the means for estimating the effect that migration will have on population trends in the urban study area. The second purpose has a more obvious application to land use planning. In industrial areas, space requirements are estimated on the basis of adopted industrial density standards, i.e.,

[1] Portions of this chapter are drawn from the author's article "Employment Forecasts for City Planning," *Journal of the American Institute of Planners*, Spring, 1954.

manufacturing workers per acre of industrially used land. In wholesale areas, space requirements are derived from various floor area standards of employees per square foot of building space in wholesaling, truck terminal, and related warehousing uses, and in business areas, office space requirements are developed on the basis of floor area standards relating employment in professional services, finance, insurance, and real estate to space taken up in this category of use. In such applications, employment forecasts thus play a vital role.

GENERAL CONSIDERATIONS OF FORECASTING

At the outset, some comment is perhaps in order concerning the skepticism sometimes encountered outside the field in the use of employment forecasts in city planning studies. Some of this reaction is warranted, especially where it is premised on the loose use of forecast data or techniques without regard to the elemental qualifications and assumptions which go with the forecast. However, where there is real understanding and prudent recognition of these limitations in city planning analyses, there are mitigating circumstances which may not be generally recognized by people outside the field.

In most applications of forecast data in land use planning—for example, in estimating industrial land requirements—there is some latitude for inaccuracy. The use of industrial employee density standards in conjunction with a forecast of manufacturing employment yields a tentative estimate of the new acreage required to accommodate normal industrial expansion. But then in the same way that civil engineers introduce safety factors which make the designed capacity of a bridge considerably in excess of maximum loads anticipated, the city planner usually provides for an "industrial reserve" or a safety factor in his estimates of space requirements which introduces into the result an increment well over the amount of land estimated to be needed to take care of normal growth and expansion.

Even if we concede the possibility of forecast inaccuracies being large enough to be critical in these calculations, the effect of such inaccuracies tends to be relatively insignificant compared with the variability in results which are possible with only slight differences in the choice of the standard used for the future employee density. Thus there may be reason for greater concern over the choice of standard to which forecast data are applied.

But apart from these considerations, there are other moderating elements in the picture. Implicit in the planning process itself as we have been viewing it is the necessity for periodically reviewing and restudying plans in the light of new and unforeseen developments. There is thus the continuing opportunity to adjust for forecast inaccuracies. Not to be overlooked, too, is the element of control which zoning and other similar plan-implementing measures exert and the effect that these may have in influencing the accuracy of the forecast.

The foregoing discussion is not to minimize the hazards inherent in developing employment forecasts, but rather to point out that city planning applications of forecast data are not so exacting in their requirements as perhaps those of labor market analysts and other consumers of forecast data. Certainly these moderating circumstances do not absolve the city planner from careful examination of the sources of data he employs and for recognizing the limitations of the forecast techniques he may be using.

It should be noted that the techniques taken up in this chapter are not concerned with prediction, but rather with methods for estimating levels of future employment, provided the assumptions which go with the techniques are found to apply during the forecast period. Some of the more obvious types of assumptions are: "continued high levels of employment with a constant rate of unemployment at roughly x percent of the civilian labor force," "no major recession," "no outbreak of war," and so on. These types of assumptions would generally be associated with the "high" estimate. Variations downward from these and other assumptions that may be involved would be set to a "low" forecast estimate. This way of looking at forecasting techniques does not preclude for planning purposes the selection of a "single best estimate;" it simply underscores the fact that forecasts are based on certain fundamental assumptions and not on intuition, divine guidance, or some special superhuman knowledge of things to come.

In some quarters, reservations of another kind are sometimes voiced, and anything to do with economic projections is viewed with suspicion. In this respect, we will simply repeat what the congressional Joint Committee on the Economic Report has observed, namely, that economic forecasting "is here to stay as long as individuals, private business, and democratic governments are free to make their own decisions. Only in an authoritarian state can we be relieved of this necessity; there, projections become commands."[2]

There are various available series of data generically included under

---

[2] Joint Committee on the Economic Report, 83rd Congress, 2nd Session, *Potential Economic Growth of the United States During the Next Decade*, U.S. Government Printing Office, 1954, p. 2.

"employment statistics." In order to be assured of internal consistency and the general accuracy of analyses undertaken, not only should distinctions between the various series be clearly understood, but also it should be ascertained that the series selected are available and the same for the whole range of study areas employed, from the nation down to the urban study area. In the more recent decades, the U.S. Bureau of the Census decennial reports carry statistics which permit direct transcription or the isolation of such series as the total labor force, the civilian labor force, total employment, nonagricultural employment, manufacturing employment, and so on. The Bureau's Census of Manufactures and Census of Business carry other series for different years, the former, for example, carrying a series on manufacturing wage earners as well as manufacturing employment, and the Bureau's *U.S. Statistical Abstract* carries average annual employment. On the other hand, the Bureau of Labor Statistics issues an average annual series on manufacturing and nonagricultural employment and a compendium of monthly state employment service figures called "covered employment."[3] There are obvious differences in some of these series, and there are frequently variations in series which on the face of it would appear to be similar, the differences occurring because of different data collection methods used in the original instance. Since there is no substitute for the investigator digging in and learning his data sources and their limitations for himself, the reader is simply alerted to these problems, and except for a few distinctions necessary to explain techniques, it is expected that he will find these things out for himself in the course of developing his own forecasts.

In the following sections of the chapter, two general groups of forecasting methods are discussed: the analytical methods and the short-cut methods. The former develop employment estimates from an analysis of the major antecedent variables which determine employment. In their most elemental form, they utilize the relationship:

$$\frac{\text{Total output}}{\text{Output per worker}} = \text{Employment}$$

and develop estimates of future employment from forecasts of production and worker output data, with a forecast being developed for each component according to an analysis of its principal antecedent variables.[4] The more commonly used short-cut methods utilize one or more series of employment statistics direct. Manifestly, they are simpler to apply and are less time-consuming to complete.

[3] For the annual series see Bureau of Labor Statistics, *Nonagricultural Employment by States: 1939–1953*, U.S. Government Printing Office, 1954; and for monthly compendium, see series in *Monthly Labor Review* published by the U.S. Government Printing Office.

[4] Future production or output is used here in a loose sense referring more precisely and correctly to *future demand*.

Both groups of methods require as a point of beginning certain estimates for the future (derived or "given") appropriate to the series being used. Thus the analytical methods require initial estimates of future total output and output per worker for the nation or the region within which the urban study area is situated from which to begin the analysis. Similarly, the short-cut methods must have an estimate of the civilian labor force, total employment, or other similar unit of measurement for some geographic area larger than the urban study area. Once a point of beginning is established, most analytical and short-cut methods utilize ratio or correlation procedures, either direct or by apportionment, as a means of connecting the initially derived or "given" data to the urban study area.

The forecaster will want to use several methods as a means of gauging the reasonableness of estimates derived. Although the methods discussed below have never been subjected to systematic statistical tests of validity, obviously the forecaster will attach greater weight to some results than to others. Until mass statistical tests can be made of these methods on a comparative basis, the importance attached to results from various methods will depend upon such factors as the liberties taken by the forecaster as necessitated by gaps in trend data, his "common sense" observations as to variations in the accuracy of procedures employed in the various methods, and so on.

The particular kinds of applications that are to be made of results from the various forecasting methods are a factor to be taken into consideration in the selection of methods. As mentioned above, population studies require estimates of total employment. Land use planning analyses require breakdown estimates for at least the manufacturing and frequently the wholesaling and warehousing-trucking components of the total, and the professional services, finance, insurance, and real estate categories. All methods presented below will yield estimates of total employment, but for purposes of developing breakdowns for special components, some methods may prove to be better than others, according to the peculiarities of the data series used in the forecast and the detail available in that series for the urban study area of interest.

ANALYTICAL FORECASTING METHODS

The analytical methods are closely tied up with the regionally oriented approaches to the study of the urban economy, and thus involve much the same order of complexity and the same limitations that were identified with these approaches in Chapter 5. Two methods are discussed below. One is an extension of input-output analysis, and the other fits within the framework of the approximation approaches to the study of regional spheres of economic influence.

The principal advantage of an analytical method is the greater accuracy theoretically obtainable by separate analysis of each individual component (total output and output per worker) that affects the final employment estimate derived. In the short-cut methods these separate effects are obscured, but in the analytical methods, the behavior of each variable in the past can be observed separately and used as a guide in estimating its likely behavior in the future. In practice, this seeming advantage may become the principal disadvantage, for with more variables to account for, there are more chances of error entering into the forecasting procedure. Whether it proves to be an advantage or disadvantage depends on the experience of the forecaster, the care with which each variable is examined for hidden influences, and the availability of suitable and reliable basic data for periods sufficiently far back in time to permit observation of trends.

Forecasts by Input-Output Analysis

In the earlier discussion of the input-output technique, our attention was centered around the derivation of the basic table of interregional-interindustry coefficients which contained the matrix of relationships in the flow of commodities between all industries within and external to a given spatial setting. In terms of our present concern, this spatial setting would be the urban study area, i.e., the Standard Metropolitan Area or whatever other delineation of this area has been settled upon for the tooling-up studies. Further, the table of coefficients, let us say, is Table 2, with Metropolitan Region I being our SMA and Regions II and III being all other areas within the sphere of economic influence of our SMA.

Now according to the analytical approach requirements, we must have as a point of beginning certain given estimates. In input-output analysis one such set of "givens" would consist of estimates of the effective demand for all the various economic lines listed in Region I or our SMA, let us say for the year 1980. Assuming adjustments have been made in the values contained in the table for anticipated changes in the local economy by 1980 as discussed in the last chapter, these future demand levels can be applied industry by industry to the adjusted coefficients to obtain the 1980 output in, let us say, constant 1955 dollars. By summing up the results for all industries in our SMA, we obtain an estimate of the total output for the forecast year. Obviously, by using a more detailed industrial classification than the one employed in our illustrative model (Table 2), it would be possible to obtain subtotals of output for manufacturing and for other desired detailed categories.

To complete the analysis, the other set of "givens" required would consist of estimates of 1980 labor productivity for all industries and for the subcategories, manufacturing, wholesaling, warehousing-trucking, and the professional, finance, insurance, and real estate services. To maintain internal consistency to the analysis, these estimates would be expressed in dollar output per worker in constant 1955 dollars for all industry and for each of the desired subcategories. If reliable estimates of this order are not available as "givens," then estimates would have to be developed on the basis of assumed levels of labor productivity based on subassumptions relative to technology, management efficiency, and so on.

With these data available, the actual employment estimates are obtained by dividing values for estimated future output by the appropriate values for output per worker. While the procedure thus described is conceptually a simple one, obviously to put it into operation involves several problems. First and foremost, except for some possible few situations where data may have been especially assembled for an input-output matrix, there are no presently available sources of data in the form needed to construct the matrix. These and other problems related to the input-output technique itself have already been covered. But assuming the necessary matrix were available, there is the further problem of the "givens" and their availability by industrial categories used in the matrix, or for that matter by broad combinations of these categories. If they are not given, it is outside the competence of the field of city planning to deal with the many variables involved in deriving estimates. These factors and the problem of technical know-how in the execution of input-output analyses thus represent deterrents in the use of this method at the present time.

Apportionment of National Output and Productivity Estimates

As the term "apportionment" implies, this is a system of analysis which determines how smaller geographical areas share in estimates (of whatever kind) previously prepared for a parent area: the nation, a region, or perhaps a State Economic Area. It is a technique which has had some use in short-cut employment forecasts but which has had more general use in population forecasts. Customarily it utilizes "step-downs" through intermediate areas until the share of the given locale of interest is determined. In each step-down operation apportionment to all parts of the whole (e.g., all regions of the nation, all subregions of the region of interest, etc.) is made and results are balanced out against the total before the procedure is carried to the next smaller set of geographical areas. In this way an interlocking relationship is worked out from the largest to the smallest area. The number of such step-downs is dependent upon how large the local area's share of the original parent area's total is likely to be (in terms of employment, population, etc.), and the larger the share, the fewer the number of intermediate step-downs required. Step-downs are usually accomplished either by ratio or by correlation procedures.

In the context of the present discussion, the apportionment technique determines first, on the basis of past trends, how each region can be expected to share in estimated future national annual production or output, and then determines on the basis of estimated future annual levels of output per worker for each region, the number of future workers this productive activity will support. Of course, the point of beginning is some reliable national forecast of both production and output per worker. Once regional apportionments have been made, the whole process is repeated on a subregional level within the region of particular interest, and apportionment of the region's share of national totals is made to subregions. The process is repeated further until the urban study area is reached. The basic requirements of this method, then, are (1) two series of data for trend analyses, one indicating past production trends and another showing past worker output trends, both being required for the whole system of geographical areas being employed in the analysis, and (2) suitable national forecasts of both production and output per worker.

Considering the total output component first and the problem of selecting a series of data, it may be noted that there are various measures of national production in common usage. Those for which statistics are reported annually are Gross National Product, Net National Product, National Income, Personal Income, and Disposable Income.[5] One or more of these income concepts are frequently used as measures of the nation's total pro-

---

[5] See U.S. Department of Commerce, *National Income Supplement to Survey of Current Business,* U.S. Government Printing Office, July 1947, p. 8. These income concepts are defined as follows:

Gross National Product is the market value of the net output of goods and services produced by the nation's economy, before deduction of depreciation charges and other allowances for capital consumption. . . . [It] comprises the purchases of goods and services by consumers and government, gross private domestic investment and net foreign investment.

Net National Product is the market value of the net output of goods and services produced by the nation's economy. . . . [It] comprises the purchase of goods and services by consumers and government, net private domestic investment and net foreign investment.

National Income is the aggregate earnings of labor and property which arise from the current

duction, with *Gross National Product* (GNP) usually favored, being considered the most stable measure of productive activity. While estimates for all five income series are summarized for individual years on a national basis, unfortunately no systematic summaries are yet available showing breakdowns as to how all states and counties share in these totals.[6]

Some studies have attempted to bridge this gap. In an effort to permit analysis of the changing economic structure of regions and smaller geographic areas relative to national trends, a recent exploratory study by Michael Cabot used *Total Income Payments to Individuals* (TIPI) as an index of production.[7] TIPI is a series of data which is most closely related to the Personal Income series, but which is closely correlated to GNP. It is broken down by states, and summaries appear annually in the July or August issue of *Survey of Current Business,* published by the U.S. Department of Commerce. By using an "effective buying income" series of data which are similar to TIPI and published annually by *Sales Management* magazine on a state and county basis, and adjusting these data to represent TIPI equivalents in constant 1951 dollars, this study shows how the nation's TIPI can be allocated to several regions, to the states, and finally to one or more counties of special interest for a particular city planning study. The approach is somewhat circuitous, but until such time as TIPI data are reported by counties, it is a reasonably satisfactory procedure for approximation purposes.[8]

---

production of goods and services by the nation's economy. . . . [These] earnings consist of the compensation of employees, the profits of corporate and unincorporated enterprises, net interest and the rental income flowing to persons.

Personal Income is the current income received by persons from all sources, inclusive of transfers from government and business but exclusive of transfers among persons. . . . Personal income is measured as the sum of wage and salary receipts, other labor income, proprietors' and rental income, interest and dividends, and transfer payments.

Disposable Income is the income remaining to persons after deduction of personal tax and other payments to general government.

Gross National Product (GNP) is considered to be the most stable measure of productive activity and to be more precise statistically than Net National Product. Net National Product is less than GNP by the amount of depreciation charges, and certain other capital consumption allowances. Theoretically Net National Product and National Income should be equal, but the latter is actually smaller due principally to certain indirect taxes received by the government which are included in the former. Personal Income is less than National Income principally by profits retained by corporations and by corporate profits taxes, after allowance has been made for net interest paid by the government and transfer payments, which are not included in National Income. Disposable Income is the smallest of the five indices and is the same as Personal Income, except it excludes income taxes.

[6] For U.S. figures from 1909 to 1928, see J. Frederic Dewhurst and Associates, *America's Needs and Resources,* The Twentieth Century Fund, 1955. For figures since 1928, see U.S. Department of Commerce, *National Income Supplement to the Survey of Current Business,* U.S. Government Printing Office, July, 1952.

[7] Michael Cabot, *A Method for Relating Population Distribution to a Changing Economic Structure,* an unpublished manuscript, University of North Carolina Department of City and Regional Planning, 1953.

[8] Figures are now available on counties in southeastern states; see J. L. Lancaster, *County Income Estimates for Seven Southeastern States,* University of Virginia Bureau of Population and Economic Research, 1952.

A suitable forecast of future national productive levels is identified as one of the needed "givens" in our second requirement above.[9] Cabot used the National Planning Association's 1951 estimates of 1960 GNP.[10] There are other more recently prepared estimates available, for example, the estimates issued in 1952 by the Paley Commission of the 1975 GNP,[11] and those completed in early 1954 by the Joint Committee on the Economic Report on the 1965 GNP.[12] All carry their own particular assumptions on national security expenditures, the general employment outlook, price levels, and so on.[13] To determine how the given future estimate of national productive levels will be apportioned among the various regions, states, and counties, Cabot converted the national GNP estimate to a TIPI equivalent and then by correlation procedures established how each successive group of areas shared in their parent area's TIPI estimates.[14] Consistent with the apportionment procedure, at each step-down level and before the next step-down analysis was begun, the TIPI values for all the subareas were adjusted as necessary to bring them into balance with the previously derived parent area TIPI figure.

Let us now consider the problem of the other component of this estimating procedure, that of selecting a suitable series on annual output per worker which would satisfactorily reflect labor productivity trends. To obtain the worker productivity data required in the analyses, it is necessary to consider the number of working units per year (hours, days, etc.) at selected time intervals into the future, and the output per worker per unit of time for these same selected time intervals. Here, too, obstacles are encountered in finding a suitable series. Small area breakdowns on the daily output per worker and the number of days worked per year are not available. To bridge this gap and to make the analysis consistent with the previously derived TIPI data, the Cabot study developed a productivity index combining these two elements in the form of a series of curves on *TIPI per*

[9] Citing the importance of considerations internal to regions which tend to be obscured in GNP projections, Walter Isard has suggested that attention be focused on regions as unit areas for income estimation and the development of estimates of future Gross Regional Product as a basis for making GNP projections. Such an eventuality would greatly simplify procedures set forth here, and the point of beginning would become the region. See Isard, "Regional and National Product Projections and their Interrelations," *Long-Range Economic Projection*, Volume 16, Studies in Income and Wealth by the National Bureau of Economic Research, Princeton University Press, 1954, pp. 429–434.

[10] Gerhard Colm, *The American Economy in 1960*, Planning Pamphlet No. 81, National Planning Association, 1951.

[11] The President's Materials Policy Commission, *Resources for Freedom*, Volume 1, "Foundations for Growth and Security," U.S. Government Printing Office, 1952.

[12] Joint Committee on the Economic Report, *op. cit.*

[13] For a summary of the basic assumptions and for selected data from all three of the cited forecasts of GNP, Joint Committee on the Economic Report, *op. cit.*, pp. 21–27.

[14] For illustrative charts and data reproduced from Cabot's work, see Chapin, "Employment Forecasts for City Planning," *Journal of American Institute of Planners*, Spring, 1954.

worker. The study developed estimates of future TIPI per worker for the nation, and then, following similar correlation procedures, established how the trends of TIPI per worker in regions related to the nation, how such trends in the states concerned related to their region, and so on down to the metropolitan counties of particular interest.[15]

Utilizing national production and worker output data, this technique thus develops estimates as to how regions and local areas share in or relate to national figures by developing and applying step-down relationships. As each step-down is accomplished, estimates of future employment are computed. By using "high" and "low" assumptions throughout, results could be presented in terms of a range within which the future employment might be expected to fall.

As noted above, ratios instead of correlation procedures could be used as another variation on the apportionment technique. In place of correlating size of subarea TIPI or subarea productivity against size of parent area TIPI or productivity, a time series is constructed expressing the smaller area increments as percentages of the parent area totals. Utilizing the same model described above, projections are made of the percentage series, and future percentage values obtained are applied to "given" absolute-figure estimates of the parent area for the forecast date to obtain absolute figures in future time for the subareas. A major advantage of the correlation procedure is the greater accuracy possible in the projection operation. Since data are plotted by size of TIPI and magnitude of productivity, they follow a more regular pattern. It is thus possible to fit a curve to the data with greater ease and less hazard than is involved in fitting a curve to a time series which is susceptible to greater fluctuations.

This particular application of the analytical approach to employment forecasts yields only estimates of *total employment* as derived from output and output per worker data. The series of data used in these analyses do not carry breakdowns by industry groups, and at present it is necessary to use short-cut methods for breaking out subtotals on the manufacturing, wholesaling, warehousing-trucking, and other desired categories.

SHORT-CUT FORECASTING METHODS

The short-cut forecasting methods are much more simply applied than the foregoing analytical methods. Since they use employment statistics direct without becoming involved in projections of total output and output

[15] For illustrative charts and data on this aspect of the analysis, *ibid.*

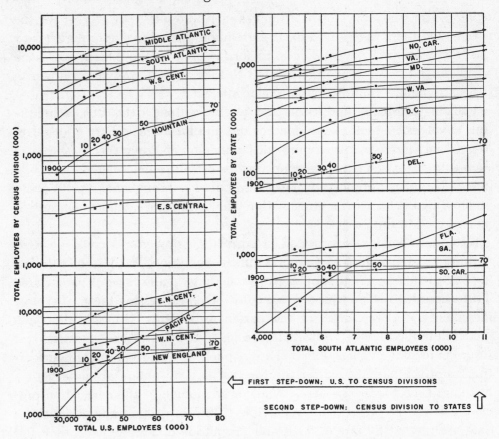

FIGURE 17.   Illustrative Charts of First and Second Step-Downs Apportioning
Estimates of Future National Employment to Smaller Geographic Areas.

per worker, the procedures generally require much less time and effort in
the actual work of carrying them out. Moreover, because there are several
employment series reported on a small-area basis the forecaster is permitted more latitude in the choice of data sources, and the mechanical task
of forecasting is generally facilitated.

There are two classes of methods in this group. While both utilize step-
down procedures in determining the urban study area's share of the "given"
estimate for a larger geographical area, one class accomplishes the step-
downs by an apportionment technique and the other employs direct step-
downs, omitting the proration analyses of all parts to the whole. The chief
weakness of the latter technique is that it ignores the manner in which the
economic structure of the region, the subregion, and the smaller subareas
selected for the step-down operation may be changing relative to the structure of all other regions, subregions, etc., that are included in each parent
area. Here too, correlation or ratio procedures can be used to accomplish
step-downs, the latter being the most commonly used.

Apportionment of National Employment Estimates

Following the same general apportionment procedures described above under analytical methods, two series of employment data may be used in this short-cut method of forecasting: the decennial census employment series (corresponds to April employment) or the average annual employment series. In the case of the latter, in order to obtain both total and manufacturing employment on an average annual basis, it is necessary to use two sources independently compiled, thus involving a problem of consistency between the two series.[16] Moreover, these two series are not available in small-area breakdowns and thus require the use of the decennial census, a third series, in estimating average annual equivalents for the selected system of small areas. Since this conversion procedure is subject to the possibility of additional error, the decennial census series is preferred, providing a single series for step-down procedures that is internally consistent

FIGURE 18.   Illustrative Charts of Third and Fourth Step-Downs Apportioning Estimates of Future National Employment to Smaller Geographic Areas.

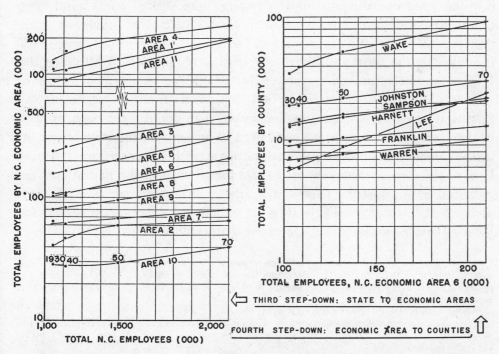

[16] For average annual total employment in the nation, the census divisions, and the states, see Bureau of the Census, *U.S. Statistical Abstract*, U.S. Government Printing Office, latest volume; and for average annual manufacturing employment, see Bureau of Labor Statistics, *Nonagricultural Employment by States, 1939–1953*, U.S. Government Printing Office, 1954.

throughout. However, it too has its limitations. Breakdowns for small areas were not undertaken before the 1930 census, and manufacturing employment is not listed as an integral part of the decennial census before that time.

Figures 17 and 18 illustrate apportionment step-down procedures in the forecast of total employment using the decennial census employment series.[17] The given national forecast of employment used in this particular illustration of the method was based on an extrapolation of the 1965 estimate of total employment contained in the study of the Joint Committee on the Economic Report, the resulting assumed estimate of 1970 national employment supplying the point of beginning for step-downs.[18] The assumptions accompanying this 1965 forecast (and presumably the 1970 estimate) were generally of a "high" order. To provide a range of estimates embracing "low" eventualities, supplemental assumptions can be introduced with corresponding variations in the magnitude of the national employment figures assumed. The system of geographical areas employed in this illustration includes four step-downs: (1) the nation to the nine census divisions, (2) the South Atlantic census division to the eight southeastern states and the District of Columbia, (3) North Carolina to the eleven state economic areas of this state, and (4) N.C. State Economic Area No. 6 to the seven constituent counties, among them Wake County (Raleigh), the urban study area for this illustrative forecast. The previously mentioned problem of fitting regression curves to data available only since 1930 is evident in the third and fourth step-downs (Figure 18).[19] Although this illustration of the method correlates size of subarea employment to parent area employment to effect the actual step-downs from one series of geographical areas to the next smaller series, data could have been ordered in time series, and ratio procedures used to accomplish the step-downs. As in the previous examples of the use of apportionment procedures, in each level of the step-down operation, figures for all parts of the parent area are balanced out against the parent area figure before the analysis is repeated at the next lower level. Table 10 gives a summary of results obtained following these procedures. Estimates are purely illustrative.[20]

[17] This illustration of the use of apportionment procedures taken from A. C. Hall, Jr., *A Forecast of Employment for the Raleigh Metropolitan Area, with a Study of Basic-Nonbasic Composition,* unpublished manuscript, Department of City and Regional Planning, University of North Carolina, 1955.

[18] Joint Committee on the Economic Report, *op. cit.,* p. 19.

[19] To alleviate difficulties encountered here, studies of employment trends by state or university agencies are sometimes available and can be used to guide the forecaster in fitting curves to his data.

[20] The curves in Figures 17 and 18 were smoothed by means of moving averages and fitted to the data by eye. Mathematical curves would normally be computed, thus yielding more valid estimates than those appearing in Table 10.

TABLE 10. Illustrative Estimates of Employment for Various Geographical Areas as Derived by Apportionment Procedures, 1970[a].

Area	1970 Adjusted Employment (000)
Census Divisions	
New England	4,200
Middle Atlantic	15,000
East North Central	16,000
West North Central	6,200
South Atlantic	11,000
East South Central	4,000
West South Central	7,000
Mountain	2,600
Pacific	12,000
U.S.	78,000
South Atlantic States	
Delaware	150
Maryland	1,350
District of Columbia	540
Virginia	1,500
West Virginia	740
North Carolina	2,100
South Carolina	820
Georgia	1,400
Florida	2,400
South Atlantic	11,000
North Carolina	
State Economic Area 1	200
State Economic Area 2	65
State Economic Area 3	450
State Economic Area 4	250
State Economic Area 5	315
State Economic Area 6	210
State Economic Area 7	80
State Economic Area 8	170
State Economic Area 9	130
State Economic Area 10	40
State Economic Area 11	190
North Carolina	2,100
N.C. State Economic Area 6	
Franklin County	13
Harnett County	22
Johnston County	30
Lee County	24
Sampson County	21
Warren County	10
Wake County	90
N.C. State Economic Area 6	210

[a] Adapted from A. C. Hall, Jr., *A Forecast of Employment for the Raleigh Metropolitan Area, with a Study of Basic-Nonbasic Composition*, unpublished manuscript, Department of City and Regional Planning, University of North Carolina, 1955.

To extend this analysis to include estimates of manufacturing employment, two alternative procedures could be followed.[21] One involves duplication of the foregoing apportionment procedures, using given national estimates of future manufacturing employment in place of total employment. The other requires a study of local trends in manufacturing employment, and by use of ratio or correlation procedures, involves the construction and projection of a curve showing the relationship between the manufacturing subcategory and total employment. Both approaches face the same limitations in not having decennial census data on manufacturing employment available prior to 1930. For large cities of the country, it is possible to get around this problem by using the Census of Manufactures series to approximate local trends in manufacturing employment for decennial years prior to 1930.[22] This adjustment procedure can be used in either of the two alter-

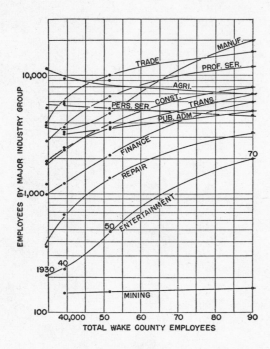

FIGURE 19. Illustrative Chart of County Employment by Major Subcategories Plotted in Relation to Total County Employment.

---

[21] Because decennial census series do not carry breakdowns in the detailed form needed to break out wholesaling and warehousing-trucking as separate subcategories, it is not feasible to develop estimates for these groupings of activities in the same way as described for the manufacturing subcategory. For estimating procedures suitable to these subcategories, see discussion of ratio methods below. Estimates for professional services, finance, insurance, and real estate services would be obtained in the same manner as described for the manufacturing subcategory.

[22] In the period prior to 1930 of particular interest here, the Census of Manufactures reports for "principal cities" rather than for counties or for Standard Metropolitan Areas that contain these cities. Thus, in order to maintain consistency to the analysis, it is necessary to adjust figures given in the Census of Manufactures for both area and the year reported in estimating decennial census equivalents.

native approaches.[23] For smaller cities, the second alternative is perhaps the most satisfactory approach. Figure 19 illustrates how the total employment estimate derived in Figures 17 and 18 can be broken out into major census subcategories by correlation procedures. However, until trends can be established over a longer period of time than is presently possible from decennial census data, results from the application of these procedures in small cities must be regarded with some reservation. Obviously three census reports (1930, 1940, and 1950) do not provide a satisfactory basis for the study of long-range trends.

Estimation by Direct and Indirect Ratio Procedures

By far the most commonly used approaches to estimating future employment in a locale of interest utilize simple ratio procedures. These procedures estimate how a particular urban study area will share in the projected employment of some larger geographic area (usually the nation). They may be used in a series of indirect step-down analyses involving successively smaller areas, until estimates for the urban study area are finally determined, or they may be used in direct local-national analyses.

As in the apportionment approach, the rationale of these procedures is based on the premise that local employment trends are a function of national trends, and given a reasonably reliable national forecast, local estimates can be derived which possess a sufficient degree of accuracy for planning purposes. Such a premise usually carries with it a corollary that the larger the employment of the local study area the greater the degree of accuracy in the final result. As in the other methods, forecasts can be developed with a series of alternate assumptions, with the end results being expressed in terms of high and low estimates bracketing a range of possibilities.

THE BASIC PROCEDURES

In the direct local-national ratio approach, percentages of local to national employment are computed for past decades from census reports and ordered in a time series. A curve is fitted to moving averages of these data

[23] In using the first approach (the apportionment procedure), step-downs of manufacturing employment below the state level must be accomplished on the rather crude basis of using "the urban study area" and "rest of state" in lieu of the system of geographic areas utilized in the third and fourth step-downs shown in Figure 18.

and projected to the desired forecast date. The value of the projected ratio thus obtained is then applied to the given estimate of future national employment to obtain the estimate of future employment in the urban study area. The step-down variant of the ratio approach follows essentially the same procedure in each successive step-down analysis. Thus curves of the employment ratios are developed and projected—the region-to-nation ratio, the state-to-region ratio, and so on. Beginning then with given employment estimates for the nation, absolute estimates of employment for each of the intermediate geographic areas are determined in turn by applying the appropriate projected ratios to absolute figures derived in the last preceding step. This step-down operation is repeated until an estimate for the urban study area is finally derived. The mechanics of this operation are identical with those of the ratio procedures used in short-cut population forecasting taken up in the next chapter. These two ratio methods are the simplest to apply and are in most common usage.

Employment forecasts in the Cincinnati and Philadelphia economic base studies follow these basic procedures, with contrasting variations suited to the particular series of employment statistics each used.[24] The Cincinnati approach worked with total labor force estimates refined down to nonagricultural employment, and the Philadelphia study, while using the Cincinnati approach as a check, placed primary emphasis on a series on manufacturing employment, finally expanding them to nonagricultural employment.[25] In the absence of suitable national forecasts at the time these studies were made, both developed national estimates appropriate to their respective approaches before deriving local estimates of employment.

CINCINNATI STUDY

Cincinnati's labor force approach began with given estimates of the United States population under selected assumptions of fertility, mortality, and immigration for the desired period of the national forecast, in this case 1970. It applied to the selected population series estimates of the percentages of total population in each major age-sex group expected to be in the

[24] Cincinnati City Planning Commission, *The Economy of the Area*, City of Cincinnati, 1946; and Philadelphia City Planning Commission, *Economic Base Study of the Philadelphia Area*, City of Philadelphia, 1949.

[25] Basic distinctions in the terms "nonagricultural employment," "employment," "civilian labor force," and "total labor force" should be borne in mind here. *Total labor force* includes all those gainfully employed and all those seeking work, including members of the armed forces but excluding housewives working at home. *The civilian labor force* is the total labor force minus members of the armed forces. *Employment* is the civilian labor force minus the unemployed segement, and *nonagricultural employment* is less than total employment by the amount of employment in farming occupations.

nation's labor force by 1970. The totaled results yielded the desired 1970 labor force estimate. This was then adjusted downward to nonagricultural employment by first applying the appropriate ratio of the expected 1970 relationship between total employment and total labor force and then subtracting out the projected employment in agriculture, forestry, and for Cincinnati's purposes, mining and fishing.

With such a national forecast of nonagricultural employment available, the Cincinnati study then developed a trend line in the ratio of local to national nonagricultural employment over past decades, extrapolated it, and applied the ratio obtained from this curve to its previously derived national nonagricultural employment estimates to obtain absolute nonagricultural employment figures for the Cincinnati metropolitan area at the desired date in the future. Manufacturing employment was derived by similar ratio procedures.

PHILADELPHIA STUDY

The Philadelphia approach developed successive interlocking relationships between numbers of manufacturing wage earners, manufacturing employment, and total employment. In the absence of suitable national forecasts, the Philadelphia City Planning Commission also developed for purposes of local analyses its own estimates of future trends of U.S. employment. This was done by fitting logistic curves to values of moving averages for three historical series of data and projecting these curves through 1980, the desired forecast period. The first series selected were absolute numbers of U.S. manufacturing wage earners from 1869 to 1949, and the other two were ratios, first, of the number of U.S. manufacturing wage earners to U.S. manufacturing employment, and then of the U.S. manufacturing employment to U.S. total employment, both covering the same span of time, 1869 to 1949. The ratios were then used to derive projections of U.S. manufacturing employment and U.S. total employment in absolute terms.

The Philadelphia forecast of local employment involved two related operations. In the first, a series of percentages of local to U.S. manufacturing wage earners were computed for the period 1869 to 1949 and smoothed by means of a moving average. A logistic curve was then fitted to the resulting series and this curve line was projected to 1980. Next, the projected percentages were applied to the projected wage-earner figures, as derived in the national forecast described above, to determine the projected number of local manufacturing wage earners in absolute terms.

The second operation expanded the foregoing manufacturing wage-earner projection to manufacturing employment, and then expanded this result to total employment. Following the same statistical procedures, two local series were developed (local manufacturing wage earners as a percent of local manufacturing employment, and local manufacturing employment as a percent of total local employment), smoothed, and the fitted logistic curves projected to 1980. Thus, when applied to the projected wage-earner data developed in the first operation, these projected percentages yielded the local forecast of manufacturing employment and total employment in absolute terms.

SPECIAL PROBLEMS RESULTING FROM MILITARY BASES

Some urban areas contain military establishments which pose a special problem in employment forecasting, particularly where the military forces represent a substantial proportion of the total local labor force. Under any circumstances forecasts in these situations are difficult, but the problem is especially troublesome when the military activity does not have official permanent status. While military employment (officer and enlisted personnel) is not included in employment totals utilized in land use planning analyses of civilian land requirements in the urban study area, obviously the military strength of the installation has a bearing on the local civilian economy. Accordingly, employment forecasting procedures must include studies of military strength as a basis for estimating future civilian employment in the area.

In general, the most feasible short-cut approach involves a segmental forecasting procedure which deals separately with the following three components of total civilian employment: (1) direct military-related civilian employment (persons employed by the military), (2) indirect military-related civilian employment (an increment composed of persons employed in retail establishments, domestic employees, etc., attributable to the presence of military personnel), and (3) all other forms of civilian employment (nonmilitary-related). Future estimates of the first two segments are predicated on future military strength. Past trends in employment in the first component are obtained by analysis of civilian payroll records of the military establishment. The indirect military-related civilian employment trends are more difficult to establish. This segment can be crudely approximated for various census years by comparative analysis with other cities of similar size not affected by military activity, but the economic structure and employment levels of which are similar to those of the nonmilitary segment of the economy of the city under study. In much the same way that service-basic ratios are developed in conventional economic base analyses, ratios are computed here for past periods of time of both direct and indirect military-related civilian employment as percents of military strength. The trend in the values of each series of ratios are then used as bases for estimating future values to be used as "multipliers" applied to the estimated future military strength of the local base. Depending upon the international situation and security policies prevailing, these estimates of future military strength can sometimes be obtained through military channels. If such estimates are not available, it is necessary (and it is desirable in any case in order to check the reasonableness of estimates secured) to estimate local military strength from national data using conventional ratio step-down procedures.[26] In thus developing these estimates, alternate "high" and "low" assumptions set to such alternatives as "war" and "normal peacetime" conditions are usually identified. Once local estimates of future military strength are available, estimates for the two military-related segments are computed in absolute terms.

The third segment of the forecast concerned with nonmilitary-related employment is developed, using the ratio procedures described above for communities where no military installation is involved. With absolute values for this last segment of local civilian employment thus prepared, the final step is simply one of summing up the three separately derived segments to obtain the estimated total future civilian employment. At best, these procedures yield very crude estimates, and consequently it is particularly important in using this kind of short-cut approach to review continually and revise estimates in the light of changing international, national, and local conditions.

ESTIMATING MANUFACTURING AND OTHER SUBCATEGORIES

In all the above applications of ratio procedures, estimates for the manufacturing subcategory of total employment are either derived in the course of the forecasting procedure itself or obtained by a relatively simple extension of it again using ratio techniques. Drawing upon trend data from the decennial census, employment estimates for professional services, finance, insurance, and real estate subcategories can also be broken out from the forecast of total employment by ratio procedures.

[26] See Bureau of the Census, *Current Population Reports*, Series P-25, for estimates of military strength by states. To illustrate the form in which these data are reported the reader is referred to Bulletin No. 132 of Series P-25 which contains a table of the estimated strength of the armed forces by state of duty and state of preservice as of July 1, 1955.

Estimates of future employment in the wholesaling and warehousing-trucking subcategories must be approximated using Census of Business and Census of Population sources. Although this procedure involves the use of two different series of employment statistics, there is presently no other alternative if these particular combinations of economic activities are to be broken out as subcategories. The following procedure is usually used in developing this estimate. From a graphic plot of national data on wholesaling employment (Census of Business series) arranged in a time series, equivalents for decennial census years are approximated. These national estimates are then expressed as percentages of total national employment (decennial census series), and the resulting ratios plotted in a time series and smoothed by means of a moving average. A curve is fitted to the data and projected. The ratio thus obtained for the forecast date may then be applied to the given estimate of future total national employment to establish in absolute terms a national estimate of future employment in wholesaling. Estimates of future national employment in trucking and related warehousing are obtained similarly using truck transportation employment data in the decennial census.

From this point on, conventional ratio procedures are followed as involved in the analysis of the manufacturing or the professional services and similar desired subcategories. Local estimates are developed either by indirect step-down ratios through intermediate areas or by direct local-national ratio procedures. While the mechanics are thus fairly simple, it should be noted that in some localities census reports may not give the needed data because of the likelihood of revealing the operations of one important firm in the area. In these instances it will be necessary to develop substitute data direct from local sources.

In summary, the freedom of choice in forecasting methods will depend on the uses to be made of results, the series of data available for the locale of interest, the general accuracy desired, and the time the analyst is willing to spend in deriving estimates. Because total output and output per worker are analyzed separately as antecedent factors affecting levels of employment, the analytical methods theoretically yield more accurate results than the short-cut methods. At the present time, however, the problem of data availability severely handicaps the use of these approaches. Furthermore, they are more complex and time-consuming than other methods. Due to these considerations, city planning agencies have favored short-cut approaches. Although these methods have never been subjected to systematic statistical tests for accuracy of results, conceptually the apportionment approach appears to be superior to the simple ratio procedure because of the manner in which it takes into account employment trends in other related areas that share in overall trends. However, within the limitations noted above, several methods should be used as a means of checking the reasonableness of estimates to be used in population and land use planning studies.

CHAPTER 7

population studies

In the last two chapters it was seen that analyses of the structure and vitality of the urban economy and the employment opportunities which the economy can support provide the means for gauging the growth potential of an urban area. These studies were identified as basic to land use planning—indeed, the starting point for all city planning. But to be entirely useful in planning analyses, this growth potential must be expressed in terms of the population it can be expected to sustain—the size of population, its composition and characteristics, and its spatial distribution. Population *size* gives an indication of the overall dimensions of the physical environment and supplies a basic yardstick for the estimation of space needs for various categories of land use. When the time element is introduced and future trends in population size are estimated, these trends become the basis for estimating future dimensions and future space needs. Investigations of population *composition* extend these analyses to such qualitative considerations as age groups, household sizes, and income composition of the population. Thus studies of population composition assist in estimating residential space requirements for various dwelling types consistent with existing and anticipated family sizes, income levels, and the needs of each segment of the life cycle. They assist in determining the amount of space needed for recreation areas, schools, and other community facilities for all segments of the population—small children, teen-agers, families, and old people. Finally, investigations of population *distribution* provide clues as to how these various land uses and facilities should be located in the urban area. Thus, population studies not only provide a means of scaling total space needs for selected land use categories at different periods of time in the future, but also give an indication as to how these total space needs should be allocated to different parts of the urban area at any particular time.

152

In much the same way that fully rounded economic studies and employment analyses require the assistance of the economist, a full-fledged study of population in the urban area requires the know-how of the demographer. He is the specialist equipped with the training and background to undertake the more complex investigations, and it is important to recognize when his skills are needed. While the city planner normally lacks the training to carry out a complete range of demographic studies, he must be prepared to execute several types of analyses. Chief among those required in tooling up for land use planning are studies concerned with (1) estimating the current population, (2) population forecasts, and (3) analyses of the composition and distribution of population. Methods involved in making these studies are taken up in the three sections of the chapter that follow below.

Sound demographic analysis is predicated on accurate and systematically recorded population data for the area under study. There are two sources commonly recognized as meeting these requirements—the complete periodic census enumeration, and a system of continuous population registration. In the United States, we employ the first approach to provide our basic source of information, whereas in some parts of the world—for example, in the Scandinavian countries—continuous registration of births, deaths, moves, separations, and so on, provides an up-to-date record at all times of general population statistics and is used in lieu of the regular census. To supplement these, a third major means of obtaining population data is by estimation. Common methods of estimation include sampling procedures, statistical or mathematical projection procedures, or the use of data series collected for purposes other than demographic analysis. Many of these methods are taken up in the first two sections of this chapter.[1]

At the outset some general observations on census sources are perhaps in order. Although the following general sources are cited to give an indication of the range of publications available, the population analyst can best learn his sources by perusing these publications for himself and locating the various data series he needs. He can thus discover the form in which each is summarized and become familiar with the limitations and changes which have been introduced from census to census. Most information employed in population analyses comes from Bureau of the Census publications, either from decennial census reports or from selected special series issued annually or on a periodic basis. The decennial reports of particular interest are those containing data by small geographic areas.[2] In recent

[1] For a fuller treatment of methods of measuring the population of a given area, see Elbridge Sibley, "Problems in Population Estimation," *The American Journal of Public Health*, February, 1944.

[2] For a listing of data available from the most recent census, see Bureau of the Census, *Key to Published and Tabulated Data for Small Areas*, U.S. Government Printing Office, 1951.

decades urban area data are found by states in three different Census of Population volumes ("Number of Inhabitants," "General Characteristics," and "Detailed Characteristics") and in the Census of Housing volumes. Supplementing these general summaries are special summaries reported by Standard Metropolitan Areas, census tracts,[3] and city blocks.[4] Vital Statistics reports are a special annual series compiled from state health department records and are used in several population forecasting techniques taken up below.[5] The Bureau of the Census periodic releases, *Current Population Reports* (see especially the P-25 series), provide estimates of current national and state population. In addition to published data, certain unpublished data are also available from the Bureau of the Census on a special request basis for the cost of photocopying the original records (e.g., enumeration district summaries), and during periods that decennial census summaries are being processed for publication, arrangements may be made to obtain at cost photostatic copies of machine tabulations in advance of actual publication dates.

The investigator can best determine these sources and understand their limitations in the framework of the specific tooling-up studies in which they are to be used. We can now proceed to review these studies—first, those concerned with estimating current population for postcensal periods; next, those employed in estimating future population prospects; and finally, those devoted to analyses of the characteristics and distribution of population in the urban study area.

ESTIMATING THE CURRENT POPULATION

Since land use planning analyses begin with the present, one of the first concerns is the current population size of the urban study area. Even if the technical work involved in developing the urban land use plan is scheduled around a decennial census period in order to have ready access to accurate and detailed population data, we know that public and private

[3] Census tracts are locally defined, permanently established small-area divisions of a city (containing from 2500 to 8000 persons) laid out with a view to permit comparisons from census to census. Data for "tracted" cities are published in *Census Tracts* bulletins, Series P-D, and in 1950 covered some 64 cities. See Bureau of the Census, *Census Tract Manual,* and other processed materials of the Bureau.

[4] Selected Census of Housing data were published in 1950 for some 213 cities in *Block Statistics* Bulletins, Series H-E.

[5] See National Office of Vital Statistics, *Vital Statistics of the United States,* U.S. Government Printing Office, published by individual years.

development is not scheduled according to census periods, and if the planning agency is to carry forward the detailed planning studies in implementation of the various features of the plan, it soon becomes involved in developing postcensal population estimates. Indeed, up-to-date population estimates are so crucial to all forms of city planning work, many planning agencies have made it a regular and continuing staff function to develop new estimates annually.

A local census, either a complete enumeration or a survey using a carefully structured sample, obviously provides the most satisfactory result. Short of this more expensive and time-consuming approach, one or more of three kinds of estimating methods may be used: (1) the migration and natural increase method, (2) the apportionment method, and (3) methods based on symptomatic data.[6] The first two methods have been used extensively by the Bureau of the Census. More in the nature of short-cut approaches with less time-consuming procedures, the third group of methods have been more widely used by city planning agencies. In general, the selection of method will depend upon the uses to be made of the estimate, the level of accuracy required, and the time and staff experience available. As indicated below, the experimental tests which have been made indicate that some methods are decidedly superior to others, but much more rigorous tests of the relative accuracy of all methods are needed before it will be possible to type them in the order of preference for specific planning or other uses.

Migration and Natural Increase Method

Of several variants of this method, two developed by the Bureau of the Census are discussed here. The Bureau's Method I was first described in 1947,[7] and its Method II was first spelled out in some detail in 1949,[8] with a later improvement of it brought out in 1956.[9] Both approaches utilize the same elemental procedure, essentially one of adjusting the last census figures of the locale of interest to reflect changes that have occurred to date, con-

---

[6] Commonly used mathematical methods, such as arithmetic and geometric projections of past trends, are not considered sufficiently reliable to be included in this résumé of methods.

[7] See Bureau of the Census, "Suggested Procedures for Estimating the Current Population of Counties," *Population—Special Reports*, Series P-47, No. 4, April 30, 1947.

[8] For a comparison of the two approaches, see Bureau of the Census, "Illustrative Examples of Two Methods of Estimating the Current Population of Small Areas," *Current Population Reports*, Series P-25, No. 20, May 6, 1949.

[9] See Bureau of the Census, "Illustrative Example of a Method of Estimating the Current Population of Subdivisions of the United States," *Current Population Reports*, Series P-25, No. 133, March 16, 1956.

sidering separately the effects of two major determinants of these changes, migration and natural increase. More particularly, both approaches are based on the following formula: "The civilian population of an area at the close of a period is equal to its population at the start of the period plus natural increase (the excess of births over deaths) during the period, plus the net migration during the period, minus the net loss of population to the armed forces. The total population is equal to the civilian population plus the number of persons in the armed forces stationed in the area."[10]

Translated into procedural steps, both approaches derive the current estimate of total population as follows:[11]

1. Civilian population at the time of last census.
2. Natural increase from last census to current date.
3. Estimated net civilian migration for the same period.
4. Net loss to the armed forces during the same period.
5. Estimated current civilian population (sum of Items 1, 2, and 3 minus Item 4).
6. Military personnel stationed in the area.
7. Estimated current total population (sum of Items 5 and 6).

The difference in Methods I and II is in the technique of estimating the net migration component, with tests by the Bureau of the Census indicating that Method II, though more time-consuming and complex, results in more accurate estimates on the average.

COMPUTING THE NATURAL INCREASE

The first ingredient of both methods of estimating the current population is the natural increase which has occurred between the date of the last census and the current date. The amount to be added for this component (in rare instances, it may be a subtraction) is simply computed from vital statistics data reported on an annual basis, and consists of differences between births and deaths as reported by place of residence, summed up for all years since the last census. Since the official date of the decennial census is April 1, care must be exercised to adjust data as reported on a calander year basis so that only the appropriate fractional parts of the census year and the terminal year are included in this estimate. In this connection the necessary adjustments can be made by linear interpolation.[12] In addition,

[10] Bureau of the Census, *Current Population Reports*, Series P-25, No. 20, p. 1.
[11] Adapted from Bureau of the Census outline of Method II. See *Current Population Reports*, Series P-25, No. 133, *op. cit.*, p. 2.
[12] See procedures suggested by the Bureau of the Census, *Ibid.*, p. 3.

certain adjustments will usually be necessary to correct for underregistration of births and sometimes deaths.[13] Since there is a lag in the publication of *Vital Statistics of the United States,* local figures for the last two or three years must be obtained from the state health department or vital statistics office or from local health agencies.

Adjustment for net migration, the other major determinant of population change, is approximated in both Bureau of the Census Methods I and II by reference to school enrollment changes from the last census date to the current date. Implicit in both approaches is an assumption that the rate of net migration for the population as a whole during this period is similar to the estimated net migration rate of school children.

NET MIGRATION BY CENSUS BUREAU METHOD I

This approach uses the total change in the elementary school enrollment from the last census date to the current date, taken as a percent of the census date enrollment as a rough indicator of net migration occurring during this period. The elementary school grades normally used are the second through the eighth grade, and in order to use this approach, data must be available for all schools of this level in the urban area on the census date and the date of the current estimate. The approach calls for a careful examination of enrollment recording techniques to insure that there is consistency in the method of counting pupils in both years (e.g., checking to see that counts for all local schools are given on a common date, checking on the consistency in the inclusion or exclusion of parochial schools, etc.). It may also require conversion of data from months used in school reports to the months involved in the population estimating procedure for both initial and terminal dates. This adjustment of enrollment data may be made by determining the monthly average change and then adding or subtracting to correct the data for the census month (April) and the month selected as the current date, or it may be estimated by linear interpolation.[14]

With the data thus checked and adjusted as necessary, the percentage change in enrollment from the last census date to the current date is computed as follows:

$$\frac{\text{Total change in enrollment to current year}}{\text{Base year enrollment}}$$

[13] See suggested procedures, *Ibid.*, pp. 3–4; for information on completeness of birth registrations, see National Office of Vital Statistics, *Vital Statistics—Special Reports,* Vol. 39, No. 4, Part II, "Data for Local Areas," January 20, 1955.

[14] See procedures suggested by the Bureau of the Census, "Illustrative Examples of Two Methods of Estimating the Current Population of Small Areas," *op. cit.*, p. 11.

To eliminate the influence of what might be considered normal change in enrollment, the percentage change in national enrollment during this period is subtracted from the local percentage thus derived.[15] After careful examination of the result for reasonableness, this figure is then used as the estimated crude net migration rate. This rate is applied to the civilian population of the study area at the last census plus one-half of the births occurring between the last census and the current date (as corrected for underregistration).[16]

NET MIGRATION BY CENSUS BUREAU METHOD II

As compared with the foregoing approach where the percentage change in school enrollment is used as a determinant of net migration, this method develops an estimate of the hypothetical enrollment based on natural increase alone, with the difference between the hypothetical and actual enrollment being used as the key determinant of net migration. More specifically, the procedure calls for the following series of steps. First, the population age groups which would be in elementary grades 2 through 8 on the current date are identified in the last census reports according to their then age-group equivalents.[17] These groups are broken out into individual years, with the current elementary school-age population tabulated as it would appear in the last census, thus showing children of preschool ages, lower-grade level school ages, and if the current date of the estimate is in the second half of the decade, including some children of minus 1 and other unborn categories. These children are "survived" year by year to the current date by applying the appropriate age-specific survival rates (determined by reference to standard life tables). The unborn children will of course appear in the analysis beginning at the date corresponding to their birth year, with the actual data on births determined from vital statistics reports. As in the other analyses above, the number of live births for the appropriate years must be corrected for underregistration. The result from following the above procedure produces an estimate of the number of elementary school-age children based on natural increase alone.

[15] Since figures on national enrollment for current dates are not available, it is necessary to substitute data on children of elementary school age in the United States; see Series P-47, *Current Population Reports*.

[16] The inclusion of half the births in this total for purposes of computing the net migration assumes that newly born persons between the time of the census and the current date were alive for only half the period and would therefore be present for net migration at only half the computed rate (or to simplify computations, the full net migration rate is applied to half the births).

[17] Probably the Bureau of the Census reasons for selecting grades 2 through 8 are first, to include a span of years where enrollment tends to be most stable, and second, to facilitate the identification of appropriate age-group equivalents in published census categories.

However, not all children of school age are in school, and it is therefore necessary to convert the elementary school-age children into an enrollment equivalent. The conversion is usually made by a ratio procedure, i.e., by noting what the number of children in school in grades 2 through 8 is as a percent of children in the elementary school-age bracket at the time of the last census, and under the assumption that the same relationship continues to the current date, this ratio (called the "enrollment factor") is used to convert the "survived" elementary school-age figure to its enrollment equivalent. The difference between the enrollment thus derived and the actual enrollment is attributed to migration. This result, expressed as a percent of enrollment at the time of the last census, is used as the net migration rate for the entire population. As in the other approach, this rate is applied to the civilian population of the study area at the last census plus one-half of the births occurring between the last census and the current date (corrected for underregistration). The analyst should consult *Current Population Reports,* Series P-25, No. 133, for detailed procedures of computing net migration under Method II.

Although there is as yet insufficient experience on which to draw conclusions concerning the validity of net migration estimates derived by use of school enrollment data, in one series of *ex post facto* tests by the Seattle City Planning Commission, it was found that net migration of school-age groups understated the magnitude of net migration for the population of all ages.[18] Using 1920, 1930, and 1940 census data, this study derived, decade by decade, the expected school age and total population considering natural increase alone, and by comparison with actual enumerated population at the end of each decade, established net migration for each population category. As would be expected, the tests showed less variation on a metropolitan basis than on a central city basis.

ESTIMATING PERSONS AWAY IN ARMED FORCES

Since World War II persons away in the armed forces have become a particularly important factor in population studies. While the military element in the nation's population in prewar years remained more or less fixed at about half a million, since 1950 this element has fluctuated from six to eight times this number, with as many as a million and a half entering and leaving the service in a single year. It is thus understandable that this segment of the population must now be given special consideration.

[18] See Robert C. Schmitt, "Differential Migration and City Population Estimates," *Sociology and Social Research,* May–June issue, 1953.

Estimates of the net loss of persons to the armed forces between the last census and the current date are made by ratio procedures. First, the most recent estimates of the losses of persons to the armed forces on a state basis are consulted in *Current Population Reports,* Series P-25. The appropriate state estimate is selected and adjusted forward to the current date by procedures suggested in *Current Population Reports,* Series P-25, No. 133. Then, assuming that losses to the armed forces in the county of interest will be in the same proportion that the county's male population 18 to 24 years old is to the state's at the time of the last census, this county-state ratio is applied to the adjusted amount of the net state losses to the armed forces between the last census and the current date to obtain an estimate of the net county losses to the armed forces during this period.

Apportionment Method

As described in the last chapter, the apportionment principle determines how systems of successively smaller geographical areas share in a previously prepared estimate for a larger geographical area, balancing subarea shares with the parent area total at each level to which the apportionment procedure is carried before proceeding to the next smaller system of geographical areas. If the previously prepared estimate is for the state containing the urban study area (obtained from P-25 Series, *Current Population Reports*), the apportionment may be made to all counties of the state or it may be made to combinations of counties as involved in the use of State Economic Areas (see Figure 11). If the previously prepared estimate is for the nation, apportionment would first be made to major census divisions (see Figure 14), then to the several states in the census division of interest, and so on down to the local level.

Two variations on this method may be employed in estimating current population of the urban study area. One approach uses previous intercensal trends as a basis for estimating allocations to smaller areas, and the other uses some suitable series of data determined to be symptomatic of population change as the guide to apportionment procedures. The first approach has had more general usage, and it was used by the Bureau of the Census in preparing postcensal estimates of state and small area population until the mid-thirties, when the migration and natural increase method superceded it. Since the group of methods taken up in the next subsection below are suggestive of the techniques involved in the second approach, only the first approach will be summarized briefly here.

As perfected by the Bureau of the Census in developing current population estimates of states, the first approach assumes that the estimated yearly increases in population since the last census can be apportioned among the census divisions and states according to the trends in the way these areas have shared in national increases in previous decades. The national estimates are originally determined on the basis of annual sampling studies carried on as part of the normal operations of the Bureau of the Census. Following the same rationale, step-downs below the state level may be made by reference to the way more localized areas within the state have shared in state increases in past decades. Obviously the smaller the system of areas used in these apportionment procedures, the more likelihood there is of encountering extreme changes in these trends and the more susceptibility there is to error in the estimating procedure.

Methods Based on Symptomatic Data

This group of methods derive estimates of the current population by reference to observed trends in data series which are found to bear a close relationship to population change and for which current data are available. Using ratio procedures to adjust the last census figures forward to the current date, they employ such series as vital statistics, school enrollment, listings in city directories, electric meter, water meter, or telephone installations, dwelling unit counts from land use surveys, registered voters, and so on. The suitability of the series is judged in terms of the consistency and accuracy of the way in which data are assembled and reported, the frequency with which the series are published (monthly, semiannually, or annually), and the degree of significance in the relationship it possesses to population trends. Obviously the series must be reported at least on the census year and the year of the current estimate in order to establish the necessary relationships.

VITAL RATE TECHNIQUE

Observing that the number of births and deaths occurring each year in a given area is roughly proportional to the size of the area's population, Donald J. Bogue has set forth a technique designed to use vital statistics data as a symptomatic measure of population change.[19] He describes the sequence of steps as follows:

1. Compute crude birth and death rates (average of a two-year base around the last census year) for the subarea and the parent area.

2. Express the crude death rate of the subarea as a ratio of the crude death rate of the parent area. Make the same computation for the birth rate.

3. Make an independent investigation of how the crude birth rates and crude death rates of the various subareas have behaved in the recent past in relation to the trend of vital rates in the parent area. If a definite change-of-ratio with the passing of time is indicated for any class of subareas, devise a set of correction factors to be applied to the ratios for the base year in order to obtain "corrected" ratios for the year of estimate.

4. Compute a crude birth and crude death rate for the parent area for the year for which a population estimate is desired. (Choose as a parent area a state or other unit for which the Bureau of the Census makes a regular postcensal estimate. The Bureau of the Census estimate can be used as a base to compute the vital rates for the parent area.)

5. Multiply the crude death rates for the parent area obtained in Step 4 by the corrected death ratio of the subarea obtained in Step 3 to obtain an estimated crude death rate for the subarea. Repeat for births.

6. Divide the estimated crude death rate of each subarea into the number of deaths registered for the year and allocated to residents of the subarea. Repeat for births. This yields *two estimates* of the subarea population, one based upon death and one based upon birth data.

7. Average the two estimates to obtain a single population estimate.

8. Adjust the population of all subareas to equal the total population of the parent area. This yields an estimate for the population as of July 1 of the year for which the rates have been computed.

Bogue made rough tests, applying the technique to assorted geographical areas: states and census divisions, cities in three states where state censuses were available, and cities in California where special censuses were available at the time he was experimenting with the technique. Where comparisons were possible, results indicated that the technique compared favorably with the migration and natural increase method.[20] Generally, it showed a greater consistency of accuracy in areas not subject to major population upheavals and in the larger geographical areas analyzed. When applied to cities (as opposed to counties containing the built-up area of these cities), it indicated a strong tendency to overestimate the population.

[19] Donald J. Bogue, "A Technique for Making Extensive Population Estimates," *Journal of the American Statistical Association*, June, 1950.

[20] Average difference of 3.6 percent per state and 1.8 percent per census division as compared with an average difference of 4.2 percent for state estimates of 1930 population, using school enrollment data as reported by Henry S. Shryock, Jr., *The Postcensal Estimation of Population in The United States*, University of Wisconsin, Ph.D. thesis, 1937.

OTHER SYMPTOMATIC SERIES

In a study of 39 counties in Washington, Robert C. Schmitt tested the following six series of symptomatic data using both apportionment and ratio procedures: live births, deaths, school enrollment, automobile registrations, voter registrations, and welfare recipients.[21] In *ex post facto* analyses, he estimated the 1950 population and then checked results against the actual 1950 returns (only preliminary returns available when study was made). Under the apportionment procedures (his "proration method"), he found the voter registration series yielded the best results (an average error of 8.7 percent), and as might be expected, he found the welfare recipient series the least accurate (an average error of 25.2 percent). Under ratio procedures (his "censal ratio method"), the enrollment-based and voter registration series yielded better results than other series (both with average error of 7.0 percent), with the "straw man" series on welfare recipients again being least accurate (average error 33.2 percent). According to several statistical tests (standard deviation and critical ratio tests as well as the arithmetic mean), Schmitt improved his results by using various combinations of weighting in these series, but points out that these results cannot be considered conclusive, indicating the possibility of differing results in other areas with differing economic conditions and differing systems of recording these series of data.

Other series of symptomatic data are used in the so-called "land use method," in the city directory method, and in estimates based on public utility data. In the land use method the ratio of the number of dwelling units to population at the time of the last census is applied to a current dwelling unit count to derive a crude approximation of the current population. Unless a local sampling survey is made to establish correction factors for changes in average household size, the method thus described assumes the same average household size that prevailed at the time of the last census. This possible source of error plus the less accurate count of dwelling units that can be obtained by simple field observation than is possible in the interview methods of census enumeration suggests that this approach has relatively less utility than some of the others.

The city directory method establishes a ratio of the number of names listed in the local directory to the population at the time of the last census, and then assuming a similar conversion factor for the current direc-

[21] Robert C. Schmitt, "Short-Cut Methods of Estimating County Population," *Journal of the American Statistical Association*, June, 1952.

tory, the factor is applied to the current count of names to yield the current estimate of population. To expedite the estimating process (and with a less accurate result), sometimes only the name of the head of the household is used in place of a full count of all names listed after his name. Sampling methods are commonly used to simplify the task of counting names. This method encounters some difficulty in establishing comparability of the area covered by the directory and that of the census area selected. Moreover, directories of this kind are frequently less complete in their coverage in fringe areas, with the likelihood of variations in this respect occurring in the compilation of the directory from one year to another. The increase in the number of water or electric meter or telephone installations since the last census date is sometimes used as a "multiplier" for estimating population change, but the inherent weakness in being unable satisfactorily to match up service areas with census areas, and the dependence of this estimating procedure upon changing economic conditions, presents limitations. While frequently refinements are introduced in these three methods as presented here, all three are several degrees removed in the level of precision possible in the estimating procedure than that obtainable in other methods described above.

Comparative Results from Various Methods

Following the completion of the 1950 census returns, the Bureau of the Census undertook a comprehensive review of postcensal estimation methods, with attention devoted to the two variants of the migration and natural increase method, Bogue's technique of using vital rates as a symptomatic series for gauging population change, and two commonly used mathematical projection methods.[22] Although the study was primarily oriented toward a reassessment of Bureau of the Census methods of estimating postcensal state population, it presents important information on the use of these methods in cities. In this particular part of the study, it tested 1950 postcensal estimates developed from 1940 census counts on 92 cities having a 1940 population of more than 100,000. On the supposition that an average of the results of two methods involving rather different assumptions would tend to eliminate extreme errors, two additional tests were made following this averaging procedure.

In recognition of the probability of differences in accuracy according

[22] Jacob S. Siegel, Henry S. Shryock, Jr., and Benjamin Greenberg, "Accuracy of Postcensal Estimates of Population for States and Cities," *American Sociological Review*, August, 1954.

to city size and the rate of population change occurring, the study also tested the results of estimates by grouping the 46 larger and the 46 smaller cities on the basis of the 1950 census, and by grouping the 46 cities with higher and the 46 cities with lower rates of change in the 1940–50 intercensal period. Table 11 shows the average percentage deviation from 1950 counts of results from these methods and according to these groupings.[23] Of the methods tested, the migration and natural increase method employing Census Method II for estimating the net migration (the one in common use by the Bureau of the Census) showed the lowest percentage deviation from actual counts, with the two averaged results showing even lower deviations. As might be expected, the larger the city and the slower the rate of change, the more accurate the result. While these tests are revealing, unfortunately they were applied to central cities rather than to counties and Standard Metropolitan Areas that contain these cities. Since central cities are rarely inclusive of the entire built-up area, with the obvious implications of differing enrollment and vital rates in suburban areas as compared with the central city, much better results could be expected for the first three methods shown in Table 11 had estimates been made on a county or Standard Metropolitan Area basis.

From the following assessment of postcensal population estimation methods, it is evident that still more rigorous testing of all methods as applied to urban areas is needed before they can be satisfactorily grouped for levels of accuracy and typed as to preference for particular kinds of plan-

TABLE 11.   Accuracy of 1940-Based Postcensal Estimates by Various Methods Measured by Average Percentage Deviation from 1950 Population Counts[a]

| | All[b] | Average Percentage Deviation | | | |
| | 92 | Population Size | | Rate of Change | |
Postcensal Estimating Method	Cities	46 Larger Cities	46 Smaller Cities	46 H-R[c] Cities	46 L-R[c] Cities
1. Migration—natural increase (Method I)	8.34	8.05	8.63	7.94	8.74
2. Migration—natural increase (Method II)	6.53	6.32	6.73	7.44	5.61
3. Vital statistics rates (Bogue technique)	9.33	9.06	9.60	10.48	8.18
4. Arithmetic extrapolation	9.60	10.27	8.92	14.79	4.40
5. Geometric extrapolation	9.33	9.97	8.69	14.24	4.42
6. Average of methods 2 and 3	4.93	4.22	5.63	5.77	4.08
7. Average of methods 1 and 2	5.96	6.04	5.88	5.98	5.94

[a] Adapted from data summarized by Jacob S. Siegel, Henry S. Shryock, Jr., and Benjamin Greenberg, "Accuracy of Postcensal Estimates of Population for States and Cities," *American Sociological Review*, August, 1954.

[b] Cities with more than 100,000 population in 1940.

[c] H-R means "high rate," L-R means "low rate."

[23] Average percentage deviation was one of five statistical tests used. For results from other measures of accuracy, see *Ibid.*

ning analyses. In this connection much more attention needs to be directed to uses of postcensal estimates in planning studies, for within this one field that makes use of current population data there is some latitude for variation in accuracy. Where the current estimate is required as the beginning point for the population forecast, the most accurate possible estimate is needed. On the other hand, where estimates are used in broad-gauge analyses of existing community facilities such as the general adequacy of park space or playground area, approximation approaches may be warranted, particularly when it is considered that the standard of space per unit of population selected will tend to introduce more variation in results of the analyses than the population figure selected.

POPULATION FORECASTS

Perhaps the single most important population study for planning purposes is the population forecast. Certainly current population estimates and studies of the present composition and distribution of population are essential as a point of beginning in planning analyses, and in the continuing task of revising and detailing features of the resulting plans. They also serve an important function in day-to-day decisions relating to all kinds of public works and land development activities. Yet frequently the original and initial comprehensive plan studies undertaken in an urban area and their subsequent major revisions can be scheduled around a decennial census period to take advantage of the detailed and accurate data available only at these particular times. But no amount of scheduling obviates the necessity for studying future population prospects, for no planning activity is fulfilling its proper function unless plans are developed within a context of a continuum of needs extending from the present into the foreseeable future.

What is foreseeable and what period into the future should be selected for population forecasts depends a great deal upon the past growth characteristics of the urban study area, how large it is, and the specific uses to be made of the forecast. Obviously the conditions that are likely to prevail within the next ten years can be estimated with greater assurance than those that develop over a longer-range period. Too, the period that is foreseeable in one community may be quite different than what would be reasonable in another. As suggested earlier, areas in the throes of a spectacular and particularly a sudden growth cycle present more difficult problems than those experiencing growth at a slower pace. At the same time this very rapidity of change makes the necessity of a population forecast more pressing. It was also noted that population estimates for small urban areas were more subject to error than estimates for metropolitan areas. The same difficulties hold for forecasting procedures, but the hazards are more accentuated.

In the face of these problems, the forecaster is confronted with differing needs as to a forecast date. Different urban land uses have different life spans for amortization, and depending upon their space-using characteristics and the relative urgency there is to reserve land for each particular use, planning analyses often require varying forecast periods. Thus the difference in the magnitude of investment between a water supply system and a park system and the difference in the gross space needs, involve differing demands in the length of the period into the future that must be taken into account. In providing for water requirements, an urban center must make a heavy initial investment in large property acquisitions, reservoir area preparations, impounding dams, and so on, and this entails looking farther into the future than is necessary in acquiring and preparing land for recreation needs. One kind of decision involves eventualities 50 to 60, perhaps even 100 years into the future, and another may involve considerations only five or ten years ahead at a time. Yet estimates suited to each decision are essential to the process of planning, and each with its varying assumptions and limitations as to accuracy must be taken into account and accorded its place in population studies.

While there is no reason why the land use plan, or for that matter the comprehensive plan, cannot be developed with variable ultimate terminal dates for varying land use categories, it is customary to present these plans in terms of a 20- or 25-year period, representing a middle course between the extremes of most estimation dates. Probably the chief reasons for affixing one common date to such plans are found in the ease it permits in setting a timetable to the plan, in measuring progress against a single target date, and in its greater clarity to the people of the community. However, detailed planning studies which stem from the plan and follow naturally from the overview that the land use plan supplies must consider the forecast periods appropriate to each facility.

Though estimates of future population are thus a requisite and vital part of planning analyses, it is noteworthy that many demographers will not involve themselves in forecasts for small areas. Traditionally they have worked with large areas—the nation, regions, and states—but they have been reluctant to engage in work on small areas because of the problem of forecast inaccuracies. They acknowledge the needs of city planners and recognize the dilemma, holding out hope that "in time, demographic research will develop more specific guides for forecasting the population of small areas than now exist."[24]

It is understandable that the population specialist leans toward this position, yet there are moderating circumstances in planning applications of forecasts that demographers are not always aware of which tend to offset the hazards of inaccuracy. In the first place, some applications are less demanding of the high levels of accuracy that demographers strive for in their own uses of population data. As Schmitt has pointed out, planning standards are sometimes variable in actual practice, and often the final decisions made will depend less on the population forecast than on the selection of the standard.[25] But more directly related to the mechanics of the land use planning process, the use of safety factors in translating forecast data into land requirements permits greater tolerance limits for error than might be required in other applications. As pointed out in the discussion of employment forecasts, this is as much of a standard practice in planning as it is in civil engineering where, for example, safety factors are introduced to make the designed capacity of a bridge much greater than the estimated maximum load that it will bear. But more fundamental than those considerations, the very nature of the planning process itself calls for a continuing activity of review and restudy, thus affording the opportunity to adjust continually for error. Moreover, as Schmitt has suggested, through plan-implementing measures such as zoning, public works programming, and so on, there is an element of control over the accuracy of forecasts.

These considerations, of course, offer no solution to the problem of improving on techniques, but rather serve only to explain some of the mitigating circumstances in the use of small area forecasts in city planning analyses. Certainly they represent no justification for overlooking the hazards involved, the fundamental limitations of small area forecasts, and the need for caution in statements concerning the results. Too, many of the limitations are of a more fundamental order than those of technique and procedure. As Harold F. Dorn implies in painting the broad picture in this respect, there are pitfalls in population estimation of a broad nature that apply to all forecasting work, for the nation as well as regions and on down to small-area forecasting.[26] The influence of economic conditions

[24] Jacob S. Siegel, "Forecasting the Population of Small Areas," *Land Economics*, February, 1953.

[25] Robert C. Schmitt, "Demography and City Planning," *Social Forces*, Vol. 30, No. 3, 1952.

[26] Harold F. Dorn, "Pitfalls in Population Forecasts and Projections," *Journal of the American Statistical Association*, September, 1950.

on the rate at which families are formed and on the voluntary control of fertility; the impact of technology and scientific developments on family life; the effect of advances in medicine on birth and death rates; and so on—these are fundamental considerations that profoundly affect the accuracy of any population forecast regardless of the size of the area being studied.

General Considerations

Before taking up the various methods of forecasting population, it would be well to sketch in some of the factors which affect results. If the effect of annexation, consolidation, and other forms of change in the territorial limits of the urban study area are disregarded, population change occurs by deaths, births, and migration. Any forecast, whether or not the method actually makes direct analysis of these three variables, either explicitly or implicitly involves assumptions with respect to each. Deaths have been traditionally the most stable of the three variables and therefore the least troublesome to forecast. Birth rates involve more complex antecedent factors, and the effect, for example, of peace or war, prosperity or depression on marriage rates and the rate at which families are formed are more difficult to assess. These factors, of course, are related to the values and attitudes held, the elusive nature of which were brought out in an earlier chapter. In this connection, it has even been intimated that the power of suggestion from advertisements of automobile manufacturers and the housing and appliance industries in "fortuitously" dropping their old two-child stereotype of the American family in favor of families with three and sometimes four and five children, may have an influence on attitudes toward family size.[27] These factors obviously make the task of forecasting births difficult.

Migration is also difficult to estimate with any degree of certainty. In his valuable bulletin on forecasting techniques, Van Beuren Stanbery succinctly summarizes the principal causes of migration as:

1. The desire for better economic opportunities. Interstate migration is largely a movement from areas with relatively low planes of living to areas with higher income levels.
2. The attraction of milder or more suitable climates in other areas.

[27] From commentary on "Baby Boom" appearing in "The Reporter's Notes," *The Reporter*, August 11, 1955.

3. Desire for better living or housing conditions. This applies particularly to short distance migration within the same general locality.
4. Movement for reasons of health, education, or retirement.[28]

Of these causes, the first is the most important, and in the average community generally is responsible for the major percentage of migration. As pointed out in the previous chapter, one major reason for undertaking employment studies is to determine the probable extent that in- or out-migration in response to economic opportunity may affect the future population prospects of the urban study area. Here again, such basic considerations as prosperity or depression, peace or war, and so on, can have a very marked influence on the volume of net migration.

This brings us to a consideration of the desirability of developing the forecast in terms of high and low estimates and the importance of identifying the assumptions coupled with these estimates. It is customary to express a forecast in terms of a range of possibilities bracketing what appears to represent the most probable range of conditions prevailing during the forecast period. This does not necessarily mean that the range is developed to cover all eventualities, i.e., from total peace to all-out war, but rather to represent the likely direction of things at the time of the forecast, with a full realization that periodically review studies must be made to reëxamine these assumptions in the light of more recent developments.

Stanbery identifies the following as *basic assumptions*, either explicitly stated or implied in most forecasts:

> The form of government and the political, economic, and social organization and institutions of the United States will remain substantially unchanged.
>
> No all-out war, internal revolution, nation-wide devastation, epidemic, or other disaster will occur.
>
> No large-scale epidemic, destruction by military action, fire, earthquake, or other disaster will occur in the area or within the geographical or economic region to which the area is closely related.[29]

In making these the characteristic basic assumptions, he implies that economic conditions are the basis for supplemental or *special assumptions*. Such conditions as "no major recession and continued full employment" might thus be identified as a "high" assumption, and "a downswing in the business cycle, with unemployment leveling off at x percent of the civilian labor force," as a "low" assumption. To such a general range of conditions assumed by the forecaster are added various others which may pertain

---

[28] U.S. Department of Commerce, *Better Population Forecasting for Areas and Communities*, by Van Beuren Stanbery, U.S. Government Printing Office, September, 1952, p. 5.
[29] *Ibid.*, p. 3.

to purely local circumstances. Thus if there is a military base in the locale, certain supplemental assumptions are introduced concerning international conditions and the general size of the armed forces. In an area
dependent on extractive resources, the conditions selected will pertain to
the degree of exploitation and the extent to which conservation measures
such as sustained-yield timber farming and selective logging are prac-
ticed, and so on. In the more common situations, assumptions may relate
to the structure and vitality of the economy, with "high" and "low" conditions, for example, being attached to "improvement" and "no change" alternatives.

As in the case of employment forecasting, the development of high and
low projections bracketing the most probable size of the future population
does not preclude the selection of a "single best estimate" for planning
analyses. This estimate may vary according to the use that is to be made
of it. Thus, "in planning the future water supply for a community, the
high population projection would probably be used to assure an adequate
supply for the largest expected population. But for estimating probable
minimum revenues from the project, the low projection might be used in
order to be on the safe side."[30]

The foregoing comments relate to the selection of a "single best estimate" from a forecast by one method with high and low alternatives. There
is also the problem of selecting the "single best estimate" from forecasts
using several methods. This involves the matter of accuracy of the various
methods, particularly as they apply to small-area forecasting. What experience is available in testing the accuracy of the different methods will
be taken up later. For the present, it can be observed that in the absence
of the needed systematic testing of results from the various commonly
used forecasting methods, most population analysts make their choice of
methods on the basis of *a priori* judgments from their experience in the
use of a few of these methods. The problem then becomes one of selecting
on these grounds the particular estimate that will be used for planning
purposes. As noted above, there may be two estimates instead of one, depending upon the use to be made of the forecast. For land use planning
purposes, a single estimate is generally used, with the choice being made
with a bias more to the high than the low side. This is based on the reasoning that it is better to err on the high than on the low side in the estimation
of space needs for housing, industry, and other land uses. The decision
is not so immediately crucial as it would appear, however, for as noted
above, the choice of standard and the extent of the safety factor introduced into analyses of space requirements are means for compensating

[30] *Ibid.*, p. 11.

for possible extreme errors in choice of the forecast estimate. In effect, the decision as to the bias to be used, if any, is postponed until the land use planning analyses are undertaken when, by means of these adjustment devices, *an effective best estimate is selected for each use,* the nature of the adjustment being dependent upon how crucial it is to provide a margin of safety for that particular use.

With these general observations as a background, we turn to a review of some of the most common forecast methods used in small area studies. Five methods or groups of methods will be summarized: (1) the cohort-survival method, (2) the migration and natural increase method, a variation on the first, (3) forecast methods based on estimates for larger geographical areas, (4) forecasts based on estimates of future employment, and (5) the mathematical and graphical extrapolation methods. The first two may be classed as analytical approaches in that they base future population estimates on an analysis of the major components of population change; the other methods are sometimes considered short-cut approaches in that they deal only with the combined effects of these components. The only one of the five approaches which yields data on age composition and sex composition directly is the cohort-survival method, although, as noted later in the chapter, crude ratio procedures are sometimes used with other methods in approximating age-sex breakdowns of the estimated future population.

Cohort-Survival Method

This method is modeled generally after the analytical approach used in developing estimates for the nation as a whole. It is the most complex of the methods taken up here, and because of the special and often very technical problems encountered in the course of the estimation procedure, it requires an experienced population analyst to execute the forecast. Briefly, it is a method that adjusts figures from the last census forward by age groups and sex groups year by year to the date of the forecast, with separate adjustments made for each of the three major components of population change: deaths, births, and net migration. A variation on this approach records the change in population by 5-year intervals, using a fertility ratio to fill in data for new persons appearing in each new 0–4 year age group. (The fertility ratio is the number of children aged 0–4, inclusive, per 1000 females of child-bearing age at the end of this 5-year time span.)

Each variable is estimated separately and adjustments are made to establish what the next year's population (or that of the next 5-year interval) is expected to be. Separate tables are developed for males and females, and additional separate tables can be developed for whites and nonwhites where large proportions of nonwhite population make it advisable to make these breakdowns. Also, a separate series of these tables is developed for low and for high estimates. Death rates (age-specific or by 5-year intervals) are determined from standard life tables. Age-specific birth rates or, alternatively, fertility ratios for 5-year intervals are estimated by reference to special studies of long-range trends in local birth rates. Net migration rates (age-specific or by 5-year intervals) are estimated by reference to studies of past trends in migration and future employment prospects. Unless wartime conditions are anticipated as one contingency of the forecast, death rates would be the same for both low and high estimates. Birth rates or fertility ratios and net migration rates would vary according to low and high assumptions that are established for the locality. As noted above, they are the most difficult to estimate. In some locales there will be available for reference use previously prepared state tables on one or more of these last variables, some possibly with an urban classification for the state as a whole. If there are such materials available, they can rarely be used without adaptation to a particular locale and a particular set of local assumptions.

Table 12 illustrates in generalized form the mechanics of the procedure for carrying estimates forward to the date of the forecast. It illustrates the variation on this method that makes the analysis by 5-year intervals and employs fertility ratios. The arrows indicate how each cohort is carried forward from the base date (in this instance the 1950 census) to the forecast date, with illustrative detail shown for tracing changes in the 1950 age group, 0–4 years. The first succession of steps derives from abridged life tables for the appropriate age groups, death rates which are used in computing the number of survivors from each age group to be carried forward to the next age bracket at the beginning of the next 5-year period.[31] In the next succession of steps, the net in- or out-migration is estimated by age groups for the same intervals of time and entered as the second adjustment shown in Table 12.[32] The sum of the survivors and

[31] For references on life tables, methods of developing abridged life tables and methods for computing survival rates from these tables, see A. J. Jaffe's Bureau of the Census publication, *Handbook of Statistical Methods for Demographers,* preliminary edition, second printing, U.S. Government Printing Office, 1951, Chapter 2.

[32] Values for net migration are developed in special studies of past trends of net migration rates for various age groups and the way in which future rates will reflect low and high assumptions of the forecasts as determined from studies of the urban economy. Past net migration rates for each 10-year age group can be established by surviving the population of one age

TABLE 12.   Sample Work Table Illustrating Forecast Procedure by Cohort-Survival Method Using 5-Year Interval —Female Table (1 of 2 Tables for "Low" Estimate)

Year	Age Groups (Females)															Total Females
	0–4	5–9	10–14	15–19	20–24	25–29	30–34	35–39	40–44	45–49	50–54	55–59	60–64	65–69	etc.	
1950	256	231	283	315	395	373	287	275	228	183	144	133	100	66		3340
1955	XXX	XXX														
1960		XXX														
1965		XXX														
1970		XXX														

XXX Survivors
±XX Net migrants

XXX Survivors
±XX Net migrants

XXX Survivors
±XX Net migrants

XXX Survivors
±XX Net migrants

the in- or out-migrants from the original age group furnish the estimate for the next higher age group at the beginning of the next 5-year period. The circled figure, the new 0–4 age group, is obtained by applying the appropriate fertility ratio to the number of females of childbearing age (usually 15–44) at the beginning of the last period.[33] Although these steps illustrate the procedure in a general way, obviously there are certain special adjustments required along the way to account for underenumeration in particular age groups, underregistration of births and deaths, and the deaths and births of migrants. Warren S. Thompson's study of metropolitan Cincinnati provides an illustration of the use of the cohort-survival method in estimating future population levels.[34]

group to the next higher age group from one census to the next census, using actual birth and death data (corrected for underregistration), with the difference at the terminal census date between the expected and the actual population in each age bracket being used to compute the net migration rate for each age group in the particular intercensal period. Five-year age-group rates are developed from the 10-year age-group rates by customary demographic procedures. See Jaffe, *Ibid.*

[33] Fertility ratio values are obtained from special studies that must be made of local trends in the past and how these trends may be expected to function in the future under low and high assumptions. In turn, these assumptions must be based on alternate estimates of the marriage rate and the number of children per marriage, or in other words, on trends in the size of completed families.

[34] Cincinnati City Planning Commission, *The Population of Cincinnati Metropolitan Area,* City of Cincinnati, December, 1945.

Migration and Natural Increase Method

This method is a simpler form of the analytical approach and is similar in many respects to the migration and natural increase method used in estimating current population. Forecasts derived from this method involve separate analyses of two components in place of three as in the cohort-survival method, and provide estimates only for the total population, without breaking out age-sex components. It starts with a current estimate of the population, and by introducing adjustments first for migration and then for natural increase on a year-by-year basis, it develops annual estimates into the future until the forecast date is reached.

Table 13 is a sample work table used in the method, illustrating the accrual aspects of the procedure. Taking up first the migration component, low and high net migration rates may be estimated by reference to past trends and assumptions as to future economic conditions (determined from study of urban economy) and other relevant factors (e.g., enrollment prospects in areas where there are educational centers). The past net migration rates may be computed by procedures similar to those cited under the cohort-survival method, except that the population is "survived" from each past census period to the next as a total rather than by age-sex groups. Using mathematical or graphical procedures, a general future trend line is first established from a graphic plot of both past net migration rates.

TABLE 13. Sample Work Table Illustrating Forecast Procedure by Migration and Natural Increase Method—"Low" Estimate Table

Year	Population (1)	Net Migration Rate (±) (2)	Net Migration Amount (±) (3)	Pop. After Adjustment for Net Migration (±) (4)	Natural Increase Rate[a] (5)	Natural Increase Amount (6)	Pop. After Adjustment for Natural Increase —Next Year's Pop. (7)
1955							
1956							
1957							
1958							
1959							
1960							
.							
.							
.							
1975							

Some forecasters introduce a crude correction step here to recognize that part of the natural increase among migrating families during year shown in the stub of the table is already accounted for before they arrive or after they leave the community. Accordingly, they apply natural increase rate to the full amount in Column 1 and to half the amount in Column 3 on the assumption that half of the births and ths in migrating families occur after in- or out-migration.

Then adjustments from this trend line in the form of supplemental curves are subjectively developed based on the low and high assumptions as to economic conditions and other factors. Among his suggestions for supplemental investigations, Stanbery lists the following considerations as aids in making these subjective determinations:[35]

1. Past relationships between the direction and volume of net migration in the area and the levels of national economic activity and rise, or decline, in per capita real incomes.
2. The relative rates of increase of employment and population nationally and in the area during decades of rapid national economic expansion (1920–30 and 1940–50), and during periods of slower expansion (1930–40).
3. Outlook for economic development and expansion of employment in the area during the period of the forecast.

On the basis of these considerations, Stanbery suggests that the forecaster then proceed to decide whether minimum and maximum net migration during the forecast period appears likely to vary upward or downward from the smallest and largest volumes of net migration observed during past decades, finally establishing low and high levels to be introduced into the analysis.

As an alternative to estimating net migration by these procedures, an approach based more directly on results of employment forecasts may be used. Local net migration as derived above for past decades is expressed as a percentage of employment in past periods of time, with the trend extended by mathematical or graphical extrapolation procedures to the forecast date. The resulting ratio is then applied to low and high estimates from the employment forecast to provide estimates of future net migration. Since this approach is based on the assumption that migration is a function of employment opportunity, obviously it is not fully applicable to such urban areas as retirement, educational, or health centers.

Estimates of future natural increase rates may be made on the basis of subjective extensions of past minimum and maximum rates somewhat parallel to the first approach above to estimating net migration, or they may be developed by reference to previously prepared vital statistics projections for larger geographical areas. Local natural increase rates for past years in time are computed from recorded resident birth and death data (corrected for underregistration). Intercensal estimates of population for rate computations (here and for net migration rates) are usually based on a linear interpolation of the population for the census figures at the beginning and ending of the decade. Under the first approach, these past rates are ex-

[35] U.S. Department of Commerce, *op. cit.*, p. 68.

amined for minima and maxima and for trend indications, and after deciding on likely low and high assumptions for the future, alternative curves of the future trend in the natural increase rate are developed. It should be noted that because of the relatively short period for which the local vital statistics contained in national summaries are available by place of residence (since 1936), and in view of the extreme depression and wartime fluctuations in births experienced in most communities for which these data are available, conventional extrapolation procedures are likely to be difficult if not unfeasible. Thus these curves will usually be based largely on a subjectively reasoned approach rather than on the extrapolation of past trends. The alternative approach uses as a guide estimated future crude birth and death rate trends previously prepared for a larger area, and by observing relationships between rates of the local and larger area in the past, develops trends for future local rates under low and high assumptions.[36]

With separate analyses of net migration and natural increase rates completed, data are transcribed to Columns 2 and 5 of the appropriate "low" and "high" tables as illustrated in the sample work table (Table 13). Using the current population estimate as the point of beginning (figure at the head of Column 1), it then becomes a simple matter of arithmetic to develop the entries in Columns 4 and 7 and arrive at a population estimate for the forecast date. Forecasts for Broome County and Monroe County in New York provide illustrations of the use of the migration and natural increase method of estimating future population.[37]

Estimates Based on Forecasts for Larger Areas

This method employs a previously prepared forecast for some larger geographical area—usually the nation, the region, or the state—and by ratio procedures establishes how the local area may be expected to share in the forecasted population of the larger area. Population ratios may be established direct between the larger area and the urban study area, or they may be developed as several interlocking series of ratios, steppingdown estimates for the larger area to the urban study area through a system of intermediate areas. The latter approach has two variations. One

[36] For use of this approach in a short-cut version of the migration and natural increase method, see U.S. Department of Commerce, *op. cit.*, pp. 71–73.

[37] Broome County Planning Board *Population Predictions for Broome County,* Broome County, New York, April, 1950; Rochester City Planning Commission, *A Study of Population Growth of Rochester and Monroe County,* City of Rochester, December, 1947.

employs *apportionment procedures in a multiphased analysis* of all parts of each parent area (the nation, the region, or the state), balancing estimates for all subareas with the parent area total before proceeding to the next step-down. The other makes *direct step-downs in a single-phased analysis,* without reference to the way other subareas of the system may be sharing in the parent area total. The procedural principles of both were discussed in some detail in the last chapter.

As brought out in the use of these techniques for employment forecasts, the population of the smaller area is expressed as a percentage of that of the larger area for past decades. These ratio values are plotted in a time series, and a curve is fitted to the data and projected to the forecast date. The projected ratio is then applied to the given future population estimate of the larger area to obtain the absolute population figures for the smaller area. Such a procedure is followed for both low and high estimates selected from the given series of estimates for the larger area (e.g., low and high estimates of the future population of the nation or the state of interest as released periodically in the Bureau of the Census, *Current Population Reports,* Series P-25). If a system of intermediate areas is used, the above-described procedure is repeated until an estimate for the urban study area is finally derived. If the apportionment technique is employed, estimates for all subareas in the selected system of geographical areas are balanced with the larger area estimate before this procedure is carried to the next smaller system of study areas.

Table 14 is a sample work table illustrating the sequence to the step-down procedure in a single-phased analysis, using the census division, the

TABLE 14. Sample Work Table Illustrating Forecast Procedure Using Previously Prepared Estimates of Large Geographic Areas—"Low" Estimate Table

Year	U.S. Population	Census Division Population	C.D./U.S.	State Population	S./C.D.	State Economic Area Population	S.E.A./S.	County Population	C./S.E.A
Census									
1900									
1910									
1920									
1930									
1940									
1950									
Estimates									
1960									
1970									
1980									

state and the state economic area as the intermediate types of areas between the nation and a county of interest. If the local study area is a city, the step-down procedure usually employs *urban* population ratios in place of ratios based on *total* population figures (giving due consideration to changes in the census definition of "urban"). The Philadelphia City Planning Commission study of its eight-county metropolitan area furnishes an illustration of this method, using a direct step-down of national urban population estimates to the local area.[38] The work of Hagood and Siegel in developing 1975 estimates of population for the census divisions of the nation presents useful methodological information on the application of the apportionment technique.[39]

A special application of this approach is usually used in areas with large military installations. Because of extreme fluctuations in troop strength that frequently occur even at the more permanent bases and in view of the semitransient character of this segment of the local population, the analysis of the separate effects of migration, births, and deaths involved in the first two methods above becomes extremely complex—so complex and with such a variety of qualifications that population analysts generally consider the use of ratio techniques better suited to these situations.

For small urban centers where the military installation tends to maintain a dominant position in the local economy, generally the most satisfactory procedure to follow is to break down the forecast analysis into three parts —one concerned with the military personnel and their dependents present in the area, one dealing with military base-related civilian population, and the other treating the nonbase-related civilian population. Separate low and high estimates are developed for each component and results are summed up for the forecast date to obtain the total population or the civilian and military population as may be desired. Analysis of the military component first deals with military strength, employing ratio techniques to establish the share that local installations may be expected to have in state or national military strength under alternative assumptions as to the future size of the armed forces, and then, by reference to past minimum and maximum levels of dependent population present, establishes assumed low and high estimates for the full component of military personnel and dependents. Next, the military-related civilian component is estimated, either by reference to previously prepared employment forecasts and the expansion of these estimates to full population equivalents (using tech-

[38] Philadelphia City Planning Commission, *Population Estimates, Philadelphia-Camden Area, 1950–2000,* City of Philadelphia, April, 1948.

[39] Margaret J. Hagood and Jacob S. Siegel, "Projections of the Regional Distribution of the Population of the United States to 1975," *Agricultural Economics Research,* U.S. Bureau of Agricultural Economics, April, 1951.

niques discussed in the next section below), or, on the basis of analyses of the past relationship between military-related civilian population and the military strength of local installations, by development of assumed future ratios to be applied to the low and high estimates of future military strength. Finally, the nonmilitary-related civilian component is estimated for the forecast date using conventional ratio procedures described above.

In larger metropolitan areas where military-related civilian employment needs are reasonably well contained by the local labor market, the foregoing approach can be simplified, using only military strength and civilian population as the components of the ratio analyses. Stanbery's population forecast for the county and city of San Diego is a well-documented illustration of this last approach.[40]

Estimates Based on Employment Forecasts

Where employment forecasts have been previously prepared for the urban study area, this method is often used as a basis for making population projections. Using the same basic ratio principle involved in the last-described method, the method expands future employment figures to labor force estimates which in turn are expanded to population equivalents. The method thus assumes fairly stable relationships between these series. Obviously the method is not suited to the study of retirement centers, university communities, resort cities, and in areas with similar kinds of special circumstances affecting these relationships.

The employment forecast, the point of beginning for analyses by this method, has been discussed at some length in Chapter 6. Two sets of ratios are computed for past periods of time—one expressing employment as a percentage of total labor force, and the other expressing labor force as a percentage of population. Each set of ratios is ordered in a time series, and curves are fitted to the data and projected. Future values of these ratios are then successively applied to expand employment estimates to population estimates. The process is repeated for low and high estimates of future employment. In this connection, Stanbery points out that forecasts by these procedures currently assume that there will be unemployment no greater than 10 percent of the labor force in the area.[41] Future

---

[40] V. B. Stanbery, *Population Analysis and Projections to 1960 and 1970, County and City of San Diego, California,* a special study for Industrial Survey Associates, San Francisco, May, 1953.

[41] U.S. Department of Commerce, *op. cit.,* p. 33.

population estimates prepared by this method are illustrated in the Detroit Metropolitan Area Regional Planning Commission's forecast.[42]

Mathematical and Graphical Methods

Of the great variety of methods falling within this category and from time to time propounded for local population analyses, those encountered most frequently include arithmetic and geometric projections, the method of least squares, and estimates based on the logistic curve. The previously described forecasting methods employing ratio techniques commonly make use of the first three of these projection methods as a means for extrapolating ratio curves forward in time. However, when applied directly to population data, especially in long-range forecasts, these methods have limited utility, it being generally conceded that no mathematical law yet discovered can wholly or consistently contain the forces governing population growth.

The arithmetic and geometric projections assume that the same forces affecting population change in the past will continue to apply in the future. Applied to data plotted on plain coördinate graph paper, the arithmetic approach results in a straight-line projection and assumes the same *numerical change* for similar periods of time. The geometric projection is represented by a straight line on semilogarithmic graph paper, signifying similar *rates of change* for similar periods of time. Under the method of least squares, an exponential equation is developed to fit a time series plot on semilogarithmic paper, and the mathematical extension of this curve provides estimates of population at selected dates in the future. The logistic curve is an S-shaped curve developed by Raymond Pearl and Lowell J. Reed based on their work with the growth phenomena of fruit flies. Their Logistic I and their subsequent modification of it in Logistic II are mathematical representations of an S-shaped curve developed from studies of the growth of national population, and the use of the curve in a local situation assumes that the population growth pattern is behaving similar to national growth phenomena. To apply this curve, the slope of the population growth curve in the local area must have passed through a decceleration period from an initially rising rate of increase. Under these circumstances a logistic curve fitted to the data is then used to establish future population estimates.

[42] Detroit Metropolitan Area Regional Planning Commission, *Population Prospectus for the Detroit Region, 1960 and 1970*, October, 1950.

Earlier it was noted that there was a need for more rigorous tests of the accuracy of postcensal methods of estimation. The need for similar, more systematic tests of forecast methods is even greater. On the basis of what tests have been made, there appears to be some agreement that the longer the forecast period, the smaller the area for which projections are made, and the more rapid the growth that occurs during the forecast period, the less accurate the results tend to be.[43] But reports on these tests have been quite inconclusive on the relative accuracy of the commonly used forecasting methods, and very little attention seems to have been given to what methods appear to be best suited for varying forecast periods, growth characteristics, and size ranges of urban areas.

Schmitt and Crosetti present some valuable information on two of the five groups of methods reviewed above.[44] In *ex post facto* analyses of 20 cities in which they "forecast" population for 1940 and/or 1950 and compared results with actual census counts, they tested the short and long forms of the ratio technique (identified above as forecasts based on previously prepared estimates of larger areas, using direct and intermediate-area step-downs), three mathematical methods (arithmetic, geometric, and logistic curve projections), and the analogy method (not included in the series of methods reviewed).[45] The five most populous urban areas in the four census regions were selected, with tests being made for both the central cities and their Standard Metropolitan Areas, and for 10- and 20-year periods. On the basis of their tests they conclude that:

1. The logistic curve, arithmetic projection, and two forms of the ratio method produced almost equally accurate results, on the average, in population forecasts for cities and metropolitan areas. These four methods were much more accurate than either the geometric projection or the analogy methods.

2. Twenty-year forecasts were less accurate—but not excessively so—than projections covering only a 10-year period.

3. Metropolitan forecasts differed little from forecasts for central cities in degree of accuracy.[46]

[43] For a comprehensive review of available tests, see Siegel, *loc. cit.*

[44] For report of tests on ratio techniques, see Robert C. Schmitt and Albert H. Crosetti, "Accuracy of the Ratio Method for Forecasting City Population," *Land Economics*, November, 1951; for report on extension of tests to other methods, see Schmitt and Crosetti, "Short-Cut Methods of Forecasting City Population," *The Journal of Marketing*, April, 1953.

[45] Considered one of the less reliable methods, this approach matches up the recent growth characteristics of the given city with those experienced by one or more other cities in the past, and then, using as a guide the recent growth trends of the prototype cities, projects the population growth of the city of interest forward in time.

[46] Schmitt and Crosetti, *The Journal of Marketing*, April, 1953, p. 424.

In generalizing on these results, they state that "the high degree of forecasting error characteristic of the ratio method indicates it to be of limited value to city planners," concluding after their later more extended series of tests that there is no foolproof short-cut approach to small-area forecasting.

Although tests of these methods used in large area forecasts do not necessarily indicate what would be best in small area work, it may be noted that studies by the Bureau of the Census of a broader range of forecasting methods as applied to states did not produce conclusive evidence of the superiority of any one method over all others tested.[47] These tests included the cohort-survival method, ratio and apportionment approaches, and arithmetic and geometric projections. While it was concluded that no method was clearly superior to the others, the cohort-survival method, the apportionment approach, and one form of the ratio technique were found to produce consistently the best showings.

Siegel's comparison of results from some 99 forecasts for small areas with 1940 and 1950 census returns brings out some interesting tendencies in the direction that errors appear to take. In these forecasts, involving all groups of methods reviewed above, he found that nearly two-thirds underestimated the population. "This type of bias appears to be characteristic of work done in the thirties and forties in the measurement of population growth to 1950. The opposite type of bias, however, may be characteristic of these same forecasts so far as population changes during future decades are concerned. . . ."[48]

POPULATION CHARACTERISTICS AND DISTRIBUTION

To round out the population series of tooling-up studies, it is important to include some brief consideration of the types of analyses of population characteristics and distribution that are useful to land use planning. While most investigations of this kind are best carried out as part of the specific land use planning analyses in which they are to be used, sometimes they may be scheduled in advance in conjunction with general demographic studies. Certainly they should be outlined at the time the above discussed studies of current and future population are planned so that the original

[47] Helen R. White, "Empirical Study of the Accuracy of Selected Methods of Projecting State Populations," *Population Index*, July, 1952.
[48] Siegel, *loc. cit.*, p. 80.

basic studies are conducted with these needs in view. Then, as and when population composition and distribution data are needed, it becomes a simple procedure of extending the original basic population studies to obtain the breakdowns in the form desired.

Population Characteristics

Of the variety of ways of breaking down the total population, urban-wide land use planning analyses generally utilize breakdowns of three kinds: age, income, and household size. Other ways of breaking down the total population—by sex, by race, by nationality, by educational background, or by other categories—may provide useful background insights into the general make-up of a city's population, but with the possible exception of racial composition, these have more limited utility in land use planning studies. While the U.S. Supreme Court has removed any vestigial legal reasons for separate attention to different racial elements of the population, city planning will continue to find special studies of racial composition of importance. But these will now be more useful in the interpretation of public response to land use planning proposals than in the actual technical analyses undertaken, and even these can be expected to become less important as racial integration problems pass into history.

Age composition data are important primarily for school and recreation planning analyses, with forecasts of age composition being of special concern in determining long-range facility needs and land requirements for school and recreation sites. As noted previously, the only type of population forecast in which age data are developed as an integral part of the projection procedure is the cohort-survival method. Where this method is not employed, a ratio technique is often used to approximate how the estimated total future population will be distributed among the various age categories. This application of the ratio technique involves the same elemental procedures followed in other applications of the technique described in this and the preceding chapter. For past census periods each selected age group is expressed as a percent of total population, and resulting ratio values for each age group are then plotted in a time series. Curves are fitted to the data for each age group, and the projected ratios for each such age group are read off these curves for the forecast year and are applied to the total population estimate for that year to obtain an approximation of the number in each age group in absolute figures. Although curves can be subjectively adjusted to reflect known trends affecting age composition (e.g., in retirement centers, an anticipated increase in inmigrant elderly couples, or changes in the rate that families are being formed, changes in the number of children per family, etc.), this technique must be regarded as a crude substitute for the cohort-survival technique which gives these factors more systematic consideration.

Another and a more refined ratio approach is illustrated in the Hagood and Siegel forecast of the 1975 regional distribution of the population in the United States.[49] This approach examines trends in each age group in relation to trends in a larger geographical area for which age composition estimates have previously been prepared for the desired forecast date. On the assumption that over a period of years the percentage distribution of the total future population among selected age groups in the smaller area will be approaching that in the parent area, the amount of the deviation in each age group of the smaller from the larger area is systematically reduced during the period it is assumed that a deviation will continue to exist. This system of adjusting ratios between the smaller and larger area according to an assumed rate at which the differentials will be wiped out might conceivably be applied in other ways, for example, by assuming a widening gap between several or all age groups of the two areas, or by assuming a widening, followed by a narrowing gap. Thus this approach adapts a ratio technique to particular reasoned sets of assumptions, with the reasoning based on comparative studies of past trends in age-group composition and trends in selected economic and social factors which appear to be affecting the two areas being compared. Hagood and Siegel used the technique to estimate the age composition of their forecast 1975 population by regions. As the technique is applied to smaller areas, the possibilities of error, of course, increase. However, balanced against these "risks" is the consideration that in the final application of the forecast data to school site and recreation area standards employed in land use planning analyses, there is tolerance for some error in either direction without materially affecting the accuracy in the calculation of land requirements.

Family income characteristics for small areas became available for the first time in the 1950 census, the data being obtained on a sampling basis from every fifth family covered in the population enumeration. While it will take another two or three decades before this information can begin to be used satisfactorily in trend analyses (assuming valid adjustment factors for the changing value of the dollar), it has considerable immediate value in housing market analyses, particularly when such studies are scheduled and executed at the time of the decennial census. For example, with

[49] For details of computations by this approach, see Hagood and Siegel, *loc. cit.*

respect to the rental market alone, in establishing how the supply of housing at various rental levels actually matches up with the number of renting families at the income levels that correspond to these rental levels, it is possible to obtain a crude picture of the under- or oversupply of rental housing which may exist for renting families of different income brackets. As will be seen in a later chapter, this kind of information has application in land use planning analyses in providing a guide for establishing the proportion of undeveloped and redeveloped land to be allocated to different residential density classes. In the future, as trend information on income characteristics can be established and applied in forecasts of the housing market, we can expect improvements in this land allocation procedure.

Household size information also has application in residential land use planning studies. Households are defined by the Bureau of the Census as being made up of all persons occupying a dwelling unit, including the related family members and also the unrelated persons who may be residing in the dwelling unit, such as roomers, foster children, wards, or employees. A household may consist of one person living alone in the dwelling unit or a group of unrelated individuals sharing the dwelling unit.[50] To be distinguished from family size data used in the 1930 census, household size characteristics became a standard item of information beginning with the 1940 census. Household size data have important applications in housing market analyses, with the percentage distribution of households by size providing guides in estimating overall space requirements for the various classes of residential structures applicable to the city under study. Studies of trends in the total number of households and the differential trends among the several typical size categories, along with studies of the rate of family formation, provide bases for estimating future household sizes. The same kinds of ratio procedures used in estimating future age composition can be used in estimating future household sizes, with investigations of economic trends, the rate of family formation, and birth rates providing the basis for the formulation of the high and low assumptions used in projections.

Spatial Distribution of Population

Not only do land use planning analyses require estimates of the future population composition for the urban area as a whole, but they also require

[50] See Bureau of the Census, *1950 Census of Population*, Volume II, "Characteristics of the Population, Part 1, United States Summary," U.S. Government Printing Office, 1953, p. 43.

an indication as to how the total population and how selected composition groups will be spatially distributed in the urban area. Thus estimates of the distribution of the future total population among the various neighborhoods have obvious implications for the study of residential areas and their community facilities. Moreover, while urban-wide age composition analyses are used in estimating the total land requirements for schools, estimates of the residential distribution of school-age children will provide guides as to how the estimated total land requirements should be allocated to the different parts of the city. Similarly, studies of the spatial distribution of various income groups and household size categories among the different neighborhoods provide clues for the geographic patterning of residential densities. The application of these population studies and the other considerations involved in establishing future density patterns are taken up in a later chapter.

For purposes of the present discussion, we will allude to two approaches to the study of population distribution. One relates to daytime population distribution, or more correctly, how people distribute themselves at different hours of the day or night; and the other is concerned with the residential distribution of population, or the place of residence where people are enumerated by the U.S. Census. The so-called daytime population kind of study has received attention in demography only recently, and this is largely because data are not generally available in the form necessary for detailed studies of this kind. What work that has been done in daytime population analysis has been concerned with current population rather than future estimates. Besides the uses that daytime population data have in civil defense studies, they have important applications in transportation and parking studies, and as noted in Chapter 3, have potential utility in studies concerned with the establishment of "density ceilings" in the central business district and industrial areas.

Developed around sources of information presently available, two techniques have been employed in estimating the accumulation of population in various functional use areas for different hours of the day or night. At the University of North Carolina, a technique was devised to order data for this purpose from origin and destination surveys used in the series of metropolitan area traffic studies undertaken coöperatively in the postwar period by state highway commissions and the U.S. Bureau of Public Roads.[51] The data available from these studies were obtained principally from home interviews on a sampling basis, supplemented by information obtained

[51] Industrial Areas Study, *Population Distribution—Spatial and Temporal*, Institute for Research in Social Science, University of North Carolina, September, 1952. This study examines daytime-nighttime population distribution patterns in Flint, Grand Rapids, Erie, Minneapolis–St. Paul, and in the Philadelphia-Camden area.

from persons traveling by car into the urban area from beyond the home interview area. Using IBM cards containing these data and beginning with the "low point" in the daily activity patterns of the normal household (usually 4 A.M.), machine tabulations of trip cards were made of the differences between the arrivals and departures of persons from each use area (composed of smaller unit zones used in the traffic surveys as reference areas for trips) for each hour of the day and night. The result was a tabulation of the approximate number of people present in each use area for all hours of a 24-hour period—a general picture of the ebb and flow of people in a metropolitan area during a particular span of time.[52] Figure 6 summarizes data obtained in one of the five urban areas covered in this study, and Figure 5 shows how results may be summarized for a city in terms of density patterns for selected hours of the day.

The second technique is one devised by the Bureau of the Census for use by civil defense agencies in studying potential disaster areas resulting from air attack.[53] It provides a rough estimate of the total daytime population during the normal working and school hours of the day, broken down by census tracts or enumeration districts. The technique begins with the residential distribution of population recorded in the last census, and then adjusts these data, first, by subtracting out, tract by tract, workers, school population, and others assumed to be away from home during the major portion of the day. It then calls for the addition of the labor force (adjusted to include commuting workers from outside the urban study area), the school population, and estimates of people away from home for other reasons into those census tracts or enumeration districts where the Census of Manufactures, local school attendance summaries, and other sources of information indicate tracts or districts of concentration. Detailed notes on these procedures are furnished in *Civil Defense Urban Analysis.*

Turning now to the second approach to the study of population distribution, namely, one concerned with the residential distribution of the popu-

---

[52] Although providing perhaps the most detailed and accurate estimates that can presently be obtained (short of a census especially designed to obtain daytime population distribution data), results from this technique are nevertheless approximate. This is true for several reasons. For example, O & D traffic survey records do not yield the actual count of people present in each use area at the beginning point of the 24-hour analysis. To obtain an estimate of the 4 A.M. distribution of population requires adjustments of residential distribution figures (customarily used as the beginning point) to account for "graveyard shifts" present in work areas at 4 A.M. Other problems relate to "walking trips" and train commuter trips which are not recorded in some of these surveys. In effect, then, results obtained by this technique tend to understate the daytime population in work areas.

[53] Federal Civil Defense Administration, *Civil Defense Urban Analysis,* U.S. Government Printing Office, July, 1953, pp. 78–81. An improved and superseding procedure developed by the Bureau of the Census is to be released early in 1957 under the title, *Population Estimates for Survival Planning.*

lation, two somewhat similar techniques are taken up briefly. The first is a general-purpose form of small-area analysis, and the second is a zonal form. Both are used in estimating how the forecast total population of the urban area as a whole can be spatially distributed to small areas, and both can be used to determine how these small-area estimates of future population break down into age groups and other subtotals of population characteristics.

In general, both techniques employ apportionment procedures, and within the limits of the holding capacity of each small area derive estimates as to how neighborhoods, census tracts, or other small areas share in urban area population growth.[54] These estimates are based on trends in the way each small area in a selected system of areas has fared relative to the urban area as a whole. Under the general-purpose technique, ratios of the population of the central city and of each of the suburban areas to the urban study area population are computed for past census periods and plotted graphically. Then, considering holding capacities and residential building trends in each component small area, these curves are extrapolated into the future. This same procedure can be repeated to determine how smaller areas such as census tracts or neighborhoods share in the above derived subtotals. This general approach is illustrated in the work of the Detroit Metropolitan Area Regional Planning Commission in estimating future population levels in the 19 development areas that have been delineated in the region surrounding the City of Detroit.[55]

As developed and applied in the Seattle urban area by Schmitt, the zonal technique utilizes groupings of census tracts in the form of a series of concentric zones around the central business district as the basic system of delineations for small-area analysis.[56] The gross density and the percentage of total metropolitan area population are computed for each zone for past census periods and extrapolated. The extrapolated densities for all zones are then adjusted to take into account holding capacities and housing vacancy rates, and these results are used to adjust percentages of total metropolitan population expected to be found in each ring. The estimate of future population for the urban area as a whole is then apportioned to the various rings using the adjusted percentages as guides. Once popula-

---

[54] The holding capacity may be considered here to mean the maximum possible population the land can accommodate at residential densities permissible under the combined application of the zoning ordinance and housing code. As discussed in greater detail in a later chapter, technically the holding capacity is the saturation point in the number of dwelling units an area can absorb under assumed densities of residential development.

[55] Paul M. Reid, *Projected Population, Detroit Region Development Areas, 1960 and 1970*, Detroit Metropolitan Area Planning Commission, December, 1950.

[56] Robert C. Schmitt, "Population Analysis of Small Areas," *Business Information Service*, a bulletin of the U.S. Department of Commerce, May, 1950.

tion estimates are obtained for each concentric zone, these totals can be apportioned to smaller areas, i.e., neighborhoods or census tracts, following similar procedures.

The purpose of this chapter has been to summarize the available methods and techniques for population analyses required in land use planning studies. It is perhaps unnecessary to draw attention again to the varying degrees of accuracy that may be expected from the use of these methods and techniques in estimating the current population, the future population, and the composition and distribution of population in urban areas. Nor is it necessary to stress that as these types of studies are undertaken one after another, each successive task, built as it is upon the preceding study, becomes vulnerable to cumulative errors. Yet as hazardous as these studies appear to be, the risks involved do not obviate the necessity for these studies. They are "musts" for urban land use planning analyses. But even with the moderating circumstances involved in city planning applications of data derived in these studies cited throughout the chapter, the population analyst is obligated to seek the maximum possible accuracy consistent with the uses to be made of the data. Meanwhile, it is hoped that as demographers can be persuaded to give greater attention to small-area population analyses in their research efforts, some of the cruder techniques discussed above can be replaced with more reliable ones that can be put to use in city planning studies.

CHAPTER 8

urban land studies

The fourth series of tooling-up investigations required in land use planning seek to describe the salient features and facts about land in the urban area and its surroundings. These studies provide information on the physical setting that accommodates the economic activity and the population which are analyzed by methods and techniques taken up in the preceding three chapters. The present chapter goes into eight types of background studies which furnish information related to the use, nonuse, and misuse of urban land—information which contributes to the analyses and decisions reached in the land use planning process taken up in Part III:

1. Compilation of data on physiographic features, mapping the urban setting.
2. The land use survey.
3. The vacant land survey.
4. Structural and environmental quality survey.
5. Cost-revenue studies of land use.
6. Land value studies.
7. Studies of aesthetic features of the urban area.
8. Studies of public attitudes and preferences regarding land use.

As these types of studies are successively described in the sections below, it will become apparent that there is considerable variability in the precision and detail to which survey and analytical techniques are carried. To an important degree, this is a reflection of the unequal attention which has been accorded these various types of urban land studies in research to date in the field of urban planning and contributing disciplines.

In general, the mapping of the urban area, as discussed in the first section below, provides the medium for recording and presenting information on the natural features of the urban setting and the manner in which these

191

have been altered and put to use in streets, blocks, and lots for urban living. Not included in the discussion of mapping below are certain other obvious investigations such as the geology and climatology of the urban area and its larger region, which round out the picture of the physiographic character of the urban setting.

The land use survey, including the classification of building and outdoor uses of urban land, has traditionally been a key investigation preparatory to all comprehensive plan studies. It classifies and records the uses of developed land according to the functional activities carried on in the urban center. Thus, in an oversimplified grouping of these activities, we have work areas, living areas, leisure-time areas, and so on, each with its assemblage of specific land uses. The land use survey results in a *land use map* and a statistical summary of the uses of the developed portion of the urban area. In effect, this map, with the base map information it contains on streets, railroads, water courses, and so on, supplies an elemental description of the man-made improvements or additions to the natural setting.

The vacant land survey classifies and records the use capabilities of the lacework residual pattern of inlying vacant parcels and the open land at the periphery not yet in urban use. This survey results in what is usually referred to as a *land capabilities map* and a statistical summary of the general characteristics of vacant and open land, considering topographic and drainage factors and the kinds of public utilities and other improvements presently serving these areas. The land use and vacant land maps thus account for all land in the urban study area.

The structural and environmental quality survey classifies and records the physical condition of structures in the city, the quality of their environment, and other factors associated with urban blight and obsolescence. This survey involves investigations of social, health, and economic as well as physical indicators of blight. It results in what is usually referred to as a *blighted areas map* and supplemental statistical summaries of the incidence of physical deterioration and obsolescence. This study indicates where there may be flexibility for replanning. The blighted areas map along with the land capabilities map furnish a picture of the areas where the major growth of the future must be accommodated—one through *urban renewal* and the other through *urban extension,* the two basic processes of urban growth.

Cost-revenue studies of land use examine prevailing public policies and practices in supplying services and facilities for various classes of land use in differing areas of governmental jurisdiction, and develop cost-revenue estimates indicating the implications for municipal finance of land development at various intensities and densities under existing or assumed changes in prevailing policies and practices. These studies are concerned with the economy of land development as a public interest consideration as opposed to the economics of development arising through the operations of builders and developers functioning within the framework of the urban land market.

As indicated in Chapter 1, studies of land values, both spatial and temporal aspects, provide clues as to the way land has been priced in the urban land market and thus what the most economic use of land might be. These studies have a direct relationship to land use and vacant land analysis and provide a basis for taking into account the implications that land use proposals hold for the structure of prevailing land values.

Studies of aesthetic features of the urban area identify distinctive locations and vistas, or foci and axes, natural features with special development potentialities, special building groupings with symbolic significance, and so on. Finally, studies of public attitudes and preferences in the use of land supply important information to be taken into account in fitting the land development plan to livability concepts of the people of the urban area. All of the foregoing list of studies contribute material which is relevant to analyses and decisions faced in the land use planning process. Existing and developing techniques used in each type of study are taken up in greater detail in the following sections of this chapter.

MAPPING THE URBAN SETTING

Since maps provide the medium for recording and summarizing data descriptive of the urban setting, it would be well at the outset to review briefly mapping needs and techniques requisite to the study of land and its uses. The need for base maps will vary with every city. Cities with an established city planning activity will generally have a selection of base maps available for mapping the urban setting and for making planning studies. Depending upon the financial resources of the planning agency, and to some extent the professional pride of the city planner and thus his office policy in keeping his basic "tools" up to date, mapping offers no problem in most such cities. It is in the smaller community where resources are limited or in the community where planning is a newly established function that the following discussion is particularly applicable. It also applies in cities where planning has never been established as a permanent and continuing service of local government, where there are periodic flurries of planning activity and then lapses of time with little or no activity.

Land use planning analyses call for a variety of maps which not only provide a basic description of the physical layout of the urban area and its physiographic features but also provide a base for plotting and analyzing information assembled in surveys discussed later in the chapter. The typical types of reference maps used in developing the base maps, the kinds of base maps, and the major steps involved in preparing planning base maps are taken up briefly in the subsections that follow.

Types of Reference Maps

Depending somewhat on the resources of the city but more frequently on the interest of the city manager, the city engineer, or some other city or county official in maintaining accurate mapped information on the city and its environs, any one or more of the following types of maps may be available:

Engineering maps.
Topographic maps.
Property or tax maps.
Miscellaneous reference maps.

The original base for these maps may be drawn from a controlled aerial photographic mosaic, from engineering surveys, or from a compilation of subdivision plats, special engineering surveys, partial aerial photography, and other miscellaneous sources.

Few cities will go to the expense of mapping beyond the corporate limits, and so, for planning purposes, where studies must be made on an urban-wide basis, the maps listed above must usually be considered reference maps. However, where the corporate limits include the planning area, or where reasonably accurate maps in one or more counties inclusive of the planning area are available at uniform and satisfactory scales, such maps may be used directly as base maps for city planning.

If available, engineering maps are usually maintained in the public works or engineering department of the city. They are generally drawn in ink on tracing linen and maintained in the form of an atlas of from two or three to a large number of sheets, depending upon the scale used and the size of the city. They are usually laid out with reference to a local, state, or U.S. Geological Survey plane coördinate system and indicate major reference and control points of triangulation, traverse, and level systems. They show street right-of-way lines and sometimes curb lines; railroad rights-of-way and sometimes track locations; streams, rivers, and lakes; culverts, bridges, and grade separations; corporate limits lines; and so on. Scales are generally 50 or 100 feet to the inch. These maps are used by the engineering force as a central set of records for all engineering work and as a point of departure for local surveys in connection with street improvements, subdivisions, and other engineering studies where accuracy is important. Such maps provide a useful reference to the planning agency in subdivision review work, site planning studies, and for all kinds of detailed investigations, including work on setback lines or street lines, the preparation of official maps, redevelopment studies, and so on.[1]

The situation with respect to topographic maps has been improving rapidly since World War II. Where previously many cities either relied upon small-scale U.S. Geological Survey maps or went to great expense to obtain engineering surveys for large-scale detailed topographic maps, the improvement and more extensive use of multiplex photogrametry equipment used in conjunction with limited ground control surveys now permit the preparation of extremely accurate large-scale topographic maps. Keyed to a grid layout of the urban area, these maps are usually prepared in the form of an atlas consisting of several sheets, the number being dependent upon the horizontal scale of the map and the extent of the built-up area. These maps are the principal reference work for the natural features of the area, indicating land forms by contour lines and showing natural drainage lines, rivers, streams, ponds, and marshy areas, some even showing wooded areas, rock outcroppings, and sink holes. Such maps generally show the used width of streets, railroad tracks, principal structures, and political boundaries. They sometimes indicate benchmarks and other triangulation and traverse monuments, depending upon the contract specifications when the mapping is undertaken. Large-scale maps prepared from engineering or aerial surveys in atlas form usually are made at 200 feet to the inch on a horizontal scale, with contour intervals at two, five, or ten feet vertical scale, depending upon the desired detail and local terrain conditions. USGS quadrangle sheets have an R.F. (representative fraction) of from

[1] The term "official map" is sometimes erroneously considered to be simply a base map prepared by the city. The term has a much more specialized meaning. An official map is a document in map form, usually recorded, which together with supplementing notations identifies existing and proposed streets, and frequently such other public facilities as existing and proposed school sites, playgrounds, parks, and so on, depending upon the scope of the official map legislation of a particular state. It is a plan-implementation instrument by which the local legislative body places on record its official intentions as to locations and dimensions of such facilities, particularly as to widenings, expansions, extensions, and new facilities.

10,000 to 65,000 depending upon the date of the survey, the practices of the original surveying agency, and the prevailing accepted scale at that time.[2] Contour intervals of these maps are generally 10 or 20 feet, depending on the topographic characteristics of the particular area involved.

Property maps (sometimes called tax maps) are usually developed from aerial photographs because of the ease in identifying fence lines, structures, and other physical features in the townscape which can be tied to property lines. Occasionally where comprehensive engineering surveys have been made, a city will use a set of reproduced tracings of the engineering maps and insert property line data on the basis of field surveys and a search of property records maintained by the city or county. In some cases, usually in small communities, a property map may be compiled entirely on the basis of recorded subdivision plats and deeds, relying on simple traverse surveys to provide controls and fill in critical gaps. These maps usually show street rights-of-way (opened and unopened streets), property lines, railroad and utility easements and rights-of-way, watercourses and lakes, and political boundaries. Maps developed on the basis of aerial photographs may show dimensions of property lines, whereas those based on engineering surveys often contain bearings as well as lengths of property lines. Scales range from 50 to 600 feet to the inch, with 50 feet being used in central areas, 100 to 200 feet in the remaining built-up areas, and 400 to 600 feet in outlying areas where acreage tracts predominate. These maps are usually developed for the tax assessor's office, but are exceedingly important reference maps for the planning agency, particularly for detailed land use surveys, subdivision review work, zoning administration, and site planning studies of all kinds.

There are a great variety of miscellaneous reference maps useful to the work of the planning agency, among them insurance maps, county and state highway maps, census maps, historical maps, and the various types of commercial maps frequently prepared for sale in larger cities. Prepared primarily for fire insurance underwriters, the insurance atlas provides useful material for planning purposes on structures, showing the outline shape, the number of stories to buildings or sections of buildings, the type of construction, and the street number of each structure or the separate address in each such structure. The planning office will frequently find county maps prepared by the county or the state highway commission useful in studies of peripheral areas where city maps leave off. Although most census maps are based on maps supplied from local sources, frequently they

[2] The R.F. system of scaling maps is commonly used by geographers where large land areas are being mapped, and is found on Army Engineer maps as well as Geological Survey and Coast and Geodetic Survey maps. On a map with an R.F. of 10,000, an inch measured on the map is equivalent to 10,000 inches on the ground, or a graphic scale of 833 feet to the inch.

will provide the only readily available source on minor civil division lines such as town, township, or borough lines.

Planning Base Maps

In urban areas where no satisfactory planning base maps are available or where for one reason or another none of the foregoing types of reference maps is completely satisfactory for city planning purposes, it is probable that sooner or later the planning office will find it necessary to prepare a series of base maps suitable for planning studies. Most planning offices will require at least two series of base maps in addition to the available reference maps described above: (1) what we shall call general-purpose maps, and (2) the detailed planning base map.

The general-purpose map is the type which cities frequently have published in quantity. It shows streets and street names, perhaps an index of street names, corporate limits lines, railroads, perhaps the major public buildings, lakes, rivers, and so on. Where this map covers the entire metropolitan area of interest, this conventional city map can be used for generalized studies, records, and displays or for rough work maps. Where the coverage does not include the entire urban area of interest, the planning agency must develop a new general-purpose base for its own special needs. Generally, this type of map should be available in three sheet sizes, ranging from the wall-display size down to a table size and letter size. These maps vary in scale for each sheet size according to the extent of built-up area and the general shape of the area covered. For example, the wall map may range from 200 feet to the inch, for the small communities 10,000 or under, to 2500 scale, and in a few cases, as much as a mile to the inch for the large metropolitan area. Table maps may vary from 500 feet to two miles to the inch, and letter size maps on 8½- by 11-inch sheets may be upward of several miles to the inch. The latter series of general-purpose maps may need to be greatly simplified by the elimination of street names, and for the larger metropolitan areas, the elimination of all but the major streets.

The other type of base, what we refer to as the detailed planning base map, merits more detailed consideration. This is a base which is prepared in atlas form, usually to the same scale as the topographic maps so that they may be used as overlay maps in conjunction with contour maps. The atlas may be keyed to the same grid system employed in the atlas of topographic sheets or it may be composed in terms of planning districts or natural planning areas as taken up in Part III. It is usually prepared in two or three series. One shows street right-of-way lines, railroads, watercourses, lakes, and civil division lines. This map is frequently combined with the second, which shows, in addition, property and easement lines. The third series have structures added. The first and second series are used for neighborhood studies and detailed studies of all kinds, and the third series are used for maintaining office records of all kinds, including land and structure uses, plots of building permits issued, a map of house numbers, zoning analyses, plots of new subdivisions, and so on.

Preparing the Detailed Base Map

Procedures for preparing the planning base map will vary from urban center to urban center according to available reference maps and the budget available for the mapping activity. Accordingly, the suggested procedures outlined briefly below must be adapted to each particular situation.

In general, the first step is the assembly of all available reference maps and the selection of one consistent series of maps as a control for the development of the new base. Scale, accuracy, inclusiveness of coverage, and street and property line data available at the selected scale are all factors which enter into the selection of the control map. The smallest suitable scale for the subsequent plot of structures on this base is 200 feet to the inch, and perhaps the largest suitable scale without involving sheets of unwieldy size or sheets too limited in the area covered to obtain relationships from block to block is 100 feet to the inch. With the possible exception of the central business district area where considerable detail must frequently be plotted and therefore the larger scale may be preferred, for most purposes 200 feet to the inch is perhaps the best multipurpose scale. It permits inclusion on a single sheet the average low-density neighborhood and conforms to a commonly used scale for aerial and topographic maps which, if not used as control maps for the preparation of this planning base, often must be used in conjunction with the planning base map in many types of city planning analyses.

The second step is the determination of the area to be mapped, which will generally be the *planning area*. This is the area expected to go into urban use during the selected *planning period*, generally a span of time from 20 to 25 years in the future.[3] The planning area will usually show all

[3] For considerations involved in selecting the planning period, see discussion under population forecasts in Chapter 7.

the present built-up area with an ample allowance for expansion beyond, especially along major highway approaches. In metropolitan areas the planning area obviously extends beyond the corporate limits of the central city to include all suburban areas considered to be functionally related to the urban center. In a few cases where the corporate limits extend considerably beyond the built-up area, the planning area may be defined to coincide with the corporate limits. Since population data are reported only by minor civil divisions, these lines may be a factor in establishing the limits of the planning area. Although somewhat arbitary so far as growth and expansion of the urban center is concerned, county or township lines may be sufficiently close to the functional delineation to be usable as the planning area. Other factors to be considered in drawing the planning area limits are locations of school attendance areas, watershed areas affecting the city water supply, limits of major drainage areas related to sanitation and storm drainage systems, outlying municipally owned property, and so on. Procedures for delimiting the planning area are taken up in greater detail in Chapter 10.

A third step is to select the coverage of individual sheets of the atlas. Where a uniform grid system is employed, this step becomes a mechanical one of laying out a grid pattern over the selected planning area. Where an attempt is made to recognize natural planning areas such as residential neighborhoods or industrial districts (see Chapter 10), each individual sheet must be composed with special care. Since no two planning districts are likely to be of the same shape or size, particular attention must be given to sheet orientation with respect to the direction of the north point and the selection of a sheet size which will contain the largest planning district to be included in the atlas. In some cases where there are odd-shaped or unusually large planning districts, it may be necessary to develop the sectional base sheet in two parts if the size of the atlas is not to become too unwieldy for convenient use on an ordinary desk or table.

Once these preliminary preparations have been completed, the successive steps which follow become somewhat mechanical operations. The result of the next steps is the preparation of what we shall call Base A, Base B, and Base C. Base A is simply a street map; Base B is Base A with property and easement lines added; and Base C is Base B with structures added. Some planning agencies may be interested in having base maps of all variations on the initial Base A. Others may be interested only in Base B and Base C, and some in Base C only. The appropriate modification to procedures summarized below can be made to fit the needs of the planning agency.

Assuming all three bases are desired, the fourth step is the preparation of a preliminary pencil drawing on tracing linen of Base A, showing the street network. If the reference base being used is sufficiently accurate for planning purposes, street right-of-way lines can be traced directly on the linen. If other reference sheets are to be used in establishing right-of-way lines, it may be necessary to trace off the center lines of the street network from the reference base, with rights-of-way dimensioned in by reference to other sources of information. Streets which are open are usually shown in solid lines, and streets which are dedicated to public use but not open are usually shown in broken lines. Base A also includes railroad rights-of-way, water courses, and political boundary lines. Political boundaries are usually shown in heavy dash and dot lines of appropriate weight to distinguish them from other lines.

From the preliminary drawing of Base A, a print is made; and to this print are added data which will be required later for Bases B and C. Property lines and easements to be used on Base B are obtained from tax maps or in the case of acreage tracts, identified on aerial photographs by reference to fence lines and use lines (after being checked against other data sources), or they are obtained from various engineering drawings, subdivision plats, deed records, and other reference maps described above. Structure data to be used on Base C are obtained from aerial photographs and insurance atlases. In general, property and easement lines are shown in broken lines of a lighter weight than those used for right-of-way lines. Property lines may be broken or unbroken lines, and easement lines are shown in dashes and dots to differentiate them from property lines. Structures are shown in bold heavy solid lines with the shapes of commercial, industrial, and public buildings following the approximate true shapes observed in photographs or the insurance atlas and with residential structures represented by symbols of uniform size, usually in the shape of an open square. All such representations of structures are located as closely as possible to actual location with reference to property lines. In residential areas, only the principal structures are shown, with sheds, garages, and other outbuildings accessory to the residential use omitted.

The result of the foregoing step completes the preliminary compilation work done in the office. The sixth step is a field check of the preliminary work sheet compiled on the Base A print. This step is usually combined with the detailed land use survey discussed later in the chapter. In this stage of the mapping activity, street and lot discrepancies are discovered on the ground. Theoretically no corrections of this order should be necessary, but in practice some changes here and there will usually be necessary. By public usage, a street right-of-way differing from the platted right-of-way may need to be recognized. In certain sections of a city, there may be considerable deviation in the lot layout discovered on the ground from that compiled from office records and subdivision maps. Recent aerial photography will usually obviate most of these difficulties in the original compilation work, but in sections not covered by photographs or where the photography is not of recent date, this field checking activity will often reveal that a superseding plat has been followed in the actual land subdivision as carried out on the ground. The field work also includes verification as to whether streets are opened or closed, visual checks of building setbacks in relation to property and street right-of-way lines, the insertion of new structures, and so on.

In the intensively developed sections of the city, field checking must generally be done on foot, but in most outlying residential areas it can be done by a "windshield survey." In peripheral sections of the planning area, distances between structures, building relationships to property lines, streams, and natural features may be estimated closely enough for planning purposes by use of the automobile speedometer, rangefinders, and similar makeshift means. In these rural sections, it is frequently simpler to make the necessary field notations in colored pencil directly on aerial photographs.

Upon completion of field work and after conducting any further investigation into official records in follow-up on any discrepancies uncovered in the field, Base A can be finally drawn in ink. From the completed Base A maps, reproduced tracings can be made and Base B data on property and easement lines added; and from the completed Base B maps a second set of reproduced tracings can be made and Base C data on structures inserted. When completed, the necessary prints can be made from these base maps, the desired data inserted with colored pencils or inks, and bound in atlas form as a set of records for analysis and general office reference use.

Because of the time and expense involved in preparing these base maps, it is most important to establish systematic procedures for keeping them up to date. Within the area of subdivision jurisdiction, it is possible to keep abreast of these changes and make additions as they occur.[4] These additions or changes can be plotted on special "correction prints" as they are formally approved. In the case of new structures or converted buildings, in cities or counties where building codes or zoning ordinances are in effect, it is possible to keep an up-to-date plot of these changes through the

---

[4] As established by local ordinance under powers granted by the state, land subdivision regulations usually provide that before land can be cut into streets and lots, officially recorded, and sold, the proposed development must go through a process of review and either be approved by the planning agency or recommended to the governing body by the planning agency for approval. The jurisdiction of these powers in some cities coincides with the corporate limits, and in some, extends sometimes as far as three miles beyond the incorporated area of the city.

building inspector. This can be done by providing him with a set of prints of Base C and arranging with him for the systematic addition of structures as building or, preferably, occupancy permits are issued. Where the planning area extends beyond the limits of the subdivision jurisdiction or in peripheral areas where building inspection procedures are not applicable, it becomes necessary to make periodic field checks to insure a complete record of changes in the physical setting. By consolidating these correction sheets and maintaining them on an annual basis, it is possible to develop comparative data from year to year on rates of change, directions of growth, and locations of conversion activity.

LAND USE SURVEY AND SUMMARY

Of all the kinds of data required in city planning studies of the urban setting, land use information is the most frequently used and has the largest variety of applications. Indeed, the existing patterns of land uses in the urban area obviously provide the base from which a development plan is fashioned for the future use of land. The land use survey supplies the data needed in defining these existing use patterns, providing information on the types and intensity of land and building uses, which taken together constitute a most elemental and necessary description of the urban setting.

One kind of summary and presentation of land use data is concerned with the total land area in urban development and is expressed in terms of the total acreage in urban use. This built-up area is frequently shown on maps. Thus by reference to land development records for selected inter-

FIGURE 20.   Use of Scatter Diagrams to Show Historical Growth Patterns in the Development of the Urban Area. (*Source:* Baltimore Department of Planning, *The Basis for a Master Transportation Plan,* Report One, 1949.)

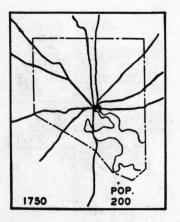
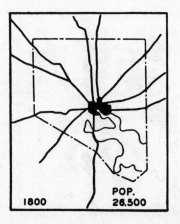
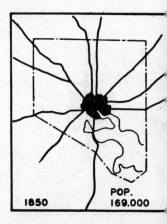

vals of time, supplemented by historical maps of the urban area, it is possible to prepare *scatter diagrams,* a visual device employed in showing historical changes in the extent of the built-up pattern of the urban area as it has expanded over the years (see Figure 20).

More commonly, land use data are summarized both statistically and in map form according to specific land use categories such as residential uses, business uses, industrial uses, and so on. Each use can be placed on a separate map (see Figure 25), or all uses can be presented compositely on one map (see Figure 24). The composite presentation is generally preferred because of its greater utility in studying use relationships. When land use data are plotted compositely by lot or land area on small-scale, general-purpose maps such as those described in the last section of the chapter, it is possible to obtain a quick visual impression of the broad patterns of land use, identify the major functional parts to the urban complex and generally observe relationships between the different parts of the city. For more detailed studies of land use patterns within small sections of the urban center, planning Base B may serve a useful purpose. When land use data are plotted according to uses of buildings and open land on a map such as Base C, a much more precise description is obtained. The latter kind of presentation is particularly useful for detailed site planning studies, rezoning analyses, and other similar types of work where detail is of paramount importance.

There are many more kinds of applications of land use data. One of the applications of immediate, direct, and obvious concern is in the preparation of a preliminary *land use plan,* a generalized land development plan which becomes the guide for the future use of land as processes of urban extension and renewal occur. But the land use survey has equally tangible uses in the whole array of transportation studies and utility expansion analyses involved in the development of the comprehensive plan

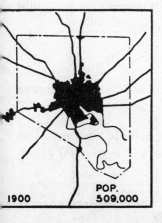
1900   POP. 509,000

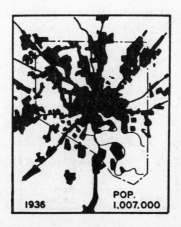
1936   POP. 1,007,000

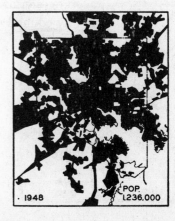
1948   POP. 1,236,000

for the urban area. In traffic analyses, land use data provide a clue as to the locations of principal traffic generators in the community, and the extent of concentration or dispersion of uses gives a means for gauging traffic intensity in various parts of the urban area. The pattern of land uses as derived from generalized land use maps is a basic reference in locating major thoroughfares, parking areas, and transit routes and terminals, and the detailed Base C type of land use presentation is fundamental in the first preliminary design of thoroughfares and parking facilities. Both the generalized and the detailed land use maps are invaluable in transit, trucking, railroad, and airport studies. Moreover, in utility studies of all kinds—in estimating existing and future needs for the expansion of water, sewerage, power, and other utility systems—land use data provide an important source of information with respect to service areas and how the demands on utilities are concentrated or dispersed within these service areas.

The applications of land use information are not restricted to urban-wide planning studies. The Base C type of detailed land use presentation is fundamental to studies of residential neighborhoods, central and outlying business areas, and organized or planned industrial districts. It is a basic reference for redevelopment and rehabilitation plans under federally aided urban renewal programs. In addition to area studies of these types, land use maps are a primary source of information for site planning work, for example, on recreation areas, school sites, housing developments, and shopping centers.

The land use map, either in generalized or detailed form, has a great variety of operational as well as planning uses. For day-to-day problems and operations, it is the city planner's "encyclopedia" for many routine and urgent matters. It provides a basis for responding to citizen petitions and council, mayor, or city manager referrals of all kinds, and it furnishes a ready reference for discussion of complaints, problems, and ideas offered by daily visitors to the planning office. The usefulness of these maps for record purposes, for subdivision review, and for zoning studies and petitions has already been pointed out. Too, the uses of these maps on day-to-day matters are not confined to the city planning office alone. Copies with acetate overlays attached for plotting purposes are frequently to be found in city council chambers and in the mayor's or city manager's office.

Land Use Classification

From the foregoing partial listing of the ways in which land use data are used in planning analyses, it is evident that before a system of classification is finally adopted, much thought and study must go into the detail and form in which data are needed in both immediate and ultimate applications. A system too narrowly conceived, too bound to one kind of application can severely handicap a planning agency's general program, and once a classification system has been adopted, later corrective changes can create many problems. Just as studies of population trends can be seriously disrupted by changes in census categories from one census to another, similarly every time basic changes in the land use classification system are introduced, the opportunities for trend studies are curtailed. More importantly, in the task of periodically adjusting long-range plans to significant new changes in trends, every revision in the classification system will present a whole series of problems in reorganizing the analytical framework employed. These problems and the sheer expense of corrective land use surveys (as distinct from the necessary periodic resurvey of land use under one classification system as discussed in a later subsection below) place a premium on care and forethought in the initial selection of a classification system.

Although there is considerable uniformity discernible in the classification systems to be found from one city to another, there is no universally recognized standard classification of land uses employed in the United States as is found in Great Britain and in many other countries abroad. There are some distinct advantages in a standard classification system. For example, standardization simplifies problems of communication among members of the profession and with the general public; it assists in determining the transfer value of analytical methods successfully employed in one city for use in the solution of problems in other cities; and it offers opportunities for comparative studies and more systematic research into urbanization trends. On the other hand, blind adherence to a standard classification system can result in an entirely inadequate appraisal of land use characteristics peculiarly local in nature or of special local interest. Moreover, standardization can involve cumbersome and time-consuming formalities in the initial adoption and subsequent amendment of a system, with attendant dangers of inflexibility and delays in the mechanics of keeping the system up to date.

Apart from the purely local requirement which may be dictated by climate, topography, local policy, and many other local factors, there are some considerations of general application worth noting at this juncture. In the first place, there are the primary uses of a classification which must be borne in mind, and there are secondary applications of land use data. The needs of a primary order may be thought of as the technical requirements of the planning agency's own on-going program, and the secondary applications are more of a service category, a service provided to public and private agencies or groups in the urban area either on a special report basis or in the form of current and continuing reports on land use changes. While the discussion here is concerned with the technical planning needs, the importance of secondary uses of the data should not be underestimated, for attention to these needs may play a useful role in strengthening the planning agency's position and general prestige in the metropolitan area.

Within the primary category, there are a variety of applications, not by any means restricted to the land use planning needs under discussion here. The range of these applications roughly corresponds to the scope of the planning agency's program:

1. Applications relating to the comprehensive plan and its various component elements.
   a. The land development plan (private and public uses, including all major land-using community facilities such as school, recreation, and other similar uses).
   b. The transportation plan (thoroughfares, rapid transit, and rail, air, and water systems of moving people and goods, and their terminal facilities).
   c. The public utilities plan (the underground, surface, and overhead distribution and collection systems, including supply, disposal, and generation facilities).
2. Applications relating to the principal plan-effectuation measures.
   a. Regulatory measures (zoning, subdivision control, etc.).
   b. Public developmental measures (public works programming and capital budgeting, urban renewal programs, etc.).
   c. Civic education and public support measures (graphic presentation requirements in exhibitions, films, television shows, publications, etc.).

The above listing is based on the usual definitions of the planning functions of a planning agency. If other functions are assigned to the agency, this list would be expanded.

Each of the above types of studies or programs has its own specifications as to the applications to be made of land use data. So, to achieve its optimum usefulness, the land use classification system must anticipate the exact needs of each application. To avoid a wasteful land use survey operation, this means that the system adopted must reflect *known specific applications,* eliminating from consideration uncertain or unexplored possible applications, as promising as they may seem, until such time as they have a demonstrated worth.

Turning now to land use planning applications of land use data, we may note two general and controlling specifications: specifications of a mechanical character that are involved in graphic presentation of the land use pattern, and specifications of an analytical character that are involved in the procedures of the land use planning process itself. The former are relatively simple, following the conventional functional breakdowns into industry, business, residence, and so on. As to the selection of these functional classes for graphic presentation, practice varies according to the scale and use of the presentation and the size and character of the urban area. In general, small-scale color presentations of land use and most black and white renditions contain relatively few land use classes so as not to detract from the readability of the map. Generally, these maps show areas of residential, business, industrial, and public-institutional uses, with vacant or nonurban areas left blank. Large-scale detailed land use maps of the Base C type can show a breakdown of these major land use classes in as much detail as desired. Generalized or detailed land use maps prepared for office reference use may show more classes than those used for public displays or in popular publications. Fewer classes are generally needed in small communities than are required in large urban centers, and within cities of similar size there may be some variation in land use categories necessary to bring out special classes of uses peculiar to one city. For example, in Washington, D.C., federal office building areas would be distinguished from other public use areas, or in cities where mining operations are carried on within the urban area, these uses would be given special identification. Table 15 presents a system of major land use categories typical of the kind used for presentation purposes, with one variant for

TABLE 15. Illustrative Major Urban Land Use Categories for Generalized and Detailed Land Use Map Presentations

Generalized Presentations by Area

Residence[a]	Industry and related uses—indigo blue
Low density—yellow	Wholesale and related uses—purple
Medium density—orange	Public buildings and open spaces—green
High density—brown	Institutional buildings and areas—gray
Retail business—red	Vacant or nonurban use—uncolored
Transportation, utilities,	
communications—ultramarine	

Detailed Presentations by Building and Open Air Use

Residence[ab]	Industry and related uses[c]—indigo blue
Low density—yellow	Extensive
Medium density—orange	Intermediate
High density—brown	Intensive
Retail business[c]	Wholesale and related uses[c]—purple
Local Business Uses—red	Public buildings and open spaces[c]—green
Central Business Uses—red	Institutional buildings and areas[c]—gray
Regional Shopping Centers—red	Vacant or nonurban use—uncolored
Highway Service Uses—red	
Transportation, utilities,	
communications—ultramarine	

[a] Low, medium, and high density or other defined density classes are increasingly being used in place of the older form of classification (one-family, two-family, and multifamily). Obviously these are not interchangeable designations.

[b] A figure for the number of dwelling units in each structure and a symbol for dwelling types (single-family, duplex, row housing, garden apartments, multistory apartments, etc.) are sometimes inserted on maps to supply supplementary information.

[c] Symbol may be used to differentiate between various subcategories.

TABLE 16.   Illustrative Classification of Uses by Conventional Major Categories as Used in Detailed Land Use Ma

Residence

Single-family
  Detached house
  Dwelling unit over or attached to other use
  Trailer (nontransient living unit)

Two-family
  Duplex
  Two attached dwelling units (semidetached units)
  Two dwelling units over or attached to other use

Multifamily
  Row housing
  Flats of three or more dwelling units
  Three or more dwelling units over or attached to other use
  Garden apartments
  Multistory apartments

Retail Business

Structures
  Retail stores and accessory storage
  Offices and office buildings
  Banks and other financial institutions
  Restaurants, bars, and soft drink establishments
  Theaters, bowling alleys, billiard parlors, roller skating rinks, etc.
  Hotels, motels, resorts, etc.
  Newspaper offices and plants

New-used auto and farm equipment sales and service establishments
Auto repair and storage garages
Drive-in services (gasoline service stations, refreshment and dairy bars, drive-in laundry and dry cleaning pickup stations, drive-in banks, outdoor theaters, produce stands, curio shops, etc.)
Miscellaneous service establishments (shoe repair shops, laundriettes, and laundry and dry cleaning outlets, barber and beauty shops, etc.)

Areas
  Used-car lots
  Farm equipment sales lots
  Trailer sales lots
  Drive-in theater grounds
  Amusement parks, carnivals, etc.
  Privately operated fair grounds
  Commercial auto, horse, dog racing tracks
  Tombstone display sales areas
  Auto graveyards
  Accessory parking and loading areas

Transportation, Utilities, Communications

Structures
  Railroad, bus, airport passenger

terminals and accessory servi
  buildings
Passenger steamship or ferry te
  minals
Electric generating plants ar
  substations
Gas works, storage tanks, ar
  distribution facilities for loc
  consumption
Telephone exchange and servi
  shops
Radio and TV studios and tran
  mitters
Transit terminal and service sho
Water treatment plants, pun
  stations, etc.
Sewage disposal plants, pun
  stations, etc.
Incinerators
Municipal, county, or state g
  rages and supply buildings

Areas
  Railroad marshaling yards
  Bus and transit storage yards
  Utilities service and storage yar
  Airport property
  Municipal dumps
  Reservoirs, aeriation beds, etc.
  Radio and TV transmitter groun
  Accessory parking and loadi
  areas

Wholesale and Related Uses

Structures
  Merchant wholesalers

maps showing uses by land areas and another for maps showing detail by buildings and land areas. It also indicates colors most commonly used for these categories. Table 16 shows an illustrative partial list of urban land uses classified into the conventional categories commonly used in detailed land use map presentations.[5]

A classification system based on the foregoing presentation requirements does not reflect the detail and the organization of uses employed in the analytical procedures of land use planning. For these purposes, the conventional system must be divisible into subclasses that are capable of recombination to form clusters of uses; for example, the whole range of uses found in residential communities, which can then be analyzed as a related group. In other words, to fulfill analytical requirements, it must be possible

[5] For a more exhaustive and indexed list of uses found in various conventional categories, see E. B. Wilkens, *Mapping for Planning*, Public Administration Service, 1948, pp. 15–25.

Wholesale assemblers
Warehouses
Trucking terminals and service buildings
Wharves, cargo sheds, and other port facilities
Wholesale greenhouses
Junk assemblers

reas
Storage yards accessory to above structures
Accessory parking and loading areas

Industry and Related Uses
ructures
Printing and publication plants
Milk and bottling plants
Baking plants
Laundry and dry cleaning plants
Lumber mills, woodworking plants, etc.
Blacksmith, tinsmith, metal working plants
Flour, feed, flax, and similar mills
Canneries
Abattoirs, meat packing and poultry-dressing plants
Tanneries
Fertilizer plants, fat-reducing works
Textile plants, dye works, clothing manufacturing plants, etc.
Chemical plants, paper mills, etc.

Refineries, oil storage, commercial gas storage
Smelters and ore reduction works
Rolling mills, fabricating plants
Railroad repair shops, locomotive works
Assembly plants
Tool and dye works
Coke ovens, brick plants, lime kilns
Stone working, rock crushing, etc.
Paint and varnish manufacturing
Tobacco redrying and manufacturing, etc.

Areas
Lumber, brick, coal and supply yards
Mines, quarries, and gravel pits
Stockyards
Accessory parking and loading areas

Public Buildings and Open Spaces
Structures
City Hall, County Court House
Local, state, or federal office buildings
Fire halls, police stations
Post office and substations
Libraries, museums, etc.
Public hospitals and health centers
Publicly supported schools and colleges

County sanitariums, orphanages, etc.
Jails, reformatories, prisons
County or state fair buildings

Areas
Parks, playgrounds, athletic fields
Public squares, gardens, and reservations
Reservations around public buildings
Public school or college grounds
County or state fair grounds
Publicly owned cemeteries
Municipal parking lots
Accessory parking and loading areas

Institutional Buildings and Areas
Structures
Privately supported hospitals, rest homes, sanitariums, etc.
Privately supported schools, colleges
Churches, missions, etc.
YMCA, YWCA, boys' clubs, settlement houses, etc.
Country clubs, other clubhouses, etc.

Areas
Grounds accessory to above structures
Institutional or private cemeteries
Accessory parking and loading areas

to break down the broad *functional categories* and lift out subcategories so that these may be regrouped with other subclasses of uses to form *analytical categories* or groups of spatially related uses which are then employed as analytical units in the land use planning process. Table 17 illustrates how certain subclasses of the pure functional categories of Table 15 can be recombined to form analytical categories and subcategories.[6] However, it must be emphasized that for purposes of preparing land use maps this classification system is no substitute for the conventional functional system, nor does it necessarily fulfill the analytical needs of other comprehensive plan studies. It simply represents a convenient form for summarizing land use data for land use planning analyses taken up in Part III.

[6] The use of symbols on detailed land use maps as cited in the footnotes of Table 15 is a useful medium for effecting recombination of functional categories into analytical categories.

TABLE 17.   A Land Use Classification System for Land Use Planning Analyses

	Industrial and Related Uses[a]
Intensive class[b]	At this extreme are establishments manufacturing jewelry, optical instruments, etc.
Intermediate class[b]	
Extensive class[b]	At this extreme are oil refineries, ship-building yards, railroad marshaling yards, quarries, etc.
	Wholesale and Related Uses[a]
Close-in class[b]	At this extreme are merchant wholesalers serving retailers, etc.
Outlying class[b]	At this extreme are wholesale assemblers, truck terminals and distribution centers, warehousing, etc.
	Region-Serving Retail and Related Uses[a]
Central business district	Retail group, office group (including wholesale agents and brokers), amusements, civic center, transportation passenger terminals, etc.
CBD satellite centers	Auto sales and service centers, farm machinery centers, farmers' markets, outlying office centers, appliance sales centers, etc.
Regional shopping centers	(Planned)
Highway service centers	Motels and related services, drive-in roadside services such as restaurants, outdoor theaters, carnivals, golf-driving ranges, etc.
	Region-Serving Recreation, Education, and Cultural Uses
Close-in class[b]	Spectator sports, museums, auditoriums, lodges, large churches, etc.
Intermediate class[b]	Medical centers, colleges, large institutions, etc.
Outlying class[b]	Golf courses, fair grounds, park reservations, etc.
	Residential Communities
Residential uses	Various residential density classes
Local business uses	Neighborhood and community shopping centers, corner groceries, and other retail outlets serving day-to-day household needs[a]
Schools	Elementary, junior, and senior high schools[c]
Recreation areas	Playgrounds, community recreation centers, local parks, etc.
Institutional uses	Neighborhood-serving churches, etc.
	Streets, Railroad Tracks, and Transit Lines[d]
	Vacant and Nonurban Uses

[a] Floor area as well as land area data are summarized for these categories. Land space taken up in railroad spur lines, parking areas, loading space, outdoor storage areas, or similar functions associated with these uses are summarized as separate subtotals of land area.

[b] Activities falling within each of these classes are defined locally.

[c] In cities where there is but one consolidated high school, such a use would be classed as a region-serving recreation, education, and cultural use.

[d] Consisting mainly of rights-of-way, this residual category is used to make acreage tabulations sum up to an urban area total.

The Land Use Survey

Once a land use classification system has been settled upon—one which recognizes presentation as well as analytical requirements—the task of planning and carrying out the land use survey can proceed. Considerations in the selection of the type of survey, the advance preparations, and the actual conduct of the survey are taken up in the pages immediately following.

TYPES OF SURVEYS

In general, two kinds of surveys have been in usage for a number of years: what we shall call the "inspection" type and the "combined inspection-interview" type. The former, being less time-consuming and expensive, is the most commonly used. However, the latter, sometimes called a real property survey, can achieve greater accuracy, and when combined with a housing survey or some other supplementing survey, may actually be somewhat less expensive when costs are allocated to the respective programs served.

The inspection survey is the simplest type of land use survey and is generally organized and executed by the planning agency primarily for its own needs. It is frequently combined with the field checking of planning base maps as noted earlier in the chapter. When these two operations are combined, data are recorded directly on the preliminary prints of the various sectional sheets as previously compiled in the office. Large-scale aerial photographs are sometimes substituted as field sheets. If field sheets are drawn to or selected at a convenient size, they can be used in both "windshield surveys" and field work on foot. While most data are plotted directly on the field sheet as the survey proceeds, some surveys have effectively reduced time spent in "windshield surveys" by use of dictaphone equipment installed in the automobile. The latter variation on the "windshield survey" involves the use of some form of property and block numbering scheme inscribed on field sheets to permit rapid recording of land use characteristics. Obviously this type of survey is not practicable for a combined mapping and land use type of survey. Where time and resources do not permit the detailed type of study as involved in surveys using Base C type maps for the field sheets, or where only the generalized type of land use information by land area is required, a copy of the general-purpose wall map cut up into convenient size sheets is frequently used for field survey purposes.

Frequently the inspection type of survey is expanded to include other investigations for planning purposes. The field survey of vacant land characteristics is often included in the land use survey. Details of this type of survey are taken up in the next section of this chapter. A general visual appraisal of the condition of structures is frequently combined with the land use survey. Appraisal techniques are covered in a later section of this chapter. Other data sometimes assembled at the time of the land use survey include racial occupancy information for general reference use, and facts relating to setbacks and sideyards and notations on incidental uses in residential areas for use in zoning analyses. Also sometimes combined with the land use survey are investigations relating to street conditions. Whether streets are open or not must be checked for purposes of completing the planning base map. With reference to paved streets, notations are sometimes made as to whether or not the street has curb and gutter, what the pavement width is, and for unpaved streets, what the used or effective graded width is. Along with data on right-of-way widths, this kind of information is used as reference material for subdivision review and for capacity analyses in thoroughfare planning studies.

The inspection-interview type of survey is generally carried out on a coöperative basis with other public agencies. The old WPA real property survey technique was the forerunner of this type of survey. Designed as a combination housing and land use survey, more than 300 of these surveys were carried out as a work-relief measure in the period between 1934 and 1940 under federal-state-local sponsorship. They were a simplified and shaken-down form adapted from an earlier experimental series of surveys known as "federal real property inventories" conducted in some 64 of the larger cities of the country.[7] In cities where there were established planning agencies, these surveys also were frequently conducted under the supervision of these agencies.

Contemporary versions of this type of survey may be jointly sponsored by planning, housing, and redevelopment agencies, and they vary in detail and content according to the interests of the sponsoring agencies. In some cities, a combination tax record and land use form has been used in inspection-interview surveys, and in others, a combination local population or school census and land use survey form has been used. Whatever the form, some basic reference map is needed in order to key questionnaire and inspection forms to a systematic property and block numbering scheme. Both key maps and data sheets or cards are used in the field.

[7] Real Property Inventories (commonly referred to as RPI's) were federally conducted surveys and were carried out as part of the Civil Works Administration program under the supervision of the Bureau of Foreign and Domestic Commerce. The improved Real Property Surveys (commonly referred to as RPS's) were conducted by state and local agencies with financial aid from the Works Progress Administration. Procedures for these surveys were developed jointly by the Central Statistical Board, the Federal Housing Administration, and the WPA, and are described in a four-volume manual, *Technique for a Real Property Survey,* U.S. Government Printing Office, 1936. For a summary of the first 204 RPI's and RPS's conducted between 1934 and 1936, see Works Progress Administration, *Urban Housing,* U.S. Government Printing Office, 1938.

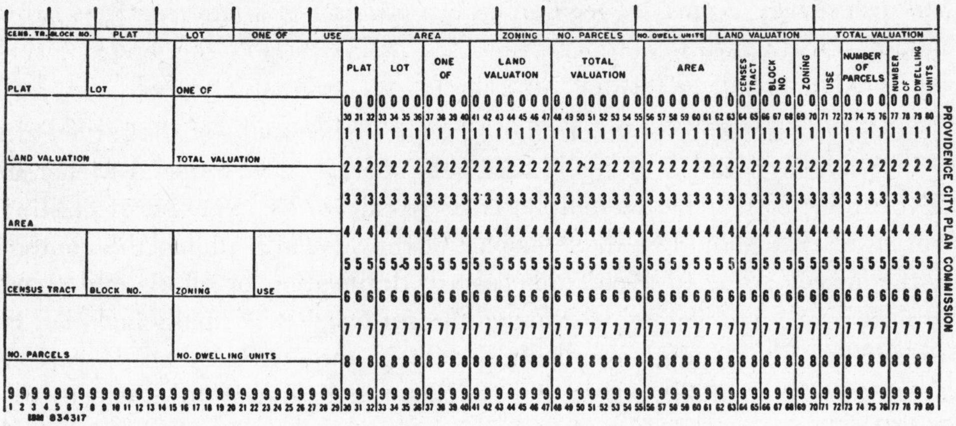

FIGURE 21. IBM Card Used in Recording Land Use and Other Planning Data. (*Source:* Providence City Plan Commission, 1953.)

The permanent form in which land use data are to be recorded has a bearing on the field data collection techniques employed. Generally, records are kept either in map or card form, or both. The finished land use map is usually developed directly from field sheets where the inspection type of field survey is employed, and in the inspection-interview type of survey, field schedules, in conjunction with various reference maps, are used in transcription of land use data to map form. Either the original field survey cards or a subsequent transcription of these data to IBM cards become the permanent record form of inspection-interview surveys. Occasionally, as in Providence, Rhode Island, land use survey data obtained from inspection type surveys are punched onto IBM cards to become a permanent record form (see Figure 21). The IBM record system is particularly useful in large metropolitan areas where machine tabulation summaries of varying combinations of the data can be quickly made for a variety of immediate and long-range planning studies.[8] In smaller cities, unless combined with tax assessment records where IBM systems of record keeping are already in use, this system of recording land use data may be too expensive to undertake, and of course, in small cities and towns, it may be unnecessarily complicated for the volume of cards involved.

[8] In reference to the Providence IBM card shown in Figure 21, the City Plan Commission there reports that the following types of tabulations have been found most useful:
1. Report showing for each lot all information on punched cards.
2. Report showing land use by census blocks, tracts, and city as a whole.
3. Report showing land use by zoning category for census tracts and for city as a whole.
4. Report showing zoning by land use category for census tracts and for city as a whole.
5. Report showing lot area classification by land use for census tracts and for city as a whole.
6. Report showing residential area per dwelling unit by census block.

ADVANCE PREPARATIONS

The key importance of determining just how the results of the survey are to be used in advance of the actual field survey, as mentioned earlier in the chapter, cannot be overemphasized. A careful examination of existing sources of data should be made as part of the step in planning the content of the survey so as to avoid unnecessary duplication of effort, and there must be a very specific predetermined use for every item finally included in the survey. Time spent in collecting data of the "we may need" variety rarely proves justified. Unless the specific use is known in advance, the exact kind of observation to be made in the field may be ill-defined, and even though the hunch was correct, the form is likely to be incorrect.

Once the type and scope of the survey has been determined, all field procedures can be set down in memorandum form or in a "Manual of Standard Field Procedures." This aspect of advance planning is most important in large urban areas where several field workers are involved, and particularly important in inspection-interview surveys. Standard practices in surveys of this kind call for one or more pretests of field schedules in order to clear up any problems of ambiguity and to eliminate or modify items which present practical difficulties of one kind or another in the field. Test surveys are also helpful in improving on standard definitions and general field instructions. After the manual is issued in final form, a formal briefing session for all field workers is held, short test surveys are made where results are discussed, and each worker is "checked out" in all aspects of his assignment. Such briefing sessions may also be held in the course of the survey where unforeseen problems develop. The purpose of these preparations and precautions is one of minimizing error due to interpretation of instructions and to secure maximum possible uniformity on all items of subjective observation or judgment.

CONDUCTING THE LAND USE SURVEY

When all foregoing advance preparations are completed, including any publicity of the survey that may be required to prepare the way for field workers where an interviewing activity is involved, the survey may be started. In inspection type surveys, outlying sections of the urban area are usually covered by automobile in a "windshield survey." In this part of the survey, at least two and sometimes three field workers are needed in each car. A driver and one or two plotters equipped with plotting boards, colored

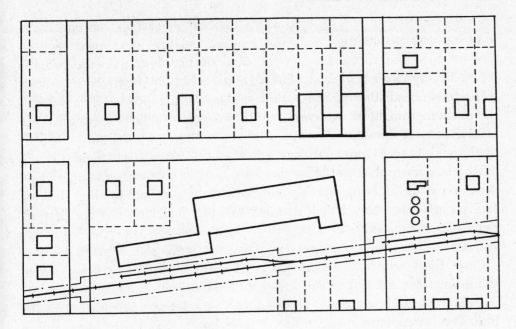

Section of a Typical Base C Print for Field Survey.

FIGURE 22.   Detailed Building and Land Use Mapping in Inspection Type
Surveys.

The Same Print After Entry of Field Notations.

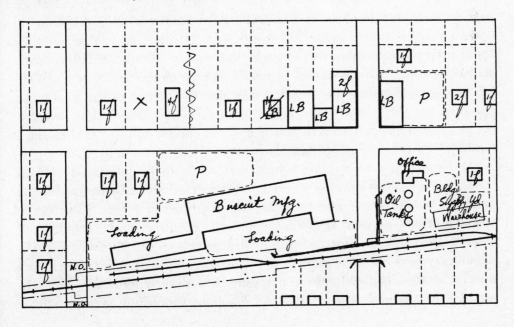

pencils, and copies of the land use classification system for occasional reference use are needed. For the more intensively developed sections where field work must be done on foot, field personnel can work individually on a block-by-block assignment basis. In inspection-interview type surveys, field workers will be equipped with clipboards, a supply of schedules, a reference map of block and property numbers, and official credentials for identification purposes.

Although there is some uniformity in the basic essentials of field plotting procedures, each planning office generally develops its own system of field notations to fit the circumstances, time schedule, and final product desired. For inspection surveys where detailed building and land use are desired, Figure 22 is suggestive of a system of field notation. The upper drawing indicates what the field worker has to start with, showing the kind of material plotted on field sheets in the office from relevant existing sources of information and maps. The lower plate shows the same drawing after the entry of field notations. It should be noted that to begin with, the Base C print contains street, railroad easement, and property lines and all principal structures. As shown in the lower plate, a notation concerning the number of families in each residential structure is made; business structures are identified along with their accessory parking (indicated by letter P in this drawing); and for industrial structures, the nature of industrial activity is identified. Storage yards, loading and parking areas, and other open areas in use are outlined and type of use identified. New structures are added; use lines are related to property lines, and where discrepancies occur, these are noted for later checking against property maps and other records back in the office; and miscellaneous notations as to whether or not a street is open (in the drawing, N.O. is used for "not open"), a residence over a business (a diagonal line drawn through structure with an LB for local business noted in the front part of the building and "1f" for one-family dwelling unit inserted over the rear portion of the structure) and other similar special notations are inserted. The memorandum or manual of instructions prepared in advance of the survey will contain standard symbols and other types of notations to be used in the field.

For inspection type surveys where results are to be presented only in terms of generalized land use by area (on Base B or general-purpose maps), there are two basic techniques. These are identified in Figure 23 as Technique A where a count of dwelling units is required, and Technique B where there is no need for assembling information on the number of dwelling units. Where the development of a land use plan is an immediate objective, either the detailed land use mapping procedure (Figure 22) or Technique A of the generalized land use mapping procedure (Figure 23) is

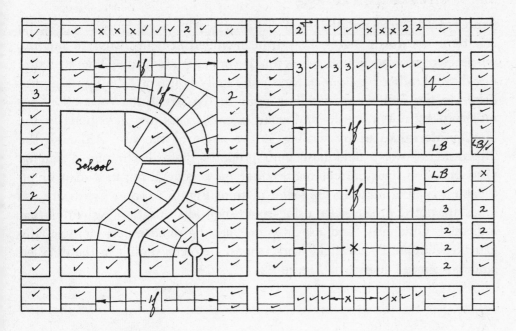

Technique A—Field Notations with D.U. Count.

FIGURE 23. Generalized Land Use Mapping by Area in Inspection Type Surveys.

Technique B—Field Notations by Area Only.

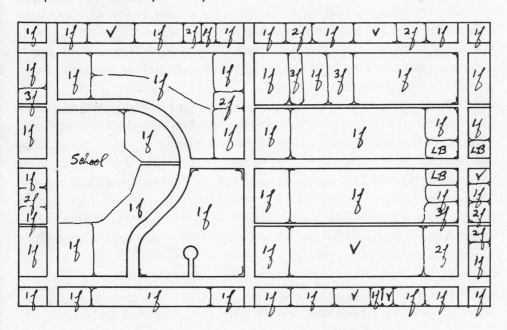

required. The field notation symbols used usually vary from city to city, and those shown in Figure 23 can be modified in many ways to suit the purposes of any particular office. In the upper plate, a dwelling structure is indicated either by a check for a one-family house or by a figure appropriate to the number of dwelling units in the structure. Vacant lots are indicated by a symbol X, and nonresidential uses are indicated by the appropriate initial or by writing in the name of the use. Although the illustration shows a field base with property lines, Technique A can be used on an ordinary street map, either on a general-purpose map or on a Base A type of map. In the lower plate of Figure 23, only aggregate use areas are noted in the field, using some such identification system as that indicated. Obviously land use mapping can be done much more rapidly using Technique B, and field work is most time-consuming in the detailed land use survey shown in Figure 22.

Presentation of Land Use Data

The results of the land use survey are generally summarized both in map form and statistically. Figure 24 shows a generalized land use map of an urban area and indicates how patterns of uses can be readily identified in this type of presentation. Figure 25, based on the pattern of uses in the same city some seven years later, shows a scatter diagram type of graphic presentation for particular uses. As indicated earlier in the chapter, color versions of land use maps which are prepared for general office reference use often carry as many as ten or more categories of uses, and by use of supplementary symbols in the Base C type of presentation, an even greater number of categories can be shown.

For most city planning purposes, land use presentations are needed at three or four different scales. For detailed work in site planning, on zoning case studies, and for various large-scale area studies, an atlas presentation on Base C maps is required. For studies of land use distribution on an urban-wide basis where planning analyses are concerned with broad patterns of uses, a generalized land use presentation is required. This may be prepared on a general-purpose wall map or on a reduced desk-size version of the map, or on both. Finally, a black and white version of the generalized

FIGURE 24. Illustrative Presentation of a Conventional Land Use Map, Johnson City, Tennessee, 1944. (*Source:* Tennessee State Planning Commission and Tennessee Valley Authority.)

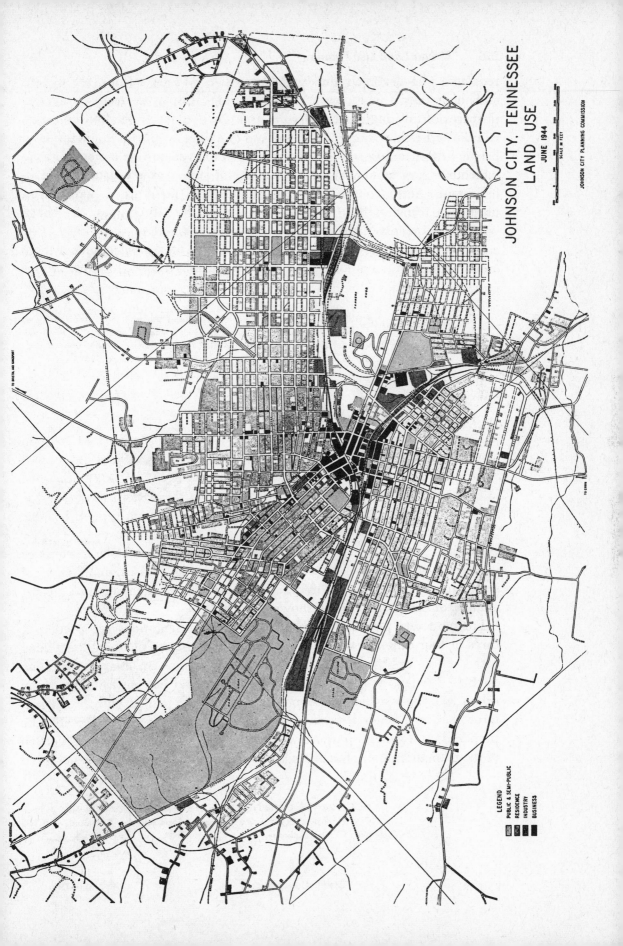

JOHNSON CITY, TENNESSEE
LAND USE
JUNE 1944

SCALE IN FEET

JOHNSON CITY PLANNING COMMISSION

LEGEND
PUBLIC & SEMI-PUBLIC
RESIDENCE
INDUSTRY
BUSINESS

land use presentation reduced to letter size will be needed for various technical reports where color overprints or transparent overlays are frequently used to single out particular areas or uses for orientation purposes.

The statistical summary of land use is typically prepared in terms of acreage devoted to each category of use employed in the survey, with an added category to summarize the acreage of land that is vacant or in non-urban use. Acreages are frequently summarized in terms of percentages, usually in terms of the developed portion of the city proper, the fringe areas, and the planning area as a whole as covered in the survey. Percentages based on *developed area* as opposed to *total area* provide a more meaningful form of summary for intercity comparisons or for comparisons

FIGURE 25.   Illustrative Presentation of Land Use with Use Categories Shown Separately, Johnson City, Tennessee, 1951. (*Source:* Johnson City Municipal-Regional Planning Commission, *A Guide to Community Growth: General Land Use Plan*, Tennessee State Planning Commission, September, 1952.)

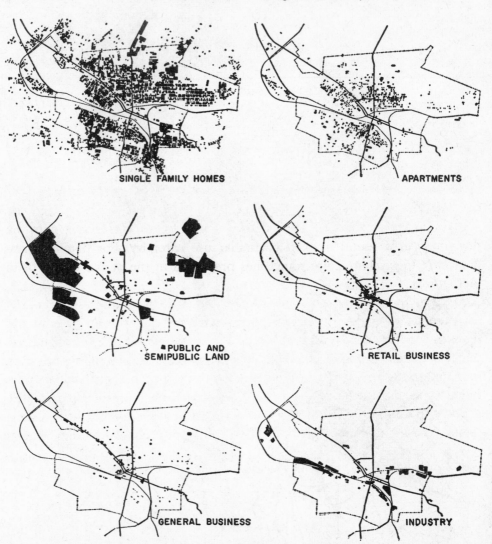

SINGLE FAMILY HOMES

APARTMENTS

PUBLIC AND
SEMIPUBLIC LAND

RETAIL BUSINESS

GENERAL BUSINESS

INDUSTRY

TABLE 18. Illustrative Summary of Land Uses, Augusta, Georgia, Planning Area, 1952[a]

Class of Use	Total Planning Area			Inside City Limits			Outside City Limits		
	Acres	Percent of Total Land	Percent of Developed Land	Acres	Percent of Total Land	Percent of Developed Land	Acres	Percent of Total Land	Percent of Developed Land
All residential	4,268.5	9.4	37.6	2,144.5	35.1	38.8	2,024.0	5.5	36.6
One-family	3,823.0	8.4	33.7	1,868.4	30.6	33.9	1,954.6	5.0	36.6
Two-family	251.3	0.6	2.2	183.3	3.0	3.3	67.5	0.2	1.2
Multifamily	194.2	0.4	1.7	92.3	1.5	1.6	101.9	0.3	1.8
Retail business	299.6	0.7	2.6	162.7	2.7	2.9	136.9	0.3	2.3
Wholesale and other[b]	441.8	1.0	3.9	185.0	3.0	3.4	256.8	0.7	4.4
Industrial[c]	814.8	1.8	7.2	257.1	4.2	4.8	557.7	1.4	9.6
Transportation and utilities	189.4	0.4	1.7	138.4	2.3	2.5	51.0	0.1	0.9
Streets and railroad rights-of-way	3,150.3	7.0	27.8	1,477.0	24.2	26.8	1,673.3	4.3	28.7
All public	1,568.6	3.5	13.9	846.3	13.9	15.3	722.3	1.8	12.4
Public	1,299.7	2.9	11.6	577.4	9.5	10.4	722.3	1.8	12.4
Military[d]	268.9	0.6	2.3	268.9	4.4	4.9	—	—	—
Institutional	597.7	1.3	5.3	300.8	4.9	5.5	296.9	0.8	5.1
Water areas	367.0	0.8	—	129.8	2.1	—	237.2	0.6	—
Vacant and nonurban	33,473.6	74.1	—	465.4	7.6	—	33,008.2	84.5	—
Total	45,171.3	100.0	100.0	6,107.0	100.0	100.0	39,064.3	100.0	100.0

[a] Adapted from Thomas H. Roberts, unpublished study, Department of City and Regional Planning, University of North Carolina, 1952.
[b] "Other" refers to a "general business," a classification used in the original study to denote uses falling between the retail and the industrial categories (includes, for example, building, plumbing, and heating suppliers, trucking terminals, amusement parks, race tracks, and other large space-using businesses).
[c] Includes extraction activities, e.g., clay extraction pits.
[d] Includes an arsenal and a military reservation (but not Camp Gordon).

between existing land use and proposed land use as set forth in a land development plan. Table 18 is a typical tabular summary of the land use survey. It tabulates acreages and the percent of the total area as well as the developed area found in each particular use category. For popular presentations, these figures are sometimes presented in pie or bar charts or in pictograms.

Acreage and percentage summaries of this order are prepared primarily as a quantitative description of land use, and are employed in land use planning analyses and in zoning studies in implementation of the land use plan. As indicated above, occasionally these percentage summaries are used to compare the urban center of interest with other centers of similar functional type and size, but since there are variations from one part of the country to another and even from one urban area to another in the same region, these comparisons have limited utility in technical studies.[9] Large

[9] For statistics on some 53 central cities, 33 satellite cities, and 11 urban areas, see Harland Bartholomew, *Land Uses in American Cities*, Harvard University Press, 1955.

variations in the way the limits of the study area are drawn, be it city limits lines, planning area, or some other defined study area, differences in topography, regional variations in residential living patterns, the differential impact of long-established planning controls which may be in effect, and many other factors introduce variations of varying magnitude. Even averaged percentage summaries for varying size cities have limited use, and certainly should not be considered as valid standards or yardsticks for land use planning, for average observed conditions in a selected number of cities will rarely measure up to positive land planning standards fitted to the needs of one particular urban center.

Although in small urban areas of approximately 100,000 or under, the generalized presentation prepared on a wall map can be used to measure land areas in various uses, Base C land use maps will yield greater accuracy and are generally the most satisfactory source for most planning studies. However, where a planning program is just getting under way and where plans are at a preliminary broad-stroke stage of development, statistical summaries drawn from a generalized land use presentation can serve a legitimate and useful interim purpose. In the more mature stages of the planning program, when preliminary planning studies are progressively refined and carried to greater detail, the more accurate measurements of land use will be required.

In the course of measuring land use acreages, it is desirable to tally measurements by the system of planning areas or districts developed for land use planning analyses (see Chapter 10). Thus planning district summaries are developed as subtotals to the summary for the urban area as a whole. The actual measurement procedures employ a simple mechanical technique. Two or more transparent overlays are used with each sheet of the land use presentation. One has all planning district and corporate limits lines drawn on it and is used as a master check sheet. Other transparencies are used to "collect" land uses, i.e., for each use category, lots and tracts are traced off and fitted together into a single puzzle-like pattern. As each lot or tract is traced, it is checked off on the master check sheet. When all areas have been taken off for each use, each planning district, and each incorporated area, the areas of the resulting saw-toothed polygons are measured with a planimeter. Averages of three measurements thus made are entered in the appropriate places in a tally work table. When all planimetering is completed and all use categories, including streets and vacant land or areas in nonurban use as separate categories, and all planning districts and separate incorporated areas are totaled, the result is checked with the area obtained by planimetering the urban area as a whole.

Keeping Land Use Data Up to Date

The work of assembling and summarizing land use data as described above represents a considerable expenditure of time and funds. It would therefore appear that every effort would be made to maintain this basic tool in up-to-date form so as to avoid a repetition of this operation in the immediate future. Yet because no systematic procedure has been developed for keeping account of changes, many planning agencies must repeat this whole operation more often than necessary.

Steps for keeping base maps up to date have already been mentioned. A simple extension of these procedures will insure up-to-date land use data, at least for all portions of the urban area included in the jurisdiction of the building codes and/or zoning ordinances in effect. As building inspections are completed or as occupancy permits are issued, the new or changed uses can be noted at the time the structure is plotted in the atlas of "correction prints," a new set of which is supplied annually to the building inspector's office. Of course, in cities not requiring occupancy permits or where this permit requirement is not enforced, some changes in use will go undetected. For example, this would be the case when changes occur from one permitted use category to another within a particular zoning district where no alterations in the structure are made. However, this type of change will normally not affect land use summaries because of the broad categories employed.

One difficulty arises where undetected violations occur, particularly in residential areas where alterations are made inside a structure to accommodate additional families—alterations which are not easily detected. Another problem relates to peripheral areas beyond the jurisdiction of building codes and zoning ordinances. As in the case of keeping base maps up to date, these outlying areas must usually be covered by special land use surveys at periodic intervals, usually once a year in portions of the urban area where there is indication of considerable building activity.

No matter what precautions are taken to keep a survey up to date, it is doubtful that a land use survey, however carefully carried out, can be depended upon for more than 10 years. Not only do changes occur which go undetected by procedures described above, but in this span of time the emergence of new analytical procedures can be expected to modify data requirements. For example, in recent time we have seen the beginnings of changes in the classification as to "light" and "heavy" industry which was developed according to the nuisance characteristics of the use, to a new classification system based on locational and space requirements of each type of industrial use. With the development of performance standards for industrial uses, more flexibility is permitted in the grouping of manufacturing activities and a much more positive approach is replacing the old negative emphasis in the classification of these uses. Similarly we may soon see a system of classes developing in business areas based on daytime population densities, where standards of maximum permitted densities or "congestion limits" become the basis for land use groupings. These and other developments in the technical requirements of this relatively new and changing field undoubtedly will make it necessary to make resurveys from time to time. Moreover, since long-range plans will be requiring major review and some revision from time to time, the timing of these resurveys will tend to fall into schedule with these periods of reassessment and restudy.

VACANT LAND STUDY

Were only a simple picture of the use and nonuse of land desired, the vacant land category in the land use survey would provide an adequate description and summary of vacant land. But since we are concerned with a basic description of the capabilities of vacant land for urban use and development, we must look at vacant and open land as something more than a residual category in the land use survey, something that is amenable to classification in some detail and the subject of special attention in land use planning.

The purpose of classifying vacant land is to determine its suitability for various forms of urban development: for industrial, residential, recreational, and other classes of land use. The vacant land study identifies the potentialities of vacant and open land for development, taking into account the physiographic features and the presence or absence of such man-made improvements to the land as streets and drainage facilities, accessibility to railroad and other transportation facilities, and the existence on or near the site of public water mains, a sewerage system, and other utilities. Whereas the vacant land study identifies these characteristics, land use planning studies as described in Part III finally determine the proposed future use of vacant areas.

As noted in the preceding section of the chapter, the total amount of vacant and open land is customarily obtained in the conventional land use survey. To obtain a more detailed classification of vacant land requires either an extension of the land use survey or a separate study. Either alternative has its problems. If vacant land is classified as part of the land use survey, such an approach cannot be entirely effective in taking into account the full range of land requirements necessary in land use planning studies, since the result of the land use survey itself is a necessary prerequisite to the formulation of these requirements. On the other hand, duplicating surveys of the urban area involved in a separate land use and a separate vacant land survey rarely can be justified.

To circumvent this dilemma, a simplified system of vacant land classification can be developed and integrated into the land use survey. This system appraises vacant land as to its general suitability for development. In the course of the vacant land analysis, it is subdivided into additional categories, and still later in the execution of land use planning analyses, it is generally extended and appropriate subdivisions made to apply to each particular use category.

Vacant Land Classification

The simplified vacant land classification system is based on two kinds of determinations: first, use capabilities from the standpoint of topography and drainage characteristics, and second, use capabilities from the standpoint of improvements available to the parcel or tract. As suggested above, later in the actual land use planning process other factors are taken into account, such as the availability of the property for development, the land value structure, cost-revenue considerations, and so on.

TOPOGRAPHIC CHARACTERISTICS

Terrain and drainage characteristics are usually determined partly from sources of information in the planning office and partly from field observations. Office sources consist of topographic maps and aerial photographs, and where these are available, they provide a suitable basis for estimating the terrain characteristics of the large open areas and rural fringe sections of the planning area. The field survey is generally confined to the classification of the scattered vacant lots and parcels interspersed in the built-up portions of the urban area. Although field surveys can be employed in the classification of all parts of the planning area (and this will be necessary where no topographic maps are available), usually they are used only to get at the characteristics of the relatively small parcels where topographic maps cannot be expected to give an entirely satisfactory or accurate assessment of prevailing conditions.

The typing of vacant land according to topographic characteristics proceeds from an initial tentative classification to successively more refined categories. In its initial and simplest version, this system of classifying vacant land contains two basic categories: prime and marginal land. Lots, tracts, or areas judged suitable for building use are classed as *prime* for urban development. Lots, tracts, or areas judged unsuitable for building without extensive preparation or modification of the terrain are defined as *marginal* land. Generally marginal land is too low (i.e., it is marshy or subject to flooding), or it is derelict land (e.g., abandoned quarries), or it is too steep to be suitable for building. Prime land is all other land. "Suitability for building" is generally a matter for local determination, since standards as to slopes that are considered economical to put into use will vary in different communities and in different parts of the country. For example, in San Francisco greater slopes are acceptable for building purposes than in middle western cities. Here the demand for land is sufficiently great and the supply sufficiently short so that greater slopes are considered economic to develop. In the Piedmont area of the South, where generally there is an ample supply of vacant or open land on level or rolling terrain located where reasonable time-distance standards are attainable once development occurs, slopes up to 15 percent are considered economical to develop.[10]

The mechanics of making this initial and preliminary evaluation of the topographic capabilities of vacant land are relatively simple. In the course of the land use survey, the scattered lots and small parcels within the built-up portion of the planning area are tentatively classified as to whether they are prime or marginal according to predetermined standards appropriate to the urban area under study. The actual notation used in plotting the land classification on field sheets will vary with the preferences of the city planner. The simplest procedure is to enter the tentative class designator on the outlined area so classified. To avoid confusion with other symbols used in the land use survey, this class designator can be circled. Thus when vacant land classification is undertaken in conjunction with the land use survey, Figure 22 and Technique A of Figure 23 would carry a circled vacant land designator in place of the X.

---

[10] The upper limit to the time people can be expected to spend in the journey to work and the extent and topography of open land areas defined by this travel radius will be key factors in establishing the slope limits for land going into urban development.

At the conclusion of the field survey and after the land use map has been prepared, this preliminary classification of vacant land can be extended to the large undeveloped tracts and open land in fringe areas of the city. This first presentation of land classification is made on an overlay tracing over the land use map. First, all vacant lots and parcels classified in the field are outlined and their appropriate classification noted from the field sheets, and then, by reference to topographic maps, the larger vacant tracts and the open land are classified. Of course, if topographic maps are not available, classification of these areas must be made in the field. Some special investigations may be necessary to establish the outlines of areas subject to periodic flooding. These facts can sometimes be obtained from local, state, or federal sources where some agency maintains official stream gauge stations. Where no such records are available, old newspaper files may carry some account useful in establishing high water marks. It may even be necessary to spot check the residents or management of businesses in certain areas to obtain first-hand accounts as to water levels during high-water periods. The end product of this initial land classification operation is a graphic representation of "buildable" and "unbuildable" areas, i.e., prime and marginal land.

For land use planning purposes, further refinement in the classification of topographic characteristics is needed. In the modern-day era of spread-out, single-story industrial plants, it is useful to introduce subclasses under the prime land category in order to identify areas with special terrain potentialities for industrial, wholesale, and related uses. Slope standards will vary to some extent from one locale to another, but within a relatively small range. For example, in the Piedmont area of the South, prime industrial land is usually limited to areas where the slope does not exceed 5 percent. In making refinements to the vacant land classification system to recognize these special topographic considerations, it is useful to introduce a tract-size criterion in conjunction with the slope differentiations that are made. Thus if the "prime" class of vacant land is to contain a special slope category for industrial and related uses, rather than opening this subcategory to every small parcel in the entire urban area, it is desirable to further refine this subclass by setting some lower limit to the size of vacant areas to be included. As brought out in Chapter 11, a tract of 5 acres or larger is a criterion sometimes used for cities, with one acre or larger being more appropriate for towns.

Once standards as to slope and tract size have been established, a refined classification system can be developed. In place of the simple two-class system, three classes can be substituted, let us say, *Class 1 Prime*, *Class 2 Prime*, and *Marginal*. Thus in the Piedmont cities of the South,

"Class 1 Prime" might be defined as all vacant areas 5 acres or more which have slopes of 5 percent or less, and "Class 2 Prime" might be defined as all other land from 0 to 15 percent slope. On the basis of the refined classification, a second overlay is developed to show the distribution of vacant land according to the new subclasses.

IMPROVEMENT CHARACTERISTICS

The final refinement of the classification system introduces further subclasses according to improvement characteristics. Thus *Class 1 Prime* land is subdivided into categories to denote whether railroad and major thoroughfare systems are in close proximity to the area and whether all the necessary utilities are available at the edge of the area. Varying degrees of combination are possible as suggested in the following list:

Subclass Designator	Improvements
1A	All improvements available.
1B	All improvements but water.
1C	All improvements but water and sewer.
1D	All improvements but water, sewer, and power.
1E	Only railroad and highway.
1F	Highway only.
1R	Raw land.

Obviously the list could be extended to include other combinations, e.g., railroad and water only, water and sewer only, and so on.

In the same way that Class 1 type of vacant land can be subclassified, *Class 2 Prime* can be detailed into subcategories of varying combination:

Subclass Designator	Improvements
2a	Platted and all improvements installed.
2b	Platted, all improvements except sewer.
2c	Platted, all improvements except sewer and water.
2d	Platted but no improvements.
2r	Raw land.

Here, too, combinations other than those listed are possible.

Obviously, a classification system which accommodates every possible combination can become unwieldy. To simplify the system and reduce the number of categories, combinations can be developed and graded to fit local needs. The footnotes of Table 19 present a simplified set of subcategories fitted to the particular needs of one small city, and generally typify the nature of the simplified vacant land classification system which evolves in the course of following the steps described above. A third and final overlay is prepared to show how vacant land is classified under this refined version of the classification system.

Presentation of Vacant Land Data

Somewhat like the land use presentation, vacant land data are generally presented in map form and in a tabular summary. The map is called a land capabilities map, and the patterns appearing on this map look somewhat like a photographic negative of the configuration of patterns appearing on the land use map. In effect, all areas in urban use are "punched out," and the resulting lacework pattern is the portion of the planning area of central interest in this presentation. A suitable color or black and white legend is developed to correspond to the various vacant land categories and subcategories and a vacant land map is prepared to show the distribution patterns of land with varying developmental capabilities.

The resulting presentation, while providing a reasonably complete picture of vacant areas, does not show, of course, areas which are *available* for urban use. Whether the property owners are willing to release their property for urban development, whether there is a clear title to the land, and whether property held in trust or restricted as to its future use by covenants running with the property, offer complications as to its use potentialities—these factors must be determined by supplementary investigations. While it would be possible to refine a "gross" vacant land presentation to a "net" presentation taking these factors into account, in practice these determinations are best left to the land use planning stage of analysis. By the time such analyses are completed and the vacant areas actually needed for urban expansion during the adopted planning period ahead are determined, there may be no immediate need to look into these matters for all portions of the area surveyed. Moreover, it is only when the whole range of considerations relating to urban expansion needs are before the city planner that he is able to reach a decision as to whether such availability factors are overriding or not. In some instances it is perfectly conceivable that "unavailable" property is of such vital importance to the sound growth and expansion of the urban center that the power of *eminent domain* would be invoked to obtain a piece of property and clear the title for the use indicated in the comprehensive plan. Obviously these determinations are made in the planning rather than the survey stages of a planning program.

TABLE 19.   Illustrative Summary and Classification of Vacant Land, Aiken, S.C., Planning Area, 1956[a]

Planning District	Class 1 Prime[b] (acres)				Class 2 Prime[c] (acres)				Marginal[d] (acres)	Total (acres)	Perc of T(
	A	B	C	Total	A	B	C	Total			
1	0.0	13.2	70.7	83.9	42.2	526.5	652.9	1,221.6	73.2	1,378.7	13
2	43.8	93.0	165.4	302.2	43.4	256.2	2,165.2	2,464.8	157.6	2,924.6	29
3	145.0	132.0	275.8	552.8	84.9	273.8	1,291.3	1,650.0	8.7	2,211.5	22
4A	3.1	7.2	90.5	100.8	63.2	66.2	253.4	382.8	0.0	483.6	4
4B	0.0	0.0	0.0	0.0	34.5	56.7	22.1	113.3	0.0	113.3	1
4C	0.0	294.9	49.5	344.4	0.0	484.5	2,025.9	2,510.4	0.0	2,854.8	28
CBD	0.0	0.0	0.0	0.0	8.5	1.0	0.0	9.5	0.0	9.5	0
Planning area total	191.9	540.3	651.9	1,384.1	276.7	1,664.9	6,410.8	8,352.4	239.5	9,976.0	100
Percent total	1.9	5.4	6.5	13.8	2.8	16.7	64.3	83.8	2.4	—	100

[a] Adapted from R. J. T. Longabaugh, A. N. Tuttle, Jr., and Shirley F. Weiss, an unpublished study, Department of City and Regional ning, University of North Carolina, 1956.

[b] *Class 1 Prime* is here defined as vacant land suitable for industrial or wholesale use, situated within 500 feet of a railroad or major thor fare, and in parcels not less than one acre, with a slope of 5 percent or under and well drained. *Subcategory A:* sewer and water line 500 feet; *Subcategory B:* water line within 500 feet; and *Subcategory C:* no sewer or water line within 500 feet.

[c] *Class 2 Prime* is here defined as vacant land suitable for residential or other nonindustrial or nonwholesale uses, with a slope of 15 p or less and well drained. *Subcategory A:* sewer and water line within 200 feet; *Subcategory B:* water line within 200 feet; and *Subcateg* no sewer or water line within 200 feet.

[d] *Marginal* is here defined as vacant land with slopes in excess of 15 percent, areas subject to flooding or marshy, and derelict land unsu or uneconomic to develop.

In addition to the map presentation of vacant areas, a tabular summary is prepared as a means of facilitating later land use planning studies of vacant land usable and vacant land required for each land use category in the foreseeable future. Table 19 typifies the tabular summary used in vacant land studies. In the same way that land use summaries are prepared in terms of planning districts and the one or more incorporated communities in the urban area, the vacant land tabulation is prepared with subtotals in order to recognize these functional and political units separately. The larger the urban area the more important is this type of summary.

STRUCTURAL AND ENVIRONMENTAL QUALITY SURVEY

As noted earlier in the chapter, urban growth is accommodated by physical renewal and expansion of the city. While expansion occurs primarily by the filling in of vacant land and by urban extension into open land, renewal is usually associated with the built-up sections of urban areas. In its broadest meaning, *urban renewal* is a form of recuperative change in the physical city by which the outworn or outmoded structures and facilities and, in time, whole areas are altered or replaced in response to pressures of economic and social change. In this sense, urban renewal is a process that has been going on as long as cities have existed and flourished. However, in the years since World War II, the term has assumed a more specialized meaning and has come to be associated with the prevention and elimination of blight. Thus "urban renewal" is now being used to refer to the planned regeneration of built-up areas through an integrated program of redevelopment, rehabilitation, and conservation.[11] We now speak of "urban renewal programs," and in this sense, urban renewal is a means of effectuating those portions of the land use plan that deal with blight prevention and elimination in built-up areas of the city.

The survey of structural and environmental quality provides the necessary information for identifying renewal areas, indicating the portions of the built-up area where there is freedom to modify the existing land use pattern. Its purpose is to identify various degrees of blight in the urban area, culminating in a generalized designation of *treatment areas*—areas for clearance and redevelopment, areas for rehabilitation, and areas for conservation.

Urban Blight and Treatment Areas

Urban blight implies deterioration or the existence of deficiencies in the quality of structures and their immediate environment. Implied also are a range of conditions which are measurable and can be defined downward or upward from a set series of "standards" which in turn are based on generally recognized criteria of health, safety, and other elements of the public interest. The standards employed and thus the range of conditions to be identified with each type of treatment area are matters of local de-

[11] Although the term "urban renewal" in some circles includes the replanning of predominantly open areas where improper land subdivision in the original instance has had a blighting effect, in the city planning field it is generally used to refer to replanning in predominantly built-up areas, with the term "reclamation" being used to refer to replanning in predominantly vacant areas. Adapting from the American Institute of Planners' definitions, all the terms we have been using can be summarized as follows:

Redevelopment is the revision or replacement of an existing land use and population distribution pattern through the acquisition of a predominantly built-up area, and the clearance and rebuilding of this area according to a comprehensive metropolitan-wide plan—a plan which reflects positive long-range land use and population policies.

Rehabilitation is the improvement or restoration of a predominantly built-up area which, though consistent with a comprehensive plan in terms of intensity of development and land use patterns, is in a stage of incipient blight. It may involve the reduction of population densities,

termination. Locally adopted standards relating to buildings, their design, occupancy, and sanitary facilities are generally specified in building, housing, fire, and sanitation codes; and environmental standards relating to the design of lots, blocks, and streets, population densities, and the type and intensity of development are included in subdivision regulations and the zoning ordinance. Where inadequate or no standards have been adopted, upgrading or setting of trial standards for survey purposes must be accomplished by reference to general standards (for example, minimum standards of health and safety for residential areas of the Hygiene of Housing Committee of the American Public Health Association[12]) or by reference to standards in force in communities of similar size and character which appear to be most consistent with local objectives.

Three types of treatment areas have been mentioned above. Clearance or redevelopment areas, the first type, are areas in which urban blight has advanced to such a degree that by local standards nothing short of clearance is physically, economically, and socially practicable. Present are what may be termed simple and complex forms of blight. *Simple forms of blight* include such physical characteristics as structural deterioration, missing sanitation facilities, structures in disrepair or lacking in elemental maintenance, presence of trash and rubbish accumulations in yards, adverse environmental influences such as noise, odors, dust, and so on, and missing community facilities such as schools, playgrounds, public water and sewerage systems, and adequate street and drainage facilities. Usually associated with simple forms of physical blight are certain social and economic indicators of blight. Social indicators of blight include presence of abnormally high rates of juvenile delinquency, venereal disease, and sim-

---

the acquisition and clearance of scattered deteriorated buildings, the repair, modernization, and provision of sanitary facilities, the provision of street, park, or other public improvements, or cleanup and maintenance work on the part of property owners.

Conservation is the preservation of predominantly built-up areas that are in "good" condition. These are the areas which are substantially in keeping with land use and population density requirements of a comprehensive plan but which require continuing systematic code enforcement, and may require public improvements to insure continued private investment therein.

Reclamation is (a) the reassembly and replanning of prematurely subdivided and relatively unsettled land which in many cases can never be put to proper use with proper population densities because of tax delinquency, clouded titles, or substandard subdivision design, and (b) the acquisition of land for public or institutional uses in areas so located or of such topographic characteristics as to be impractical, unsafe, or unhealthful for standard private development.

Urban extension is the acquisition and development (or the restriction of the use) of open unsubdivided land to provide for sound expansion of existing small urban centers or for the creation of completely new towns in the hinterland of existing metropolitan centers.

[12] Committee on the Hygiene of Housing, American Public Health Association, *Planning the Home for Occupancy* and *Planning the Neighborhood,* Public Administration Service, 1948; see also their pamphlet on *A Proposed Housing Ordinance,* American Public Health Association, 1952.

ilar results from other health and welfare indices; and economic indicators include concentrations of tax delinquent and tax title properties, declining property values, and presence of an abnormally large number of building vacancies. *Complex forms of blight* are said to exist when an area contains a mixture of incompatible land uses (the classic illustration being the glue factory located in the residential area), obsolete or impractical layout of lots, blocks, and streets, unsafe and unhealthful conditions existing or possible when marginal land is in use, particularly land subject to floods, marshiness, or tidal flows. In terms of local standards, simple forms of blight may be present to such a degree that these factors alone constitute a basis for designating an area for clearance and redevelopment. Even if simple forms of blight have not advanced to the degree where local standards would call for clearance, if complex forms of blight are present, clearance and redevelopment obviously offer the only ultimate rational type of treatment for the area.

The second type of treatment area is the rehabilitation area. This is an area where usually only simple forms of blight are present, and where the overall degree of blight, according to local standards, has not progressed to the stage where so-called "rehabilitation measures" will not restore the area to standard condition. Rehabilitation measures include such activities as spot condemnation of structures, enforced building repairs, or provision of missing sanitary facilities through code enforcement, a public improvements program for the provision of missing community facilities, and a campaign for voluntary cleanup, painting, and improved building maintenance standards.

Conservation areas, the third type of treatment area, make up the balance of the built-up portions of the city. They are areas in what might be termed "standard condition"—the areas to be protected from urban blight and to be maintained at least at their present standard of development. Strict and continuing enforcement of zoning and a minimum housing standards ordinance and vigilance as to the maintenance of community facilities and private property are key conservation measures.

While the foregoing distinctions are generally recognized in professional planning circles, other groups such as real estate and home building organizations use these terms in other connotations. For example, it is not uncommon to find rehabilitation and conservation being used interchangeably, nor to find a whole array of differing meanings in use from city to city or even in one locality. It is thus most important that these terms be carefully defined to avoid any unnecessary confusion and misunderstanding.

With this introduction to the characteristics of blight and how various gradations in quality are linked with various forms of treatment, it is appropriate now to consider briefly the types of surveys and their potentialities for land use planning analyses. It must be noted at the outset that for land use planning purposes, as desirable as it may be, it is not often feasible to undertake on a metropolitan-wide basis the more elaborate types of surveys of structural and environmental quality that have been developed in recent years. Nevertheless, it is important to be familiar with the alternatives so that should opportunity permit a more elaborate survey, this may be used in lieu of the less exacting alternatives. Not to be overlooked in this connection are the increasingly promising opportunities for undertaking more detailed types of structural and environmental quality surveys jointly with urban renewal and public health agencies. It should also be noted that, up to this time, research on measuring the quality of structures and their environment has been devoted almost exclusively to residential uses and areas. Of necessity, then, this review of appraisal techniques deals only very generally with that part of the survey that relates to business, commercial and industrial areas.[13]

APHA APPRAISAL TECHNIQUE

Perhaps the most precise and comprehensive type of survey for use in residential areas is the American Public Health Association's appraisal technique.[14] Including provisions for the appraisal of environmental as well as dwelling conditions, it employs a penalty scoring system applied item by item for various features in the structure and its surroundings that have been found to be diagnostic of urban blight. It can be used to measure both the extent of deviation from minimum standards and the detailed nature of housing conditions which adversely affect the health, safety, or the essential livability of dwelling units and their residential environment. The

[13] In this connection, it should be noted that some exploratory work in the appraisal of non-residential areas of cities was initiated in 1955 in St. Louis under a "demonstration grant" of the Housing and Home Finance Agency. The reader is alerted to follow this and other similar efforts that seek to furnish more satisfactory appraisal techniques in measuring the quality of business, commercial, and industrial areas.

[14] Committee on the Hygiene of Housing, *An Appraisal Method for Measuring the Quality of Housing: A Yardstick for Health Officers, Housing Officials and Planners,* Part I, "Nature and Uses of the Method," 1945, Part II, "Appraisal of Dwelling Conditions," 1946, Part III, "Appraisal of Neighborhood Environment," 1950, American Public Health Association.

technique was developed, tested, and refined to its present form over a
period of years by a group of public health specialists, city planners, sociologists, and others composing the membership of the Association's Committee on the Hygiene of Housing.

Under this technique, two separate appraisals are made: one of dwelling
conditions, and one of the quality of the environment. Dwelling appraisals

FIGURE 26. Illustrative Map Presenting Results from the Use of the APHA
Technique for Appraising the Quality of Housing, Philadelphia, 1949. (*Source:*
Philadelphia City Planning Commission, *Philadelphia Housing Quality Survey,*
1951.)

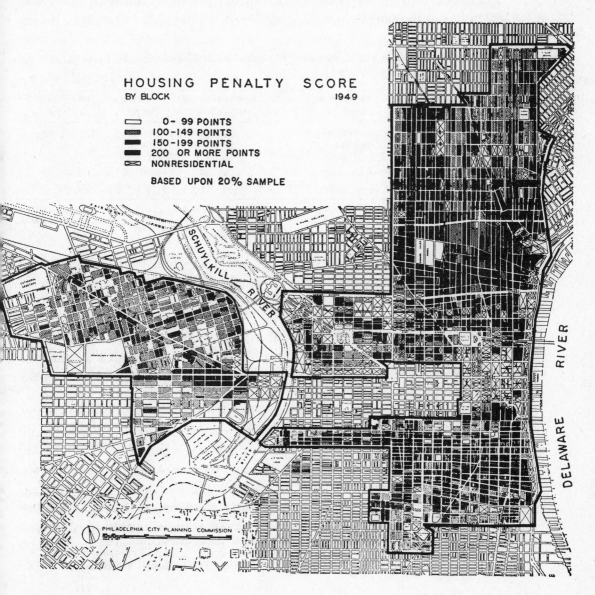

are made on an individual dwelling unit basis and include items on deterioration, maintenance and state of repair, safety and sanitation factors,
adequacy of heating and lighting, degree of room crowding, and so on.
The environmental quality schedule covers such items as land crowding
(defined in terms of coverage and adequacy of yard space), lineal feet
frontage of inimical land uses on the block, adequacy of water and sewerage
facilities in the block, adequacy of schools, recreation areas, and other
community facilities in the area, and the extent of hazards and nuisances
in the area from traffic, railroads, and industry. The scores obtained from
these two schedules can be combined to give a "housing score" as shown
in the illustrative results from the use of this technique in Figure 26. Table
20 indicates the range of quality possible in the use of the technique, show-

TABLE 20. Summary of Gradations in Housing Quality Under APHA Appraisal Technique[a]

Gradation of Quality	Environmental Score	Dwelling Score	Total Housing Score
A—Excellent to good	0–19	0– 29	0– 49
B—Acceptable	20–39	30– 59	50– 99
C—Questionable	40–59	60– 89	100–149
D—Substandard	60–79	90–119	150–199
E—Unfit for habitation	80 and over	120 and over	200 and over

[a] Committee on the Hygiene of Housing, *An Appraisal Method for Measuring the Quality of Housing: A Yardstick for Health Officers, Housing Officials and Planners*, American Public Health Association, 1945.

ing the corresponding range of penalty scores for each of the environmental
and dwelling schedules and for the combined total of both. Blocks with
Grade E scores generally fall into areas classed as clearance areas, and
those with Grade C tend to be classed as rehabilitation areas, with blocks
carrying a Grade D quality score being assigned to clearance or rehabilitation areas according to the nature of the items which have the highest
penalty ratings and the scores prevailing in the surrounding blocks. Blocks
with Grades A and B scores will usually be classed as conservation areas.

The APHA technique can be used for both a complete house-to-house
coverage of an urban area or a sampling survey of the area. Under federally
assisted urban renewal programs of slum clearance and area rehabilitation,
low-ratio sampling surveys have been used for screening purposes, i.e., for
identifying in generalized form the treatment areas. Such a survey is then
followed by a house-to-house or high-ratio sampling resurvey in the areas
tentatively identified in the screening survey as most in need of attention.
For land use planning purposes, the first screening survey is usually the
only coverage necessary. This survey may involve either the use of an

abbreviated schedule or the conduct of a low-ratio sampling study employing the full schedule.

CONTINUOUS REAL PROPERTY INVENTORY

In cities where a positive code enforcement program has become accepted practice and is adequately financed, there is an opportunity to develop and maintain records of structural and environmental quality on an up-to-date basis. Under a well-organized program of this type, a record is maintained on every structure and its environmental character. At periodic intervals each structure and its premises are reinspected. While such inspections cannot go into great detail since they are made primarily to ascertain the conformance of structures to code provisions, the very act of reinspection at regular intervals permits the keeping of records in the form of a continuous inventory. Obviously, such a source of information, especially if data are summarized on IBM cards, can readily be used in the identification of treatment areas for land use planning purposes.

CENSUS OF HOUSING AND LAND USE SURVEY SOURCES

Short of a continuous real property inventory, an APHA-type of special survey, or a study combined with some other inventory such as the land use survey, a property appraisal study for tax purposes, or one conducted in conjunction with a housing market analysis, the only remaining alternative for the evaluation of structural and environmental quality is the use of standard sources of data such as are available in the decennial Census of Housing and in the planning agency's own map and land use records. Such sources are crude substitutes for surveys especially designed for the measurement of structural and environmental quality, but they are by no means unsuitable for the identification of treatment areas in the generalized form required for land use planning purposes. Although they present a variety of mechanical problems as noted below, many and perhaps most planning agencies find it necessary to resort to these sources.

For those portions of the urban area in residential use, the conventional sources of information are the U.S. Census bulletins entitled *Census Tracts,* the bulletins entitled *Block Statistics,* and the Base C type of land use maps. Census data can be used in measuring simple forms of blight relative to structural condition and dwelling unit sanitary facilities. For each type of treatment area, the analyst can specify as a yardstick the

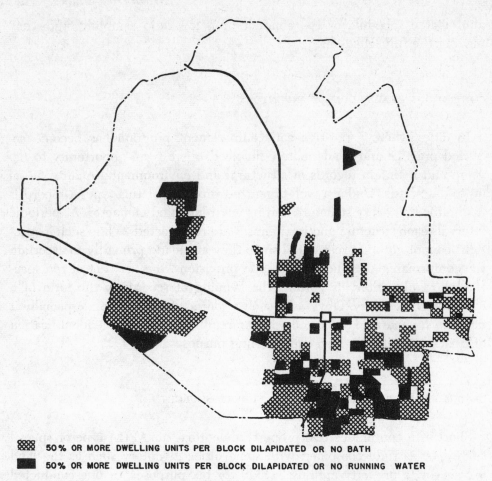

☒ 50% OR MORE DWELLING UNITS PER BLOCK DILAPIDATED OR NO BATH

■ 50% OR MORE DWELLING UNITS PER BLOCK DILAPIDATED OR NO RUNNING WATER

FIGURE 27. Illustrative Map Showing the Use of Census of Housing Data in Plotting Gradations in Housing Quality, Raleigh, N.C., 1950.

range of allowable proportion of dwelling units in residentially used portions of blocks which may have sanitary or structural deficiencies. Then by reference to these Census of Housing bulletins, each block or census tract can be classified and tentatively assigned to a particular treatment category. Figure 27 is suggestive of the way in which blocks can be studied by graphic plots of Census of Housing data prior to the classification of areas for renewal treatment.

In *Block Statistics* and *Census Tract* bulletins there are two combinations of data reported and available for use in analyzing small unit areas: dwelling units in dilapidated structures or *without running water,* or dwelling units in dilapidated structures *with running water but without private bath.* However, the form in which the data are thus combined in census summaries presents difficulties in establishing the exact kind of deficiency, particularly in the failure of these summaries to separate out units in dilapidated structures from those with various deficiencies in sanitary facilities.[15] Where the base year of the land use planning study falls in a postcensal year, there is also the problem of bringing census data up to date.[16] The unavailability of data in the form of *Block Statistics* in the unincorporated fringe areas presents still another problem.[17]

The other sources of information by which the quality of residential areas may be evaluated are Base C land use maps. Such sources provide data relative to certain complex forms of blight such as obsolete or impractical platting and street layout, mixed land uses, and high land coverage. Although presenting certain obvious complications as to measurement and evaluation, other sources of information sometimes used are changes in assessed property values, number of tax delinquencies, proximity to uses considered to have adverse effects on residential property, and so on.

Here again, by reference to locally adopted standards, a range of deficiencies can be established for each selected criterion of environmental quality. Thus if residential densities are used as a criterion, by reference to zoning ordinance standards, ranges in the proportion of lots in a block below standard can be established to correspond with each type of treatment area.[18] Or if mixture of uses is selected as a criterion, ranges in the proportion of lineal feet frontage of inimical uses in a block for each type of treatment area can be established and used as a basis for classifying blocks, and so on. After both structural and environmental criteria have been thus applied, a crude composite scoring system is sometimes devised to assist in the final delineation of treatment areas. To make for greater consistency in this task, weights are sometimes assigned each of the selected

[15] In the "dilapidated or no running water" category, a crude way of isolating the number of dwelling units in dilapidated structures from those reported to be without running water is sometimes possible by reference to plots of dwelling units connected to the public water distribution system at the time of the census. Such plots are commonly maintained in the city hall in connection with the enforcement of housing and sanitary regulations. By reference to this information, it is possible to estimate the probable number of dwelling units recorded in this dual category which are dilapidated only, at least in all areas where dwelling units are known to be connected to the water system.

[16] Crude adjustments can sometimes be made on the basis of city hall records of changes brought about by code enforcement activities. This source of information plus observations during the land use survey on structure removals can be used in making adjustments for dwelling units brought up to standard or eliminated. In this connection, there is no way, short of a field survey, for determining the number of dwelling units changing in status from standard to substandard categories since the census date.

[17] In some cities census tracts extend into unincorporated fringe areas within one or more counties. In such cases for those items of the Census of Housing reported by tracts (except for persons per room ratio, the form of summary parallels that employed in *Block Statistics*), a reasonably satisfactory approximation of the distribution of substandard dwelling units can be made on the basis of field checks as to locations of areas of dilapidated-appearing structures.

[18] Where zoning ordinances do not carry density provisions, it will be necessary to devise trial standards by reference to lot size standards in subdivision regulations or by reference to general standards adapted to the local situation.

criteria to assist in making the final allocation of blocks into one of the three treatment categories. Unless exhaustive statistical tests are made, the analyst should avoid imputing any special accuracy to such a "scoring system," if, indeed, it can be dignified by such a term in the first place. Though it is far too subjective and crude to be construed as a valid scoring system, it can assist in systemizing the application of judgment in the course of designating areas for possible clearance, rehabilitation, and conservation.

Factors of blight in business, wholesale, and industrial areas, which have not been given the attention in research and study that housing areas have received, are more difficult to identify and evaluate. Land use maps provide one source of information, particularly as to platting and street layout. Tax records will indicate tax delinquencies and changes in assessed valuations. Special field checks of vacancies and general structural conditions also provide a crude basis for classifying these areas for various forms of treatment.

When all use areas in the built-up portion of the urban center have been classified into treatment areas according to locally adopted standards of structural and environmental quality, a map showing the generalized patterns of these treatment areas is prepared. This is the *map of urban renewal areas.* In those portions of the urban area identified for clearance and redevelopment, there is a full measure of freedom for modifying the land use pattern. While in areas earmarked for rehabilitation only minor changes in land use are generally possible, there is some flexibility for modifying the intensity of development through the spot elimination of substandard structures.

The presentation of urban renewal areas by the foregoing procedures is based on the extent that urban blight is present in the respective treatment areas. Subsequent analyses in Part III of location and space requirements may indicate additional areas where land use patterns need revision. Although for practical reasons it is highly unlikely that large areas of this kind could be altered in use and intensity of development, it is possible that certain clearance and redevelopment areas may be enlarged because of considerations other than urban blight.

For land use planning purposes, the foregoing kind of analysis yields a summary of acreages expected to become available for reuse through clearance operations during the planning period. By following procedures similar to those employed in establishing the use potentialities of vacant land, it is possible to apply to renewal land a classification system such as that presented in Table 19. The final result of following this procedure is a summary of the supply of renewal land by planning districts tabulated according to topographic characteristics and the level of improvements available at the site. Obviously the designation of certain areas for clearance and redevelopment will involve in later analyses acreage deductions for various land use categories in the tabular summary of existing land uses such as that shown in Table 18. Similarly in subsequent land use planning analyses, it will involve deductions in the inventory of dwelling units available during the planning period.

COST-REVENUE STUDIES

The kinds of urban land studies covered so far have been largely concerned with the development of a basic description of the physical characteristics of land in the urban area as a step in tooling up for land use planning. But along with these characteristics of urban land, the decisions finally reached in the land use planning process must take into account the public costs of supplying community facilities and services to land as these compare with tax revenues received. While it is beyond the scope of this summary treatment of the subject to go into basic and the very complex questions of tax structure and public finance, available techniques for determining cost-revenue relationships for different uses of land under prevailing policies and levels of service will be briefly reviewed.

Related, but in many respects distinct from land value studies (which are concerned with the economic worth of land and its improvements on the open land market), cost-revenue studies aim to provide information on the governmental costs of supplying public improvements and services to urban land as these costs relate to the revenue available to finance such improvements and services. For purposes of land use planning, these studies are concerned most directly with cost-revenue comparisons for various uses of land at varying locations and at varying densities and intensities of development. Thus a primary element that must be taken into consideration in reaching land use planning decisions is how much it will cost to provide public improvements and services at particular locations in relation to revenues that can be anticipated at these locations. But density and intensity of development are related to location. Thus for residential development, it is important to investigate differentials in cost-revenue relationships in fringe areas where scattered settlement patterns tend to occur as opposed to those of the more concentrated development found in closer-in locations. It is also important to know what the differential effects on these cost-revenue relationships will be when development occurs in these locations at low, medium, and high densities. By the same token, in industrial, commercial, and retail business areas, it is important to know how these relationships will differ in developments ranging from an intensive to an extensive use of the land.

However inadequate methods of analysis have been in the past, cost-revenue studies have long been employed in various special-purpose investigations. For example, they have been undertaken to estimate the magnitude of the financial drain that blighted areas and slums represent to a city, to evaluate the financial implications to the central city of "the flight to the suburbs," and to set forth the fiscal considerations of annexation for the annexing city and for the area being annexed. Only in the years since World War II have the applications of these studies to land use planning begun to receive serious recognition, and since 1950 an increasing number of cost-revenue studies have been initiated.[19]

The earliest studies have had a strong influence on methods in use in the past 20 years.[20] But in the years since World War II, deficiencies in the methods of computing costs and revenues have been noted.[21] While a great deal more research is needed in perfecting methods of conducting cost-revenue surveys, some valuable guidelines for these surveys are beginning to emerge. In the following pages, these are summarized as taken from the work of George H. Esser.[22]

Methods of Analysis

The methodological problems in estimating the allocation of costs of public improvements and services to specific use areas are more complex than those involved in estimating revenues. Indeed, much more research is needed before available methods will be entirely satisfactory for direct application in land use planning studies. For example, most work in this

[19] For an exhaustive and critical review of studies undertaken up to 1955, see Ruth L. Mace, *Fiscal Aspects of Land Use Planning*, an unpublished study, Department of City and Regional Planning, University of North Carolina, 1956.
[20] These include such studies as R. B. Navin, *An Analysis of a Slum Area in Cleveland*, Cleveland Metropolitan Housing Authority, 1934; and *The Income and Cost Survey*, Boston City Planning Board, 1935.
[21] See Ralph M. Barnes and George M. Raymond, "The Fiscal Approach to Land Use Planning," *Journal of the American Institute of Planners*, Spring-Summer, 1955.
[22] George H. Esser, *Urban Growth and Municipal Services: Uses and Methods of Cost-Revenue Analysis*, Institute of Government, University of North Carolina, to be completed in 1957.

field has been concerned with cost allocation for residential areas,[23] and fully satisfactory methods for the study of industrial, wholesale, and business uses have yet to be developed. Of necessity, then, the approaches discussed here deal primarily with cost-revenue analysis for residential uses.

Early work and most of the more recent studies which attempt to allocate costs for public improvements and services to residential uses have relied heavily on approximation techniques in making measurements of the cost incidence, without checking what it actually costs to provide improvements and services to a given area. Moreover, they have made allocations generally on the basis of assessed valuations, with some variations (for example, costs of road construction and maintenance have been assigned to residential uses in terms of the lineal feet of improvements or services involved). The faulty assumption implied here is that assessed valuation is a reliable measure of services consumed. While frankly recognized in most studies as a means of getting around the complexities of making actual measurements of cost, the very use of such approximation approaches has obscured two factors which are considered crucial to obtaining reliable results.

The first such factor relates to the base which is to be used in cost allocations: the need for an approach which recognizes that some costs are more properly chargeable to the *community as a whole* while other costs can be traced more directly to *properties* alone. A concrete illustration based on a widely accepted public policy in street improvement work will serve to point up the reasoning behind the differentiation being made here. When a street is under consideration for paving, its financing is usually accomplished in one of two ways. If the street is a major traffic artery which is used by all the people of the community, the cost of paving is generally made chargeable to the entire community, i.e., out of general funds. On the other hand, the cost of paving a local street which is used primarily by the residents of a particular area is usually financed by property assessments charged against abutting property owners who directly benefit by the improvement. One is a cost that is chargeable to people of the community as a whole, and the other is a cost chargeable to property. Following the same general reasoning, cost-revenue analysis should differentiate between (1) costs which are essentially property-related and (2) costs which involve improvements and services for the people of the community as a whole.[24] Examples of costs considered to be chargeable to people in the

[23] For example, see the very valuable work of William L. C. Wheaton and Morton J. Schussheim, *The Cost of Municipal Services in Residential Areas*, Housing and Home Finance Agency and U.S. Department of Commerce, 1955.

[24] It is interesting to note that the division of functions among the metropolitan government of Toronto and its several constituent municipalities roughly corresponds to the distinction being made here for purposes of cost-revenue analysis. In general, the metropolitan govern-

TABLE 21. Cost Measurement of Residential Area Activities, Greensboro, N.C., 1956[a]

Basic Operational Activity	Self-Supporting	Activity Performed by	Unit of Activity	Unit of Cost[b]	Method of Finance	Unit of Time	Unit of Incidence	Residential Portion	Unit o[f] Reside[ntial] Co[st]
Police patrolling[c]	—	City	Patrol car beat	$51,264	Operating	Annual	15,000 people	50%	$25,63
Detective	—	City	Per patrol car beat	8,635	Operating	Annual	15,000 people	50%	4,31
Fire fighting									
Station	—	Purchase	Pumper company	72,182	Bond	30 years	10,000 people	75%	54,13
Engine	—	Purchase	"	20,623	Capital	10 years	10,000 people	75%	15,46
Equipment	—	Purchase	"	34,339	Capital	10 years	10,000 people	75%	25,75
Company	—	City	"	48,802	Operating	Annual	10,000 people	75%	36,60
Fire alarm									
Boxes	—	City	Box	155	Capital	30 years	—	100%	15
Circuit	—	City	Wire-mile	150	Capital	30 years	—	100%	15
Fire prevention	—	Company personnel	—	—	—	—	—	—	—
Traffic signing									
Initial	—	City	Sign	12	Capital	4 years	—	100%	1
Replacement	—	City	Sign	5	Operating	4 years	—	100%	
Street paving	Assessment (partial)	Contract	Street-mile	22,295	Revolving	15 years	—	100%	22,29
Paved street maintenance									
Resurfacing	—	Contract	Street-mile	10,388	Revolving	15 years	—	100%	10,38
Other	—	City	Street-mile	398	Operating	Annual	—	100%	39
Sidewalk construction	Assessment	—	—	—	—	—	—	—	—
Street signing	—	City	Sign	18	Capital	10 years	—	100%	1
Garbage collection	—	City	Collection route	11,139	Operating	Annual	750 houses	100%	11,13
Machine cleaning	—	City	Street-mile	61	Operating	Annual	—	100%	6
Building inspection	Fee	—	—	—	—	—	—	—	—
Street lighting	—	Contract	Lamp	22	Operating	Annual	—	100%	2
Water and sewer construction	Assessment and rates	—	—	—	—	—	—	—	—
Water	Rates	—	—	—	—	—	—	—	—
Sewer	Rates	—	—	—	—	—	—	—	—

[a] David L. McCallum, *A Case Study of the Cost of Governmental Activities in Single-Family Residential Areas of Different Density*, unpublish[ed] manuscript, Department of City and Regional Planning, University of North Carolina, 1956.
[b] Includes apportioned cost of supplementary activities.
[c] Local records not maintained on a basis to permit use of more precise measurement units.

urban area as a whole are schools, libraries, recreation, health and welfare services, traffic regulation, major streets, and so on. Examples of costs considered to be incident to particular parcels of land are residential street, water, and sewerage systems, some aspects of police protection, fire protection, and so on.

ment assumes responsibility for functions that serve the people of the urban area as a whole, and the several municipalities assume responsibility for property-related functions. A similar distinction is made in both the Miami and Pittsburgh metropolitan government proposals.

It is recognized, of course, that the classification of these improvement and service costs into one or the other category is not always a clear-cut choice and that there is a gray area between the black and the white where choices will tend to be somewhat arbitrary. Yet if no attempt is made to differentiate between these two classes of cost, the effect is to conceal actual costs incurred by the municipality in the development of new property. Thus in place of residential areas being "a net liability" in cost-revenue comparisons as is commonly concluded when a single base for cost allocation is used, under the more realistic two-class system of cost allocation, all but unsoundly developed property, particularly slums, will generally show up as paying their fair share of property-related costs. However, as will be seen in the illustrative material below, there can be a wide variation in the extent to which land development at various densities is contributing to the costs for improvements and services for the community as a whole.

The second conceptual consideration is the necessity of recognizing that different parts of the urban area will require different levels of service. For example, the central, intensively developed sections of the city usually require higher levels of fire protection than the suburban fringe areas. Within the central area, business uses may require more frequent garbage collection than residential areas. Thus levels of service may vary with the density of population, the use of the land, the powers and functions of the governmental unit having jurisdiction in the area and their policies, and so on. Moreover, since these conditions and policies vary with urban area, cost experience in one area may have little transfer value in another.

Turning now to cost allocation procedures, we refer to a pilot study made by Esser and McCallum in Greensboro, North Carolina.[25] This study aimed to develop and apply a methodology of measuring the incidence of improvement and service costs to residential property. It made detailed investigations of the operations and service areas of various municipal agencies under the prevailing quality and intensity of service permitted under existing financial policies of the city. Table 21 presents a summary of these cost measurements.[26] Next, these cost data were applied to a land area at the fringe of the city considered prime for residential development. Designs were developed for this area at alternative residential densities, with development into lots of 6, 9, 18, and 36,000 square feet. Table 22 is a summary of annual and amortized capital costs of public facilities and services for future periods of time, and indicates how costs vary according to density.

[25] David L. McCallum, *A Case Study of the Cost of Governmental Activities in Single-Family Residential Areas of Different Densisty,* unpublished manuscript, Department of City and Regional Planning, University of North Carolina, 1956.

[26] For a detailed discussion of the derivation of cost data, see *ibid.*

TABLE 22. Annual and Amortized Capital Costs for an Illustrative Fringe Area Residential Development Designed to Varying Densities, Greensboro, N.C., 1956[a]

	Minimum Lot Size (in square feet)							
	6,000		9,000		18,000		36,000	
Annual and Amortized Periodic Costs	Subdivision Total	Average per House[b]	Subdivision Total	Average per House[b]	Subdivision Total	Average per House[b]	Subdivision Total	Average per House[b]
Annual Costs								
Police patrolling	$ 5,991	$ 6.41	$ 4,544	$ 6.41	$ 2,288	$ 6.41	$ 1,314	$ 6.41
Detective	1,009	1.08	765	1.08	385	1.08	221	1.08
Pumper company	12,833	13.73	9,732	13.73	4,901	13.73	2,815	13.73
Other paved street maintenance	2,974	3.18	2,872	4.05	2,114	5.92	1,691	8.25
Garbage collection	13,887	14.85	10,530	14.85	5,302	14.85	3,045	14.85
Machine cleaning	456	.49	440	.62	324	.91	259	1.26
Street lighting	1,607	1.72	1,430	2.02	902	2.53	660	3.22
Total	38,757	41.45	30,313	42.75	16,216	45.42	10,005	48.80
General activities[c]	3,004	3.21	2,349	3.31	1,257	3.52	775	3.78
Total annual costs	41,761	44.66	32,662	46.06	17,473	48.94	10,780	52.59
Amortized Capital Costs, Years 1–4								
Fire station	$ 633	$ 0.68	$ 480	$ 0.68	$ 242	$ 0.68	$ 139	$ 0.68
Fire engine	542	.58	411	.58	207	.58	119	.58
Fire equipment	903	.97	685	.97	345	.97	198	.97
Fire alarm boxes	62	.07	52	.07	41	.11	47	.23
Fire alarm circuit	15	.02	15	.02	14	.04	11	.05
Street signing—initial	117	.13	96	.14	66	.18	30	.15
Street paving	11,105	11.88	10,727	15.13	7,895	22.11	6,316	30.81
Street signing	97	.10	88	.12	49	.14	36	.18
Total	13,474	14.41	12,554	17.70	8,859	24.81	6,806	33.63

General activities	1,044	1.12	973	1.37	680	1.92	554	2.00
Interest on bonds	184	.20	140	.20	70	.20	40	.20
Total, years 1–4	14,702	15.72	13,667	19.27	9,615	26.93	7,470	36.43
Total, annual and amortized capital costs, years 1–4	$56,463	$60.39	$46,329	$65.34	$27,089	$75.88	$18,251	$89.02
Amortized Capital Costs, Years 5–15								
Less traffic signing—initial	$ −117	$−0.13	$ −96	$−0.14	$−66	$−0.18	$ −30	$−0.15
Less general activities[c]	− 9	− .01	− 7	− .01	− 5	− .01	− 2	− .01
Plus traffic signing—replacement	+ 49	+ .05	+40	+ .06	+28	+ .08	+13	+ .06
Plus general activities[c]	+ 4	+ .00	+ 3	+ .00	+ 2	+ .01	+ 1	+ .00
Net change, years 5–15	− 73	− .08	−60	− .08	−41	− .11	−18	− .09
Total, years 5–15	14,629	15.64	13,607	19.19	9,575	26.82	7,453	36.35
Total, annual and amortized capital costs, years 5–15	$56,390	$60.31	$46,269	$65.26	$27,048	$75.76	$18,233	$88.93
Amortized Capital Costs, Years 16—								
Less street paving	$−11,105	$−11.88	$−10,727	$−15.13	$−7,895	$−22.11	$−6,316	$−30.81
Less general activities[c]	− 861	− .92	− 831	− 1.17	− 612	− 1.71	− 489	− 2.39
Plus resurfacing	+ 5,174	+ 5.53	+ 4,998	+ 7.05	+3,679	+10.31	+2,943	+14.36
Plus general activities[c]	+ 401	+ .43	+ 387	+ .55	+ 285	+ .80	+ 228	+ 1.11
Net change, years 16—	− 6,391	− 6.83	− 6,173	− 8.71	−4,543	−12.73	−3,634	−17.73
Total, years 16—	8,238	8.81	7,434	10.48	5,032	14.09	3,819	18.62
Total, annual and amortized capital costs, years 16—	$49,999	$53.47	$40,096	$56.55	$22,505	$63.03	$14,599	$71.20

[a] David L. McCallum, *A Case Study of the Cost of Governmental Activities in Single-Family Residential Areas of Different Density*, unpublished manuscript, Department of City and Regional Planning, University of North Carolina, 1956.
[b] Discrepancies in adding columns caused by rounding numbers.
[c] A 7.75 percent factor used as a measure for apportioning costs of general activities.

Revenue estimates from these residential developments include property taxes (developed on the basis of building trends and actual tax assessments derived from a representative sample of residential properties in the ranges indicated) and the probable income from gasoline, beer and wine, intangible, and franchise taxes. The final cost-revenue comparisons derived from this analysis are presented in Table 23. From this table it is seen that under prevailing local service levels and financial policies for the provision of improvements and services in this city, residential areas developed to sound standards at any one of the listed densities would return their fair share of property-related costs. The figures appearing opposite the "difference" item in the stub of Table 23 indicate how much a house and lot at the quoted price ranges at different densities will be contributing toward the costs of community-wide improvements and services. Particularly noteworthy is the relatively small difference in this figure in similarly priced developments with 6000 and 9000 square-foot lots, suggesting that from a cost-revenue standpoint, this city might adopt 9000

TABLE 23. Cost-Revenue Comparisons for an Illustrative Fringe Area Residential Development Designed to Varying Densities, Greensboro, N.C., 1956[a]
(Costs expressed in dollars per dwelling unit per year)

	Lot Size and Price Range						
	6000 sq ft	9000 sq ft		18,000 sq ft		36,000 sq ft	
	$7000–9000	$7000–7500	$11,000–12,000	$12,500–13,500	$20,000–21,000	$19,000–20,000	$40,000–41,000
1956–1961							
Revenue[b]	$69.01	$67.19	$ 93.10	$104.51	$164.75	$155.67	$278.69
Annual operating costs	45.08	46.47	46.47	49.48	49.48	53.12	53.12
Amortized capital costs	15.46	19.01	19.01	26.67	26.67	36.17	36.17
Total costs	60.54	65.48	65.48	76.15	76.15	89.29	89.29
Difference	8.47	1.71	27.62	28.36	88.60	65.38	189.40
1961–1971							
Revenue[b]	79.03	77.20	103.11	114.52	174.75	165.68	288.71
Annual operating costs	45.08	46.47	46.47	49.48	49.48	53.12	53.12
Amortized capital costs	15.39	18.92	18.92	26.55	26.55	36.08	36.08
Total costs	60.47	65.39	65.39	76.03	76.03	89.20	89.20
Difference	18.56	11.81	37.72	38.49	98.72	76.48	199.51
1971——							
Revenue[b]	79.03	77.20	103.11	114.52	174.75	165.68	288.71
Annual operating costs	45.08	46.47	46.47	49.48	49.48	53.12	53.12
Amortized capital costs	8.55	10.22	10.22	13.83	13.83	18.35	18.35
Total costs	53.63	56.69	56.69	63.31	63.31	71.47	71.47
Difference	25.40	20.51	46.42	51.21	111.44	94.21	217.24

[a] David L. McCallum, *A Case Study of the Cost of Governmental Activities in Single-Family Residential Areas of Different Density*, unpublished manuscript, Department of City and Regional Planning, University of North Carolina, 1956.
[b] From 1956 to 1959, it is estimated that revenue from property taxes would range from 89 percent of the total revenue for the 6000 square foot property to 93 percent for the higher valued 36,000 square foot property. From 1961 on, it is estimated that revenue from property taxes would range from 76 percent to 90 percent, respectively, of the total revenue.

square feet as a minimum lot size without making an appreciable difference in net cost.

Applications to Land Use Planning

The above-described pilot study is indicative of the kinds of tests it is possible to make in developing a land use plan. By applying such tests to all areas proposed for residential development and redevelopment, it is possible to estimate the impact of future development on a municipality's fiscal structure. Ultimately, when similar detailed cost measurement methods are available for cost-revenue comparisons of business, wholesale, and industrial areas, it should be possible to assess the net cost implications of providing improvements and services as set forth in the entire land development plan.

At the same time, it is well to recognize that the "break-even" point in municipal finance involves considerations which are outside the scope of land use planning and the tests we have been discussing. While land use planning can and should give proper consideration to optimum cost-revenue relationships in the land use patterns proposed in a land development plan, more fundamental readjustments may be called for in the basic tax structure of the urban area and in the governmental arrangements for tax administration. Thus there is a need for caution to avoid distorting land development standards, where remedial action is more properly obtained in the tax field. Studies which seek to establish a break-even point, concluding that homes costing less than a certain amount will upset this break-even point, should be used cautiously unless keyed in with a basic reexamination of the tax structure.

Where remedial action gets into questions of tax structure, these lead to problems of tax relationships among the various governmental jurisdictions to be found in metropolitan areas. While solutions to these problems are not within the scope of land use planning, they have implications for the way in which cost-revenue studies are approached. Obviously cost-revenue tests will encounter variations in service policies among these various jurisdictions. Suburban municipalities can be expected to pursue policies of quite a different order than those being followed by the central city, and among suburban communities there may be some range of variation. These policies may be in conflict with one another, and they may well continue thus until metropolitan government becomes a reality. The task of testing land use planning proposals for cost-revenue relationships under these circumstances is difficult enough for the central city planner, but the task for suburban city planners is even more difficult. In the face of these problems, the soundest approach would seem to be the pooling of effort on the part of the various planning agencies in the metropolitan area in the development of one urban-wide land use plan that is sound in every other respect, and then jointly to test such a plan for its cost-revenue implications under alternative combinations of service policies. The very act of focusing attention on different combinations of consistent and inconsistent cost-revenue relationships may hasten the time when financial policies are developed on a metropolitan-wide basis.

LAND VALUE STUDIES

As brought out in Chapter 1, the structure of land values in the urban area has a very considerable influence on the way in which individuals seek to use land for various purposes, in various locations, and at various densities. While traditionally the city planner has been preoccupied with social objectives—what we have referred to as public interest considerations—he cannot proceed far in his land use planning studies without taking into account value-use relationships of urban land. He encounters too many forcible illustrations of these relationships in his day-to-day work not to be aware of their implications. The repeated approaches to planning commissions for the rezoning of corner lots for filling stations and the continual requests of all kinds for rezoning properties from one category to a "lower" category are manifestations of urban land market forces.

Land use planning proposals and the subsequent implementing decisions reached in the system of use districts and permitted densities and intensities of development adopted in a zoning ordinance seek a balance between the economic and "social" use of land. Of necessity, then, a very vital part of the tooling-up process for land use planning is an investigation of the structure of land values. It indicates whether various proposed locations for particular uses or groups of uses are feasible in terms of land costs, whether individuals, firms, or developers are likely to take up the land in the use and intensity of development that may be proposed from a public interest point of view.

Since it is the very nature of the real estate market that land and building values are constantly changing, it is never possible to obtain a precise picture of the pattern of values. The task of appraising the value of property is an extremely complex and time-consuming kind of study. By the time a study is completed, in the course of the survey itself, some of the details have undergone change. Fortunately the needs of land use planning are such that changes in detail have little direct consequence. It is the broad pattern of values, their general gradations upward or downward, and their trends of change which have most direct application to the work of the city planner for the generalized level of detail with which he is working in his land use planning analyses.

Land values are normally computed in urban areas on a front-foot basis and on an acreage or area basis in fringe areas and in open country. In calculating the value of a particular urban lot or tract, applied to the front-foot unit values are adjustment factors to take into account varying lot or tract depths and corner influences. Valuations of structures and other improvements are estimated separately by reference to rates of depreciation applied to original costs, to depreciated replacement costs, or by other means.

Valuation data are presented in map form to show the geographic patterns of values. Land and building values may be presented separately or in the form of a combined property value map. For the study of vacant and open land, the pattern of land values alone are needed; for the study of renewal areas and other built-up areas where the public acquisition of land and buildings may be involved, the combined form of property value map is generally needed.

In general, market value appraisals, even on a sampling basis, provide the most accurate source of information for constructing land value maps. Where no recent comprehensive study of property values has been undertaken or where no funds are available to finance such a study, assessed values as prepared by the city and county tax offices are frequently used as a substitute source of information. These values usually bear only very approximate relationships to true market values, and such relationships may vary from one part of the city to another. According to local assessment practices, assessed values are usually pegged under the estimated "true" value by some established percentage relationship. Figure 28 illustrates a land value map based on assessed valuations. Various critical areas on such maps can be crudely spot-checked by reference to known sales prices in land or property transactions at dates corresponding to those of the tax information. These investigations serve to evaluate in a rough way the extent to which assessed valuations deviate from market values for land and properties in different locations. Rough indications of trends in land values in different parts of the urban area may be noted by reference to an historical series of land value maps, i.e., graphic presentations of the pat-

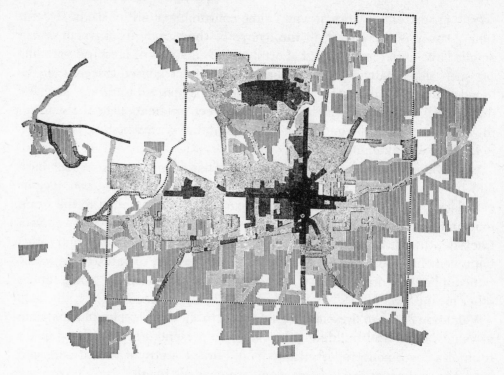

FIGURE 28. Illustrative Map of Assessed Land Values, 1948, Greensboro, N.C. The highest front-foot values are shown in black, with the wide vertical hatch being the lowest and the blank areas being either tax-free or assessed on an acreage basis. The expected decrease of values outward from the CBD is graphically illustrated by the fingerlike extensions of high-value land following the main radials. The large pocket of high-value land north of the CBD is the country club rseidential district, and the scattered small pockets are shopping centers or industrial tracts. (*Source:* Greensboro, N.C., Department of Planning, "Land Use Plan, Greensboro Metropolitan Area," 1948.)

terns of values such as that shown in Figure 28 for past intervals of time. However, to insure comparability, adjustments must often be made to correct for changes in relationships between assessed and market values, and in the change in the value of the dollar during the periods under observation.

STUDIES OF AESTHETIC FEATURES OF THE URBAN AREA

Along with the more utilitarian features of urban land, land use planning is also concerned with the perceptual aspects of the urban environment, its aesthetic qualities, and the preservation and development of natural features in a manner calculated to enhance these qualities for the enjoyment of city residents. Seemingly this aspect of land use and development would require no special emphasis, for aesthetics has long been linked with the basic objectives of city planning—indeed, as we have seen, the very origins of city planning and its early development possessed a strong aesthetic orientation. Yet as the field has developed and matured and as the kinds of tasks city planners are called upon to undertake have multiplied, taking them into engineering, economic, and social science investigations of all kinds, the aesthetic aspects of land development have sometimes been slighted as "old shoe" or "frilly." Fortunately, this point of view appears to be only a transient phase in the maturing of the profession, and since World War II, urban aesthetics has assumed a far more important role in the total approach to urban development.

Perhaps more responsible for the lull in this aspect of land use planning is the inherently fugitive character of norms as they apply to aesthetics and the difficulties of defining and ordering aesthetic factors into anything approaching an analytical framework. However, some recent research into the perceptual qualities of cities is beginning to point the way toward a more systematic approach to the creative use of aesthetic features in land use planning, one that is developing more on a reasoned and less on an intuitive basis. Kevin Lynch has observed that urban areas possess distinct and recordable qualities that affect an individual's perceptual satisfactions from the urban environment.[27] In addition to the generally recognized factor of size, he suggests that density, grain, the outline or shape, and the internal pattern of cities are all dimensions of the urban area that can be observed. These affect the pleasantness of city living, the subconscious or conscious awareness, the positive and negative response that people experience in following the daily path to and from work, in making shopping trips, or in taking an occasional outing. The placement of key functional areas and buildings, the location of circulation routes, and the siting of residential and other areas in relation to each and every other feature, and how they relate to the sun, prevailing winds, and existing vistas—all of these considerations are elements of aesthetics which enter into the land use planning task.

Sydney H. Williams has developed a method for studying the aesthetic characteristics of cities consisting of what he terms a "visual survey."[28] This survey consists of two parts: one which identifies three-dimensional characteristics of the city's site and the man-made features which have been added to the site, and a second which records significant paths and vantage points from which the city can be visually perceived. For purposes

---

[27] Kevin Lynch, "The Form of Cities," *Scientific American*, April, 1954.
[28] Sydney H. Williams, "Urban Aesthetics," *The Town Planning Review*, July, 1954.

of the first part of the survey, he has developed a classification of city sites into six basic ground forms:

1. Level, or gently sloping or rolling sites.
2. Sloping sites, backed by hills or steeper slopes.
3. Valley, or gorge sites.
4. Amphitheatrical, or fan-shaped sites.
5. Bowl-shaped sites.
6. Ridged, or hilltop sites.

Williams then classifies man-made features into the following five forms:

1. Urban textures.
2. Green areas.
3. Circulation facilities.
4. Paved open spaces.
5. Individually significant architectural masses, including vertical, slablike, massive, and horizontal forms.

For purposes of the second part of the survey, he has developed five ways in which the city may be perceived: the panorama, the skyline, the vista, the urban open space, and through the experience of the individual in motion.[29]

On the basis of this system for studying the perceptual aspects of the city, the observer may actually conduct a "visual survey" in the field and record the features about the city that are important to take into account in both land use planning and the more detailed later stages of site planning. Important ground forms can be sketched or noted directly on a map by reference to topographic maps and aerial photographs and by field observation. Man-made features particularly important to preserve and visually accentuate in subsequent planning studies can be outlined or spotted, and significant skyline views, vistas, and open space systems to be utilized and enhanced in future development can be similarly noted and supplemented by sketches. A sketchbook and photo album record of the important features observed in the field would provide a valuable additional means for summarizing data collected in the field.

ATTITUDE STUDIES AND LAND USE

One final form of investigation warrants consideration in this list of tooling-up studies. This is an attitude or public opinion study which seeks

[29] The reader is referred to the illustrative sketches that Williams has prepared to portray the distinctions in these several ways of perceiving the city. *Ibid.*

to get at expectations and preferences of people in a particular urban area as to the way the city should develop. By "feel" city planners have long felt that certain forms of civic design, certain kinds of patterns of land use and transportation appeal to urban dwellers more than others, that these patterns elicit a higher degree of satisfaction and result in a fuller city life and more stable forms of group behavior. Yet little effort has been directed toward determining through available social science research techniques what conscious or unconscious attitudes of livability can be identified among groups and the unorganized citizenry in general and whether city planners' concepts of livability, in fact, match up with prevailing citizen attitudes.

There is a wide variety of questions affecting land use planning decisions which should be included in an attitude study—questions which may evoke differing responses from one community to another, and questions which have not yet or may never reach a stage of public recognition or acceptance such that general consensus is deemed to prevail. These involve such questions as the separation versus the intermixing of ethnic and income groups in the residential areas of a city, or the intermixing or separation of "high-rise" and single-family dwelling types; attitudes concerning individual yards around the dwelling versus community property as found in large-scale housing developments; and so on.

Although public opinion survey techniques have reached an advanced stage of development, city planning agencies have yet to make use of them as a tooling-up kind of survey of the same level of importance as the other kinds of urban land studies we have covered in this chapter. Some early exploratory work of the Princeton Bureau of Urban Research[30] and the recent Detroit surveys of the University of Michigan[31] and Wayne University[32] indicate the potentialities of sampling surveys for providing answers to these kinds of questions on an objective basis. However, while the survey research techniques have been developed to an advanced degree, much work remains to be done in perfecting the mechanics of interviewing in order to get at the latent as well as the more articulated notions of livability that people may hold.[33] Until the results of this kind of research become available and can be tested, however, we can expect only limited use of attitude surveys.

[30] Bureau of Urban Research, *Urban Planning and Public Opinion, A Pilot Study,* Princeton University, February, 1942.

[31] See annual and special Detroit area reports of the Survey Research Center, University of Michigan.

[32] Arthur Kornhauser, *Detroit as the People See It,* Wayne University Press, 1952.

[33] With Robert L. Wilson, the author has an exploratory study under way on this general problem entitled *Livability in the City: Attitudes and Urban Development,* an Institute for Research in Social Science project, University of North Carolina.

CHAPTER 9

transportation and land use

The types of studies covered in the four preceding chapters can be termed tooling-up studies in the sense that they are *prerequisite* analyses to the land use planning study. Studies of the movement of people and goods in the urban area, whether by automobile, or other means of transit, involve investigations that are more properly regarded as *paralleling* analyses. That is to say, the land use plan cannot be developed independent of transportation plans any more than transportation planning can proceed independently of land use planning. It is self-evident that business districts, industrial areas, and residential sections of the city simply cannot serve their functions unless there is easy movement of people and goods to and from or between these areas. By the same token, thoroughfares with their related parking facilities and the urban transit and transport systems make little sense unless they are planned in conjunction with the pattern of land uses they are intended to serve.

It is beyond the scope of this book to go into a description of theory, methods, and practice of transportation planning. However, apropos of the foregoing observations, it is appropriate to sketch in some of the fundamentals of thoroughfare planning as they shed light on the elemental relationships that exist between land use and traffic.

TRAFFIC AND LAND USE RELATIONSHIPS

Traffic pertains to the movement of vehicles which transport persons and goods for various purposes to various places. The overall direction and magnitude of movement is established by a *traffic volume survey*. The purposes of movement and the places encompassed in these movements are obtained through an *origin and destination survey*. Volume measurements are obtained by traffic counts, procured by persons or by mechanical devices recording traffic at selected stations throughout the thoroughfare network. The O & D survey obtains information on intra- and intercity movements, and the most reliable data are obtained by home interviews (usually organized on a sampling basis), supplemented by information procured by stopping a sample of the vehicles passing through the "cordon line," a line drawn around the urban interview area. Special information on commercial movements is obtained from truck and taxicab operators. Results of the traffic volume survey provide a measure of the total movement over the system of streets surveyed, showing the actual *travel lines* of all traffic in the aggregate. Although surveys permit summaries of movements by 15-minute intervals, results are usually mapped for the peak hour or a 24-hour period. The O & D survey results can be used to establish for various trip purposes, for similar time intervals, *desire lines*, i.e., what the travel lines would be if straight-line routes were provided between various origins and destinations. The results also show the mode of transportation and the relative importance of these desire lines at different times of the day for each mode.

While these surveys provide a description of the extent and nature of person- and goods-movements, they do not explain directly the factors that produce these movements. These explanations are bound up in the land use arrangements of the city and the nature of activities carried on in various functional use areas. Like the land use planner, the transportation planner is interested in future needs. He must estimate the future traffic characteristics of an urban area so that he may develop solutions for the future movement of people and goods. While there are a number of variables involved such as automobile ownership rates, transit usage factors, time-distance considerations, income levels, and residential densities of the city under study, there are nevertheless definable relationships between land use and traffic.

In their work of identifying and classifying the nature of traffic movements in relation to land use, Mitchell and Rapkin suggest that not only does land use provide explanations of traffic, but much about the urban pattern of development is explainable by the movement requirements of establishments within major use areas. "Specialization of urban activities makes it necessary for establishments and their members to communicate with each other, and consequently there is a pervasive tendency for establishments to make accessibility a major locational consideration. The

258   *Urban Land Use Planning*

pattern of land uses is thus a large dependent system in which choice of location of an establishment is made in terms of spatial distribution of others with which it interacts. For some this means access to the largest number of persons, firms, or households—a central location; for others it means convenience in regard to an inexpensive channel of goods-movement; and in still other cases it means actual proximity."[1]

Some recent studies have gone a step further and developed empirically some relationships between traffic and land use, some suggesting general formulas for the estimation of traffic-generating potentials of various functional use areas. Based on the analysis of a number of O & D surveys, one of these studies has developed a series of curves for estimating the residential termini of city-generated traffic of the CBD.[2] The study measured the extent that these movements vary with time-distance and compactness of development and how they vary with city size and the population-vehicle ownership ratio. Another study suggests that the trip generation of business areas involves a factor of competition which can be measured in terms of Reilly's "law of retail gravitation" (see reference to Reilly in Chapter 5).[3] Another study has organized the findings from these studies into a procedure for predicting peak-hour traffic patterns—what the reorientation of traffic movements might be by the creation of a new shopping center or the construction of a new highway facility such as an expressway.[4] These studies represent exploratory investigations of traffic-land use relationships and suggest ways of approximating the traffic changes that might be expected by introducing changes in the existing land use pattern.

The problem of estimating future traffic ten and twenty years ahead is far more difficult and involves careful analysis of the behavior of each major variable in each particular urban area separately. It is probable that certain "universals" in the behavior of these variables can be definitively established in the future, and under specified conditions, used for estimating purposes in any locale. But until rigorous tests can be made, the safest course of action would appear to be one of studying the behavior of these variables and estimating their effects in each particular urban area.

In the most comprehensive long-range study of this kind ever undertaken, J. Douglas Carroll, Jr., has formulated the traffic-land use relation-

[1] Robert B. Mitchell and Chester Rapkin, *Urban Traffic, A Function of Land Use,* Columbia University Press, 1954, p. 132.
[2] F. Houston Wynn, "Intra-City Traffic Movements," *Factors Influencing Travel Patterns,* Bulletin 119, Highway Research Board, 1955.
[3] Alan M. Voorhees, Gordon B. Sharpe, and J. T. Stegmaier, *Shopping Habits and Travel Patterns,* Special Report 11-B, Highway Research Board, 1955.
[4] Alan M. Voorhees, "A General Theory of Traffic Movement," *Proceedings of the Annual Meetings of the Institute of Traffic Engineers,* 1955.

ships in the Detroit metropolitan area, and applying them in conjunction with 1980 estimates of land use and population distribution of the Detroit Metropolitan Area Regional Planning Commission, has developed a long-range traffic forecast for this area.[5] Since this study provides a prototype for traffic-land use analyses for predictive purposes, it is useful to summarize the general procedure that was followed:

> First, the effect of certain variables [cars per dwelling place, distance from city center, income index, and net residential density] on the number of trips which members of a dwelling unit make on an average day is studied. From this analysis, it becomes clear that the number of trips made by residents of the Study Area can be reliably predicted if such factors as car ownership and distance from the city center, for example, are known. Such a prediction provides an overall control or reference figure. Next the relationship between trip generation and land use is explored. Using trip purpose as the key for determining how many trips go to each land use type, trip volumes are deduced for each major category of land activity at given distance ranges from the city center. It is shown that zone by zone [for purposes of small area analysis, the Study Area was subdivided into 254 zones], the trip termini by land use can be accurately measured and, from these measurements, reliably predicted. Finally, it is shown that, knowing the total trips in the system, and the trip termini in each zone, it is possible to predict the traffic movements between zones.[6]

PRINCIPLES OF THOROUGHFARE PLANNING

The above observations on traffic and land use suggest some of the basic principles of thoroughfare planning. In general, most of these principles derive from some of the same elements of the public interest which are so fundamental to land use planning, namely, public safety, convenience, economy, and amenity, with public health being involved to a less extent. In very general terms, principles specify that the trafficways plan must:

1. Derive from a thorough knowledge of travel that is taking place today, its component parts, and the factors that contribute to it, limit it, and modify it.
2. Conform to and encourage the land development planned for the area.
3. Serve the future traffic demand.

[5] Detroit Metropolitan Area Traffic Study, *Report on the Detroit Metropolitan Area Traffic Study*, Part I, "Data Summary and Interpretation," July, 1955.
[6] *Ibid.*, p. 77.

4. While being consistent with the above principles and realistic in terms of travel trends, be economically feasible.[7]

Expressed more concretely, the San Francisco Department of City Planning has made the following principles an integral and basic part of their Trafficways Plan:[8]

1. The system of trafficways should consist of two principal functional types:
   a. Radial routes, linking the downtown metropolitan district of the city with the outlying working and residential areas and other important traffic generators and with the gateways leading into and out of the city; and
   b. Circumferential or crosstown routes, intersecting the radial routes, linking the various community areas of the city, collecting and distributing radial traffic, and by-passing through traffic around areas of highest traffic concentration in and near the downtown metropolitan district of the city.

2. The system of trafficways should be so designed that the several types of facilities composing it—freeways, major thoroughfares, and secondary thoroughfares—are located between or skirting, rather than cutting through, residential communities and neighborhoods. In order to keep residential neighborhoods free from extraneous through-traffic movements, the trafficways should be spaced an average minimum distance of one-half mile apart, except in areas of highest population density where traffic volumes require closer spacings.

3. The system of trafficways should be coördinated with the trafficways system of adjoining cities and counties and with the system of state highways. Sections of state highways within the city should be so located and designed that they will be in harmony with all aspects of the comprehensive Master Plan of San Francisco.

4. The system of trafficways should be designed to accommodate public transit vehicles, where appropriate, without interference with traffic flow on through-traffic lanes.

5. Opposing flows of traffic on thoroughfares in the trafficways system should be separated wherever possible by a central dividing or median strip. In areas where streets are narrow and widening is not feasible, this principle may be met by application of one-way street controls on parallel streets.

6. The number of intersection conflict points on the trafficways system should be decreased by means of grade separations, channelization, and appropriate restrictions on turning movements. All remaining intersections should be provided with such traffic signals or stop signs as may be necessary for safe and efficient vehicular operation.

[7] *Ibid.*, p. 13.
[8] San Francisco Department of City Planning, *Transportation Section of the Master Plan of the City and County of San Francisco*, May, 1955, mimeo., p. 1.

7. Lane widths for moving traffic and for parked vehicles on trafficways should conform wherever possible to widths necessary to obtain maximum traffic capacity per lane, as expressed by established standards.

8. All thoroughfares in the trafficways system should be adequately provided with clearly visible directional signs, name signs, and route signs, and with traffic warning and control signs and signals sufficient to prevent hazardous driver delays or uncertainties.

9. Wherever physical conditions permit, major thoroughfares should be given expressway treatment, limiting direct access from abutting property to through-traffic lanes. In such cases where considerable access to adjoining property is necessary, independent service roadways, parallel to but separated from the through-traffic lanes, should be provided.

10. Wherever appropriate and physical conditions permit, major thoroughfares and secondary thoroughfares should be given parkway treatment, providing landscaped strips along either or both sides, and stopping places at outlook points or other points of interest or scenic attraction.

Pursuant to such statements of principles, guiding standards for the design and layout of the thoroughfare plan are generally developed.

CLASSIFICATION OF MOVEMENTS AND TRAFFICWAYS

As suggested in the above illustrative statement of principles, thoroughfare planning analysis is predicated on the clear recognition of certain elemental traffic movements. As would be expected, the classification of movements derives from the land use areas served. Thus, in the movement of people, there are home-to-work, home-to-shopping, home-to-recreation, and other land use-related movements. In the movement of goods, there are delivery or assembling movements from retail to residential areas, from wholesale to retail areas, from industrial to commercial areas, and so on. The thoroughfare counterparts to these major systems of movement are classified variously. As noted above, San Francisco identifies two major *functional classes* of trafficways—the *radial* and the *circumferential* (sometimes called a crosstown or loop). A third functional class of thoroughfare sometimes distinguished from these two primary classes is the *connector*, which, as its name implies, serves as a connection between two or more major radial or circumferential systems of movement or between major focal points of traffic.

Another system of classification in general usage specifies the *design classes* of streets. According to the size of the urban area and local preferences, it may consist of upward of three classes. The National Committee on Urban Transportation has suggested four classes: the expressway system, the major arterial system, the secondary arterial system, and the local street system.[9] As illustrated in the above San Francisco classification system, only the first three classes of systems are used in the trafficways plan.

The expressway system generally includes freeways, all parkways with full control of access, and those expressways where there is at least partial control, e.g., where there are limitations of intersections at grade, prohibition of private driveway connections, and so on. The major arterial system consists of all major streets and those expressways and parkways with lower-order controls over access. The secondary street system consists of the connectors between the local street system and the higher-order systems and feeder streets which pick up and distribute traffic within residential neighborhoods and communities. Not generally included in the thoroughfare network is the residual class, the local street system which is designed primarily to provide access to adjacent land uses.

COÖRDINATED LAND USE AND THOROUGHFARE PLANNING

This "thumbnail sketch" of selected elements of thoroughfare planning would not be complete without reference to the interrelatedness of thoroughfare studies and parking, which is essentially the terminal facility for traffic movements, or of trafficways and transit planning as complementing facilities for moving people in urban areas. All have their place in the total transportation study. Many land use planning decisions are contingent upon the analyses undertaken in these studies just as decisions reached in planning for these facilities will be contingent on land use planning analyses.

Of all the transportation studies, the thoroughfare study is perhaps the most pivotal to land use planning. The same observation can be made vice versa. Consequently each can and should be organized to relate to the other. By proper timing of the work of each, both should proceed con-

[9] National Committee on Urban Transportation, *Better Transportation in Your City—How to Get the Basic Facts on Urban Needs and Services,* review draft of manual in preparation for publication, February, 1956.

currently from preliminary generalized stages of study through the later more detailed plan-formulation stages. Occasionally pressures develop which force work ahead on the thoroughfare plan without coördinate provision for work on the land use plan. While the basic traffic surveys can be and usually are carried out independently of land use studies, analyses of the results of these surveys, particularly analyses which are concerned with traffic forecasts, cannot proceed validly without related work on the urban land use plan. Thus if no official arrangements have been made for the land use planning task by the time this forecast stage is reached, either informal provision for land use planning must be made within the transportation planning program or the work will have to be suspended. The same may be said of a situation in reverse, i.e., the situation where land use plan studies are scheduled without concurrent provision for thoroughfare studies.

PART III

land

use

planning

WE COME NOW to the land use planning process itself. It is a process which looks to the basic theoretical orientations set forth in Part I for its conceptual guidelines. Drawing on the information developed from the kinds of studies set forth in Part II, it seeks to fashion a balanced and integrated set of proposals for the future use of land in the urban area which are generally consistent with theoretical precepts and yet workable in every practical sense of the meaning.

It is useful at the outset to consider broadly the relationship of urban planning to public policies, particularly developmental policies. As suggested in the Introduction and as is evident throughout Parts I and II, city planning is viewed as a process —a series of evolutionary and rationally organized steps which lead to proposals for guided urban growth and development. Various meanings have been ascribed to "developmental policies" or, more specifically, "urban land use policies." Some view these policies as something akin to a statement of general principles for planning, and they are thus formulated before plans are developed. Others consider them to be embodied in the plans themselves, and when a plan is officially adopted, the proposals contained in the plan become official urban land use policies. Still a third usage considers them to be statements of the directions in which the urban area should move in order to achieve the objectives of, and implement the proposals contained in, a plan. For example, in this sense policies might take the form of general specifications for zoning, urban renewal, and so on. In the usage of the term here there are present elements of all these meanings.

Urban land use policies *are considered here to be a series of guides to consistent and rational public and private decisions in the use and development of urban land. They are maxims to guide land development decisions in principle. They give direction to the urban planning process, but they also become conditioned by the findings and proposals developed from the planning process. We may conceive of the formulation of policies as proceeding from the general to the particular, with each level of policy making supplying the foundation for subsequent more detailed policy determinations. But within the planning process the preparation of a specific plan proposal for the coördinated development of urban land is in many respects contingent upon a variety of prior policy decisions. Thus in a very fundamental sense the planning process must play an important role in supplying policy alternatives and pressing for decisions from the earliest and broadest level of policy formulation on down to the more detailed levels of policy determination. This aspect of the planning function can therefore be considered one of supplying alternatives at progressively more detailed levels of decision making, with each successive stage in policy formulation building on previously made choices of a more general character.*

To illustrate, the hierarchy of policy decisions might follow roughly in this order. Perhaps the highest order of policy decision could be viewed as a choice between urban development stabilized at a certain level (measured in terms of economic development, employment, population, land area in development, and so on) and urban development proceeding on an indeterminant and noncontainment basis. Conceivably there could be gradation of several choices here rather than these two extremes. In any case, involved in this illustrative choice are

268

a variety of social, economic, and public interest considerations relating to public finance, health, safety, convenience, and the general amenities of urban living. A decision on the first alternative— containment of urban development at a particular level—would involve in the planning implementation of the decision an emphasis on balance within the limits of a known size of ultimate growth. A decision on the noncontainment alternative would involve an incremental approach to the development of land, transportation, and community facilities, one which accommodates the needs of growth as and when they occur, but still according to a plan.

A second level of policy decision might relate to the basic orientations in the way land development and transportation systems are to be accommodated. Although there are gradations here too, this decision might be posed as a choice between concentrated expansion concentric to existing patterns of development and dispersed expansion to a polynucleated array of outlying centers. In its purest form the first land development alternative involves the presumption of a single major center with functionally related suburban outlets of business and radial developments of industry and commerce generally concentrated along existing or proposed railroads and highways. The indicated transportation system is essentially the conventional web pattern consisting of major radial arteries and transit routes fed by auxiliary crosstown, feeder, and local service systems. In the purest form of the second alternative, though the downtown area of the central city would continue as the dominant center for certain metropolitan-wide functions, it is supplemented by functionally differentiated or somewhat independent centers of business and industry, each providing a

269

*substantial proportion of the employment and serv-
ices for its own surrounding localized area. Here
we are dealing with high-order freeway and rapid
transit systems providing interconnections between
centers, with a series of lower-order web systems of
circulation emanating from each major terminus of
the higher-order systems.*[1]

*Following from the above succession of decisions
are many other related policy considerations. For
example, a third-order series of policy decisions
might relate to homogeneity versus heterogeneity
of development among functional use types and
among various activities within each use type. They
might involve questions of intensity of development,
what might be referred to as "open-order versus
closed-ranks" development patterns. Along with intensity would be questions of density of use: high,
medium, or low residential densities and high, medium, or low daytime population densities, and so
on. These decisions again bring into play social, economic, and public interest considerations, the decision seeking to strike a balance in such factors as
cost-revenue implications for local finance, health,
safety, convenience, and the desired level of amenities to urban living.*

*The above illustration is indicative of the kind of
hierarchy of considerations involved in policy-
formulation, with policies at each level feeding into
the planning process and the findings of the planning process subsequently feeding back into policy
decisions. Now obviously many public policy de-*

[1] John T. Howard's description of these alternate policies as applied to the Washington, D.C., metropolitan area provides an excel-
lent detailed illustration of the planning implications involved in this
level of decision-making. See John T. Howard, "A Planner's Philosophy for the National Capital Region," an address delivered before
the American Civic and Planning Association and reprinted in the
Congressional Record, February 21, 1956, pp. A1602–A1604.

cisions affecting urban development emerge with-out following such an idealized sequence, indeed, probably in very few American communities have urban development policy and planning developed in any way approaching such a sequence. But while the full sequence may not be achieved, it is impor-tant to note that policy decisions generally do tend to evolve from the general to the particular. In this connection it should also be noted that where de-cisions are made out of sequence, the point of entry into the hierarchy automatically tends to force de-cisions of a higher order without the opportunity for deliberate consideration of the broader or more ele-mental choices involved in these higher-order deci-sions. It might be noted, too, that there is a dynamic aspect to the foregoing more or less static rendition of the relationships between policy and planning. Just as we think of planning as a continuing process, we must also view policy formulation as a continu-ous activity. That is, policies may be reconsidered and modified from time to time under changing cir-cumstances. Entire new ones, some being the ob-verse of policies previously in effect, may be adopted, setting in motion a whole new cycle of policy and planning.

The so-called progressive planning approach *is a system of planning analysis which provides a logical counterpart to this conceptual approach to policy-making.*[2] *Now fairly widely accepted as a basis for planning analyses, this approach can be summarized in the following six-point sequence:*

1. Develop a first estimate of existing conditions and significant trends in the urban area. *In scope this es-*

[2] First perfected in test demonstration studies by the National Re-sources Planning Board at the beginning of World War II, the "pro-gressive planning approach" was later set down in *Action for Cities*, Public Administration Service, 1945.

timate encompasses the full range of planning studies; as to detail, it is abbreviated and general, to be progressively rounded out as the program proceeds.

2. Determine the principal and most pressing problems and needs, briefly evaluate them, and develop an interim program. *This stage involves the development of a generalized sketch plan intended to serve as a starting point for later phases of the program. As current problems and needs come more fully into perspective and the longer range aspects of the program get under way, the interim sketch plan is progressively refined.*

3. Formulate a detailed program indicating priorities for undertaking component studies of comprehensive plan. *This is the step which determines the end product and the time schedule to be followed.*

4. Carry out detailed plan studies according to program and priority. *This phase is essentially one of progressive refinement of studies initiated earlier on an abbreviated basis and presented in generalized form.*

5. Integrate various plan studies into comprehensive plan. *This is the stage in which the individual plan proposals are synthesized and inconsistencies and conflicts are eliminated.*

6. Revise plans as conditions alter their applicability. *This will be a continuing activity of observing trends, revising studies and adjusting plans.*

Following what might be regarded as a circular *rather than a* straight-line *sequence, this approach gears directly into the cycle-like sequence described above by which policies become formulated and adopted. As policy decisions are reached of a broad and general nature, planning solutions can be developed in generalized form. As these solutions are reviewed and decisions are reached of a more detailed order, the planning process picks up from there to carry the solution to a more detailed stage.*

272

Thus both policies and plans are progressively refined to the point where an acceptable plan proposal emerges. But as conditions alter the applicability of earlier findings and proposals, policies and plans are reviewed and often modified. This explains the emphasis in the field on planning *rather than on* plans.

The approach set forth in the foregoing paragraphs supplies a conceptual framework for the analytical procedures of land use planning taken up below. It is thus clear that the city planner utilizes techniques of analysis that are variable in their detail, the level of detail being fitted to the stage that has been reached by the city council and planning commission in the formulation of public policy. While the city planner is not barred from proceeding immediately to the most detailed level of land use planning, by moving too far ahead of policy decisions he runs the risk of assuming policy choices which never materialize, thus removing his proposals from the realities of political action and eventual fulfillment.

In the following pages the analytical procedures are organized and presented primarily in terms of the most generalized approach, with supplemental material supplied at various stages of the analysis to indicate the nature of some of the more detailed types of studies that might be undertaken in refinement of the initial generalized land use planning study. This approach has been selected because research simply has not yet supplied the detailed and reliable analytical techniques needed for refined studies in many aspects of land use planning, and it is felt that one approach developed at a consistent level of detail throughout will provide a clearer picture of the land use planning process. Chapter 10 presents an overview of the entire analytical frame-

work; Chapter 11 takes up location requirements for various uses of land; Chapter 12 sets forth approaches for estimating space requirements for each of these uses; and finally, Chapter 13 discusses the applications of these analyses in the design of the urban land use plan.

the plan and its analytical framework

In no aspect of the planning process is the city planner dealing with more fundamental, more important determinants of guided physical expansion and renewal than he is in the development of the land use plan. Land use data assembled and plotted as described in Chapter 8 record these patterns as they have occurred in the past, whether in haphazard or in guided form. The land use plan reflects a carefully studied estimate of future land requirements for expansion and renewal, showing how development in the urban area should proceed in the future to insure the best possible physical environment for urban living, the most economic use of land, and the proper balance in use from a cost-revenue point of view. Fundamentally, then, the land use plan embodies a proposal as to how expansion and renewal should proceed in the future, recognizing local objectives and generally accepted principles of health, safety, convenience, economy, and the general amenities of urban living.

DEFINITIONS AND APPLICATIONS

While there appears to be general agreement on these fundamentals of land use planning, there are in usage a variety of connotations to the term "land use plan." As might be expected, "land use map" is sometimes loosely and interchangeably used with "land use plan," especially among lay groups such as planning commission members and citizen groups in general. Even among professional planners, this confusion is not entirely unheard of. More prevalent and similarly a source of confusion is the interchangeable use of "zoning plan" and "land use plan." Finally, considerable vagueness persists as to the functional relationship of the land use plan to the comprehensive or master plan.

Although distinctions between these terms are made below for purposes of clarifying the land use plan concept employed herein, it should be remembered that in American city planning practice there is as yet no full agreement on these meanings. Nevertheless, there is considerable agreement on some terms in professional circles. The land use map is generally recognized for what it is, simply a map showing how the land and structures on the land are used for urban purposes at a particular time, past or present. The land use plan is generally recognized as a proposal for the future use of land and the structures built upon the land. As a proposal, it is more than a map; it embodies a whole array of principles and the assumptions and reasoning followed in arriving at this proposal. Thus, while the land use map is a factual description of the urban setting, usually as it exists today, the land use plan is a generalized but scaled presentation of a scheme for the future development of the urban area.

The so-called "zoning plan," as an adjunct to a zoning ordinance is generally conceived as a scheme of districting an urban area for purposes of regulating use, density of population, coverage of lots, bulk of structures, and so on. Zoning is one of several legal devices for implementing the proposals for land development as set forth in the land use plan. As a legal instrument, it is exacting in detail. The land use plan is concerned with use and intensity of development but is generalized in form. The usage of "zoning plan" in place of "zoning map" in some cases may be intended to convey the notion of a proposal as opposed to an officially adopted map of zoning districts, but even as a proposal the zoning plan is, or should be, aimed at *achieving* the objectives of the land use plan. Thus the latter is a prerequisite of the former. Indeed, no zoning ordinance and its accompanying districting scheme are likely to be comprehensive in scope and sound in content unless based on a previously prepared land use plan. Illustrations of the map form of the land use map, the land use plan, and the zoning plan are shown in Figure 29.

Apart from these rather elemental distinctions, there are variations in the connotation attached to "land use plan" when it is properly used to refer to a generalized proposal for the future development of an urban area. In many parts of the country, by legislative definition or by common usage, the "land use plan" is used to refer to that portion of the master plan which is devoted to proposals for industrial, commercial, business, and residential uses—the so-called *private uses* of land, the public uses being covered by the term "community facilities." In other cases, while being construed as a part of the master plan, proposals for both *public and private uses* of land are considered to be a part of the land use plan.

For example, San Francisco is guided by the following statement from its city-county charter:

> The master plan . . . shall include a land use plan showing the proposed general distribution and the general location and extent of housing, business, industry, recreation, education, and other categories of public and private uses of land, and recommended standards of population density and building intensity.[1]

This is the essential meaning of the term as it is used here. But within the framework of the "progressive planning approach," there is some latitude for variation in the extent of detail that may appear in such a plan at any particular time. Thus it may be viewed as *a preliminary land use plan* (or generalized land use plan) where its emphasis is in presenting a first general but comprehensive estimate of land use requirements relative to location and amount of land to be reserved for each public and private use. As pointed out earlier, the analytical framework presented here is developed to correspond to this general level of detail. The preliminary land use plan is usually developed concurrently with the preliminary thoroughfare plan, and these two generalized studies in combination provide a point of departure for the development of the comprehensive or master plan, either as the first such plan to be adopted or as a major revision of an earlier such plan.

As time permits more detailed study, the generalized land use plan is progressively refined into the master land use plan, which is a part of the comprehensive or master plan and may be published either as individual master plan reports for residential, business, industrial, recreational, and other areas or as an integrated master land use plan study. Thus in the framework of this concept, *the comprehensive plan* is a synthesis of these component, more detailed plans, including not only systems of use areas, but all forms of circulation and their terminal facilities and all kinds of utility requirements, the rudiments of which were first outlined in overall form in the preliminary land use plan and the preliminary thoroughfare plan.

Inherent in the progressive planning approach is a recognition of the need for an overall general plan to guide day-to-day operational decisions of the planning office and to provide a basis for rational solutions for zoning and subdivision control problems, urban renewal programs, and similar pressing needs until such time as the comprehensive plan is developed. The generalized land use plan serves this need. For purposes of these decisions and actions, such a plan may be adopted by the planning commission to give it official interim status.

[1] San Francisco Department of City Planning, *Land Use Section of the Master Plan of the City and County of San Francisco,* January, 1953, mimeo., p. 1.

FIGURE 29. Illustrative Forms of the Land Use Map, a Preliminary Land Use Plan, and a Preliminary Zoning Plan. (*Source:* Seattle City Planning Commission, 1955.)

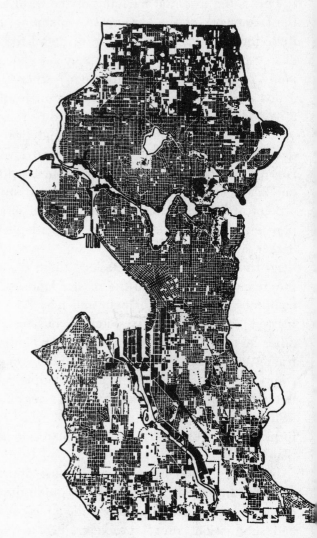

LAND USE MAP

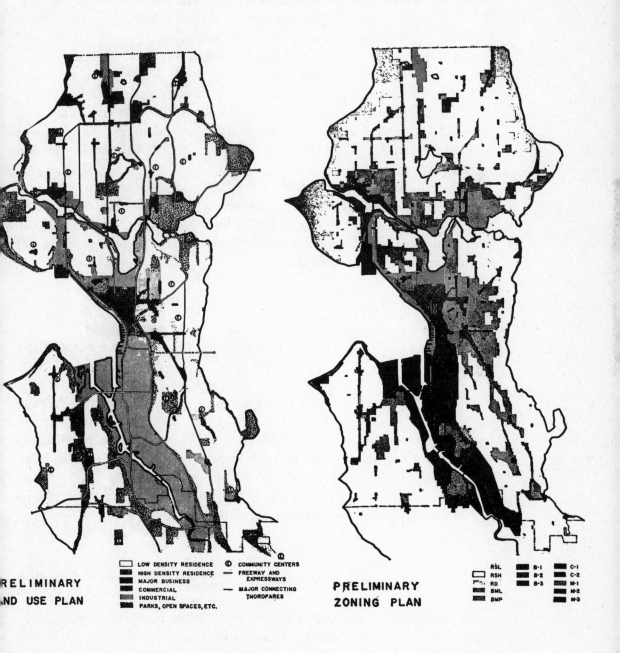

**PRELIMINARY
LAND USE PLAN**

**PRELIMINARY
ZONING PLAN**

The generalized land use plan (hereafter referred to sometimes as the "land use plan") serves a variety of purposes. Where decisions on public facilities must be made prior to the adoption of a comprehensive plan, it serves as a guide to reaching these decisions, particularly in land acquisition for such public facilities as schools, playgrounds, firehalls, and so on. It becomes a useful guide to private developers, particularly promoters of large-scale developments such as residential communities, shopping centers, organized industrial districts, and so on. As previously mentioned, it is a guide for zoning, subdivision control, and urban renewal studies. And finally, it is of invaluable assistance to public and private agencies concerned with utilities and transportation. It indicates areas where water, sewerage, and private utility systems are likely to encounter new or increased demands in the future, and in so far as the future land use pattern is a factor, it provides the necessary kind of information for making rational decisions concerning major airports, military air bases, transit extensions, railroad routing, and so on.

With this general introduction to the land use plan, we may now turn to the analytical procedures. At the outset it is helpful to obtain an overview of these procedures first in terms of what the table of contents of a land use plan report would show, and then in terms of the sequence which would be followed in the technical studies.

ELEMENTS OF THE LAND USE PLAN STUDY

Although there can be many variations in the way they are grouped and presented, in general the basic elements of the study will include the following: a statement of local objectives; a discussion of existing trends in the use, nonuse, and misuse of land; a presentation of future land use requirements including a statement of the principles to be followed and the assumptions made; a description of the land use plan and its proposals; and recommendations for the implementation of the plan.

Statement of Objectives

The statement of objectives in the land use plan report broadly identifies what it is hoped the plan, and subsequent refinements of it embodied in the comprehensive plan, will achieve in the urban area. The goal-making function is generally that of the planning commission, although it is usually the task of the city planner to set forth the alternatives. Objectives in general form are set forth at the outset of the study, but as the work proceeds and problems and issues are brought more clearly into view, refinements and modifications will generally be introduced. In the transition period from the time of the completion of the preliminary land use plan to the time of the adoption of the more detailed land use proposals of the comprehensive plan—often extending over a period of several years— there is an opportunity to reëxamine the first statement of objectives. During this period, observations of public reaction are made by formal and informal contacts with citizens, through public hearings, and in the editorial columns of the press, all these channels providing a subjective basis for the reformulation of objectives. Still a virtually untapped means of identifying the values and attitudes of both the organized and unorganized segments of the urban population is the sampling public opinion poll discussed in an earlier chapter. The exploratory work noted in the Detroit area indicates the potentialities of sampling surveys for providing a more objective basis for the identification of goals.

While there may be similarities in objectives in a broad sense, the priority and emphasis will tend to vary from one city to another. The statement of recommendations at the end of the report will generally reflect priorities and emphases as locally determined. The following statement of the San Francisco objectives taken from the land use section of its master plan is illustrative of broadly stated land use planning objectives:

1. Improvement of the city as a place for commerce and industry by making it more efficient, orderly, and satisfactory for the production, exchange, and distribution of goods and services, with adequate space for each type of economic activity and improved facilities for the loading and movement of goods.

2. Improvement of the city as a place for living, by aiding in making it more healthful, safe, pleasant, and satisfying, with housing representing good standards for all families and by providing adequate open spaces and appropriate community facilities.

3. Organization of the two principal functional parts of the city—the working areas and the community areas—so that each may be clearly distinguished from but complementary to the other, and so that the economic, social, and cultural development of the city may be furthered.

4. Protection, preservation, and enhancement of the economic, social, cultural, and aesthetic values that establish the desirable quality and unique character of the city.

5. Coördination of the varied pattern of land use with public and semi-

public service facilities required for efficient functioning of the city, and for the convenience and well-being of its residents, workers, and visitors.

6. Coördination of the varied pattern of land use with circulation routes and facilities required for the efficient movement of people and goods within the city, and to and from the city.

7. Coördination of the growth and development of the city with the growth and development of adjoining cities and counties and of the San Francisco Bay Region.[2]

The first six objectives are sufficiently general in statement so as to apply to most urban areas. In a more detailed formulation of objectives, however, one could expect considerable variation between urban areas.

Existing Conditions and Future Needs

With the objectives set forth, the next section in the land use plan report is generally a description of the urban setting as it is today. This usually consists of a presentation of the results of the urban land studies, including maps and tabular summaries as discussed in Chapter 8.

Following the summaries of existing land use characteristics, the use capabilities of vacant, open, and renewal land, and so on, there is a major section concerned with the summary of future land use requirements. This describes requirements of both a qualitative and quantitative character. In the former category is a statement of principles setting forth relationships to be observed in setting aside areas for various land uses. This statement deals with the *relationships in the broad patterns of use areas and the location criteria for each specific class of use* employed in the design phase of the plan. In the second category is a statement of *space requirements for each class of use.*

Proposals and Implementation

Once the land use planning requirements have been presented, the section of the report devoted to the plan itself follows naturally. Here, in accord with objectives, the limitations of the existing pattern of uses, and the principles and requirements previously established, the basic features of the plan's design are presented. The map presentation of the plan appears here, along with a descriptive summary of its basic features.

[2] *Ibid.,* p. 2.

Finally, the last section of the report formulates a tentative program for the implementation of the plan. If the plan is adopted by the planning commission, the program assumes some official significance and provides the basis for interim action on developmental matters until such time as the comprehensive plan is adopted and its implementing program supersedes the interim one. Broadly, this program is customarily concerned with zoning, subdivision control, a housing code, and similar regulatory measures, and a public works expenditure program, an urban renewal program, and similar developmental measures for public and private action. The importance of zoning as a measure for regulating use and intensity of development in both expansion and renewal areas has already been noted. Concerned primarily with site development standards and other site planning requirements, subdivision regulations provide an additional means for controlling the character and intensity of development in expansion areas. Among other purposes served, the housing code regulates the number of persons permitted per room and thus in combination with other regulative measures controls the density of population according to land use plan proposals in this respect. Public works programming insures that utilities, street improvements, and community facilities are provided in expansion and renewal areas as needed. It represents an important means of channeling growth into the desired areas for expansion and of discouraging it in other areas. Urban redevelopment under federal-local financing arrangements and both public and private measures employed in rehabilitation programs provide important means for implementing the land use plan in renewal areas. Organized and administered as complementing and related elements of one integrated urban improvement program, these are the types of measures commonly used in implementation of the plan. This final section of the report deals with each measure as may be appropriate to each particular locality.

GENERAL SEQUENCE TO TECHNICAL STUDIES

With this organization of the general elements of the land use plan *report* in mind, we can now proceed to outline the major phases in the work of carrying out the land use planning study—*the procedures*. Planning the technical work procedures is a crucial part of the whole operation. Once the nature of the end product has been identified as set forth above, it is important to chart the sequence to the land use planning analyses as a basis for overall guidance and economy of staff effort. This sequence can be organized into three phases.

Initial Spadework

DELINEATION OF STUDY AREAS

The first phase is best labeled as "initial spadework." It is essentially concerned with completing and bringing together the results of tooling-up studies needed in the land use planning analysis. But as pointed out in Part II, in summarizing the data needed from these studies, it is necessary to identify a system of study areas to be used in these analyses. As a practical matter, these delineations must be made in advance of land use planning studies. They include the "planning area" and the subdivision of this larger area into subplanning areas, what we have termed "planning districts."

In general, the *planning area* includes the dominant urban center of special planning interest, the adjoining incorporated or unincorporated areas built up in urban uses, and the vacant land or open country beyond which is expected to go into urban development by the end of the planning period, generally a 20- to 25-year span of time. In some metropolitan centers, where there are one or more separate planning agencies functioning in segments of the total metropolitan planning area, local expediency may dictate the usage of the term "planning area" in each locality to refer to its area of planning jurisdiction as defined by state act, the municipal charter, or local ordinance. In the context of the usage here and for comprehensive land use planning studies, it is a larger area. It is larger than the urbanized area, but generally smaller than the Standard Metropolitan Area as defined by the Bureau of the Census.

DEFINING THE PLANNING AREA

The actual procedures employed in delineating the planning area are based on the following considerations. Once the built-up area is roughly defined, the resulting outline is extended outward into open country, considering the general growth prospects and the likely directions of expansion as affected by natural and man-made features. These features include the broad pattern of natural drainage areas, especially the sections of the area which are economic to sewer, and such special features of the area as lakes and hills which are likely to attract growth, the pattern of highways, transportation facilities, and so on.

The extent of area likely to go into development is approximated in terms of square miles by using a rough average density of persons per square mile existing in the presently built-up area and applying this figure to crude estimates of the increase in population of the county or counties, the towns or townships, or the incorporated areas, whichever appears most appropriate to local circumstances for approximation purposes. The resulting rough estimate of the total amount of land likely to go into development is then distributed around the perimeter of the built-up area according to anticipated directions of expansion activity and other factors cited above. Finally, the resulting outline is generalized to follow lines readily identified on the ground, such as watercourse lines, ridge lines, highways, civil division lines, and so on. As noted earlier, these lines may be drawn to follow civil division lines entirely for convenience in statistical analyses of census data. Whatever basis is used, such delineations of the planning area are tentative and may be subject to revision for land use planning purposes according to suggestions made in Chapter 12.

DEFINING PLANNING DISTRICTS

The delineation of planning districts within the planning area involves other factors. Planning districts may be either natural areas or somewhat arbitrary areas useful primarily for analytical purposes. In urban areas where there has been a long-established planning program and residential neighborhoods, or other forms of natural planning areas have been previously identified and are established for planning purposes, the planning districts employed for land use planning may be identical with these. Appropriate extensions of this system of districts to allow for new neighborhoods may be necessary. Planning districts of this type usually aim to recognize the service area of an elementary school, but often must be modified according to the number of people or families present and the density of population in relation to the existing school plant, and the physical barriers present such as railroads, thoroughfares, watercourses, and large areas of nonresidential use.

In situations where no such delineations have been previously made, a somewhat arbitrary system of planning districts may be used or developed for analysis purposes. These may follow census tract boundaries or some other previously developed breakdown of the urban area into small statistical areas. There are certain very obvious advantages to using census tract breakdowns, namely, those of having census data available for the system of subareas to be employed in land use planning analyses. In urban centers which have not been tracted or in situations where it is considered more expedient to depart from census tract lines, a rather simple procedure can be employed. This is based on a rather crude, but nevertheless useful division of land use categories into those which for land use planning purposes are studied on an urban-wide basis, and those which are tied to local subareas (see the breakdown in Table 17). In the former category are industrial areas, wholesale areas, the central business district, institutional areas, upper-level schools, and recreation areas serving the city as a whole. In the latter category are residential areas and their service facilities such as elementary schools, local shopping centers, playgrounds, and local parks.

Once the industrial, wholesale, institutional, and other land areas not tied to residential community analysis have been identified and blocked out on a map, only the balance of the urban area—the living areas—needs to be broken down into planning districts. The simplest procedure to follow is first to trace off on an overlay placed over the land use map the pattern of existing residential areas. In order to include in the system of planning districts new undeveloped areas as well as the existing built-up areas, the resulting pattern is then extended out to the limits of the planning area by blocking in all vacant and open land areas identified in the vacant land analysis as potentially suitable for residential use (for example, all of Class 2 Prime type of land as defined at the foot of Table 19). Then on the basis of readily recognized barriers, such as railroads, thoroughfares, watercourses, or large nonresidential areas, a perimeter outline is drawn in generalized form. Planning district dividing lines are then drawn, similarly generalized and following major barrier lines, so that planning districts are not much in excess of one mile in the longest dimension and contain or can accommodate roughly from 1000 to 5000 persons each, according to prevailing densities. The general concept employed here is a series of planning districts which represent multiples of the elementary school service area.

The planning districts as previously delineated or as identified by the above procedures are numbered or named for convenience of reference in the subsequent land use planning analyses.

COMPLETION OF TOOLING-UP STUDIES

Once a system of study areas is defined, the results of various prerequisite studies can be summarized in terms of these areas. It is recognized that these studies may have been completed earlier and published for general planning purposes, but if data have not been summarized by these study areas in a form usable for land use planning analyses, "completion" may mean reëxamination of earlier studies. The prerequisite studies include an analysis of the urban economy, employment and population studies, the land use and vacant land surveys, and other studies discussed in Chapters 5, 6, 7, and 8. Scheduled concurrently with this work are the paralleling preliminary thoroughfare plan studies.

Local priorities may dictate the initiation of work on the land use plan before the formal completion of work on prerequisite studies. If this should be the situation, tooling-up studies should be sufficiently advanced to have produced the following minimum required information:

Current and forecast urban area *population*—total and by school-age groups.

Current and forecast urban area manufacturing, wholesale and office-related *employment*.

Map and tabular summary of *existing land use* by planning district.

Map and tabular summary of *vacant and renewal land* characteristics by planning district.

Summary of current *stock of dwelling units* by structure type and by planning district.

Summary of currently *substandard dwelling units* by structure type and by planning district.

Data on cost-revenue relationships for developments in varying locations, at varying densities and intensities of use, and information on the general pattern of land values and their trends in the urban area should be available early in the analytical sequence.

Estimation of Future Land Requirements

The second major phase in the sequence is the development of what might be termed *qualitative* and *quantitative* land use requirements. This phase goes to the very heart of the analytical procedure. In the first part of this phase—the one relating to qualitative aspects of the analysis—principles and standards governing the location of individual uses and the relationships between uses are formulated, and a schematic land use diagram is prepared. This is a first sketch study for the future pattern of uses, showing in principle "desirable" use relationships and locations. It serves as a reference for the study of space requirements and a guide and beginning point in the development of a preliminary plan.

The estimation of space requirements, the quantitative aspect of the analysis, is the most complex and time-consuming part of the analytical procedure. Essentially it is concerned with the estimation of the acreage required to accommodate the expansion anticipated during the planning period for each use category. Built into the procedure is a means for adjusting estimates of land requirements that are derived so as to reflect anticipated future public or private renewal activity and any displacement of existing uses occasioned by these processes of change. Although the final product of these studies is expressed in terms of acreage, the intermediate analyses made in arriving at space requirements utilize different measurement units, e.g., employees, dollar sales, dwelling units, population, and so on.

As intimated above and in the earlier discussion of land use classification, space needs for region-serving uses are dealt with first. These are uses studied on a planning area basis—uses not directly tied to residential communities such as industry, wholesale and region-serving retail business, recreation, education, and cultural uses. Following these analyses, space requirements for uses associated with residential areas, namely, housing, schools, recreation, local business, and neighborhood-type church uses, are analyzed as an interrelated group of uses. In place of the planning area, here the planning district becomes the primary unit area of analysis.

The tabular and mapped summary of the supply of vacant and renewal land previously classified according to various topographic and improvement characteristics should be available for reference use in these analyses. According to the preferences of the analyst, estimates of space needs for all uses may be completed before trial geographic distributions of uses are attempted (by reference to the previously developed schematic location diagram), *or*, as the acreage requirements for each use are developed, trial distributions may be made to areas defined as vacant and renewal land. In the latter approach a cumulative record is maintained in both tabular and map form of trial land use proposals. In some respects, the "dimensioning-in" of space requirements on a trial basis as the space needs for each use are derived is the more convenient alternative since the derivation of space requirements for some uses is contingent on the manner in which space needs of other uses are distributed. On the other hand, if the first approach is followed, proper adjustment for this contingency may be made later. In either approach, it must be emphasized that at this phase of the study, location and space requirements are developed and tested irrespective of potential conflict (thus the continual reference to *trial* distributions above).

Design of Land Use Plan

The third and final phase to the procedure is a design stage. This stage involves the collation of preliminary proposals as to location and distribution of various types of land uses as developed in the preceding phase of the work and the preparation of the preliminary land use plan in firmed-up form. By the time the design phase in the sequence is reached, at least a first schematic presentation of the preliminary thoroughfare plan should be available. Also at this stage, the visual survey and cost-revenue, land value, and if available, attitude studies come into play in some detail. With all this information at hand, then begins a "cut and fill" process, a process of ironing out conflicts in location. These are of two orders: conflicts between the land use pattern and the thoroughfare scheme, and conflicts between the different land uses. Each land use category is reviewed for the economic feasibility of development in the locations indicated, considering the fiscal abilities and legal authorities of the one or more municipalities and counties which may be involved for realizing the plan in the planning period.

Once location conflicts are brought into harmony, space requirements are reëxamined as necessary and the space needed for each use is brought into overall balance. The final result is the best practical, most economical, and attractive design for all uses, fitted to the topography and the existing land use pattern and articulated with the circulation system.

CHAPTER 11

location requirements

Location requirements take the form of guiding principles and standards for the placement of uses on the land. Involving a whole range of physical, economic, and social considerations, these requirements are concerned with the location of each individual use in relation to every other use and to the transportation and utility systems of the urban area. In their most elemental form, they relate to health, safety, convenience, economy, and the general amenities of urban living. They involve consideration of danger from floods and other health and safety hazards, the nearness or remoteness of one use from another in time and distance, their compatability and the social implications of these uses to the people of the community, the economic feasibility of developing particular uses in particular locations considering the pattern of land values and site development costs, the practicalities from a cost-revenue point of view, and livability and general attractiveness as factors of location.

How these considerations are expressed in terms of principles, and how principles are subsequently translated into standards of location are fundamentally matters of local determination. Different urban areas will have different natural advantages, different fiscal capabilities, different concepts of convenience, amenity, and livability in general. Theoretically these differences should result in different emphases from city to city in statements of principles and standards. However, in practice most such statements are very similar. They are similar partly because in their fundamentals all such statements stem from a common core of widely recognized general principles of design, and partly because few cities have yet attempted detailed investigations of public attitudes concerning such factors as amenity and convenience, which are less conducive to standardization than such other elements of the public interest as health and safety.[1]

[1] See previous references to the potentialities of attitude studies for city planning in Chapters 3 and 8.

General principles relating to the location of land uses customarily identify three major functional areas in the urban complex: the work areas, the living areas, and the leisure-time areas. The major work areas consist of those parts of the city devoted to manufacturing, trade, and the services. The living areas are viewed as the residential communities and their accessory community facilities such as neighborhood stores, playgrounds and local parks, and elementary schools. The leisure-time areas are generally considered to include the major educational, cultural, and recreational facilities of the urban center consisting of colleges, museums, concert halls, libraries, colosseums, golf courses, large public parks and wildlife reserves for hiking, picnics and outings of all kinds, and similar facilities.

In the broadest possible context, principles relating to these three areas generally read somewhat as follows:

Work areas should be located in convenient proximity to living areas where there are nearby interconnecting transit and thoroughfare routes to insure easy access back and forth, and should be in convenient proximity to other work areas where uses accessory to one another have access to interconnecting truck routes. Some work areas should be in locations accessible to heavy transportation facilities and large capacity utility lines. Work area locations should provide sites adequate in size, economic to develop, and attractively situated for the particular uses intended.

Living areas should be located in convenient proximity to the work and leisure-time areas where there are nearby transit and thoroughfare routes to insure easy access back and forth. They should be in convenient proximity to large open spaces and should include smaller open spaces to insure an open-order character of development, with residential areas in easy walking distance of accessory community facilities. They should be located in areas protected from traffic and incompatible uses, in areas economic and attractive to develop, and in areas where desirable residential densities with a range of choice can be assured.

Leisure-time areas should be located in convenient proximity, by thoroughfare and transit, to living areas. Cultural activities and spectator sports should be central and on sites adequate for their purposes, and major parks and large open spaces should be located so as to take advantage of natural or unusual features of the landscape and provide for a variety of outdoor recreational and other activities.

In such a statement, such terms as "convenient proximity," "easy access," "adequate in size," "easy walking distance," "economic to develop," and "desirable densities" immediately pose problems of definition. These are points in the statement of principles where definitions will vary somewhat according to the size of the urban area. Here, too, value and policy questions are involved which vary from city to city, even within the same general size range. Definitions of these terms appear in the standards as adopted to fit a particular local situation.

The factors involved in a more detailed formulation of principles relating to the location of land uses are suggested below according to the category of land use. It should be noted that, with some exceptions, this listing recognizes the same location groupings developed in the land use classification scheme shown in Table 17.[2] It should also be noted that even this listing is very general in form. While it is in keeping with the generalized character and level of detail required for the preliminary land use plan, location factors are considered in greater detail in the course of developing the comprehensive plan.

MANUFACTURING AREAS

1. Reasonably level land, preferably with not more than 5 percent slope, capable of being graded without undue expense.
2. Range of choice in close-in, fringe, and dispersed locations.
    Extensive Manufacturing: large open sites for modern one-story buildings and accessory storage, loading and parking areas in fringe and dispersed locations, usually 5 acres as a minimum, with some sites 10, 25, 50, or 100 or more acres depending on size of urban area and economic outlook for industrial development of extensive lines of activity.
    Intensive Manufacturing: variety of site sizes for modern one-story or multiple-story buildings and accessory storage, loading and parking areas in close-in and fringe locations, usually under 5 acres.
3. Direct access to commercial transportation facilities; in fringe and dispersed locations, access to railroad, major trucking routes, cargo airports, and, in some urban areas, deep water channels; and in close-in locations, for a major proportion of sites, access to both railroad and trucking routes, with the balance adjoining trucking thoroughfares, or if appropriate, port areas.
4. Within easy commuting time of residential areas of labor force and accessible to transit and major thoroughfare routes directly connected with housing areas.

    [2] A number of uses which involve certain special location factors or are popularly regarded as possessing certain nuisance characteristics have been grouped together as a miscellany under the heading "public service facilities." Such uses will be found distributed among other headings of the land use classification system in Table 17.

5. Availability of utilities at or near the site such as power, water, and waste disposal facilities.

6. Compatibility with surrounding uses, considering prevailing winds, possibilities of protective belts of open space, development of "industrial parks," and other factors of amenity both within the manufacturing area and in relation to adjoining land uses.

WHOLESALE AND RELATED USE AREAS

1. Reasonably level land, preferably with not more than 5 percent slope, capable of being graded without undue expense.

2. Range of choice in close-in and fringe locations, site sizes usually under 5 acres.

3. Direct access to trucking routes and major street system for incoming goods and outgoing deliveries; frontage on a commercial street or in well-served wholesale centers essential; railroad access for minor proportion of sites or centers.

4. Suitability for development of integrated centers, with consideration for amenity within the development and adjoining areas.

REGION-SERVING BUSINESS AREAS

1. Adjoining heavy traffic flows, central to their tributary trade area.

   Central Business District: locations close to peak flow of traffic and pedestrians where retail, professional, financial, and related services can be conveniently accommodated in subcenters easily accessible to adequate parking, transit, and regional transportation services for clientele and employee groups patronizing or working in CBD.

   Regional Business Centers: (a) regional shopping centers: location close to two major arterials tributary to trade area (50–100,000 families within 30 minutes); site adequate for peak parking and a complete line of shop and store types, eating and entertainment facilities, and branch business and financial services sufficient to fill several hours of a shopper's time (30 to 175 acres); and (b) satellite CBD centers (office centers, automobile sales and service centers, appliance centers, farmers' market and service centers, etc.): locations on intersection of radial and circumferential arteries and on one or more major transit routes, with adequate parking and service areas.

   Highway Service Centers: locations in outlying areas on major highway approaches to urban area where sites are adequate for integrated design of drive-in services and motel accommodations and proper consideration is given to highway safety, roadside beauty, and general amenity of adjoining uses.

2. Suitability for development as one center internally arranged, where appropriate, in an integrated series of subcenters, with consideration for parks and other open spaces, approaches, and general amenity within the area and in adjoining use areas.

PUBLIC SERVICE FACILITIES

1. Suitable locations, adequate in size for following uses, as determined by special studies: civic center, subcenters, and general civic services; cemeteries; water works, sewage disposal facilities, and garbage and refuse disposal facilities; gas works, power plants and substations, and communications facilities; transit yards and service facilities; railroad terminals, marshaling yards, and service facilities; port facilities; overland bus and union truck terminals and servicing facilities; helioports, landing strips, and major airports; military installations; and so on.

REGION-SERVING RECREATION, EDUCATION, AND CULTURAL FACILITIES

1. Reasonably level land for facilities involving structures, accessory parking and active recreation areas, with perhaps not more than 5 percent slope, capable of being graded without undue expense; for large open spaces and public reservations, land with a variety of natural features and no limitations as to slope and drainage characteristics (often includes land not practical for other urban uses).

    Major Parks, Public Reservations, and Golf Courses: acreage sites in fringe and outlying areas, ranging from gently rolling terrain for golf courses to topography with variable features for parks and reservations.

    Colleges, Medical Centers, and Institutions: fringe locations on level to rolling terrain in areas protected from traffic and incompatible uses; site adequate to accommodate buildings, accessory parking, outdoor uses, and grounds, with due consideration to approaches and amenity of surroundings.

    Cultural Facilities, Large Churches, and Spectator Sports: level sites in central locations (out of high-value areas) adequate to accommodate building, accessory parking, and landscaping, with due consideration to approaches and general amenity of surroundings.

2. Suitability of unusual land forms and natural drainage creeks for incorporation into an integrated open space system in urban area, serving as natural breaks between functional use areas and providing connective links between recreation areas and large public and institutional open areas.

3. Direct access to major thoroughfare and transit or stage routes with direct and easy connections to the residential communities of the urban area.

RESIDENTIAL COMMUNITIES

1. Terrain with variety, offering fairly level, rolling, and hillside sites depending on topographic characteristics in the urban area, but avoiding steep or irregular sites and low or poorly drained areas; slope usually under 15 percent.

2. In close proximity to major thoroughfares and transit system with direct connections to work and leisure-time areas; bounded but not penetrated by major streets; and internally served by a system of collector and service streets fitted to the terrain with due consideration to drainage, sunlight, and views.

3. Suitability for integrated design of residential areas and their related shop-

ping, school, church, and recreation facilities, including the community-serving and the neighborhood-serving facilities.

Local Shopping Facilities: sites adequate for shops, accessory off-street parking and loading, and landscaping; convenient to specific local tributary trade areas and accessible for receiving goods: (a) neighborhood-serving store group within convenient walking distance of families served (within convenient driving range, in low-density areas), with due consideration for pedestrian access and amenity of surrounding areas; and (b) community-serving shopping center on major radial thoroughfare, usually at the intersection of a major crosstown street, situated toward in-town edge of tributary trade area, and located with due consideration for integrated design of center and amenity of adjoining areas.

Schools: reasonably level sites, with upper-level schools within convenient commuting range and lower-level schools within easy walking distance of age groups served (except in low-density areas, where convenient driving range rather than walking distance becomes crucial consideration); sites adequate for buildings, recreation facilities, and landscaping, and located with due consideration for safety of children and amenity of surroundings.

Churches: reasonably level sites, adequate for parking and landscaping, and convenient to potential membership; for neighborhood-serving churches, walking convenience important, and for community-serving churches, accessibility to major street system important.

Playground Areas and Parks: (a) reasonably level playground and recreation center sites, usually in conjunction with schools, within easy walking distance of age-groups served (within convenient driving range, in low-density areas), and adequate for appropriate active recreation facilities and circumscribing planted strips; and (b) quiet parks on steep, level, or low sites and fingers of open space along watercourses and in low areas, integrated with active and passive recreation areas and the larger open space system of the urban area according to the opportunities offered by land forms in locale.

4. Range of choice in residential densities, with high densities in close-in and intermediate locations, in close proximity to permanent open spaces and nearest to the thoroughfare and transit systems and community-serving shopping centers; with lowest densities on the more steep portions of usable terrain and generally in the more outlying locations.

These are illustrative of the kinds of factors which would be covered in a detailed statement of guiding principles for the location of various functional use areas within the framework of the land use plan. Again it should be noted that there will be variations from one urban area to another. Cities in mountainous areas will have emphases differing from those in the Great Plains; climate will produce differing emphases; resort, government, transportation, and other specialized centers will have their special considerations; and even the size of the urban area will be a factor in playing up certain features and deëmphasizing others.

LOCATION STANDARDS

Standards are a set of yardsticks established for measuring the excellence of quality in elements of the community's makeup, in this case, use locations. Standards established in laws generally take the form of *minimum standards* which have come to be recognized as necessary in the public interest. For planning analyses, we use *"desirable" standards,* an excellence of quality somewhere between the minimum and optimum situation —something practicable to achieve in the great majority of applications. In this sense, standards are not absolute, but more in the nature of guides or criteria to be followed under average circumstances. Where there is a marked range of variation in circumstances, variable standards of location may be warranted.

Convenience Standards

As suggested above, standards supply measurement units for terms appearing in the statement of principles. In dealing with standards for the location of uses, time and distance criteria are primary units for the measurement of convenience. Thus "close proximity," "convenient driving range," "easy walking distance," and "accessible to railroad, transit, or utilities" are defined in time or distance standards, usually in terms of minutes or miles of travel.

For purposes of the preliminary land use plan, these convenience standards are usually locally established adaptations from general standards developed by nationally recognized authorities from long experience and intimate familiarity with the testing and use of varying standards. Access standards adopted by the Committee on the Hygiene of Housing for time and distance relationships between the dwelling and various community facilities are widely used as general standards.[3] However, adaptations must be made in each locale on the basis of judgment and general observation of prevailing community habits. Compiled from the land use plan studies for an urban area of about 100,000 population, Table 24 serves to illustrate

[3] Committee on the Hygiene of Housing, American Public Health Association, *Planning the Neighborhood,* Public Administration Service, 1948, p. 9.

the form in which such standards are expressed for generalized land use planning analyses. Obviously these standards are based on a certain set of local conditions with respect to terrain, prevailing residential densities, local transportation systems, school and recreation policies, and other considerations which would not necessarily be duplicated in another community of the same size or even in the same region.

TABLE 24.   Illustrative Time-Distance Standards for Selected Uses in Urban Area of 100,000 Population[a]

Use or Facility	Controlling Standards
Employment centers	20 to 30 min
Central business district	30 to 45 min
Local shopping center	½ mile or 10 min
Elementary school	½ mile
Junior high school	1 mile or 20 min
Senior high school	20 to 30 min
Playgrounds and local parks	½ mile
Playfields and recreation centers	1 mile or 20 min
Public park or reservation	30 to 60 min

[a] Greensboro, N.C., unpublished land use planning studies, 1948.

For later studies in refinement of the preliminary land use plan, convenience standards should be developed on the basis of much more detailed study. For example, in the case of time-distance between residential areas and places of employment, the controlling standard used for illustrative purposes in Table 24 in all probability would be replaced by a series of several standards. Sampling attitude surveys can be expected to identify a variety of variables such as cost and pleasantness of travel which would provide a basis for the development of more exacting specifications, probably taking the form of variable standards. The location of the employment center itself may be found to be a factor to be recognized in location standards. Thus, where employment centers are planned for peripheral locations, lower time-distance standards may be indicated than those used in more centrally located employment centers. "The value which a worker places on time, and the degree to which he is willing to make a specified journey to work will depend upon many variables. Age, sex, race, occupation, economic class, cultural group, reason for working, will all be important determinants of the evaluation of the journey to work by individuals. No gross generalizations can be made as to the 'optimum' journey to work, nor can generalizations be made as to how far employees as a whole are willing to journey to their jobs."[4] However, for particular

[4] Planning Advisory Service, *The Journey to Work: Relation Between Employment and Residence*. Information Report No. 26, American Society of Planning Officials, May 1951, p. 5.

segments of the population situated in particular sections of the urban area, standards may be developed which on the average match up with dominant preferences as to travel times or distances to various functional use areas considering convenience, cost, and other factors.

Similarly, in more detailed studies of school needs, variable standards may be substituted for the single crude standard used in the preliminary land use planning analyses. A map of school sites with half-mile circles described around each site provides only the very crudest measure of location adequacy. Even when time zones are substituted for distance circles, variations in concepts of convenience in different parts of the urban area suggest that variable standards may be more realistic than one uniform standard. These concepts will vary with different residential densities, different income groups, and so on. Similar observations may be made concerning shopping facilities and recreation areas. Indeed, convenience standards for all uses should be carefully reëxamined and refined as work proceeds from the preliminary land use plan toward the comprehensive plan.

Performance Standards

Another form of location standard is the so-called "performance standard." Deriving from health, safety, and to some extent, the amenity elements of the public interest (as opposed to convenience as taken up above), in present usage performance standards provide criteria for testing the degree of hazard or nuisance from land use activities creating smoke, dust, noise, glare, odor, or fumes, or from activities generating traffic or producing wastes. To date they have been largely applied to industrial and related activities, although they have applications for other uses, e.g., tests of glare, noise, and traffic associated with spectator sports, recreation uses, carnivals, revival meetings, and so on.

Since Dennis O'Harrow's study in 1951, much attention has been given to the use of performance standards as a basis for the location of industrial activity.[5] Borrowed from earlier applications in building codes, the principle of the performance standard is based on the use of tests to determine whether a particular industry (or, originally, a particular building material) conforms with established basic criteria or standards of acceptability. Largely associated with industrial zoning, performance standards are increasingly being used as the basis for determining the location qualifica-

[5] Dennis O'Harrow, "Performance Standards in Industrial Zoning," *Planning 1951*, American Society of Planning Officials, 1952.

tions of various industries for admission to particular classes of zones. The degree to which hazards and nuisances are brought under control through technological and planning measures becomes the test. The performance approach renders obsolete the old basis of zoning under which industries were arbitrarily grouped into "light," "heavy," and "unrestricted" manufacturing districts.

It should be noted that performance standards are as yet imperfectly developed, some being more highly developed than others. Thus research on standards of smoke pollution, dust, glare, and noise is more advanced than what has been accomplished with fumes and odors. The measurement of most of these nuisances presently requires special equipment, and for interpretation of findings, some technical knowledge is necessary. Moreover, being a tool of zoning, performance standards presently focus on minimum rather than "desirable" standards. However, recognizing that the land use plan provides the basic rationale for a system of zoning districts, we may anticipate that with the advancement of research, upgraded forms of performance standards will be used in the future as general location criteria in land use planning analyses.

Security Factors of Location

Security factors pose still another order of location criteria—criteria that are based in some measure on public safety but perhaps more fundamentally on national well-being. With the atmosphere of unsettled global conditions following World War II and the prospect of international tensions continuing for an indefinite period into the future, increasing attention has been centered on security factors of planning. Historically a factor in the layout and development of individual cities, security now encompasses nations, indeed continents. While protection of the populace is of fundamental concern, the protection of industrial areas, the means for prosecuting war, is an objective of particular concern.

The great concentration of the nation's industrial resources in a relatively few metropolitan areas has grave implications for national well-being in event of an enemy attack. The vulnerability of these resources and the cities in which they are located prompted the establishment of a national industrial dispersion program. Launched in 1951 when the President announced a national policy for industrial dispersion, the program is based on voluntary action of localities and industrialists. Urging that future plants be built outside highly industrialized or densely populated areas and away from military installations, the policy established that, as a condition to receiving federal defense-production assistance (available to new defense plants in the form of accelerated tax amortization privileges and loans), new plants must conform to certain dispersal criteria.[6] Having been revised to keep pace with postwar improvements in thermonuclear weapons, these criteria now call for the placement of defense plants beyond large industrial or population concentrations.[7] The distance that a new plant is required to locate beyond these concentrations is determined on a case-by-case basis, considering "the proper functioning of our urban economies, the size of the particular urban target area, the destructive power of a large-yield weapon suitable for that target, proximity to strategic military installations, and the degree of damage the proposed facility could sustain and still remain operable."[8]

Without going into the many and varied arguments that this program has precipitated or its relative ineffectiveness in the period it has been in operation, we may note that it is steadily gaining support.[9] While solutions to our national security are basically within the province of foreign policy and military preparedness programs, reasons for a strong and realistic dispersal program are compelling. Certainly dispersal is not a phenomenon entirely foreign to the normal processes of decentralization, and if a program can be fitted to forces already at work in the economy, it is reasonable to expect some progress can be made in making the program effective in the future. "The trend that is occurring as a result of normal economic forces is not of a scale or at a rate which will reduce industrial centralization and congestion to any marked degree in the near future. The existence of such a trend, however, raises the possibility that industrial decentralization in certain sections of the economy might be accelerated and to a significant extent attained through various incentives, without introducing diseconomies or inefficiencies."[10]

If the importance of a dispersal program is accepted, it becomes apparent that the urban land use plan offers an important means for effectuat-

[6] For statements of criteria and techniques of analysis, see U.S. Department of Commerce, *Industrial Dispersion Guidebook for Communities*, U.S. Government Printing Office, 1952, and amending Defense Mobilization Order I-19, issued by the Office of Defense Mobilization, January 11, 1956.

[7] Defined as the area enclosed by a line drawn through the centers of a number of contiguous four-mile diameter circles each of which encloses either defense-supporting plants with a combined employment of 16,000 industrial workers or a residential population of 200,000. See Victor Roterus, a news article, *The Journal of Commerce*, April 3, 1956.

[8] *Ibid.*

[9] For a summary of these arguments, the shortcomings of the program in the past, and opportunities for the future, see Bureau of Business and Economic Research, *Industrial Dispersal*, Studies in Business and Economics, University of Maryland, March, 1956.

[10] William L. C. Wheaton, "Minimum Density and Spacing Requirements for Metropolitan Dispersion," *Project East River*, Part V-B, Associated Universities, Inc., 1952, pp. 15b–16b.

ing workable dispersal objectives within any particular metropolitan area. The extent to which national dispersion criteria can be integrated into local industrial development principles and standards should be the subject of a special study. While certain general principles of dispersal may be applied in the preliminary land use plan, the application of dispersal criteria in detail are probably best undertaken in the refinement and extension of the preliminary land use plan.

TRIAL APPLICATION OF PRINCIPLES AND STANDARDS

Once location requirements for each major class of land use have been established as set forth above, it is possible to develop a sketch applying in schematic form to the urban area of interest the requirements thus derived. While analyses of space requirements in the next phase of the study may modify this tentative selection of locations and final determinations must thus be made in the synthesizing process of the design phase, nevertheless for these later phases of land use planning, it becomes a guide and a beginning basis for the development of the preliminary land use plan.

At this point, a number of the tooling-up studies mentioned in Chapter 8 come into play. Among them are: the land capability study, blighted areas study, cost-revenue study, land value study, visual survey, and attitude studies. Although detailed applications of these studies are not warranted at this stage of the study, each one serves a reference purpose in blocking out locations in schematic form. The land capabilities analysis brings to bear studied consideration of the terrain and drainage conditions and the utility and transportation services available in different areas. The blighted areas study shows what sections of the city are expected to be available for redevelopment during the planning period and indicates land capabilities in areas slated for renewal. According to assumed future development policies and levels of service of governmental units in the area, cost-revenue studies will indicate preferred use locations at varying intensities of use, and land value studies will indicate the economic feasibility for the use of land contemplated at these locations. The visual survey identifies locations where there are distinctive views and other similar features which are important developmental assets to be considered in the placement of various uses. Finally, attitude studies will provide a picture of dominant public preferences and expectations in the future development of the urban area.

The mechanics of developing the schematic plan are relatively simple. Using the land use map as a base, locations for the future use of land in the planning area in both vacant and renewal areas are blocked out on overlays. Normally the locations for each use are first roughed out on individual overlays, and then, by examining them in cumulative or superimposed form, a trial scheme is eventually developed in which the major conflicts are provisionally resolved and location proposals for all uses are combined and shown on one sketch map. With location requirements thus established, the analyst is ready to estimate space requirements as taken up in the next chapter.

CHAPTER 12

space requirements

In shifting the focus of the land use planning study from the derivation of location requirements to the estimation of space needs, fundamentally we are seeking a basis for scaling the land area needed to accommodate growth in the urban area expected in the next 20 to 25 years. More particularly, having established in principle *where* each category of use should be located in the future, we are now interested in estimating *how much* land will be needed for each such use. Once these estimates are available, it is then possible to firm up the preliminary land use plan, initially "testing out the various locations for size" and eventually arriving at a plan reflecting the best possible balance in land utilization that is commensurate with the generalized level of study employed in analytical procedures throughout the whole sequence of study. This final balancing task is taken up in the last chapter.

In this chapter the whole range of tooling-up studies of Part II are brought into play. Studies of the urban economy, employment, and population provide measures of the growth potential, and the several kinds of urban land studies indicate the general character of existing development and provide the basis for determining the space-using characteristics of various land use categories developed to their present intensity of use.

While techniques for estimating space requirements vary according to the class of land use, there is a common methodological pattern to the analysis of all classes. Integrating into the procedure the kind of trial tests alluded to earlier for checking the space needs of each land use against the supply of land as the various use categories are successively analyzed, the operation can be summarized as consisting of three major steps. The first involves a recapitulation of the existing characteristics of development for the particular land use category being studied. Thus the present distribution of the use between inlying and outlying locations is examined,

303

and variations in the intensity of use in each of these parts of the urban area are determined.

The second step is directly concerned with space requirements. It involves first the derivation of space standards appropriate to each class of use and then the application of these standards to the appropriate growth index previously developed. Density standards are employed for industrial and residential uses, with employees per net or gross acre of land used for manufacturing purposes being the measure for the former, and families or dwelling units per net or gross acre of land used for residential purposes being the measure for the latter. For schools and certain types of recreation areas, local adaptations of general empirical standards of minimum site sizes for designated multiples of school or total population are customarily used as standards. For retail business uses, standards are based on trade area population or the volume of retail sales per unit of retail floor area, and wholesale standards are based on wholesale employment per unit of wholesale area. Thus in such analyses the measure of growth is generally taken from the employment, population, or some other forecast, and the estimate of space requirements is obtained by applying the standard to this growth increment.

The third and final step in this analysis is the balancing of space requirements as derived in the preceding step against the supply of land. The supply of land is all vacant land, summarized in a form somewhat like Table 19, plus all land slated for clearance during the planning period under an urban renewal program, summarized in a similar form. The balancing of need against supply is done separately for each class, with the acreage needed for each use being compared with the supply listed under the classification appropriate to that use in the table of vacant and renewal land. Cumulative tallies of deductions from the vacant and renewal land summary are maintained as the analysis of space requirements for each use is successively completed. Overlays are prepared showing the distribution of the vacant land taken up by each use and the distribution of residual vacant land after each deduction is made. The deduction tallies are usually maintained in subcategories according to the basic characteristics of the vacant land originally employed in the vacant land classification system (see illustrative Table 19). Thus if deficiencies should be encountered in the supply of land classified for one use, vacant land with alternative use potentialities can be considered for reclassification to the use class where the shortage develops. If such a reclassification is impractical or does not fully accommodate these deficiencies, then it will be necessary to extend the limits of the planning area, classify the additional vacant land thus brought into the planning area, and revise the summary of the supply of land upwards accordingly.

Generally, however, the limits of the planning area tend to be drawn rather generously in the first instance, and so this balancing operation will usually show a surplus rather than a shortage in the supply of vacant and renewal land. The surplus can run so high that the delineation of the planning area may appear unrealistic. However, so long as the total excess of land is not unreasonable, i.e., it is not over what is considered locally to be an adequate allowance for flexibility (usually roughly 25 percent of the total amount of land estimated to go into use during the planning period), there is no particular need to contract the boundaries of the planning area. In this connection it should be noted that such a flexibility factor is over and above the safety factors introduced in the course of detailed calculations made in the analyses of space requirements as discussed in the various sections of this chapter below. Such a flexibility factor allows for deviant choices of individuals and firms who may acquire land in excess of the estimated need, and it allows for land which may be held out of use because of personal preferences or whims of a few property owners or because of legal complications which make the land unavailable for immediate development.

If the surplus of vacant land is considerably in excess of estimated needs plus the flexibility allowance, it is usually desirable to tighten up the planning area delineation initially assumed, to bring it more in line with what space requirement analyses show to be a planning area of practical size. This, of course, involves acreage deductions from the appropriate classes in the land use and vacant land summaries. In the actual sequence of procedures employed in determining space requirements, the contraction of planning area boundaries, if it is found to be necessary, is made after running through the analyses for all classes of land use.

The whole trial distribution procedure in which space needs are balanced against supply of vacant and renewal land must be viewed of course as tentative until the final design phase of the land use planning is reached, for it is only at this phase of developing the land use plan that location decisions can finally be reached. However, the trial distribution of total space requirements is an essential step in reaching these final decisions.

The balance of the chapter describes the techniques in common usage for estimating space requirements of each class of land use. Uses not tied to small-area analysis are taken up first, followed by uses customarily analyzed by planning districts, namely, the residential communities and their accessory community facilities.

MANUFACTURING SPACE REQUIREMENTS

For purposes of a generalized result such as is required in the preliminary land use plan, estimates of space requirements for manufacturing areas are usually obtained in four steps as follows:

1. Determine the salient characteristics of existing manufacturing uses in the urban area, existing industrial densities, and the prospects for future manufacturing activity as determined in previous studies of the urban economy.

2. On the basis of these studies and considering modern-day industrial plant requirements, develop local standards for future industrial densities.

3. Apply industrial densities to future manufacturing employment estimates to obtain estimated land requirements.

4. Determine from summary of vacant and renewal land how supply matches up with estimated need, and, referring to location requirements, make a trial distribution into areas considered prime for industrial use, carrying over the surplus for reallocation in the vacant land tally.

The first step above is the equivalent of the industrial survey carried out in later comprehensive planning studies. For an abbreviated type of study involved in the preliminary land use plan, it consists of organizing data assembled in the land use survey and the study of the economy, and determining existing industrial densities.

Existing Industrial Densities

Two types of breakdowns are prepared to describe these characteristics of existing manufacturing uses: first, a summary of the acreage and employment of manufacturing establishments for the *urban area as a whole* broken down by density classes of manufacturing activity; and then a breakdown of the totals in this summary *by central city and by outlying incorporated and unincorporated fringe areas* making up the balance of the planning area. Converted to industrial densities, the first breakdown provides a measure of the intensity of development in the urban area as a whole for the selected density classes of manufacturing activity, and the second provides a crude indication as to how the intensity varies by density class from the central city to outlying areas.

Industrial density is defined as the number of manufacturing employees per gross industrially used acre.[1] As applied to particular density classes, it refers to the gross industrially used acres in that class. The term "gross" refers to all land within the property lines of the plant site, including building areas, landscaped grounds, parking and loading areas, outdoor storage and waste disposal areas, and to half of the area of all drives, streets, highways, or railroad spur lines bordering the property.

The number and the definitions of density classes of manufacturing activity in common usage vary from one city to another. Depending somewhat on the size of the urban area and the nature of manufacturing activity present, a breakdown by density classes may or may not be necessary. For example, in urban areas under 100,000 with a fairly diversified character of manufacturing activity, a breakdown by density classes may unnecessarily complicate the analysis and thus prove to be impractical. For larger urban centers, two or more classes may be required. Probably for most land use planning purposes, not more than two or three density classes will be required. The Detroit Metropolitan Area Regional Planning Commission has settled upon two broad density classes, extensive and intensive manufacturing areas, with a range of subcategories for special uses.[2] The "intensive" category was defined as including all manufacturing activities with 40 or more workers per net industrial acre, with "extensive" applying to those activities with fewer than 40. The Philadelphia City Planning Commission study employed three density classes, intensive, intermediate, and extensive, with differing definitions to suit the needs of its area.[3]

Density Standards for the Future

Having examined the density characteristics of existing manufacturing activity in the urban area and the range of variation from central to outlying areas, the next and second step is the development of density stand-

[1] Some planning agencies use the "net" measurement, which includes the industrial building site plus outdoor storage, parking, and loading areas, presumably eliminating undeveloped portions of the industrial site, bounding or internal streets, and railroad spurs included in a "gross" measurement. However, this usage is generally connected with analyses of existing manufacturing areas, rather than in the context of land use planning studies for future industrial areas. For estimating future land requirements, gross measures which include streets, railroad spurs, and similar service facilities are simpler to apply to vacant and open land in dimensioning the land use plan.

[2] Detroit Metropolitan Area Regional Planning Commission, *Industrial Land Use in the Detroit Region*, February, 1952, mimeo., p. 7.

[3] Philadelphia City Planning Commission, *Industrial Land Use Plan*, December, 1950, pp. 8–9.

ards to be used in estimating space needs for industrial expansion in the future. These are generally developed as adaptations of the existing densities, considering modern-day trends in site sizes among various industrial uses. Densities for activities which the study of the urban economy suggests are likely to develop in the area in the future and would be entirely new to the area are generally estimated on the basis of studies made in other cities where these activities presently exist.

Illustrative of this general approach, the Department of Planning in Greensboro, North Carolina (planning area of about 100,000 population), adopted in 1948 a single general density standard of 30 manufacturing employees per gross industrial acre.[4] This compares with a then existing industrial density of 37.3 manufacturing employees per gross industrially used acre. This was considered adequate in this area for modern one-story plants and their parking, loading and storage spaces. In Philadelphia, standards adopted are:[5]

Density Class	Workers Per Acre	
	Net	Gross
Intensive	147	50
Intermediate	40	18
Extensive	18	6

As an average gross density for all manufacturing, Cincinnati has used 30,[6] Copenhagen, 20,[7] and the British new towns, 30.[8]

Estimating Space Needs

The foregoing type of standard when applied to the appropriate estimates of *increases in manufacturing employment* is sometimes used as a basis for determining the amount of land required for new industry. To make allowances for replacements of existing industrial plants in character with contemporary trends toward the spread-out one-story type of development, it is more common to apply the locally derived density standards to appropriate estimates of *total forecast manufacturing employment*. The difference between this result and the acreage presently in manufacturing

[4] Greensboro (N.C.) Department of Planning, *Land Use Plan, Greensboro Metropolitan Area*, offset, 1948, p. 26.
[5] Philadelphia City Planning Commission, *op. cit.*, pp. 8–9.
[6] Cincinnati City Planning Commission, *Industrial Areas*, June, 1946, p. 46.
[7] *Storkobenhavn*, udarbejdet 1947, Egnsplankontoret.
[8] Patrick Abercrombie, *Greater London Plan 1944*, His Majesty's Stationery Office, 1945, p. 52; and T. A. Jeffreys, "New Towns Technique," *Journal of the Town Planning Institute*, November–December, 1946, p. 12.

use is then taken to be the estimated additional land needed for industrial use. Since all plants cannot be expected to rebuild to these standards during the planning period, the latter approach in effect introduces a "built-in" safety factor to allow for a greater industrial growth than is foreseen under normal circumstances.

Even with the introduction of such a safety factor, the resulting estimate of space requirements is generally regarded, especially in small urban areas, as insufficient to cover the contingency of very large installations desiring to locate in the area. To cover such an eventuality and at the same time to give some recognition to the importance of protecting prime industrial sites in anticipation of needs even beyond the immediate planning period, frequently a planning agency will earmark additional areas as "industrial reserves." There is no standard practice in estimating space requirements in this category. It is largely a subjective matter, tempered somewhat by the supply of land in fringe and dispersed locations appropriate for industrial use. In urban areas situated in level country where there is virtually an unlimited supply of open land adjacent to highway and railroad transportation facilities and within reasonable range of existing utility lines, it is less important to provide an industrial reserve. In hilly and mountainous areas, the protection of prime industrial land is a matter of considerable importance, and planning agencies are much more likely to provide for an industrial reserve.

The foregoing procedures apply in arriving at *overall estimates* of industrial space requirements for an urban area. In the large metropolitan area it may be desirable to differentiate between inlying and outlying areas in the density standards adopted. Higher land values and the additional taxes usually involved in incorporated portions of the urban area may dictate as a practical consideration a dual system of density standards, with a higher range of densities for density classes located in the inlying areas than those being used for corresponding classes in the outlying areas. In many urban areas, by "natural selection," the intensive, intermediate, and extensive density classes distribute themselves in inlying, fringe, and outlying locations more or less automatically in recognition of these practical considerations, and it is thus unnecessary to employ a dual-standard system.

Trial Distribution Scheme

Having arrived at an estimate of the total amount of land needed for future industrial growth broken down by density classes, the final step is one of matching up the supply of vacant and renewal land having industrial use potentialities with the estimated need for industrial land. In this step the acreage requirements for future industrial expansion are tentatively dimensioned into areas considered to be prime land for industrial use as established by the previous analysis of location requirements. (This would be Class 1 Prime land in the illustrative classification system of Table 19.) Whether or not the single or dual system of density standards is being employed, gross allocations are first made on the basis of proportions of total industrial expansion expected to occur in the central city of the urban area and in the outlying portions.[9] This procedure provides a crude control in the dimensioning process. This proportion is estimated on the basis of observed past trends in the rates of industrial growth in these two portions of the urban area, but considered in the light of the supply of vacant and renewal land in the central city available for the absorption of industrial development. Once tentative allocations have been made on this basis, allocations are made to each of the two portions of the urban area by density classes. The *pro rata* share of expansion in each portion of the urban area is tentatively dimensioned into vacant and renewal areas according to estimated proportions of subtotals each density class will absorb in the future. The final result may be summarized as indicated in Table 25.

TABLE 25.   New Space Requirements for Industrial Areas, 19xx

Density Class	Acreage Requirements			
	Central Areas[a]	Fringe Areas[a]	Outlying Areas[a]	Total
Intensive	xx	xx	xx	xxx
Intermediate	xx	xx	xx	xxx
Extensive	xx	xx	xx	xxx
Planning Area total	xx	xx	xx	xxx

[a] As a practical necessity, these areas are usually differentiated by designation of the central city as constituting "central areas," suburban incorporated cities as "fringe areas," and unincorporated areas at the outskirts of the planning area as "outlying areas." This table obviously applies to large metropolitan areas and would be simplified when used for smaller urban centers.

After a trial distribution has been made, the surplus land not required in the foregoing allocation process is earmarked for possible absorption by other land use classes according to analyses to follow. Appropriate overlays are prepared identifying land allocated for industrial use and the residual areas available for other uses. It should be emphasized that the

[9] In large metropolitan areas, it may make more sense to group certain suburban communities with the central city for purposes of these breakdowns, and in some it may be possible to establish an intermediate ring of incorporated communities between the central city and the outlying fringe area as in Table 25.

above allocations of land for future industrial use are tentative at this stage of the analysis. As noted earlier, these remain tentative until the final design phase of the land use planning procedure is reached.

Detailed Industrial Planning Studies

The above crude procedures for the estimation of space requirements are reasonably satisfactory for purposes of the generalized or preliminary land use plan. However, as attention is directed toward revision and refinement of these first investigations, looking toward the development of a comprehensive plan, studies of a much more detailed nature covering a wider range of considerations are required. The general character of these later, more detailed studies is indicated below.

DETAILING THE SPACE NEEDS

The above-described approach to estimating space requirements is geared to analyses of general aggregates of manufacturing activity. In effect, the broad groupings of manufacturing activity for which employment data are reported in the Census of Population have imposed limits on the level of detail that is possible. Furthermore, to the extent that the land use survey is planned and conducted to furnish data of a general-purpose character, this basic source of information imposes similar limitations. Consequently, when the comprehensive plan studies come to focus on industrial space requirements, it is generally necessary to undertake an industrial survey, often a combined survey of industrial and wholesale activities.

Essentially this survey is an establishment-by-establishment study involving interviews with the management. Although the content of the survey may be partly dictated by the needs of coöperating promotional groups and others interested in industrial development, for industrial land use planning purposes, the planning agency will want to obtain such detailed information as: past and present employment by shift; total land area within the property lines of each establishment and how this area is taken up by the plant and auxiliary buildings, by outdoor storage and waste areas, and by parking and loading facilities; floor area data; water-using, waste-disposal, and other operating characteristics of the activity; transportation and utility services available to the plant site; and so on. Such surveys must be carefully structured to the data requirements of space analyses undertaken later in the study.

Dorothy A. Muncy's research into space requirements for industry provides considerable insight into the kind of detail required for more advanced analyses.[10] Her work indicates ways of classifying industries in much greater detail than is customarily used in preliminary land use planning studies, and among other things, suggests the advisability of using floor area standards and of computing industrial densities on the basis of shift employment as opposed to total employment. Her studies of floor space per employee, structural density (ratio of the ground area of the factory and its accessory structures to the total land area of the plant site), and other site relationships provide important clues for the derivation of more precise industrial density standards for various classes of manufacturing activity. All these considerations should be taken into account in detailed land use planning studies of industrial space requirements.

PLANNED INDUSTRIAL DISTRICTS

In connection with more detailed studies of industrial land use, investigations should include consideration of organized or planned industrial districts. Just as entire residential communities or shopping centers are now planned and built as integrated developments, modern-day industrial areas are increasingly being developed as planned industrial districts. Usually an enterprise under one management for marketing industrial sites on a sale or long-term lease arrangement, these developments are laid out in acreage lots of varying size especially designed for modern industrial operations. Employee parking and loading areas are required; water, waste, power, and fire protection facilities adequate for contemporary types of industrial operations are provided; and special attention is given to railroad and trucking facilities, and in some cases, to water and air transportation. Some of the more enterprising developments are conceived as "industrial parks," reserving areas for special common facilities such as lunchrooms, exhibition space, and recreation and park areas, and providing for control over landscaping and the architectural design of structures.

Based on the experience of some of the pioneering organized industrial districts, manuals are available describing methods of planning, organizing, financing, and developing these industrial districts.[11] Although oriented

[10] Dorothy A. Muncy, *Space for Industry, An Analysis of Site and Location Requirements*, Technical Bulletin No. 23, Urban Land Institute, July, 1954.

[11] See Theodore K. Pasma, *Organized Industrial Districts*, a U.S. Department of Commerce publication, Government Printing Office, June, 1954, and Milburn L. Forth and J. Ross McKeever, *Planned Industrial Districts*, Technical Bulletin No. 19, Urban Land Institute, October, 1952.

mainly toward detailed site planning and development work, they provide useful insights into general land use planning requirements. Of particular interest is the general magnitude of these developments. One analysis of tract sizes of established industrial districts indicates that 80 percent of the districts have tracts of less than 500 acres. The average tract is about 454 acres. Of the older, established districts, the average acreage comes to 1182.[12] In identifying acreages of this magnitude for possible development as planned industrial districts, the land use plan must not only take into consideration topographic, transportation, utility, and other requirements normally associated with studies of industrial needs, but it must also give special attention to land ownership patterns and the actual availability of tracts for the industrial use contemplated. Obviously, the availability of unsubdivided land in as few ownerships as possible with clear land titles is an important consideration affecting the feasibility of developing such districts.

SPACE NEEDS OF WHOLESALE AND RELATED USES

Of all the major use categories customarily included in the land use plan, the class referred to as "wholesale and related uses" is generally treated with the least specificity. Indeed, it is often combined with manufacturing or given only vague recognition in a "general business" category. This is, of course, a reflection of the lack of attention accorded the wholesaling function in planning research and the need for studies which define the space-using characteristics of wholesale uses and provide techniques especially suited to the measurement of space requirements.[13]

It has been common practice to relegate to this category all commercial uses of a nonindustrial and nonretail nature. Yet an investigation of the range of uses that thus fall within such a category clearly suggests the need for some form of subgrouping within this category, possibly some reallocation of uses to industrial or CBD office categories in recognition of variations in function, location, and space-using characteristics. While a great deal of further research is needed in this general area, for purposes

[12] Pasma, *op. cit.*, p. 7.

[13] In recognition of this research need, an exploratory study in this problem area was made in 1954–55 with the aid of the Institute for Research in Social Science, University of North Carolina. Much of the material from this section of the chapter is drawn from this study. (George M. Beaton, *Planning for Wholesale and Related Functions*, unpublished study, Department of City and Regional Planning, University of North Carolina, 1955.)

of the preliminary land use plan, three general subgroups warrant recognition: wholesaling and warehousing proper, trucking and related warehousing, and the subcategory "other." This categorization is dictated primarily by standard employment data available in the Census of Business and the Census of Population which are used in conjunction with land use information for the estimation of space requirements. Of these three subcategories, the first two submit to a crude form of systematic analysis, with space requirements for the "other" subcategory being developed on a case-by-case consideration of the uses which fall within this miscellaneous group locally.

Of the Census of Business' five-category classification of wholesalers, four categories could be included under our classification *wholesaling and warehousing proper:* merchant wholesalers, manufacturers' sales branches and offices, wholesale agents and brokers, and wholesale assemblers.[14] The fifth category, petroleum bulk stations, is more appropriately included in the final miscellaneous classification called "other," since it possesses distinctly special space-using characteristics. Merchant wholesalers generally predominate in this first class, and employing warehouses for assembly, storage, and distribution of goods are the establishments traditionally associated with wholesale uses. They include retail distributors, who deal in commodities for retail outlets, and industrial distributors, who deal in goods bought for further processing or for business consumption. Manufacturers' sales branches and offices, a mixed group, function in effect to by-pass merchant wholesalers. As the name implies, they are the manufacturers' own outlets. Sales branches require warehousing as well as display space, while sales offices require only display and office space for taking orders, which are then handled directly from the manufacturing plant. Wholesale agents and brokers are middlemen who require only display and office space.[15] They do not handle or acquire title to goods but only arrange sales between producers and retailers or wholesale merchants. Wholesale assemblers, who collect farm output for distribution to other wholesalers or to retailers, include farm-produce packers, shippers, coöperative marketing associations, and storage stations (e.g., grain elevators, tobacco warehouses, cotton gins, milk depots, etc.).

[14] The Bureau of the Census defines wholesale establishments as "those productive units which are engaged in selling merchandise to retailers, to industrial, commercial, institutional, or professional users or to other wholesalers, or acting as agents in buying merchandise for or selling merchandise to such persons or businesses." The wholesale part of a business is counted as a separate establishment if it is operated functionally on a separate basis, and where businesses deal in both retail and wholesale trade, the business is classified in the category with the majority of sales. (*Source:* Bureau of the Census, *U.S. Census of Business: 1948,* Volume IV, Wholesale Trade—General Statistics, U.S. Government Printing Office, 1952, p. 2.)

[15] In line with comments above, manufacturers' sales offices and wholesale agents and brokers would be more properly classified with CBD office uses for detailed land use planning studies.

The *trucking and related warehousing* category as used here refers to common carrier trucking facilities. These are the trucking firms which require terminals for assembly and breakdown of truck-load lots in connection with over-the-road hauls, and include accessory warehousing, repair and service facilities, and employee dormitories and similar services. They serve largely manufacturers and wholesalers, deriving only about 10 percent of their business from CBD activities.[16]

With this brief introduction to wholesale and related uses, we may now examine techniques for estimating space requirements. This analysis includes a sequence of four steps:

1. Analyze the characteristics of existing wholesale and related activities in the urban area.
2. On the basis of anticipated growth in wholesale activity as determined in studies of the urban economy and expected changes in the intensity of use, estimate future ratios of land area per employee for inlying and outlying locations.
3. Apply these ratios to future wholesale employment estimates to obtain estimated land requirements.
4. Determine from summary of vacant and renewal land how supply matches up with estimated need, and, referring to location requirements, make a trial distribution into areas identified as having potentialities for this use, earmarking the surplus for use in subsequent analyses of other uses.

A more detailed explanation of these steps to the analysis follows.

Existing Wholesale Areas

For the generalized results required in the preliminary land use plan, the first step is simply one of organizing data assembled in the land use survey and studies of the urban economy and employment in a form suitable for evaluating the general character and intensity of development in areas presently used for wholesale purposes. The acreages of wholesale use for the urban area as a whole are abstracted from the land use summary, including breakdowns by subcategories for wholesaling proper, trucking, and other related uses. If these wholesale breakdowns were not compiled in the original summary of the land use survey, remeasurements of land areas in wholesale use of course would have to be made. In addition, summaries by major subdivisions of the urban area are required, and in

[16] See Planning Advisory Service, *Motor Truck Terminals*, Information Report No. 21, American Society of Planning Officials, December, 1950.

order to permit comparative analyses with employment data, usually the central city and the balance of the planning area are the selected sub-areas. Summarized in percentages, these breakdowns by area give a crude indication of the relative concentration of wholesale uses in the inlying and outlying portions of the urban area.

By recapitulating wholesale employment data by the same functional and areal categories,[17] and applying these to acreage figures, it is possible to compute existing ratios of employees per wholesale acre for each of these categories and for the urban area as a whole. Measures of the existing intensity in the use of wholesale land (the percentage coverage of land areas by wholesale structures) may be computed from Base C land use maps or by reference to insurance atlases.

Future Land Area Ratios

With a knowledge of the characteristics of existing development in wholesale use, it is possible to proceed to the development of standards of wholesale acres per employee. For purposes of the preliminary land use plan, the most expedient procedure in developing such standards at present is one of examining existing ratios for their sufficiency and subjectively upgrading those which appear to possess inadequacies for the character and intensity of development judged reasonable for the future. Thus if existing development as a whole in any one of the three functional sub-categories of wholesaling, in either the inlying or outlying areas, appears to be crowding the land by comparison with some selected local "model" development or modern developments elsewhere, appropriate adjustments upward may be made. Such elements as the percentage of the land covered by structures and the observed adequacy of parking, loading, and service areas would provide the basis for making these adjustments.

It should be noted that the floor space per employee is a more valid basis for developing standards than land area per employee. In later detailed studies in revision of the first crude estimates developed by the above procedures in preliminary studies, a special establishment-by-establishment survey (probably combined with the industrial survey suggested earlier) would be designed and conducted to obtain, among other things, floor area data. Floor area ratios would then be used as base standards,

---

[17] Census of Business employment figures are available separately for major cities and Standard Metropolitan Areas. Crude adjustment of SMA figures to a planning area basis is made by reference to local sources of employment data for establishments beyond the planning area but inside the SMA.

with land area ratios developed from these base standards by applying appropriate parking standards and expansion factors to take into account loading and other on-site space requirements.

Using data compiled in a survey of industrial and distributive land uses made in Nashville and Davidson County, Tennessee, in 1954 by the Nashville Planning Commission, Beaton followed this approach in developing standards of land area per wholesale employee in this urban area.[18] Floor area ratios for some 87 establishments covered by the survey were computed, and by reference to questions of adequacy of space that were addressed to the management of these establishments as part of the survey, standards of the floor area per employee for future wholesale development were derived. Results obtained suggested that in the Nashville area, for wholesaling proper, 1000 square feet of floor space per employee, and for trucking and related warehousing, 3500 square feet per employee were reasonable average standards for the urban area as a whole (the study did not use separate standards for inlying and outlying wholesale structures). Then by reference to coverage data and the observations of the management concerning the adequacy of the site, both of which were obtained in the survey, conversion factors were developed to express floor area ratios in land area ratios. For petroleum bulk stations, land area ratios were computed direct. These investigations resulted in the following standards for the survey area as a whole:

Activity	Acres per Employee
Wholesaling proper[a]	0.032
Trucking-warehousing	0.103
Petroleum bulk stations	0.344

[a] Merchant wholesalers, manufacturers' sales branches, and assemblers only.

The study also dealt with variations in ratios of land area per employee for central, intermediate, and outlying areas.

Future Space Requirements

Once space standards for future wholesale development have been derived, space requirements can be estimated by applying these standards to estimates of future employment developed as described in Chapter 6. Land requirements would be broken down to show the space needed by the end of the planning period for each subcategory of wholesale activity

[18] Beaton, *op. cit.*, pp. 84–91.

and for the central city and the remainder of the planning area. Table 26 indicates the kind of summary of space requirements which should finally emerge from these analyses. The "extensive" and "intensive" subcategories at the head of the table are shown to indicate the possibility of using dual standards. Thus in the central city, there may be intensive wholesale developments near the CBD and more extensive types in outlying locations. By the same token fringe areas may require dual standards.

TABLE 26.   New Space Requirements for Wholesale and Related Uses, 19xx

| Wholesale Categories | Acreage Requirements | | | | | |
| | Central City | | Outlying Area | | Total | |
	Ext.[a]	Int.	Ext.[a]	Int.	Ext.[a]	Int.
Wholesaling and warehousing proper	xx	xx	xx	xx	xxx	xxx
Trucking and related warehousing	xx	xx	xx	xx	xxx	xxx
Other (petroleum bulk stations, etc.)	xx	xx	xx	xx	xxx	xxx
All wholesale and related uses	xx	xx	xx	xx	xxx	xxx

[a] "Ext." is an abbreviation for "Extensive," "Int." for "Intensive."

An alternative but less reliable approach sometimes used in estimating space requirements in preliminary land use plans utilizes an index of wholesale activity as a "multiplier." Such an index is constructed from a wholesale sales series and projected by ratio procedures using a forecast of Gross National Product or some other national income series. This approach assumes that space requirements will increase in proportion to the forecast increases in wholesale activity. Thus a 20 percent rise in the index would mean a 20 percent base increase in total space requirements. The approach next makes certain assumptions relative to changes in space requirements of existing wholesale establishments in line with observations of the local scene, such as trends toward decentralization and a more spread-out type of building development, corrections for inadequate loading, parking, and other on-site facilities accessory to existing wholesale establishments. Finally, a safety factor is introduced to allow for unforeseen increases in wholesale activity and to provide some flexibility to incoming wholesale concerns in choice of sites.

The Greensboro preliminary land use plan illustrates these procedures.[19] In 1948 this study estimated an increase of 23.5 percent in wholesale activity during the planning period. Thus the then existing space devoted to this use was increased by an equivalent percent. On the basis of observed past trends in the area in this respect, it was then estimated that in the next 20 years 75 percent of the existing wholesale development in the central business district would move to outlying wholesale areas at half the existing intensity of development. This assumption necessitated a net in-

[19] Greensboro Department of Planning, *op. cit.*, p. 27.

crease in wholesale land then existing in addition to the 23.5 percent increase, with subtractions in the downtown area and additions in intermediate and outlying areas. Finally, this study determined that these combined new land requirements should be increased by 50 percent to provide a safety factor for unforeseen contingencies.

Trial Distribution Scheme

The final step in the procedure compares the supply of vacant and renewal land judged to have wholesale use potentialities with the estimated need as established by procedures described above, and makes a tentative distribution of these acreage requirements according to location criteria established by studies discussed in Chapter 11. Using the same procedure employed in the analysis of manufacturing areas, allocations are first made to central city and outlying portions of the urban area on a proportional basis to serve as a control in the dimensioning process. Here too, proportions are estimated on the basis of observed past trends of growth in these two segments of the urban area relative to one another, and on the supply of vacant and renewal land in these areas available for wholesale development, particularly considering any ceilings on growth imposed by space limitations of intown locations. Of course, this procedure must recognize any assumptions previously made concerning decentralization of wholesale uses. Then, in the framework of these controls, total acreage requirements are tentatively dimensioned into vacant and renewal areas previously identified as having potentialities for wholesale use or into areas carried over in the surplus tally as not needed for manufacturing uses. The map of vacant and renewal areas and the overlay of surplus industrial lands provide ready references for this dimensioning process. Finally, all land not needed to fill out space requirements for wholesale and related uses is carried over in the surplus land tally for absorption in other use categories in analyses that follow, and the accompanying overlay map is modified to show the locations of the surplus vacant land available at the conclusion of this analysis.

SPACE REQUIREMENTS FOR REGION-SERVING BUSINESS AREAS

Perhaps the most complex and difficult problems the average metropolitan area faces today are found in the business areas, particularly in the central business district. Foremost among these are traffic congestion and the lack of adequate parking. Although the immediate concern of investigations described below is with land use, proposals for the movement of people and goods to and from and within the central area and certainly the storage of vehicles during business hours of the day profoundly affect land use planning proposals. Indeed, these transportation elements are large space-using activities themselves. Obviously, if optimum parking conditions prevailed, vast areas would be taken up in storage of cars, even if the space were provided in multideck mechanized parking lofts. And if it were feasible to finance the drastic surgery that would be required in central areas so that all people with destinations in the CBD could drive there and find terminal parking space, great swaths would have to be cut through built-up areas in all directions simply to accommodate the traffic. These costs would be staggering. Even if the auto millennium were here and every person entering the CBD daily had an automobile enabling him to make the trip by car, the overall costs for completely "automobilizing" the CBD would be astronomical. Thus transit becomes an important leveling factor in striking some kind of practical balance—transit planned in effective balance with automotive transportation and its parking requirements.

The integrated solution to these problems is the subject of special CBD improvement studies.[20] While the kind of generalized approach to these problems involved in developing the preliminary land use plan falls far short of providing solutions in the detail that ultimately will be required, they do assist in identifying the broad relationships involved and the general outlines of solutions that must be worked out in later refined types of studies.

For purposes of a preliminary plan and the generalized result desired, a very broad-gauge type of approach to the estimation of business space requirements is generally used. For the fully detailed analysis of space needs undertaken in comprehensive plan studies, a whole array of specialized investigations of retail, service, office, and other commercial functions is required. Although detailed floor area analyses, purchasing power studies and other specialized types of investigations are alluded to at the end of the discussion below, our main concern here is with a type of analysis commensurate in detail with those undertaken in space analyses of other uses. It should be noted that, as a beginning point in these preliminary studies, analyses of space needs assume a continuation of the present

---

[20] For a compendium of proposals growing out of such studies taken from a variety of cities, see Planning Advisory Service, *Programs for Central Business District Improvements*, Information Report No. 80, American Society of Planning Officials, November, 1955.

balance in the use of automotive and transit modes of transportation. In the final design stages of the generalized plan, when a preliminary transportation plan becomes available, adjustments may be necessary in order to bring these initial assumptions into harmony with those of transportation studies.

As noted in Chapter 11, three types of region-serving business areas are involved in this general use category. These are the central business district, various satellite business centers, and highway service centers. The satellite centers include certain decentralized CBD-type business activities seeking larger and lower value sites and escape from the downtown congestion (e.g., auto sales and service centers, office building centers, etc.), and the so-called "regional shopping center," the type of facility planned and engineered for the automobile age. Since fully satisfactory estimates of space requirements for regional shopping centers and highway service centers involve specialized investigations not normally feasible for inclusion in preliminary land use planning analyses, these types of business areas will be taken up briefly at the outset before attention is centered on the CBD and its satellite business centers.

Regional and Highway Service Centers

Decisions relative to developing regional shopping centers require particularly exacting studies because of heavy initial investments involved in this type of center. These include purchasing power analyses, investigations of buying habits, surveys of family expenditure patterns, and a variety of other studies. Having removed these studies from the scope of the present approach, and with the relatively limited experience with this new type of business area generally available to serve as a guide, for purposes of the preliminary land use plan the only feasible procedure for the present is simply to insure that, if such a center seems warranted, a generous reservation of land is made for it in the most strategic location. General guides in this respect were presented in Chapter 11.

Space requirements for highway service types of business areas are dependent upon studies of both inter- and intraregional traffic movements and the make-up of these movements. According to the characteristics of this traffic, one or more types of business centers may be warranted. Thus, along major tourist routes, these studies may indicate the need for tourist service centers. For these centers site sizes will be conditioned by space requirements for one or more modern motel accommodations on sites easily seen from the highway yet set back from the noise of passing traffic, plus their accessory restaurant and automobile service facilities. Along major trucking routes, a few sites for facilities to serve the 24-hour schedules of the trucking industry should be anticipated. Special sites for these needs will be less important where truck terminal centers are planned in peripheral locations.

In addition to these transient forms of business, highway service centers may be warranted to cater to the needs of the local metropolitan area, providing for outdoor theaters, drive-in refreshment and produce stands, auction centers, automobile service areas, and so on. In the average small and medium-size metropolitan area, say 250,000 or under, where site planning review requirements are anticipated in the implementing zoning provisions, a single type of highway service center may suffice. In the larger metropolitan areas, two or three types of highway service centers may be desirable to meet the needs of specialized service facilities. The number and spacing of these centers will normally be determined on the basis of estimates of purchasing power to be tapped from either transient or localized sources or both. The space requirements for any particular center will depend upon the number and character of facilities estimated to be needed in each such center and how they can be provided within the framework of an integrated site plan. For preliminary land use planning purposes, these analyses are necessarily very general, and since aggregate space requirements are somewhat nominal as compared to those of other land uses, the generalized land use plan frequently carries only symbols as to strategic locations and the spacing of such centers in outlying rural sections of the planning area, specifying in the text of the plan the criteria to be employed in the future establishment of these highway service centers.

Study of CBD Characteristics

Turning now to the central business district and satellite business centers, the analysis of space needs entails a sequence of three steps:

1. Delineate the CBD study area and satellite business centers and analyze existing space usage by floor area and ground area.
2. On the basis of this analysis and studies of retail business trends in the primary trade area, develop estimates of probable changes in intensity of use, parking needs, and so on, and determine future space needs.
3. Determine from vacant and renewal land summary the amount of land available for CBD expansion and determine what additional space is

expected to become available due to decentralization moves of whole-sale and manufacturing uses presently in CBD. Establish space deficit, if any. As necessary earmark for CBD expansion strategically located areas, and summarize data on areas presently in other uses needed for CBD expansion. Repeat these space investigations for satellite centers.

The first step involves the definition of the CBD study area and any satellite business centers which exist at present or are anticipated to develop, and the compilation of floor area and acreage data relative to uses located in these areas from Base C type of land use maps and supplemental sources. Since what may reasonably be expected to be the limits of the future CBD cannot be firmly established until the full sequence of this analysis is complete, the CBD study area as defined in this first step is tentative. In general, it is drawn so that it is overly generous in extent. The delineation recognizes the directions in which the CBD is currently expanding, and is traced out to include immediately adjoining areas in wholesale and manufacturing use previously identified as being likely to relocate in outlying areas during the planning period. It also recognizes locations of any adjoining renewal areas, and is drawn to include the major portions, if not all of the "inner loop," the major belt street ringing the CBD as defined in the preliminary thoroughfare scheme.

It should be noted that the CBD study area is therefore larger than the CBD as it is seen today or as defined by various empirical methods for research analyses of CBD structure. Nevertheless, such empirical methods are useful in defining the CBD core which can then be used as a basis for delineating the larger study area. Particularly useful in this respect is Murphy and Vance's "central business index method."[21] Defining the central business district in terms of whole blocks, this method utilizes two general tests, supplemented by special rules to take care of civic center uses and special situations. A block in which the ratio of the total area in central business uses on all floors to the total ground floor area has a numerical value of one or more would be included in the CBD. In the terminology of the authors, this block would have a "central business height index" of one or more. Any additional blocks where the percentage of the floor area on all floors in central business uses is 50 or more would also be included. The terminology used here is "central business intensity index." Central business uses are defined as those involved in "the retailing of goods and services for a profit and the performing of various office functions."

Once a CBD study area is tentatively defined, major subfunctional areas are defined, recognizing principal concentrations of retail shopping, enter-

---

[21] Raymond E. Murphy and J. E. Vance, Jr., "Delimiting the CBD," *Economic Geography*, July, 1954, pp. 209–219.

tainment, finance, offices, and such other functional groupings as represented by the civic center or the wholesale district and manufacturing areas which may be present. In this connection, unless special attention was given in the land use survey to the detail required in the analysis of the CBD study area and satellite business centers, a special resurvey may be required.[22] Assuming the necessary detailed information is available, in each subfunctional area, acreages occupied by structures in each dominant class of use, acreages devoted to off-street parking lots, and the residual acreage (alleys, landscaping, outdoor sales space, etc.) are tabulated. In addition to these subarea summaries, an overall summary for the entire study area is developed in two parts, one to show ground acreages by major class of use, and the other to show floor area for retail uses and office uses broken down into subtotals as to area on the first floor and area above the first floor.

In addition to the CBD analysis, it is necessary to investigate the characteristics of any distinct satellite region-serving business centers that exist in the metropolitan area. Generally, similar procedures are followed in delineating and analyzing these centers. For scattered region-serving business establishments, a miscellaneous "all other" category is used in area tabulations.

Future Space Requirements

Having established the existing physical characteristics of the CBD study area and satellite centers, the second step draws on this information and, by using crude proportions relating space to the appropriate "multiplier," develops estimates of future space requirements. A crude estimate of the needed increase in aggregate floor space to be devoted to retail uses in the CBD and all satellite centers may be computed in proportion to the increase in population expected during the planning period in the primary trade area.[23] Sometimes a retail sales index is used as a "multiplier" in lieu of of retail trade area population growth. A rough measure of the needed in-

[22] In this connection, the reader should be familiar with the detailed kind of CBD survey developed by Murphy and Vance, *ibid*, pp. 204–209.

[23] Murphy and Vance report that there appeared to be no significant relationship between floor space and primary trade area population in the nine small-city CBD's they studied, but their studies do not take into account all region-serving retail areas—retail floor space situated in satellite business centers and in scattered locations as well as in the CBD proper. Certainly further study is needed covering more cases and experimenting with different definitions of floor area identified with the retail function and different delineations of the tributary trade area before the use of a population "multiplier" is rejected or unconditionally accepted as a method of estimating space requirements.

crease in aggregate floor space to be devoted to office use may be computed proportional to the increase in employment expected during the planning period in the professions, finance, insurance, real estate, and similar office-related categories of the employment forecast. Once the aggregate increments of increase have been determined, they are allocated to the CBD and satellite business centers in proportion to the assumed extent that each will share in the overall increases. These percentages are based on existing proportions adjusted subjectively to reflect observed trends or any planned modifications in these areas which might alter these trends.

Next, according to assumptions as to an average height of building in which this aggregate floor space will be accommodated in the CBD and each center, estimates of the amount of additional ground floor area which will be needed in all business areas during the planning period are developed. Next, according to locally adopted standards relating parking space to floor area, the amount of additional ground area in off-street parking required (1) to accommodate the new retail and office uses, and (2) to make up deficiencies in off-street parking for existing retail and office uses, is estimated and added to this acreage in all business centers. Then, on the basis of observations of existing relationships between the loading and yard areas to retail floor area of the present retail shopping areas, standards considered reasonable and adequate for the new retail development in the CBD and for outlying centers are adopted and applied, and the amount of space needed for these purposes is added into these cumulative totals. Finally, these totals are adjusted upward by an amount judged to be adequate to allow for drives, landscaping, and waste area and to provide a safety factor for unforeseen needs not covered in the foregoing analysis.

To illustrate this procedure, the 1948 land use planning analysis in Greensboro, North Carolina, is again cited.[24] This study dealt only with the CBD and did not differentiate between retail and office functions, and therefore did not use separate growth "multipliers." In terms of conditions then prevailing, the following assumptions were considered in the study to be reasonable:

1. Additional floor area needed will be 23.5 percent of present floor area.
2. This expansion will take place in structures of an average height of 1.75 stories.
3. One square foot of off-street parking will be required for every two square feet of ground floor retail area, and for every three square feet of space on upper floors.
4. One square foot of loading and yard area will be required for every 20 square feet of total retail floor area.

[24] Greensboro Department of Planning, *op. cit.*, pp. 28–31.

5. To all the above land area, 20 percent should be added for landscaping, drives, and waste areas.[25]

These assumptions are of course purely illustrative, and in another setting where different conditions prevail, an entirely different set of standards would be adopted.

The foregoing procedures apply in estimating space requirements for retail and office functions. For other functions, such as civic center needs and its accessory parking areas, rail, bus, and possibly helicopter terminal facilities and their accessory parking areas, central park areas and other uses to be accommodated in the CBD, special estimates of space requirements are necessary. (Techniques for estimating space needs for these functions are taken up under other sections of this chapter.) The sum total of these needs, when added to the acreage presently in use for retail shopping and office purposes, yields a grand total of the net area required for the future development of the CBD.

Dimensioning the Future CBD

Finally, these total net space requirements are fitted into the block pattern of the CBD study area and other centers that exists or as this pattern may be modified by street adjustments or by renewal measures. The process of "dimensioning in" space needs in the CBD takes into account criteria previously established and such tempering elements as the prevailing directions of expansion, land values in the central area, the preliminary thoroughfare scheme, the pattern of railroads in or near the CBD and other relatively fixed features, natural or man-made. Close-in vacant and renewal areas are first examined for their suitability as expansion areas for the CBD. Then the manufacturing, wholesale, and general commercial areas in the downtown section expected to become available by the natural processes of decentralization and succession are investigated for their adaptability to CBD uses. Finally, any additional area needed may involve the earmarking of acreage for CBD purposes from residential areas, usually areas where old residences have been converted into rooming houses or light housekeeping apartments (sometimes referred to as the

[25] This study added to the total space required as determined from applications of these assumptions an additional increment of acreage amounting to roughly 20 percent to serve as a flexibility factor.

"area of transition") bordering on the present central business area. While clearance of limited portions of these occupied areas may be achieved by blanketing them into clearance areas under the local public renewal program, for the most part stimulation for clearance and redevelopment into new CBD uses during the planning period must come from indirect means such as zoning changes, stiffening of fire regulations, promotional programs, and so on.

The problems of guiding expansion of the central area along sound and orderly lines and controlling the speculative forces commonly present in areas of transition are particularly acute and difficult. Planning proposals are dealing here with an area which is largely built up and where properties (usually composing an area much larger than can be absorbed in the foreseeable future) are valued by their owners for a use that may not develop for a great many years, if at all. These problems of plan implementation are beyond the scope of this discussion. However, it is clear that much more positive implementation measures are required in central areas, perhaps along the lines of a central business improvement district authority contemplated in St. Paul, Minnesota,[26] backed with new forms of redevelopment powers.

Following the dimensioning process, any increments of vacant and renewal land not taken up in these analyses are entered in the surplus land tally, and any necessary modifications in the overlay maps keyed to the tally are made. In the central areas of the city this step may involve very few if any changes in the tally and key maps. Finally, data are summarized relative to areas tentatively identified for use invasion. Table 27 illustrates the way in which these analyses may be summarized. Since most if not all new acreage requirements involve invasions into built-up areas, therefore making the summary of vacant and renewal land of relatively limited utility, it is usually simpler to prepare this table in terms of *total space needs* rather than in terms of new space needs as done in other use analyses. While space requirements for the central park areas, the civic center, and public service uses requiring central locations are taken up later in the chapter, these needs are recapitulated in the table as part of the CBD space summary. This table also records the deductions in acreages presently in other uses so that these may be taken into account in space analyses of other affected use categories. Not shown in the table but necessary for later analyses of the housing inventory is a tabulation of the number of dwelling units affected, by type of structure.

[26] Organizing Committee of the St. Paul Central Business District Authority, *Downtown St. Paul*, City of St. Paul, August, 1943.

TABLE 27.   Total Space Requirements for CBD and Satellite Region-Serving Business Centers, 19xx

Type of Center and Use[a]	Net Acreage of Ground Area					
	Total Needs	Residence	Deductions from Other Uses			
			Wholesale	Mfg.	Other	Total
Central business district	xx	x	x	x	x	xx
Retail uses	xx	x	x	x	x	xx
Office uses	xx	x	x	x	x	xx
Civic uses and parks	xx	x	x	x	x	xx
Transportation uses	xx	x	x	x	x	xx
Other uses	xx	x	x	x	x	xx
Satellite business centers	xx	x	x	x	x	xx
Center A	xx	x	x	x	x	xx
Center B	xx	x	x	x	x	xx
Etc.	xx	x	x	x	x	xx
Other scattered	xx	x	x	x	x	xx
Total	xx	x	x	x	x	xx

[a] Acreage figures for each center and type of use include parking, loading, and other miscellaneous areas associated with these uses.

Later Detailed Investigations

As noted at the outset of this discussion of region-serving business areas, a variety of more exacting investigations are necessary in the refinement of this first generalized approach as the planning agency moves toward the development of a comprehensive plan. This is not to imply that there are highly developed techniques available for all phases of these investigations. On the contrary, the tools available for these purposes are variable in their precision and adequacy, and when these investigations are initiated, it soon becomes evident that there are a great many aspects of business area analysis which are urgently in need of research attention.

One series of studies which should be included among these later detailed investigations includes analyses of purchasing power, family expenditure patterns, and consumer buying habits. Such analyses are used mainly for the study of retail functions or business areas, having only limited application to office functions.

Contemporary techniques for making detailed estimates of retail space needs require estimates of the effective buying income in the retail trade area and how it is distributed among various income groups. This information is obtained in conjunction with a survey of family expenditures. Typical family expenditure patterns of these various income groups are spelled out for purposes of identifying the major kinds of retail facilities that are associated with goods and services purchased. In this connection, it has been found that the volume of goods and services purchased bears a relationship to the floor space required to handle the indicated volume of business. Once a measure of the volume of business by income group for various retail categories has been determined, a study of patronizing habits is made to establish what places the different income groups in various sectors of both the immediate urban area and outlying portions of the trade area select for what kinds of purchases. Besides providing insight into the many and complex variables affecting consumer purchase habits, this study provides a means of linking the spatial distribution of total space in retail use with the spatial distribution of the various income-group families patronizing these business areas.

While the Census of Business provides data on retail sales for various categories of establishments, the only means presently feasible for connecting these sales with the income and geographic distribution of families making the purchases reflected in these sales is through the above kinds of studies. Since forecasting techniques are most satisfactory if developed in terms of population units in these analyses—in this case the family—we therefore need family expenditure information for various income levels represented in the trade area, and according to the way these income groups are distributed spatially.

The procedures for these analyses can go into great detail, and their most detailed applications are found in shopping center analyses. Robert M. Lillibridge's analysis of a center in a Chicago redevelopment area gives perhaps the clearest and most systematic summary of the steps involved,[27] and shows how the Bureau of Labor Statistics' family expenditure studies may be used for estimation purposes in lieu of a sampling survey of families.[28] The Real Estate Research Corporation's analysis of Englewood Plaza in Chicago, an illustration of a study using a sampling survey, introduces an interesting geometric zonal and sector scheme for the analysis of families potentially served by this facility.[29]

Whether the study is centered on a particular shopping facility or its scope is the entire range of business areas in the city, there are obviously

[27] Robert M. Lillibridge, "Shopping Centers in Urban Redevelopment," *Land Economics*, May, 1948.
[28] Lillibridge used the 1935–36 BLS family expenditure studies (see Bureau of Labor Statistics, U.S. Department of Labor, *Family Expenditures in Selected Cities, 1935–36*, Volumes I–VII, U.S. Government Printing Office, 1940–41). Although published in less detail, the 1950 BLS surveys cover more cities and reflect more current buying habits (see Bureau of Labor Statistics, U.S. Department of Labor, *Family Income, Expenditures, and Savings in 1950*, Preliminary Report [revised], U.S. Government Printing Office, June, 1953).
[29] Real Estate Research Corporation, *Economic and Legal Analysis, Perimeter Plan for Englewood Plaza*, published by the author, 1953.

variations in the techniques that can be employed in pursuing the basic procedures—variations in short cuts that may be taken and variations in the methods of assembling data required at various stages of the analyses. But most techniques begin with the family or household as a unit, and by analysis of expenditure patterns of various income groups, build up estimates of gross retail sales for various retail locations. These estimates broken down by store type are translated into floor space, which in turn can be expanded into acreage requirements by using appropriate parking ratios, loading area factors, and so on.

Forecasts involve a variety of intangibles and uncertainties about the future which are difficult to assess. Buying habits are affected by changes in technology, fashion, and whim, which in certain lines are difficult if not impossible to anticipate with any reliability. (For example, in the entertainment field the widespread purchase of television sets has had an effect upon family expenditures for the movies.) Moreover, changes in patronage habits are difficult to anticipate. The place of patronage is affected not only by such elements as parking, traffic congestion, and the physical convenience and attractiveness of the business center, but also by customer loyalities, which depend upon management policies on such things as sales, opening and closing hours, merchandising practices, and other similar factors.[30] Changing income levels and inflationary-deflationary forces also offer formidable problems in forecasting. While these difficulties would seemingly raise serious questions as to the utility of these detailed analyses, it should be remembered that these sources of possible inaccuracy would have a relatively limited effect on the acreage space requirements, since parking and off-street loading areas constitute such a large proportion of the total space needs.

SPACE NEEDS OF PUBLIC SERVICE FACILITIES

What we refer to here as a "public service" group of uses is composed mainly of use activities which commonly appear on land use maps as either "public and semipublic uses" or "transportation, utilities, and communications." If existing land uses have been grouped and summarized following

[30] See series of studies of shopper attitudes, C. T. Jonassen, *Downtown vs. Suburban Shopping*, 1953, and *The Shopping Center Versus Downtown*, 1955, Bureau of Business Research, Ohio State University. Latter study also published as *Shopper Attitudes*, Special Report 11-A, Highway Research Board, 1955.

the pattern proposed in Table 17, the space needs for uses listed in this group would normally be analyzed as part of the functional category in which they fall in this table. Thus the civic center, the central post office, the state and federal functions, the various passenger stations, and headquarters for the various public utilities requiring access to the general public would be included in the CBD, possibly with branch offices or facilities in satellite business areas or community shopping centers. Similarly, such facilities as freight terminals, railroad marshaling yards and service facilities, port installations, power plants, gas works, and garbage and refuse disposal plants might be studied in conjunction with manufacturing uses, thus forming the category referred to in Table 17 as "industry and related uses." Some uses with special location considerations—uses which do not properly fall within any of the broad functional use categories, such uses as cemeteries, water works, sewage disposal plants, power substations, and airports—would continue to be handled as special uses. All these miscellaneous public service uses are grouped together for purposes of this discussion simply to emphasize their special nature and the necessity of reserving space for them in addition to that which may be provided for under the general use category in which they fall.

For the most part, space requirements for these facilities are determined on the basis of special studies of the individual needs of each facility and the site size dictated by these needs. Obviously, the variety of special investigations involved in arriving at accurate space requirements for each type of facility are more appropriately covered in the comprehensive plan studies.[31] For the level of detail required in the preliminary land use plan, the need for new or expanded public service facilities, especially the large space users, is established on the basis of interviews with the appropriate public or company officials. Crude estimates of space needs are made facility by facility based on the judgment of these officials, any pertinent special investigations they or their consultants may have made in the recent past, and the general experience with the particular facility that may be gained from other cities. Some of the general considerations involved in estimating space requirements for civic center and subcivic center facilities are taken up briefly below.

[31] For the reader's convenience, some of the references for these more detailed studies are listed as follows: Planning Advisory Service, *Cemeteries in the City Plan*, Information Report No. 16, July, 1950; *Municipal Waterfronts: Planning for Commercial and Industrial Uses*, Information Report No. 45, December, 1952; and *Helioports in the City Plan*, Information Report No. 52, July, 1953, all issued by the American Society of Planning Officials; Civil Aeronautics Administration, *Airport Design*, January, 1949, *Community Airport Requirements*, January, 1950, and *Airport Planning*, July, 1952; and for highly technical installations such as power plants, railroad marshaling yards, and railroad service facilities, few of which are treated in city planning sources, standard engineering texts in these fields should be consulted.

Except in a few of the very large metropolitan areas, the civic center is usually situated on the edge of the retail shopping section of the central business district. The site selected and the intensity with which the site is developed are often markedly influenced by the pattern of land values, although other important considerations such as the accessibility to the major street network and transit system are also involved. Generally, the site should be near but not in the high-value area and out of the path of retail expansion; it should be in an area where there are good approaches and adequate space for a pleasing grouping of buildings, for open green areas and for parking space, and in general, sufficient space for the proper setting and symbolic treatment normally associated with the civic center. Some facilities such as fire or police stations or an auditorium located in the group may impose special requirements as to location. For example, these facilities require a location which permits easy and quick access to the thoroughfare system. All these factors are considered in principle in connection with the establishment of location requirements as taken up in Chapter 11.

The estimation of space requirements for the civic center must first take into account the functions to be housed in the center: the city hall, the county courthouse, state and federal buildings, if any, the public library, museums, the civic auditorium, and any other types of functions that may be contemplated. Once decisions have been reached on the activities ultimately to be accommodated, it is then necessary to determine how intensively the site is to be developed: whether buildings are to be low, one- or two-story, or multistory buildings. This decision is dependent to some extent on land values and the size of the chosen site and to some extent on design objectives in the massing and grouping of buildings on the site in relation to approaches and vistas. However, once decisions have been reached on the character of buildings to be provided, space needs then become a matter of summing up the ground area required for these buildings and the areas determined to be needed for accessory parking, public grounds, and related park areas. Of course, floor space requirements of each function to be housed in the center, present and future, are essential to the study. Initially, for purposes of site selection, these may be rough estimates assembled on the basis of preliminary scaled diagrams of alternative space arrangements for each function. The architect should be available for consultation at the earliest possible stage of these studies, and certainly in the execution of site development sketches and studies.

Subcivic Centers

There are certain public service functions which must be organized on a district basis. Thus, except in the case of very small communities, fire stations are provided in selected locations to serve certain subareas of the city. In the large metropolitan areas, it eventually becomes necessary to decentralize a number of these functions. However, it is not always feasible to consolidate in the same subcenters all decentralized civic functions. While there is need for branch offices at outlying focal points where the public can pay utility and tax bills, secure permits and licenses, and in some sections of the community, have access to public health personnel for routine clinical examinations, at the same time efficient police and fire districting may call for substations at entirely different locations.[32]

In this connection, it will be helpful to outline some of the location criteria and other factors which affect the derivation of space requirements of branch facilities for public service functions. In general, branch municipal offices should be located near the focal point of several residential neighborhoods, preferably near or adjoining community shopping centers. According to the overall districting system and other specialized needs of each facility, there may be consolidated with the branch municipal office a fire station, a precinct police station, a health clinic or station, or a branch library.

The extent of fire districts and local service areas which govern the location of fire stations is strongly influenced by the recommendations of the National Board of Fire Underwriters who set standards for the administrative organization, equipment, and location of fire stations for fire insurance rating purposes. Intensively developed high-value areas (usually contained in special "fire districts" defined in the city's fire code) require higher-order standards than other sections of the urban area. For example, for pumper companies, a direct street-travel distance to business and industrial areas of no greater than three-quarters of a mile is recommended, and for compactly developed residential areas, a distance no greater than a mile and a half; for ladder companies, standards of maximum direct travel distance are one and two miles, respectively. In San Francisco, a general firehouse service radius of one-half mile is recommended, although variations would be permissible, depending on property valuations, building intensi-

---

[32] For a detailed evaluation of these considerations and the facility requirements taken up in the next few paragraphs, see Cincinnati City Planning Commission, *Public Service Facilities,* January, 1947.

ties, population densities, the pattern of trafficways, and so on.[33] The actual space requirements for firehalls are dependent upon the type of fire company and therefore the size of ground floor area in the firehall, any outdoor facilities required for practice drills, the visual clearance needs for the particular site, landscaping, and so on.

District or precinct police stations are located on the basis of other criteria. Since contact with the public is not of primary importance, the location of these stations is determined by the district lines and by the speed and efficiency of moving personnel and equipment into these established service areas. Police districts in commercial areas and close-in densely populated areas are usually small and patrolled on a beat system, while outlying districts are larger and are covered by patrol cruisers. On the other hand, public health centers, clinics, or stations are generally needed only in certain areas of the city. Generally, the out-patient department of the city hospital contains the specialized facilities for the city as a whole, with clinics and stations for routine examinations being provided in the densely populated areas where the disease incidence rates tend to be high. Obviously, there would be only a few instances in which the application of the individual location criteria for fire, police, and health stations would result in the same location.

The provision of branch libraries depends not only on the population size of the library system's service area, but also on local policy matters such as separate school and public library systems versus a combined system, the use of bookmobiles, and so on. American Library Association standards call for all residential areas being within the service area of a public library, and where a branch library system is the adopted local policy, a local service-area radius of not more than one mile is recommended.[34] In making adaptations of these standards to local needs, San Francisco favored, in principle, large branches serving 25 to 50,000 population, but recognizing that in areas of low population density or in situations where barriers exist, a service-area population of 10 to 15,000 may be warranted. The facility should be located in or adjoining a community shopping center or some similar center which is a point of congregation for the residents of the service area. The space requirements are determined by the ground floor area of the ultimate-size building required, parking areas for automobiles and bicycles, and landscaping.

Post offices generally seek business center locations. In addition to the independent or central post office in the downtown area, outlying post

[33] San Francisco Department of City Planning, *Report on a Plan for the Location of Firehouses in San Francisco*, August, 1952.

[34] San Francisco Department of City Planning, *Report on a Plan for the Location of Public Libraries in San Francisco*, April, 1953.

office "stations" are provided in cities of medium size and upwards. Stations outside the corporate limits of the area served by an independent post office are called "branches." Stations and branches are located at the focal points of shopping, usually in large community shopping centers. They may be in government-owned buildings, but post office policy calls for leased quarters as a general rule. Since all mail deliveries originate from the independent post office, space requirements for stations and branches are minimal.

SPACE FOR REGIONAL RECREATION, EDUCATION, AND CULTURAL USES

As in the other categories of land use discussed so far, for the generalized result required in the preliminary land use plan, this class of use also employs only broad-gauge estimating techniques. For most of this category of region-serving uses, the same general procedural sequence followed in other land use classes applies equally well here. Thus the first step is an analysis of the existing facility in terms of its adequacy for the population groups served and the sufficiency of the site size for the particular facility developed there. In the light of these findings and available general standards adapted to the local situation, the second step first derives total acreage requirements for the correction of existing deficiencies and the accommodation of future growth, and then distributes the total acreage thus derived to appropriate vacant, renewal, or sometimes occupied sites in the urban area according to location criteria previously developed as discussed in Chapter 11. The final step involves deductions from the supply of vacant and renewal land for the indicated tentative uses, with appropriate notations sketched in on overlays indicating locations of areas absorbed for region-serving recreational, educational, and cultural uses, and those areas still unearmarked for specific use at the conclusion of this series of analyses.

Recreational Uses

The region-serving recreational uses encompass a variety of facilities with divergent location needs. At one extreme are the spectator sports involving ballparks, public stadiums, boxing arenas, and other facilities for regularly scheduled sports events and the occasional exhibition matches. These require inlying or intermediate locations directly accessible to the transit and major traffic-handling routes. Also found in central locations are the downtown parks in or near the CBD. At the other extreme are country parks or large public reservations in the outlying reaches of the planning area that are developed for picnicking, hiking, nature walks, boating, and other forms of activities for family excursions and organized group outings. These facilities are usually accessible only by car or stage. In between, at the edges of the built-up portions of the urban area are public and private golf courses, race tracks, fair grounds, botanical gardens, zoos, and other large space users. These usually locate close enough to the built-up area so as to be near the end of public transportation routes and near major traffic radials.

The estimation of space requirements for these recreation areas and public open spaces employ two criteria, one based on population and the other based on site size. The population standard indicates the number of people served per facility, and thus, when used in relation to the forecast population of the planning area, provides a rough measure of the number of facilities required. When a minimum site-size standard is applied to the number of facilities thus derived, a crude estimate of the minimum acreage of space is obtained for each type of facility. Final space requirements are an upgraded version of these minimum needs, with higher standards, in effect, achieved in the course of fitting facilities to particular sites. Table 28 summarizes some of the commonly used standards. In addition to these rather specific types of facilities, most cities have a general system of park and open space. Within this system fall the central parks, the miscellaneous small sitting areas in the central business district, squares, monument sites, and various historical plots (with or without structures) that have some special local, state, or national significance.

Obviously, the general open space system of an urban area is less amen-

TABLE 28.   General Standards for Region-Serving Recreational Facilities

Type of Facility	Population Standard	Minimum Site-Size Standard
Major natural parks	1 park/40,000	100 acres/park
Public golf course	1 hole/3,000	100 acres/18 holes
County fairgrounds	1/county seat	special[a]
Public stadiums	1 stadium/100,000	special[a]
Botanical garden	1/metro. area	special[a]
Zoo	1/metro. area	special[a]

[a] Site-size estimated according to size of facility appropriate to size of region served, facilities desired, and parking and service areas needed.

able to quantitative analysis and ill-adapted to the use of space standards, the amount of space provided being more a subjective determination, considering such factors as the natural drainage patterns in the urban area, the character of the terrain and the aggregate amount of land considered uneconomic to develop for other uses. In this respect, the financial ability of public agencies with maintenance functions is sometimes an important limiting factor. However, such maintenance costs must be considered in relation to potential expenses incurred by public agencies in dealing with drainage and other problems which develop when some of these areas are pressed into use. To circumvent the problem of these maintenance costs, in some urban areas low-lying or steep areas are acquired and left in woodland strips and city forest reserves where maintenance costs are minimal.

Educational, Cultural, and Medical Centers

As in the case of public service facilities, space requirements for colleges, museums, music or art centers, medical centers, and various kinds of institutions requiring substantial acreages are estimated on a case-by-case basis. For preliminary land use planning purposes, these requirements will usually be determined on the basis of interviews with administrative officials in charge of developmental programs for these institutions and their estimates of the expansion anticipated during the planning period. Where institutional personnel or their consultants have prepared within recent time estimates of long-range developmental needs of the institutions concerned, these may be used *in toto*, with little or no adjustment. Where estimates are obviously subjective approximations, they should be checked for their reasonableness and possibly modified according to experience drawn from studies elsewhere.

Most colleges maintain a master plan for the development of their campuses. The enrollment in many educational institutions is the population equivalent of a small city, and with the millions of dollars of investment that a university represents, it is to be expected that it would maintain a planning staff. From the viewpoint of the city in which it is located, competent campus planning will materially assist in relating the institution's plans with the general plans for the urban area as a whole. Encompassing some of the same general considerations involved in planning for the civic center grouping of structures, campus planning studies must delve into other factors, especially higher education enrollment trends as they are distributed among the various private and public institutions in the region and how the local university or college may be expected to share in these future enrollment trends.

Another kind of institutional grouping of facilities is the modern-day medical center. In recent years, there has been an evident trend, particularly in large metropolitan areas, for hospital facilities to gravitate together to form distinct medical centers. Sometimes a foundation grant or state and federal funds have provided the means for establishing such centers, and usually the presence of one or more medical schools has formed the core for these centers. The advantages of economy and efficiency in administration, the convenience to the doctors, and the opportunities for specialization are obvious, but these must be balanced against other considerations, for example, the depressing effect that the very large center may have on patients, especially those who are hospitalized for long periods of time. Among other objectives, it was to get away from the "warehousing" of patients at some distance from their families and friends that the Peckham Center experiment in England was undertaken.

Again, developmental studies by these institutions themselves will facilitate general planning in the urban area, at the same time assuring a far-sighted approach to their own expansion needs. Indeed, a number of the larger centers are now maintaining their own master plans with their own planning staffs. In the case of the smaller medical centers, the local planning agency may furnish planning assistance.[35]

SPACE NEEDS OF RESIDENTIAL COMMUNITIES

We come now to the final category of uses, the residential communities of the urban area. These are the largest users of space, consisting mainly of residential uses proper, but also including accessory community facilities. As brought out earlier, analyses of residential areas cannot be divorced from consideration of their related community facilities, the location and space requirements for local shopping centers, churches, schools, and local recreation areas being interrelated with considerations of density, location, and character of the residential developments they are serving. In order to take these relationships into account on a scale that is meaningful, space

[35] A valuable reference for these studies is available from Planning Advisory Service, *Zone Locations for Hospitals and Other Medical Facilities*, Information Report No. 50, American Society of Planning Officials, May, 1953.

requirements are analyzed within the framework of localized planning districts.

Since the number and extent of new community facilities depend mainly upon estimates of the location and density of new residential development, this discussion of space requirements for residential communities begins with housing requirements, then takes up local shopping centers, schools, and recreation facilities in that order, and finally considers residential communities as a whole. Space requirements for churches are usually omitted at this generalized stage of planning, these needs being more appropriately considered in detailed comprehensive plan studies. In keeping with the generalized result desired, it should be noted that throughout, analyses are pitched to an "approximation" level of accuracy where subjective estimates and assumptions are introduced at various steps in the procedure in substitution for what would become objective determinations in the later comprehensive plan investigations. The general character of some of these later more detailed studies is indicated at the end of this section of the chapter.

Residential Space Requirements

The sequence of the analysis of residential area requirements falls into the following steps:

1. Organize data relative to the existing supply of dwelling units and density of development and summarize by planning districts.
2. Develop working assumptions as to future residential trends, and on the basis of these assumptions, determine additions to total supply of dwelling units required and estimate how this total is to be allocated to assumed future housing types and residential density classes.
3. On the basis of the supply of vacant and renewal land suited to residential development and its approximate effective net holding capacity by planning district, make tentative allocation of additions to total dwelling unit stock for the several density classes to the various planning districts.
4. Summarize space requirements and population estimates by planning district.

The key unit of measurement normally employed in residential area analyses is "the primary family,"[36] but in this somewhat abbreviated approach

---

[36] In the Seventeenth Decennial Census, "a primary family consists of the household head and all persons in the household related to him by blood, marriage or adoption."

TABLE 29.   Current Stock of Dwelling Units, Acreage in Residential Use, and Net Densities in Urban Area by Housing Type, 19xx

Planning District	Single-Family			Two-Family			Row Housing		
	D.Us.	Acres	Density	D.Us.	Acres	Density	D.Us.	Acres	Densit
1	xx	xx	xx	xx	xx	xx	xx	xx	xx
2	xx	xx	xx	xx	xx	xx	xx	xx	xx
etc.	xx	xx	xx	xx	xx	xx	xx	xx	xx
Subtotal central city	xx	xx	xx	xx	xx	xx	xx	xx	xx
10	xx	xx	xx	xx	xx	xx	xx	xx	xx
11	xx	xx	xx	xx	xx	xx	xx	xx	xx
etc.	xx	xx	xx	xx	xx	xx	xx	xx	xx
Subtotal fringe area	xx	xx	xx	xx	xx	xx	xx	xx	xx
Planning area total	xx	xx	xx	xx	xx	xx	xx	xx	xx

"the household"[37] is used as a crude substitute term. Thus population data, being the original yardstick of growth, are translated into household data, which in turn can be expressed in terms of dwelling units, and through the medium of residential densities, dwelling units are ultimately converted to acreage equivalents, the end product desired in this analysis.

1. *Existing housing supply.* The first major step is one of organizing data concerning existing residential areas into a form suitable for such an analysis. This involves first a summary of the existing stock of dwelling units, a summary of existing acreages in residential use, and a summary of prevailing net densities—all by planning district. For control purposes, planning districts are grouped into central city districts and fringe area districts, with subtotals developed for each of these portions of the planning area. Dwelling unit counts are taken from the land use survey field sheets (see Figure 22 or 23A); acreages are read off the tabular summary of land uses; and net densities are computed from these two series of data. Table 29 illustrates the form of the summary, using five classes of housing types. These housing types correspond to residential classes used in the land use survey, the original selection of classes having been made with this type of analysis in mind. The selection of housing types in the first instance is governed by what is typical to a particular urban area. Usually large metropolitan areas will have a greater variety than small urban areas.

[37] In the same census, "a household consists of all persons who occupy a dwelling unit. Included are the related family members and also the unrelated persons, if any, such as lodgers. A person living alone in a dwelling unit, or a group of unrelated persons sharing a dwelling unit as partners, is considered a household."

Garden Apts.			Multistory Apts.				Total	
D.Us.	Acres	Density	D.Us.	Acres	Density	D.Us.	Acres	Density
xx	xx	xx	xx	xx	xx	xx	xx	xx
xx	xx	xx	xx	xx	xx	xx	xx	xx
xx	xx	xx	xx	xx	xx	xx	xx	xx
—	—	—	—	—	—	—	—	—
xx	xx	xx	xx	xx	xx	xx	xx	xx
xx	xx	xx	xx	xx	xx	xx	xx	xx
xx	xx	xx	xx	xx	xx	xx	xx	xx
xx	xx	xx	xx	xx	xx	xx	xx	xx
—	—	—	—	—	—	—	—	—
xx	xx	xx	xx	xx	xx	xx	xx	xx
—	—	—	—	—	—	—	—	—
xx	xx	xx	xx	xx	xx	xx	xx	xx

Thus the selection of land use classes and consequently the format of Table 29 must be developed in terms of predominant housing types typical of the urban area under study. Where there is reason to believe new housing types will be introduced into the local housing market during the planning period, additional types will appear in the later stages of the analysis.

Another summary developed at the outset sets forth the trends in conversion and new construction activity. Table 30 illustrates the form used in this summary. The table is compiled from building permit records, usually for the past five- or ten-year period. Reading horizontally, it shows the relative emphasis between conversion and new construction in any planning district, and within the new construction category, the relative emphasis between the various housing types. Reading vertically and used in conjunction with a map of planning districts, the table indicates the sectors of the urban area where conversion activity is most pronounced and which areas appear to be preferred ones for new construction. By reference to this summary and annual building permit plots (prepared in map form as discussed in Chapter 8), it is possible to establish the important directions of residential expansion.

2. *Estimates of future need.* The second step develops and applies working assumptions relative to future residential area requirements. Attention is first focused on procedures for estimating the total number of new dwelling units needed by the end of the planning period, either by conversion or from new construction, and on procedures for approximating the distribution of new construction both as to housing types and as to classes of

TABLE 30.   Recent Trends in Distribution of New Additions to Housing Stock, 19xx to 19xx

Planning District	Total Number D.Us. Added	Percent in Conversions	Percent in New Construction by Housing Type				
			Single-Family	Two-Family	Row Housing	Garden Apts.	Multistory Apts.
1	xxx	xx	xx	xx	xx	xx	xx
2	xxx	xx	xx	xx	xx	xx	xx
etc.	xxx	xx	xx	xx	xx	xx	xx
Subtotal central city	xxx	xx	xx	xx	xx	xx	xx
10	xxx	xx	xx	xx	xx	xx	xx
11	xxx	xx	xx	xx	xx	xx	xx
etc.	xxx	xx	xx	xx	xx	xx	xx
Subtotal fringe area	xxx	xx	xx	xx	xx	xx	xx
Planning area total	xxx	xx	xx	xx	xx	xx	xx

residential density. The end product of the first series of assumptions is a tabular summary such as that presented in Table 31. Involved here are assumptions as to (1) changes in household size during the planning period, (2) losses in the existing stock of dwelling units, and (3) changes in the vacancy rate.

a. *Household-size assumptions.* As already pointed out, household size is a key element in making the transition from population estimates to dwelling unit requirements. On the basis of a study of trends in the change in average household size, assumptions are made as to the average size of household by the end of the planning period. These assumptions are presumed to reflect changes (1) arising out of net population increases, and (2) developing from shifts in living patterns within the surviving population such as changes relative to family size, doubled-up living conditions, and so on. By applying the present average household size to the present population and the assumed future household size to the estimated future population, the difference between these two results provides a crude unadjusted estimate of the total new dwelling unit requirements as shown in Row 1 of Table 31. In this connection, it is useful for control purposes to develop separate assumptions for central city and fringe area planning districts. For example, in the Greensboro study, it was assumed that 1948 average household sizes of 4.78 for the central city and 5.41 for fringe planning districts would become 3.6 and 3.8, respectively, by the end of

T ABLE 31.   Derivation of Total New Dwelling Unit Requirements, 19xx

	Number of Dwelling Units	
Sequence of Steps	Central City	Fringe Areas
1. Crude unadjusted estimate of D.Us. needed	xx	xx
2. Plus net losses in current stock of D.Us.	xx	xx
Losses by public renewal programs	xx	xx
Losses by use invasions	xx	xx
Assumed catastrophe losses	xx	xx
3. Plus allowance for vacancy rate	xx	xx
Total: Adjusted crude estimate of D.Us. needed	xx	xx
Assumed conversions	xx	xx
Assumed new construction	xx	xx

the planning period in 1965, subsuming a declining family size and elimination of all doubling-up of families.[38]

b. *Assumptions on D.U. losses.* Estimates of losses in the current stock of dwelling units by the end of the planning period are covered under three categories: dwelling units eliminated through public renewal programs, dwelling units eliminated by use invasions, and dwelling units lost by fire and from other catastrophes. Dwelling units included in the first category consist of all dwelling units in clearance areas as defined by techniques discussed earlier, all substandard structures in rehabilitation areas, and finally an assumed allowance of the present stock of standard housing that is judged likely to fall into the substandard category by the end of the planning period. The latter assumptions are usually based on local observations as to past rates of deterioration (rough comparisons between the last two Censuses of Housing) and the anticipated effectiveness of local rehabilitation and conservation programs during the planning period. Either by actual count or by estimate, these losses are recorded for the appropriate planning district in Table 32.

Losses by use invasion occur principally in central areas, and these can be tallied up from previous studies of the CBD. This estimate can then be adjusted upward to cover any losses tentatively identified in previous space need analyses in manufacturing, wholesale, and other use areas. By actual count or by estimate, losses from this source are recorded for appropriate planning districts in Table 32. In the Greensboro study these losses and those resulting from assumed local renewal activities were grouped together, and it was found that the combined effect of eliminations under the separate assumptions relating to each category of loss in the central

[38] Greensboro Department of Planning, *op. cit.*, p. 35.

344   *Urban Land Use Planning*

TABLE 32.   Estimated Distribution of Dwelling Unit Losses by Planning District, 19xx

| Planning District | Current Stock D.Us. | D.Us. Removed by Type of Loss | | | | D.Us. Remaining by 19xx |
		Renewal	Invasion	Catastrophe	Total	
1	xxx	x	x	x	x	xx
2	xxx	x	x	x	x	xx
etc.	xxx	x	x	x	x	xx
Subtotal central city	xxx	x	x	x	x	xx
10	xxx	x	x	x	x	xx
11	xxx	x	x	x	x	xx
etc.	xxx	x	x	x	x	xx
Subtotal fringe area	xxx	x	x	x	x	xx
Planning area total	xxx	x	x	x	x	xx

city area amounted to 6 percent of the then total existing dwelling unit stock. Then, pointing out that dwelling units in fringe areas were, for the most part, in newer structures, the study assumed that half the central city rate, or 3 percent of the then present stock of fringe dwelling units, would need replacement by the end of the planning period.[39] This particular procedure for estimating fringe area losses was used in this study because of the unavailability of housing census data at that time for these outlying portions of the planning area. In other situations where there are census tract summaries available, there are of course other approaches which can be used as discussed earlier.

Assumptions relating to the third category of losses, those attributed to fires or other catastrophes, are based on local observations of past rates of loss, adjusted downward for anticipated improvements in fire-fighting potential, and the expected effectiveness of local renewal programs and code enforcement activities during the planning period. Distribution of these losses by planning districts as summarized in Table 32 is based on observations as to concentrations of fire calls during the past and expectations as to how renewal programs and other similar measures will alter these concentrations in the future. Illustrating again from the Greensboro study, local observations resulted in the assumed total losses of 20 units a year in the central city and 10 units a year in the fringe areas.[40]

[39] *Ibid.*, p. 35.
[40] *Ibid.*, p. 35.

c. *Vacancy rate assumptions.* Estimates of dwelling unit replacements to cover these three categories of losses are tallied by planning district as shown in Table 32 and summarized in Row 2 of Table 31. The final entry made in Table 31, Row 3, increases the cumulative total to make allowance for a normal vacancy ratio. This ratio should be applied to the sum of the Row 1 entry and the current stock of dwelling units (see Table 29). Although a 5 percent vacancy ratio has been in common usage in estimating future requirements in the past, this rule-of-thumb figure may not be suited to all situations. In this respect, special seasonal studies may be desirable in urban areas having significance as resort centers.

d. *Conversion-new construction assumptions.* With all three segments of need for new dwelling units covered, results are totaled as indicated in Table 31, yielding an adjusted crude estimate of total new dwelling unit requirements. The final working assumption to be made in this phase of the analysis is the expected allocation of this total between conversions and new construction by the end of the planning period. This brings the analysis to the point of considering the second series of assumptions, namely, those concerned with the distribution of the total need for new dwelling units by housing and density types.

The working assumptions relative to housing and density types assist in making the transition from dwelling unit requirements to space requirements. Thus, having arrived at estimates of the total additional units required during the planning period, we are first concerned with assumptions as to how this total can be expected to break down into housing types. Although some types of housing market analyses (see discussion at the end of the chapter) attempt to establish consumer preferences in this respect, for the generalized result required in this analysis, assumptions are usually based on trends in the crude distribution characteristics reflected in recent additions to the housing stock. These trends can be approximated by analyzing building permits on an annual or five-year basis for past increments of time and observing changes in the proportions devoted to each housing type (see Table 30). On the basis of these observed trends, assumptions are made relative to the future distribution of housing types. As a check on the reasonableness of such assumptions, figures in Table 29 can be converted to percentages and the distribution of the present stock of dwelling units among housing types can be compared with that proposed for future additions to the housing supply. In the Greensboro study results of such an analysis led to assumptions that the total new units added to the housing supply by the end of the planning period would be distributed 6 percent to conversions and 94 percent to new construction, and that the

94 percent in new construction would be distributed 73 percent to single-family units, 8 percent to two-family, and 13 percent to multifamily.[41]

e. *Residential density assumptions.* The final set of assumptions are concerned with the further breakdown of housing types into density types. However, before this breakdown can be made, decisions must be reached concerning a classification of "density types," a term used here to represent *the range of assumed densities (in terms of dwelling units per acre) at which development in the future will take place.* Assumptions in this respect are generally based on locally adopted "density standards," here used to represent *a classification of proposed maximum permissible residential densities.* Both the average assumed densities and the adopted standards as to maximum permissible densities can be expressed in "net" and "gross" terms.[42]

Net residential density standards have a very specific and direct application in the development of the zoning ordinance in implementation of the land use plan. They are used in setting up the various density districts within categories of land to be zoned for residential use. *Gross residential density standards* are also sometimes used in zoning ordinances in provisions relative to group housing developments. Gross residential density standards should be distinguished from *neighborhood density standards* which are sometimes used in the so-called "community development districts," special districts recognized in zoning ordinances for the integrated development of entire residential communities.[43]

On the other hand, land use planning procedures employ what in effect amounts to higher-order "standards." The various types of *assumed average net residential densities* are primarily significant in estimating space needs for developed or partially developed areas, and as brought out later in this section of the chapter, after consideration of local shopping, school, and recreation space requirements, the various *assumed average neighborhood* densities become significant yardsticks in estimating space requirements in areas presently undeveloped or in large clearance areas made available under public renewal programs.

The net residential density standards employed in any urban area are usually a local adaptation of generally recognized national standards considered to be consistent with sound principles of healthful housing. Table 33

---

[41] *Ibid.,* p. 36.

[42] *Net residential density* refers to dwelling units per acre of land area actually in use or proposed to be used for residential purposes, and *gross residential density* is computed on the basis of net residential land area plus traversing streets, alleys, and drives, and one-half of bounding streets and one-quarter of bounding street intersections.

[43] *Neighborhood density* refers to dwelling units per acre of land area in use or proposed for development as a neighborhood area including residential land, areas for local shopping, school, and public open spaces, and land taken up in streets.

presents general standards recommended by the Committee on the Hygiene of Housing of the American Public Health Association.[44] This range of net densities is commonly used as a guide in examining net densities presently existing in the urban area of interest (derived as shown in Table 29) for purposes of developing local standards as to maximum permissible densities for future development.

TABLE 33. Net Residential Density Standards[a]

	D.Us. Per Net Acre	
Dwelling Unit Type	Desirable	Maximum
One- and two-family		
1-family detached	5	7
1-family semidetached or 2-family detached	10	12
1-family attached (row) or 2-family semidetached	16	19
Multifamily		
2-story	25	30
3-story	40	45
6-story	65	75
9-story	75	85
13-story	85	95

[a] Committee on the Hygiene of Housing, American Public Health Association, *Planning the Neighborhood*, Public Administration Service, 1948, p. 39.

These standards will not be concerned alone with the higher-order densities possible in open-land portions of the fringe areas. The range of standards adopted must recognize that for inlying renewal areas designated for clearance, lower-order densities must usually be provided for. As another practical consideration, the range of proposed net densities must usually recognize what can be expected to emerge in any large vacant areas already subdivided but as yet undeveloped. These will often be of a lower order than standards adopted for open land areas. Of course, if the subdivision pattern imposed on the land is below general standards to a serious extent, it would be a function of the land use plan to propose higher-order local standards, with specific implementing recommendations for any necessary steps to achieve replanning.

As would be expected, illustrations of locally adopted net residential density standards exhibit considerable variation. Presented here for illustrative

[44] Committee on the Hygiene of Housing, American Public Health Association, *Planning the Neighborhood*, Public Administration Service, 1948.

purposes are standards adopted in Providence, Greensboro, and San Francisco. Providence's land use plan proposed the following standards within the city proper:[45]

Square Feet of Lot per D.U.	Families per Net Acre	Persons per Net Acre[a]
5,000	9	30
3,500	13	45
2,000	20	75
1,500	29	100
1,000	43	150

[a] Computed from this study's estimate of probable average number of persons per family at end of planning period.

In contrast, Greensboro, in its 1948 study for the entire urban area, employed the following:[46]

Housing Type	Proposed Minimum Standard		Assumed Average for New Development	
	Sq Ft of Lot per D.U.	D.Us. per Net Acre	Sq Ft of Lot per D.U.	D.Us. per Net Acre
Single-family	9,000	5	10,000	4
Single-family	6,000	7	7,500	6
Two-family	4,800	9	6,000	7
Row and garden apt.	3,600	12	4,500	10
Walk-up apt.[a]	2,000	22	2,500	18
Multistory apt.[a]	1,000	43	1,000	43

[a] Policies adopted since 1948 rule out densities of the order indicated for both of these housing types.

In San Francisco, the following were used as general guides within the city proper:[47]

Density Class	Housing Types Primarily Included	Maximum Persons per Net Acre
Low	Single-family detached and single-family row dwellings	55
Medium	Two-family and low 2- and 3-story multiple dwellings	100
High	Medium and high multiple dwellings	220

The above data from Greensboro illustrate the dual classification of density categories, one column presenting net residential density standards and the other showing assumed average net residential densities.

[45] Providence City Plan Commission, *Master Plan for Land Use and Population Distribution,* Publication No. 4, 1946, p. 21.

[46] Greensboro Department of Planning, *op. cit.,* pp. 24, 37.

[47] San Francisco Department of City Planning, *op. cit.,* pp. 3–4.

f. *Allocation assumptions by type and density.* Once standards have been
established, and from these, assumptions made as to average net densities
at which future development will occur, it is then possible to extend the
breakdown by housing types to a more detailed form, recognizing the assumed density types. This involves making assumptions as to how single-
family units will be allocated to the density types appropriate to this class
of residential use, how two-family units are to be allocated, and so on. For
lower-order densities (i.e., densities of lower standard), generally the percentage allocation will be guided by observations as to the supply of subdivided land and renewal land which originally influenced the choice of
these density classes. For higher-order densities, assumed allocations will
usually be based on observed recent trends of the rates at which land has
gone into development in lot sizes reasonably similar to those included in

TABLE 34. Allocation of Total New-Construction Dwelling Units by Housing
and Density Types and Derivation of Total Acreage Requirements, 19xx

Density Type	Housing Types	Assumed Av. No. D.Us./Net Acre	Total Requirements D.Us.	Acreage
Density A	xxxxxxxxxxxxx	x	xxx	xx
Density B	xxxxxxxxxxxxx	x	xxx	xx
Density C	xxxxxxxxxxxxx	x	xxx	xx
Density D	xxxxxxxxxxxxx	x	xxx	xx
Density E	xxxxxxxxxxxxx	x	xxx	xx
Density F	xxxxxxxxxxxxx	x	xxx	xx
etc.	xxxxxxxxxxxxx	x	xxx	xx
Planning area total	—	—	xxx	xx

Note: This same general tabular format is used for separate summaries of central city and fringe
areas.

the upper-order selections of residential densities. Using the Greensboro
study for illustration purposes, this analysis resulted in assumptions of 25
percent of new single-family units on 10,000 square-foot lots and 75 percent on 7500 square-foot lots; all two-family units on lots 6000 square feet
per unit; and multifamily units allocated 60 percent on lots 4500 square
feet per unit, 30 percent on lots 2500 square feet per unit, and 10 percent
on lots 1000 square feet per unit.[48]
The results of the foregoing analyses thus yield a tabular presentation
such as that shown in Table 34. It should be noted that this table summarizes requirements only for new construction, conversions being excluded from this part of the analysis on the assumption that for the most

[48] Greensboro Department of Planning, *op. cit.,* p. 37.

part they will not involve additional land. This is in extension of the work already completed and summarized in Table 31 and prepares the way for the next step concerned with the allocations of total dwelling unit requirements to the individual planning districts. Table 34 can be used as a prototype for separate tables, one on the central city and another on the fringe area subtotals.

3. *Fitting space needs to land supply.* The third major step in the sequence to the procedure in analyzing residential space requirements is one of establishing *approximate effective net holding capacities* of the various planning districts and making a tentative allocation of total dwelling unit requirements to planning districts which is within the ceilings indicated by these holding capacities. The *holding capacity* of a planning district is the number of dwelling units the vacant and renewal land in the planning district will accommodate according to a prescribed pattern of residential densities. The *net* holding capacity excludes allowance for streets, and the *effective* net holding capacity excludes areas unavailable for development due to whims of property owners, legal entanglements, and so on. Holding capacities are *approximate* at this stage of the analysis since space requirements for community facilities and resulting reductions in effective net holding capacities are still to be determined. As in analyses of all the preceding classes of land use, only a tentative allocation of dwelling units is made here, since all location decisions are subject to review and possible revision in the design phase of land use planning procedures.

a. *Holding capacity analyses.* To determine approximate effective net holding capacities, two steps are involved. In the first, a tentative generalized pattern of residential densities is developed, showing how net density standards would be applied to the urban area as a whole, considering locational requirements previously developed, the pattern of existing densities in built-up areas, and the use capabilities of vacant and renewal land as previously determined. The second step focuses on the vacant and renewal areas in this pattern of residential densities. Using assumed average net density figures (in place of the net density standard figures), approximate net holding capacities are computed planning district by planning district and tabulated by density type. These figures are then adjusted downward district by district by crude percentage correction factors appropriate to each district to convert them into effective net holding capacities. For planning districts in built-up or partially developed portions of the urban area, these deduction percentages are based on prevailing practices with respect to purchase of double lots and what is known concerning the unavailability of vacant tracts of land in the planning district. For planning districts in open country, correction factors are approximated on the basis of those derived for nearby developed or developing areas which have a character similar to that contemplated in these planning districts. Although reasonably appropriate for the generalized results of preliminary land use planning, these subjective methods are of course superseded by special investigations in comprehensive plan analyses of residential requirements. The result of the foregoing steps is a tabular summary such as that presented in Table 35 and an overlay or key map identifying by density types the vacant and renewal land to which planning district holding capacities refer.

TABLE 35.   Approximate Effective Net Holding Capacity of Vacant-Renewal Land Suited for Residential Development, by Planning District

Planning District	Number of Dwelling Units by Density Type							
	A	B	C	D	E	F	etc.	Total
1	xx	xx	xx	xx	xx	xx	xx	xxx
2	xx	xx	xx	xx	xx	xx	xx	xxx
etc.	xx	xx	xx	xx	xx	xx	xx	xxx
Subtotal central city	xx	xx	xx	xx	xx	xx	xx	xxx
10	xx	xx	xx	xx	xx	xx	xx	xxx
11	xx	xx	xx	xx	xx	xx	xx	xxx
etc.	xx	xx	xx	xx	xx	xx	xx	xxx
Subtotal fringe area	xx	xx	xx	xx	xx	xx	xx	xxx
Planning area total	xx	xx	xx	xx	xx	xx	xx	xxx

The holding capacity total for the planning area as derived in Table 35 is usually considerably in excess of total dwelling unit requirements as derived in Table 34. Of course, if the planning area holding capacity is under the estimated dwelling unit total requirements, the planning area must be enlarged according to procedures previously described.

b. *Estimating distribution of new D.Us.* The final operation in this third major step of the procedure is one of distributing new dwelling unit requirements to the various planning districts within the holding capacity ceilings shown in Table 35. This is a "cut and fill" process of allocating dwelling units to planning districts by density types within the limits of the controlling density type quotas set forth in Table 34. For the various density classes, preference is given first to planning districts with land previously determined as prime for residential use, which are situated in the directions where there appears to be the greatest preference for building new homes. Location criteria as developed in Chapter 11 and the preliminary thoroughfare study (being developed concurrently with the land use plan) may indicate other sectors of the urban area which should receive emphasis in this allocation process. Other considerations are the rate at which scattered vacant lots in the older areas can be expected to fill in and the extent to which condemned or destroyed units will be replaced on their original sites. These factors have a bearing on the distribution of new units.

Along with these positive factors, certain limiting factors should be considered in the allocation process. For example, planning districts falling in general areas which cannot be economically served by water, sewer, and

TABLE 36.   Total New Dwelling Unit Requirements by Density Type Tentatively Distributed Among Planning Districts, 19xx

| Planning District | Total New D.Us.[a] | No. New D.Us. by Conversion[a] | No. D.Us. from New Construction by Density Type | | | | | | | |
			A	B	C	D	E	F	etc.	Total[a]
1	xxxx	xx	xx	xx	xx	xx	xx	xx	xx	xxx
2	xxxx	xx	xx	xx	xx	xx	xx	xx	xx	xxx
etc.	xxxx	xx	xx	xx	xx	xx	xx	xx	xx	xxx
Subtotal central city	xxxx	xx	xx	xx	xx	xx	xx	xx	xx	xxx
10	xxxx	xx	xx	xx	xx	xx	xx	xx	xx	xxx
11	xxxx	xx	xx	xx	xx	xx	xx	xx	xx	xxx
etc.	xxxx	xx	xx	xx	xx	xx	xx	xx	xx	xxx
Subtotal fringe area	xxxx	xx	xx	xx	xx	xx	xx	xx	xx	xxx
Planning area total	xxxx	xx	xx	xx	xx	xx	xx	xx	xx	xxx

[a] Total and subtotals match up with those at the foot of Table 31.

other utility lines would be deëmphasized. Similarly, it would be important to recognize unfavorable soil conditions in areas which are likely to remain beyond the public sewer service area and which therefore would depend upon septic tanks for sewage disposal. The land use plan must recognize these and other similar factors, and through its implementing recommendations it actually exerts some control in seeing that these limiting factors are respected.

Results of this allocation process as finally balanced against the requirements in Table 34 and kept within the ceilings of Table 35 are summarized in a form such as shown in Table 36. It should be noted that the table includes a column on conversions. While not directly necessary in the derivation of residential space requirements, estimates of the distribution of conversions among planning districts during the planning period is made as part of this process so that population distribution data can be computed for purposes of community facility analyses. Allocation of conversions is made on the basis of the previously prepared map showing the proposed pattern of maximum permitted residential densities and considering those planning districts where the pressures for conversion are apt to be greatest, principally those containing the large old, outmoded homes frequently found ringing the central business district.

TABLE 37. New Residential Space Requirements by Density Type Tentatively Distributed Among Planning Districts, 19xx

Planning District	Net Addition in Residential Land by Density Type (Acres)							
	A	B	C	D	E	F	etc.	Total
1	xx	xx	xx	xx	xx	xx	xx	xx
2	xx	xx	xx	xx	xx	xx	xx	xx
etc.	xx	xx	xx	xx	xx	xx	xx	xx
Subtotal central city	xx	xx	xx	xx	xx	xx	xx	xx
10	xx	xx	xx	xx	xx	xx	xx	xx
11	xx	xx	xx	xx	xx	xx	xx	xx
etc.	xx	xx	xx	xx	xx	xx	xx	xx
Subtotal fringe area	xx	xx	xx	xx	xx	xx	xx	xx
Planning area total	xx	xx	xx	xx	xx	xx	xx	xx

4. *Summary of space needs and population.* The fourth and final step in the analysis of residential area requirements summarizes tentative new space needs, and according to the assumed average household size, determines the tentative distribution of the total population by the end of the planning period. In this connection, it should be noted that the population distribution estimates thus derived provide a more refined result than that obtained by methods described in Chapter 7. Table 37 represents the form of the summary showing how total acreage requirements developed in Table 34 are distributed by planning district. Table 38 indicates the form in which the future population by planning district is summarized.

TABLE 38. Approximating the Distribution of Total Planning Area Population by Planning District, 19xx

Planning District	Current			By End of Planning Peroid				
	Pop.	D.Us.	H'hold Size	Existing D.Us. Remaining 19xx	D.Us. Added by 19xx	Total D.Us. by 19xx	H'hold Size	Pop.
	1	2	3	4	5	6	7	8
1	x	x	x	x	x	x	x	x
2	x	x	x	x	x	x	x	x
etc.	x	x	x	x	x	x	x	x
	–	–	–	–	–	–	–	–
Subtotal central city	x	x	x	x	x	x	x	x
10	x	x	x	x	x	x	x	x
11	x	x	x	x	x	x	x	x
etc.	x	x	x	x	x	x	x	x
	–	–	–	–	–	–	–	–
Subtotal fringe area	x	x	x	x	x	x	x	x
Planning area total	x	x	x	x	x	x	x	x

Explanation: Columns 1 through 3 show the derivation of the existing household sizes by planning district. Column 1 figures are estimated by methods described in Chapter 7, and Column 2 is a summary of the dwelling unit count appearing in Table 29 as obtained from the land use survey. Approximations of the household sizes by the end of the planning period are derived in Columns 4 through 7. Column 4 comes from Table 32 and Column 5 from Table 36, with Column 6 representing the sum of entries in these two columns. Using previously assumed future household sizes for the central city and fringe area and using Column 3 as a guide, household sizes of the future are approximated, first on a proportional basis and then adjusted on a subjective basis, considering the previously derived distribution of housing types and expectations as to the planning districts which will attract families with children, those which will attract childless couples, and so on. Estimates of population by planning district appearing in Column 8 are finally computed from entries in Columns 6 and 7. Obviously this whole process is an extremely crude one. Yet it is a reasoned approach to making subjective judgments, and until the needed research can supply more objective techniques, such an approach is the only alternative. In any case, it may be considered sufficiently accurate for the generalized character of the result desired.

Local Business Space Requirements

As previously noted, it is not practicable to include in a preliminary land use planning analysis the detailed kind of investigation of retail space requirements involved in purchasing power and similar studies. Moreover, for the generalized result desired in the preliminary land use plan, this level of detail is not warranted, particularly when it is considered that the space required is very nominal in comparison with that for other land use categories.

ESTIMATING STANDARDS

Fairly crude rule-of-thumb procedures are usually employed in the preliminary land use plan for estimating space requirements of local retail business areas. They begin with estimates of total space requirements for combined community and neighborhood type facilities. These estimates are made on the basis of local adaptations of empirically derived general standards such as those summarized in Table 39. As illustrations, the Greensboro study, omitting the larger form of shopping center, estimated neighborhood space requirements using 0.65 acre per 1000 population as a standard,[49] and in San Francisco, 0.75 to 1.00 acre per 1000 population was used for the combined requirements of both neighborhood and community types of shopping centers.[50] In adapting such yardsticks to local needs, it should be borne in mind that detailed test applications of general standards to a particular locality may show that variable standards should be developed for neighborhoods and communities of different density characteristics. Thus a suburban residential development of acreage plots may have a different order of standard than one in densely developed apartment areas.

TABLE 39. Crude Standards for Estimating Space Requirements of Neighborhood and Community Shopping Centers

Selected Neighborhood Population Sizes in Residential Communities of 30–50,000	Acres of Combined Community-Neighborhood Shopping Area per 1000 Population		
	Parking Ratios[a]		
	2:1	3:1	4:1
5000	0.7	0.9	1.1
2500	0.8	1.0	1.3
1000	1.1	1.5	1.8

[a] Parking ratio is here defined as the square feet of parking space for every square foot of ground area covered by store buildings.

Using some such locally adopted standards of shopping space per 1000 population served, crude estimates of the total shopping space required are developed community by community for each assemblage of planning districts which are considered to approximate a residential community. When such a standard is applied to existing population figures, it is common to find that in many residential communities by these standards local business is overexpanded. Often the business is scattered and interspersed with residences. If there is still an oversupply when the standard is applied to the forecast population, subtractions are indicated for these communities.[51] In other residential communities, additions to existing retail business acreage will be indicated.

[49] *Ibid.,* p. 34.

[50] San Francisco Department of City Planning, *op. cit.,* p. 3.

[51] It might be observed parenthetically that it is an important function of the land use plan to identify the major centers to be retained, and by omission, the areas and the scattered establishments which are proposed to be retired. The nonconforming use provisions of a zoning ordinance developed on the basis of the land use plan, if sufficiently stringent and if enforced,

SPACE NEEDS BY FACILITY TYPE

The first step thus provides a gross indication of space needs by residential communities. The succeeding steps use these gross estimates as guides in deriving more refined and superseding estimates. The second step divides the combined standard into its two components. On the basis of observed local trends in the existing distribution of local retail space between community shopping centers and local neighborhood outlets, the combined yardstick is split into separate yardsticks for each of these two functional types of shopping facilities.[52] If a system of residential communities has been identified within the framework of planning districts, the yardstick for community shopping centers is sometimes applied to the estimated future population of these community areas to obtain guides on a residential community level. In some urban areas where residential communities are not identified as intermediate analytical areas, the community shopping center yardstick is applied on an urban-wide basis. Similarly, using the neighborhood portion of the original yardstick and applying it on a planning district basis, space requirement guides are obtained at the localized level. The estimates of future population by planning district as summarized in Table 38 are used in this analysis.

TRIAL DISTRIBUTION SCHEME

The third and final step first examines within the framework of location criteria previously developed the existing pattern of shopping centers and develops a tentative scheme of strategic sites for retention, for expansion, and for the development of entire new centers. Then, using the foregoing yardsticks as general ceilings, estimates of space requirements for each site are derived. Finally, these estimates are summarized on a planning district basis for community shopping centers, neighborhood facilities, and a combined total in a form such as that indicated in Table 40. This analysis cannot go into the details of store types for each site. Although practice in approximating site sizes varies, one method is to select typical inlying,

---

over a period of time can assist scattered businesses in becoming reëstablished in centers. From the standpoint of the poorly located businesses, the land use plan provides a guide to finding relocation sites in expanding areas where businesses, under modern zoning provisions, are assured strategic locations with ample room for off-street parking and loading areas and other essential requirements of the modern shopping center.

[52] In urban areas of approximately 100,000 and under, the community shopping center functions are commonly performed by the central business district, and consequently this step does not apply. This was the situation in Greensboro, which may explain to some extent the difference between the above-cited Greensboro and San Francisco systems of standards used.

midtown, and outlying community and neighborhood centers presently existing, analyze the facilities for the range of services provided and the space allotted, and derive typical site sizes which would approximate space needs for each type of center in these typical locations. At sites in fully developed areas, parking space is usually the principal space need. The provision of off-street parking lots and the amount of space allowed must be considered in terms of such practicalities as land values, the appeal and risk involved to public and private agencies available to undertake the development and management of such facilities, the prevailing and probable future character of on-street parking restrictions, and so on. At developing midtown and outlying sites, off-street parking requirements in a new or revised zoning ordinance can be anticipated, using higher-order space allowances. In outlying undeveloped areas, space allowances can approach those of planned shopping centers with the highest standards of off-street parking and loading spaces and the provision of planted areas.

The final result of this analysis as summarized in Table 40 indicates tentative proposals for the amount of land to be retired from local business use in its present location and for the amount of land to be added to each planning district for community shopping centers and for neighborhood facilities. Accompanying such a table as part of the working materials of this analysis would be a key map identifying actual locations of additions

TABLE 40. New Space Requirements for Local Business Centers by Planning District, 19xx

Planning District	Net Reduction in Space (Acres)	Net Additions in Space (Acres)								
		Community Shopping Centers			Neighborhood Facilities			All Local Business Facilities		
		Invasion	V & R[a]	Total	Invasion	V & R[a]	Total	Invasion	V & R[a]	Total
1	xx	x	x	x	x	x	x	x	x	x
2	xx	x	x	x	x	x	x	x	x	x
etc.	xx	x	x	x	x	x	x	x	x	x
	—	–	–	–	–	–	–	–	–	–
Subtotal central city	xx	x	x	x	x	x	x	x	x	x
10	xx	x	x	x	x	x	x	x	x	x
11	xx	x	x	x	x	x	x	x	x	x
etc.	xx	x	x	x	x	x	x	x	x	x
	—	–	–	–	–	–	–	–	–	–
Subtotal fringe area	xx	x	x	x	x	x	x	x	x	x
	—	–	–	–	–	–	–	–	–	–
Planning area total	xx	x	x	x	x	x	x	x	x	x

[a] V & R is an abbreviation for "vacant and renewal land."

and reductions. Obviously, some planning districts will have both additions and subtractions. Because community shopping centers serve areas sometimes covering as many as five and six planning districts, entries in the table for these facilities will appear only for planning districts in which these centers happen to be located. In some instances, space requirements allowed for some community and neighborhood facilities will be split among two or three planning districts where district boundaries pass through sites of these facilities. It should be noted, too, that the V & R column in the summary of net additions for all facilities contains the data required in analyses of gross residential densities taken up later in the chapter. This entire analysis of local business space requirements is, of course, tentative and may be subject to revision in the final design phase of the land use planning procedure. In this connection, net additions in retail space may involve invasion of land previously counted as part of the residential land supply, and net reductions in retail space may have the reverse effect. These are illustrative of some of the "cut and fill" adjustments which must be made in the final design phase.

School Space Requirements

Although involving different measurement units, the basic method used in estimating space needs for schools is very similar to that employed in estimating space needs for local business areas. This method involves first a determination of the number of facilities needed, and then on the basis of estimates of space needed for each facility, space requirements are assigned to the appropriate planning districts in which each such facility is located. As in the space analyses for other land use classes, crude approximation techniques are employed rather than the more detailed and accurate techniques used in studies for the comprehensive plan. Thus in place of using the survival techniques in estimating future school enrollments as cited later in the chapter, we use crude ratio techniques, estimates of enrollment being a key element in determining the number of schools required.

STUDY OF EXISTING SCHOOL PLANT

For purposes of the preliminary land use plan, space requirements are derived in the following sequence of steps. First, pertinent data concerning the present school system or systems in the urban area and long-range school policies are assembled. This involves preparing summary tabulations of past enrollments for each school; totals for each administrative school jurisdiction falling within the planning area, public and parochial (or increments thereof, where a school board's jurisdiction is partially within the planning area); school capacities as measured by the number of classrooms of standard size (generally 30 square feet per pupil, with a maximum of 25 to 30 pupils per classroom); school site sizes in acres; and presently prevailing and proposed changes in school board policies with respect to the organization of the system or systems (i.e., 6–3–3;8–4, or other breakdown of grade organization) and the community use of schools and recreation facilities.

ESTIMATING FUTURE ENROLLMENTS

The second major step is one of estimating future total enrollments in the planning area according to the anticipated typical future grade organizations of the systems involved, and approximating the distribution of this future school population by planning district. The ratio method for estimating future total enrollments examines all school systems as if they were a single system, and according to the typical grade organization, develops historical series for past decades showing the percentages, for example, that elementary, junior high, and senior high school age groups in the population are of the total population at each census enumeration. These percentage series are then extrapolated and applied to the population estimate forecast for the end of the planning period as discussed in Chapter 7 to yield crude estimates of the future school-age composition of the population. Two additional percentage series are then developed, the second being required only where there is a parochial system involved in the urban area: (1) the proportion of each census-enumerated school age group enrolled in each level of the grade organization, and (2) the proportion of enrolled children in each level of the school system enrolled in public schools. Each percentage series is arranged in a time sequence and extrapolated, and the resulting crude estimates of future proportions applied to the above derived estimates of school-age population. The results are a series of estimates of future total enrollment broken down as to elementary, junior high, and senior high school levels (assuming here a 6–3–3 system) and by public and parochial systems (assuming both systems are present).

The next operation is one of distributing planning area totals to the various communities and planning districts for each type of school and each school system. This distribution is made on a crude basis following proportions in the way the future total population is distributed by planning districts as previously summarized in Table 38. The resulting crude allocation of total future enrollment to planning districts by type of school and for each separate school system (where this situation exists) is usually subject to further adjustment. For planning districts in fringe area locations where the land is open or where residential development is just commencing, by reference to household size data in Table 38, crude upward adjustments are made, recognizing that the pattern of the proportion of children attending school to total population which will emerge here will be above average, tending to correspond with recent experience in this respect in existing new developments. Such upward adjustments for peripheral areas of course will involve compensating downward adjustments in the inlying planning districts, probably in conversion areas, and in planning districts with large numbers of small apartment accommodations. Again, household size data in Table 38 will provide guides for these adjustments. Obviously, data developed by such crude techniques will have limited significance for school-building programing until they can be substantiated by the more detailed studies mentioned below at the end of this section of the chapter. However, for generalized land use planning purposes they are sufficiently accurate to indicate general locations where concentrations of school children may be expected in the future, and thus where school sites should be reserved.

TRIAL SCHEME OF SCHOOL SITES

In the third major step, the existing school locations are examined in terms of approximations as to the future concentrations of school-age population and the location requirements previously developed, and, considering the general age and adequacy of existing school buildings, the adequacy of existing school sites, and the availability of vacant or renewal land for new sites, a tentative scheme of school sites is developed for the urban area for each school type and each school system. Such a scheme would give particular attention to new sites and those existing sites which by standards cited below require additional land or, in other words, special attention to locations where additional land will be needed. At the same time, locations should be noted where schools are likely to be abandoned and where land in these sites may be expected to become available for other uses. In developing this tentative scheme, comments of local school authorities would be invited and drawn upon to the fullest practicable

Table 41. General Standards for School Site Sizes

Type of School	Minimum (Acres)	Desirable Minimum (Acres)	Preferred Range (Acres)
Elementary	5	5 + 1 per 100 ultimate enrollment	10–25
Junior high	10	10 + 1 per 100 ultimate enrollment	25–50
Senior high	20	20 + 1 per 100 ultimate enrollment	40–100

extent, and, of course, what advanced planning that has been undertaken by these authorities or their consultants would be taken into consideration.

SUMMARY OF SPACE NEEDS

The fourth and final step is the development of the summary of new space requirements by planning districts. On the basis of such generally recognized "preferred" standards as those reproduced in Table 41, local site-size standards are adopted and applied. Space requirements are then compiled on a planning district basis for each type of school for all systems of schools as presented in Table 42. Since junior and senior high schools serve communities which will encompass a number of planning districts, entries in these columns in Table 42 will appear only for the plan-

Table 42. New Space Requirements for Schools by Planning District, 19xx

	Net Additions in Space (Acres)											
	Elementary			Junior High			Senior High			All Schools		
Planning District	Invasion	V & R[a]	Total	Invasion	V & R[a]	Total	Invasion	V & R[a]	Total	Invasion	V & R[a]	Total
1	x	x	x	x	x	x	x	x	x	x	x	x
2	x	x	x	x	x	x	x	x	x	x	x	x
etc.	x	x	x	x	x	x	x	x	x	x	x	x
	–	–	–	–	–	–	–	–	–	–	–	–
Subtotal central city	x	x	x	x	x	x	x	x	x	x	x	x
10	x	x	x	x	x	x	x	x	x	x	x	x
11	x	x	x	x	x	x	x	x	x	x	x	x
etc.	x	x	x	x	x	x	x	x	x	x	x	x
	–	–	–	–	–	–	–	–	–	–	–	–
Subtotal fringe area	x	x	x	x	x	x	x	x	x	x	x	x
	–	–	–	–	–	–	–	–	–	–	–	–
Planning area total	x	x	x	x	x	x	x	x	x	x	x	x

[a] V & R is an abbreviation for "vacant and renewal land."

ning districts in which these schools happen to be located. In small urban areas, usually under 100,000 population, there may be only one consolidated high school. Some sites may be split among two or three districts if they happen to be located on district lines. As in the previous analyses, the V & R column in the summary for "all schools" will be of particular interest in the later discussions of gross residential densities.

Local Recreation Space Requirements

As noted earlier in discussions of location requirements, recreation facilities serving residential communities are usually classified according to general age groups served and according to whether they are active or passive. For active recreation facilities, space requirements are developed on the basis of two criteria: (1) a population yardstick to indicate the total acreage required for each type of area, and (2) a minimum site-size criterion. A population yardstick is also used as a general guide in estimating space requirements for passive recreation areas. Since passive recreation areas are often integrated into an urban-wide system of public open space as previously discussed, such a yardstick is often simply a means of checking space allotments already made to insure that each planning district measures up to minimum standards.

RECREATION AREA STANDARDS

Generally recognized crude standards for local recreation facilities are reproduced in Table 43. Even such crude standards may not fit the conditions of all urban areas, and where warranted local adaptations should be developed. In more detailed studies of recreation space requirements in extension of those developed for the preliminary land use plan, variations in these standards would be developed according to density classes of residential development.[53]

Obviously, an important consideration in the application of such standards is the pattern of school sites and the recreation facilities provided in these areas. Thus some of the space requirements for playground areas will be satisfied by facilities on elementary school sites, and recreation center or playfield space needs, at junior and senior high school sites. While there

[53] See detailed standards of the Committee on the Hygiene of Housing, *op. cit.,* pp. 48–49.

TABLE 43. General Standards for Local Recreation Areas

Facility or Area	Population Standard	Site-Size Standard
Playground	1 acre/800 population	3–6 acres
Local parks	1 acre/1000 population[a]	2 or more acres
Recreation center	1 acre/800 population	15–20 acres
or playfield	1 acre/800 population	10–30 acres

[a] Varies according to residential densities ranging from 2 acres per 1000 population in areas of multifamily dwellings down to three-quarters of an acre per 1000 population in single-family developments.

may be presently unreconciled conflicts in school board and recreation commission policies with respect to joint use of recreation facilities, the probabilities are that in the long run, cost considerations will dictate integrated planning of active public recreation facilities and school site facilities. At the same time it should be remembered that location criteria, population yardsticks, and site-size considerations may dictate the provision of active recreation areas in addition to or separate from what may be available at school sites.

TRIAL SCHEME OF RECREATION AREAS

Once local recreation standards have been established, space requirements are estimated in the following manner. Referring to the general urban-wide pattern of open spaces and the system of existing and proposed school sites previously developed, a tentative schematic plan of recreation sites is developed for each type of facility. In this study scheme, attention is given to the availability of surplus public lands, abandoned school sites, and tax title lands. Considered, too, are the ideas and previous proposals of recreation and park officials or their consultants. The final result of this process is a scheme of sites with areas dimensioned according to the locally adopted standards of desirable (as opposed to minimum) site size and balanced off against gross requirements as determined by population standards. With acreages compiled by planning district, the result is summarized in tabular form as shown in Table 44. Comments made concerning procedures in tabulating school data apply equally well here, namely, that in the case of facilities serving a larger residential community, such as playfields and recreation centers, Table 44 will show entries only for those planning districts in which the facilities happen to be located. Again, the V & R data under "all facilities" have special significance for the analysis of gross residential densities which follows.

Table 44.　New Space Requirements for Local Recreation Areas by Planning District, 19xx

	Net Additions in Local Recreation Space (Acres)											
Planning District	Local Parks			Playgrounds			Playf'ds-Rec. Ctrs.			All Facilities		
	Inva-sion	V & R[a]	Total	Inva-sion	V & R[a]	Total	Inva-sion	V & R[a]	Total	Inva-sion	V & R[a]	Total
1	x	x	x	x	x	x	x	x	x	x	x	x
2	x	x	x	x	x	x	x	x	x	x	x	x
etc.	x	x	x	x	x	x	x	x	x	x	x	x
	–	–	–	–	–	–	–	–	–	–	–	–
Subtotal central city	x	x	x	x	x	x	x	x	x	x	x	x
10	x	x	x	x	x	x	x	x	x	x	x	x
11	x	x	x	x	x	x	x	x	x	x	x	x
etc.	x	x	x	x	x	x	x	x	x	x	x	x
	–	–	–	–	–	–	–	–	–	–	–	–
Subtotal fringe area	x	x	x	x	x	x	x	x	x	x	x	x
	–	–	–	–	–	–	–	–	–	–	–	–
Planning area total	x	x	x	x	x	x	x	x	x	x	x	x

[a] V & R is an abbreviation for "vacant and renewal land."

Space for Residential Communities as a Whole

This subsection on residential community space requirements serves two functions. First, it directs attention to any revisions in net residential space requirements which may be necessitated by the results of the subsequent analyses of community facility requirements and the preëmption of land for these purposes that may have been tentatively included as residential land in the first place. Second, it focuses attention on effective gross holding capacity and gross residential density concepts which have special significance in estimating space requirements in the presently undeveloped planning districts or in districts with large clearance areas becoming available under public renewal programs.

FINAL ADJUSTMENTS IN NET SPACE NEEDS

The data developed in terms of net effective holding capacities in the analysis of residential areas will continue to serve an important purpose in developed and partially developed planning districts where streets are in

TABLE 45. Allocations of Residentially Suited Supply of Vacant-Renewal Land to Local Community Facility Uses by Planning District, 19xx

Planning District	Total V & R^a Land Suitable for Res. Communities	Space Rqts. of Community Facilities From V & R^a Supply of Land				V & R^a Land Remaining for Residential Use
		Local Bus.	Schools	Recreation	Total	
1	xx	x	x	x	x	xx
2	xx	x	x	x	x	xx
etc.	xx	x	x	x	x	xx
	—	–	–	–	–	—
Subtotal central city	xx	x	x	x	x	xx
10	xx	x	x	x	x	xx
11	xx	x	x	x	x	xx
etc.	xx	x	x	x	x	xx
	—	–	–	–	–	—
Subtotal fringe area	xx	x	x	x	x	xx
	—	–	–	–	–	—
Planning area total	xx	x	x	x	x	xx

^{a} V & R is an abbreviation for "vacant and renewal land."

place or dedicated, for in these areas, estimates of space needs based on gross data do not apply. Thus on the basis of the space requirement summaries appearing in Tables 40, 42, and 44, a summary such as that shown in Table 45 is prepared, recapitulating space requirements for community facilities and giving the amount of vacant and renewal land remaining for residential use in each planning district after deducting the total land absorbed by these community facilities. Then a new Table 35 of final effective net holding capacities is prepared. These revisions, in turn, may involve revisions in the distribution of dwelling units among planning districts (see Table 36) and in the distribution of acreage requirements by planning district (see Table 37). While it is possible that these revisions will involve several repeated trial computations extending into revisions of community facility estimates of space needs in order to balance off the supply of land with the combined space needs of all relevant uses, it is more probable that adjustments will be relatively minor since community facility space needs make up only a very nominal part of the total.

ESTIMATING GROSS SPACE NEEDS

The final matter of concern is the development of estimates of space requirements for entire residential communities which may be expected to develop in outlying planning districts during the planning period. These requirements are analyzed in terms of effective gross holding capacities and gross residential densities. These data are prepared primarily for planning districts with large amounts of open land or containing large areas earmarked for clearance and redevelopment as residential communities. The procedure is relatively simple. The figures in the last column of Table 45 are adjusted downward for the appropriate planning districts by an amount which it is estimated will accommodate needed streets. This adjustment is crudely approximated on the basis of observed existing proportions of total land area devoted to streets in presently built-up planning districts as recorded in the summary of existing land uses, and on the basis of subjective allowances for the character of the terrain in each planning district of interest. In the more detailed analyses of residential communities, special adjustments for each class of residential density are recommended. Such detail is not warranted in the broad-gauge analyses employed in developing the preliminary land use plan.

With an adjustment made in the supply of vacant and renewal land available for residential use to allow for streets, procedures then follow those previously outlined. A tabular summary of effective gross holding capacities is prepared for the appropriate planning districts following the format of Table 35. Next a table similar to Table 36 is developed, showing for the planning districts of interest any changes in the distribution of dwelling unit requirements by density type, considering changes in the holding capacity ceilings developing as a result of a shift from a net to a gross presentation of data. The final step is the summary of space requirements for the appropriate planning districts as shown in Table 46.

From Preliminary to Refined Studies

The foregoing procedures for the analysis of residential communities are especially designed for preliminary land use planning. While the basic framework in the more detailed comprehensive plan studies is similar, at certain points in the procedures, specialized studies are introduced to sharpen the analyses, substituting more precise estimating techniques for the approximation approaches employed in certain stages of the work described above. Thus, in residential area studies, a housing market analysis would be a "must"; in school plant investigations, a more reliable forecasting technique would be introduced, and more detailed studies of the existing school plant would be made; in shopping center analyses, a detailed

TABLE 46.   Derivation of Gross Space Requirements for Entirely New Residential Communities in Selected Planning Districts

Planning District	Net Acreage Requirements by Use Class									
	Residential Use by Density Type							Community Facilities	Allowance for Streets	Gross Acreage Rqts.
	A	B	C	D	E	F	etc.			
X	x	x	x	x	x	x	x	x	x	xx
Y	x	x	x	x	x	x	x	x	x	xx
Z	x	x	x	x	x	x	x	x	x	xx

survey of existing floor space in local business use and a purchasing power and family expenditures study would be undertaken (see references to these studies in earlier section of this chapter); and studies of church space needs would be introduced.[54] These are a few of the kinds of studies which would be undertaken in detailing the first preliminary planning analyses. Undoubtedly, as research is conducted into various aspects of land use planning procedures for residential communities, some elements in the above framework will be superseded by improved methods and techniques in both the preliminary and later stages of land use planning. To indicate the general character of these more detailed studies at the present stage of research development, the first two areas of investigation cited above will be briefly alluded to in the following paragraphs.

HOUSING MARKET ANALYSIS

In a valuable monograph on theory and methods of housing market analysis, Rapkin, Winnick, and Blank define this kind of a study as "a process that attempts to identify and measure the forces that produce change in the size and utilization of the housing inventory and thus influence the distribution of dwelling units among the population."[55] Thus it is essentially an analysis of supply and demand conditions in the housing market. Broadly, supply is concerned with "how much of the product will be made available at different prices when costs (of various kinds) and the organization of the industry are taken into account," and demand, with "how much of the product the public will buy, given its income, tastes, and the price of the product (relative to the prices of other goods)."[56]

[54] For a useful reference on church planning needs, see Robert C. Hoover and Everett L. Perry, *Church and City Planning*, Survey Guide 2, Bureau of Research and Survey, National Council of the Churches of Christ in the U.S.A., November, 1955.

[55] Chester Rapkin, Louis Winnick, and David M. Blank, *Housing Market Analysis*, a Housing and Home Finance Agency research monograph, U.S. Government Printing Office, December, 1953, p. 1.

[56] Louis Winnick, "Housing Market Analysis," *Journal of Housing*, December, 1955, p. 432.

The procedure outlined in the above framework for the analysis of residential areas is essentially aimed at determining existing and long-range housing need as opposed to housing demand. The most important elements missing in this framework is first, an analysis of the housing inventory by rent and price categories compared with the rent-paying and purchase ability of the population under study, and second, a study of choice factors which affect demand, given rents and prices that match up with the financial abilities and desires of this population to take up housing at these rentals and prices. While the above framework introduced assumptions as to choice, to be firmly based, these assumptions must be geared to market forces.

Now obviously, market analyses have their greatest utility in terms of short-run eventualities. Over long-run periods, there are a great many intangibles in the matter of tastes, income levels, family sizes, and other factors which are difficult to anticipate. Yet if assumptions concerning the future can be framed in terms of an intimate knowledge of the workings of the present housing market, long-range planning proposals affecting the future market are more likely to prove practicable than had market factors been entirely ignored. The residential areas portion of the land use plan is a long-range proposal which seeks to fulfill future housing needs, but is attuned as closely as possible to realistic market factors. Thus the housing market analysis provides valuable insights into the economic factors likely to influence proposals based purely on social need. Properly evaluated and introduced into the studies for residential land use planning, these factors can be used in framing more studied assumptions, setting more detailed developmental specifications, and preparing a plan that is reasonably possible of attainment and yet does not compromise the important social objectives sought in the plan.

The techniques of housing market analysis are adequately described elsewhere and are beyond the scope of this discussion.[57] On the supply side, they involve surveys of a somewhat different order than the studies heretofore described, although some of the basic types of data will obviously be similar.[58] On the demand side, a whole new array of investigations are introduced, including sampling studies which delve into both the future housing intentions of people as well as their past behavior in the selection of housing.[59] Finally, it should be noted that the whole market analysis

[57] See Rapkin, Winnick, and Blank, *op. cit.*

[58] See Fitzhugh L. Carmichael, *How to Make and Use Local Housing Surveys,* a Housing and Home Finance Agency research monograph, U.S. Government Printing Office, April, 1954.

[59] An example of the results of a study of consumer intentions is seen in *Greater Seattle Housing Market Survey,* Bureau of Business Research, University of Washington, 1948; some of the most recent techniques are cited by Chester Rapkin, Louis Winnick, and Ned Shilling, *Program for Eastwick Housing Market Development Analysis,* Institute for Urban Studies, University of Pennsylvania, 1954.

process is extremely complex and requires the skills of persons trained or experienced in this specialty.

SCHOOL PLANT PLANNING

Another illustration of the character of the more detailed work to be carried out in comprehensive planning studies is found in school plant planning analyses. In preliminary land use planning, investigations go only into sufficient detail to permit the identification of a general pattern of school sites as they relate to other space-using facilities in residential communities. Although school officials may be, and usually are consulted at this first stage of planning, the generalized character of these first studies are such as to be more fitted to the needs of general planning than to the work of the school board itself. The more detailed studies in extension of these first investigations, therefore, aim not only to provide more studied general planning information with which to develop the comprehensive plan, but to supply the school board with a service in which it has confidence as a basis for programing school plant needs. Essentially, this means that the planning agency is functioning in a service capacity and that, even though the planning agency conducts the studies, the school plant plan which emerges must for all purposes be the school board's plan.

On the surface of it, such an approach may appear to be simply a matter of "changing hats," i.e., writing in the name of the school board on the face of school planning reports as sponsor or cosponsor. But it goes more deeply than this. It involves an appreciation of a schoolman's point of view, and more specifically, a full understanding of educational objectives and school board policies as they impinge on school plant planning. For the city planner, long-range planning is primarily tied up in physical needs of the school plant; for the school administrator, long-range planning includes, as well, future curriculum considerations, future personnel requirements, and future budget needs for these as well as for the school plant.

There are a number of basic policy matters which impinge on school plant planning. Among them is the organization of the school system and the probabilities of change in the future, say, from an 8-4 to a 6-3-3 grade system, or from a 6-3-3 to a 6-3-3-2 system in which a junior college program is introduced into the traditional 12-grade organization. Another policy consideration concerns the community use of school facilities, not only in school-sponsored adult education programs, but in programs sponsored by other agencies or groups, for example, the recreation commission, or drama, music, and other similar civic groups. Still another policy matter relates to pupil transportation and the use of school buses or special transit passes to extend the attendance areas of schools beyond the traditional walking distance service radii. A related consideration is the basis for the establishment of attendance areas of the individual schools and the policy with respect to the admission of pupils from beyond the school district as a whole.

Though seemingly less tangibly connected with school plant planning than such administrative policy considerations, there are educational objectives which must be taken into account. Indeed, as self-evident as it seems, the basic objectives relating to the scope of the program, the curriculum content and the methods of education are the most fundamental determinants of the character of the school plant. In all its several connotations, the "community school" concept involves an educational philosophy calling for different spatial arrangements within and without the school than those involved in the more traditional philosophy. For example, when used in the sense that the teaching of the three R's is accomplished in the context of special studies, projects, or problems centered in the home community, the concept involves different yardsticks of space utilization in school buildings as a means of checking the adequacy of the school plant. If educational objectives include "camping education" programs, this would be reflected in different standards of school site sizes, and so on.

Thus education objectives and administrative policies can dictate variations in the approach to school plant planning. This places a premium on an approach in which the school authorities share in the planning process. Finally, as a practical matter it must be recognized that the school plant plan is effectuated by the school authorities. Thus if they can be persuaded to spare time from their day-to-day administrative burdens to participate in the planning process at critical points along the way, there is greater likelihood that the plan will be carried out.

Again, it is noted that consideration of the methods and techniques employed in these more detailed studies of space requirements are beyond the scope of the present discussion. Survival methods of estimating future enrollments are well covered elsewhere,[60] and the specific requirements of the elementary and secondary school plants and their sites have been treated in detail in specialized publications.[61] These more exacting kinds of studies, predicated on the above kinds of guiding considerations, however, clearly fall within the comprehensive planning stage of the progressive planning approach.

[60] See Planning Advisory Service, *Planning for School Capacities and Locations,* Information Report No. 36, American Society of Planning Officials, March, 1952; see also New York Commission on School Buildings, *Enrollment Handbook: Classrooms for How Many?* December, 1952.

[61] See National Council on Schoolhouse Construction, *Guide for Planning School Plants,* W. D. McClurkin, Peabody College, Nashville, 1953.

the land use plan

Implicit in the theoretical formulations of Part I and in the procedural sequence which has been unfolding in the chapters of Parts II and III is an emphasis on plan*ning,* and more particularly on land use plan*ning.* Though there has been this emphasis on process (indeed, it has supplied the syntax for our approach to land use planning), nevertheless it must be recognized that, to have utility, plan*ning* must produce some tangible and concrete results in the form of plans, in this case a land use or land development plan. So we come to a point in the process in which it is necessary to congeal the somewhat fluid results obtained so far into a plan, recognizing, of course, that in the framework of the progressive planning approach we are in the culminating stage of but the first cycle of a continuously evolutionary sequence.

Up to this point in the land use planning process, the city planner has been drawing primarily on the science of planning, with only secondary attention to the art of planning. He has been assembling, collating, and analyzing facts within the framework of a prescribed methodological approach to problem solving. On the basis of these facts he has been measuring and describing existing urban conditions in terms of locally derived concepts and standards of livability, and he has been estimating and interpreting discernible trends which can reasonably be expected to influence living conditions in the future. In other words, following certain defined principles and standards of land use planning, he has been determining location and space requirements for each urban land use category for the purposes of establishing the form of corrective action in renewal areas and of presenting guides for growth and development in expansion areas. Finally, he has made trial applications of these requirements and obtained a tentative fitting to those land areas requiring renewal and those available for expansion.

The city planner is now ready to apply himself to what is primarily the design phase of land use planning. His task is to translate these previously derived requirements into a well-articulated scheme for land development in the urban area which both reconciles conflicts in location and scales into the revised locations the space needs for each category of land use. He now examines all the individual use requirements as an interrelated group of requirements, and he views the use proposals cumulatively derived in the manner described in Chapter 12 as they fit into one coördinated pattern of uses. In addition, with a tentative transportation scheme now available, he seeks a synthesis of the land use with the circulatory requirements so that the preliminary land use and transportation plans which subsequently emerge are mutually compatible. Although in dealing with these relationships the city planner is entering upon a phase of the work which is concerned with the purest fundamentals of land use planning design, it must be remembered that design has been involved throughout the process, particularly in the derivation of location requirements.

DESIGN CONSIDERATIONS

As noted above, the final design phase of land use planning begins by taking the cumulatively derived product of the Chapter 11 and 12 types of analyses and subjecting it to two compatibility tests—first, a test for the conflict between land use and transportation requirements, and second, a test for inconsistency among the use relationships examined as a pattern or group of uses. Although cited here as separate tests for purposes of describing design considerations, in actual application they tend to be linked together, since readjustments in the scheme to achieve compatibility in the one set of relationships usually involve compensating readjustments in the other.

Transportation and Land Use

It should be observed at the outset that since thoroughfare and land use planning studies rarely proceed entirely independently of one another, it is not as though interrelationships were being explored for the first time at this juncture. Not only are the basic principles of design of each recognized in the other in such a way as to automatically give some attention to these interrelationships from the very beginning, but usually there are opportunities for cross-checks as each study proceeds along a seemingly independent line of investigation. However, since each will tend to be swayed in its emphasis by its own particular orientation, this synthesis stage is essential if results of either are to fall into a harmonious and comprehensive framework.

CENTRAL AREA

In the central area of the city the basic circulation principles call for an inner loop surrounding the CBD somewhat on the order of a giant traffic circle. This loop serves as an interchange between radial routes converging on the downtown area and permits drivers to select their points of entrance into the CBD without the necessity of entering the CBD's internal street system. In principle, the all-day, low-price parking areas fringe the inner loop, providing a quick means of siphoning off traffic at inbound times of the day to keep it from penetrating the CBD itself. At outbound times, traffic is fed from these parking terminals directly onto the loop and thus to the radials which drain the CBD. Closer in at the edges of the CBD are the higher-price parking lots for short-term parkers. In the large metropolitan areas, the inner loop is sometimes ringed by a higher-order expressway type of facility with interconnections provided by ramp streets at designated intervals.

The land use plan for the CBD both influences and is influenced by the location of the inner loop (and any auxiliary expressway loop that may be warranted). CBD land use planning studies establish the general location of the loop, but thoroughfare planning studies set the location in greater detail, considering such factors as future desire lines of traffic (in turn, influenced by the CBD plan), the selection of streets available from the existing street pattern that are adaptable and feasible for inclusion in such an inner loop, the conflicts posed by railroads and transit, and so on.

But within the framework of a general plan for the CBD, these are third- or fourth-order considerations. As noted in the Part III introductory discussion of public policy and planning, there are a hierarchy of policy considerations which underlie and precede these determinations. Among them are policy determinations relative to the balance that the land use plan is to reflect between the central and outlying region-serving business centers and the related determinations as to the balance between transit and automotive modes of transportation. The distribution of region-serving business functions has obvious implications for the size of the area the CBD will encompass, and decisions relative to modes of transportation affect the extent of parking areas to be provided as well as the capacity to be built into the downtown street system. These determinations, in turn, may be dependent on higher-order considerations relative to concentrated growth concentric to the existing built-up area versus dispersed expansion to a polynucleated series of outlying centers, and so on.

OUTLYING AREAS

Concentric to the inner loop, there are intermediate and outer loop systems of crosstown streets or parkways supplying interconnections between industrial areas, wholesale districts, and various residential communities in the urban area. Intersecting these crosstown streets are the major radials: the expressways and major thoroughfares which radiate outward from the CBD to outlying residential areas and employment centers.

Here again, land use planning considerations influence and are influenced by thoroughfare planning requirements. The intersections of major radial and circumferential streets are the strategic locations for satellite region-serving business centers and for community shopping centers. In some

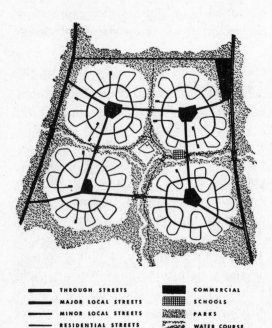

THROUGH STREETS
MAJOR LOCAL STREETS
MINOR LOCAL STREETS
RESIDENTIAL STREETS
TRAILS

COMMERCIAL
SCHOOLS
PARKS
WATER COURSE

FIGURE 30. Generalized Application of Residential Community Design Principles. (*Source:* Philadelphia City Planning Commission, *Preliminary Far Northeast Physical Development Plan,* January, 1955.)

such centers, a perimeter loop with its own web system of radials and cir-cumferentials subordinate to, but integrated with the larger metropolitan web system may be required. The design of this subordinate system of ma-jor streets must be closely coördinated with the design of the business cen-ter and surrounding residential areas. Similarly, outlying employment cen-ters such as organized industrial districts may be the focal points for other subordinate web systems of radial and crosstown routes which must also be related to surrounding use areas and to the larger metropolitan system of major streets. Finally and fundamental in residential community design, every effort is made to locate the metropolitan and more localized radials and circumferentials so that they bound rather than penetrate or truncate any particular system of neighborhoods that compose each residential com-munity. This general principle is illustrated in Figure 30. It should be noted that within residential communities there are various lower-order major streets, one supplying interconnections between neighborhood centers (see Figure 30), and still another supplying a means of collecting or distributing traffic within each neighborhood (see Figure 30) or sometimes bounding the neighborhood (see Figure 31). All these various subordinate systems of major streets, whether they serve business centers, industrial areas, or residential communities, obviously must be fitted to the use areas they serve and to the surrounding pattern of uses.

Use Relationships

Related to the foregoing considerations are the interrelationships intrin-sic to uses themselves—relationships between industrial areas and residen-tial communities, between region-serving recreational, educational, and cultural areas and residential communities or business centers, and so on. The basic principles for these relationships have been set forth in the loca-tion requirements discussed in Chapter 11. But there remains the task of checking the trial pattern of uses developed in the sequence of analyses in Chapter 12. This involves not only tests for compatibility, but also checks to insure that proposals for the use of vacant and renewal areas are, in fact, the best use of these areas. Even though the vacant land classification sys-tem employed in the first instance would tend to preclude basic miscalcula-tions, it is necessary to establish that the peculiar sequence followed in Chapter 12 in the analysis of major use categories has not introduced any distortions in the pattern of use relationships.

Under this category of design considerations are the tests for such basic

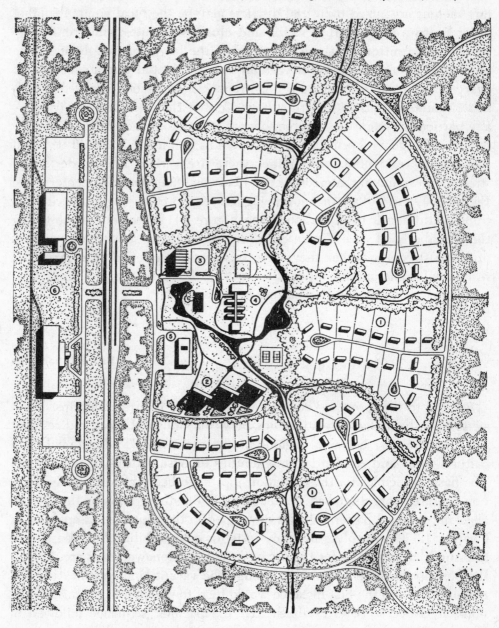

FIGURE 31. Illustrative Application of Neighborhood Design Principles. (*Source:* Atlanta Metropolitan Planning Commission, *Up Ahead,* 1952.)

① SINGLE-FAMILY DWELLINGS   ④ SCHOOL

② MULTI-STORY APARTMENTS   ⑤ SHOPPING CENTER

③ CHURCH   ⑥ INDUSTRY

elements as the convenience between use areas, the relationship of prevailing winds to industrial and residential areas, or the way in which glare from business areas or the noise and gasoline fumes from traffic in business or employment centers may interfere with the amenities of residential communities, and so on. Also involved at this juncture are checks to ascertain the general compatibility of the trial pattern of uses with the structure of land values, and tests to establish whether in the particular locations selected the densities proposed for residential areas and the intensity of development proposed in commercial and industrial areas yield a favorable cost-revenue relationship. These elements plus the aesthetic considerations in the use of natural and man-made visual assets intrinsic to the setting of the city and the arrangements of use areas in this setting, and citizen attitudes and preferences on such things as differential densities within any single residential area, the siting of industry under performance standards in areas traditionally closed to industry—these considerations all enter into the summary reëxamination of use relationships.

PREPARING THE PLAN

On the basis of these design considerations, the earlier trial scheme for the location and distribution of future land uses can be shaped up into its final version, what we have termed here the preliminary land use plan. The creative aspects of this final synthesizing process of design are not readily described in words, but it may assist in picturing the rudiments of this process to summarize briefly its mechanics and the form in which the results are presented.

Design of the Plan

The design of the plan is the culmination of repeated tests and retests of alternative arrangements in the pattern of uses, considering location and space needs previously specified and the density and intensity of development prescribed in the course of deriving these needs. The scope of these tests will of course be guided by the above kinds of design considerations. Overlays are used in the testing process. Over the trial scheme of uses cumulatively derived is inserted an overlay of the trial thoroughfare scheme. Next, an annotated overlay is prepared, identifying the conflicts in transportation and land use and the inconsistencies or awkward elements in use relationships. In general, tests of conflicts with transportation systems begin with the CBD and are carried from there to outlying sections of the urban area. Concurrently or separately, according to the preferences of the land use planner, the workability of use relationships are established in both their localized and their broad patterns.

The overlay with annotations of conflicts and other problems then becomes the reference work for the design analyses. By other overlays, different solutions to each problem are tested in sketch form. Where a solution has implications for other aspects of the plan not previously noted on the reference overlay, special additional adjustments which go with that particular solution may become involved. Thus each problem is studied individually and finally in combination until a scheme emerges with all elements in balance and harmony. With a decision reached on a scheme, the final task of the operation is the recapitulation of the summary of space allocation adjusted to this final version of the preliminary land use plan.

Plan Presentation

The general scope and content of the report on the land use plan was outlined in Chapter 10. Of primary concern here is the tangible form that the map presentation takes as a means of visualizing the end product of the design process. A number of factors dictate the form and detail employed in the presentation, principal among them being the size of the urban area and the purpose to be served by the presentation. Generally the land use plan is a combined presentation of the principal elements of the thoroughfare network and the pattern of proposed uses. The generalized version of the Detroit Metropolitan Area Preliminary Land Use Plan shown in Figure 32 illustrates the value of this combined presentation, supplying a visual explanation as to how various major functional use areas are to be tied together and developed in balanced relationship to one another.

To provide a fully meaningful picture of use relationships, the presentation must show the entire metropolitan area pattern of proposed uses. While the official presentation of a plan prepared for adoption may be restricted to the incorporated area, the studies incident to the plan will have taken the entire urban area into the scope of investigations. Generally, the use patterns shown on the map include as many of the major use categories employed in analytical procedures as the scale of the presentation will permit. Very often in large metropolitan areas two presentations are necessary —one which shows the entire metropolitan area in generalized patterns, and another which shows the detailed categories by small subareas on a larger scale. This was done in the Detroit study. Thus while Figure 32 gives the generalized presentation of the preliminary land use plan for the met-

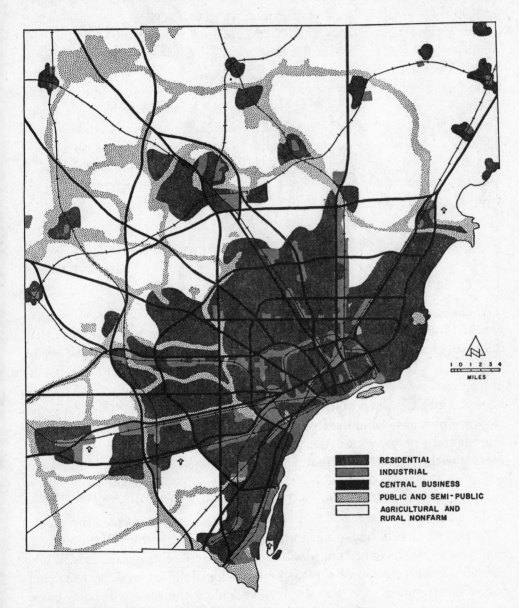

MILES

RESIDENTIAL
INDUSTRIAL
CENTRAL BUSINESS
PUBLIC AND SEMI-PUBLIC
AGRICULTURAL AND
RURAL NONFARM

FIGURE 32.   Illustrative Preliminary Land Use Plan for a Large Metropolitan Area. (*Source:* Adapted from 1953 Annual Report, Detroit Metropolitan Area Regional Planning Commission, 1954, frontispiece.)

LEGEND

■	INDUSTRIAL – MANUFACTURING
■	INDUSTRIAL – EXTRACTIVE
▥	COMMERCIAL
▦	RESIDENTIAL
▦	RECREATION
▦	PUBLIC AND SEMI-PUBLIC
▨	UTILITIES
▦	AIRPORTS
▦	AGRICULTURAL
▦	VACANT SUBDIVIDED
□	VACANT

FIGURE 33.   Land Use Map (left) and Preliminary Land Use Plan (right) of a Residential Community Within a Large Metropolitan Area. (Source: Detroit Metropolitan Area Regional Planning Commission, 1954.)

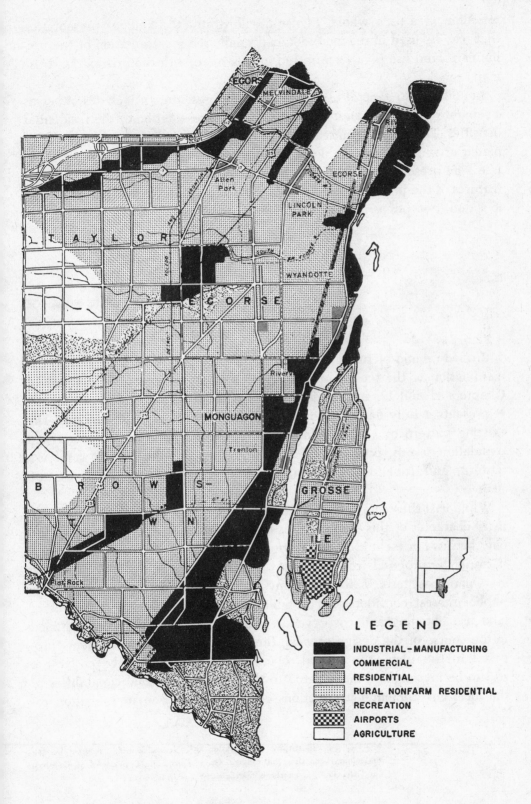

ECORSE

MELVINDALE

Allen Park

LINCOLN PARK

ECORSE

T A Y L O R

E C O R S E

WYANDOTTE

RiverV

MONGUAGON

Trenton

B R O W S-
T W N

GROSSE

STONY

ILE

Flat Rock

LEGEND

■	INDUSTRIAL-MANUFACTURING
▓	COMMERCIAL
░	RESIDENTIAL
⋅	RURAL NONFARM RESIDENTIAL
⋯	RECREATION
▦	AIRPORTS
☐	AGRICULTURE

ropolitan area as a whole, Figure 33 illustrates the kind of presentation that may be used in the more detailed small-area representation of the preliminary land use plan (contrasted in this plate with the existing land use map).

In addition to general use categories, the presentation includes either as a separate plate or as an overlay a graphic representation of the residential densities. This presents in scaled form the distribution of density types tabulated as illustrated in Table 37. Using the Greensboro Preliminary Land Use Plan presentation as an illustration, Figure 34 shows all nonresidential features of the plan, and Figure 35 shows the pattern of distribution of various density types as proposed in 1948.

LAND USE PLAN AND PUBLIC FINANCE

Firmed up and pictured in this form, the preliminary land use plan is the culmination of the tooling-up studies of Part II, the planning analyses of Chapters 11 and 12, and the synthesizing design steps of this last chapter. It presents a fully harmonized proposal for renewal and expansion of the existing pattern of land development in scale with future economic and population trends, fitted to the natural setting and the existing land use pattern, and functionally integrated with a preliminary transportation plan.

While it is thus complete as a scheme for land development, the preliminary character of this plan requires further emphasis. It is preliminary not only because of technical qualifications cited throughout Part III, but also because the proposals contained in this plan have still to be subjected to systematic cost tests. While "economy" along with health, safety, and other public interest considerations is built into the basic design principles of land use planning and cost-revenue relationships are carefully examined in the course of the design process, the costs of public improvements proposed in the plan—the capital, operating, and maintenance costs—are still to be investigated and related to the long-run financial capabilities of the local governmental jurisdictions concerned. Such an investigation re-

FIGURE 34. Illustrative Presentation of Nonresidential Features in the Preliminary Land Use Plan. (*Source:* Greensboro, N.C., Department of Planning, *Land Use Plan, Greensboro Metropolitan Area,* 1948.)

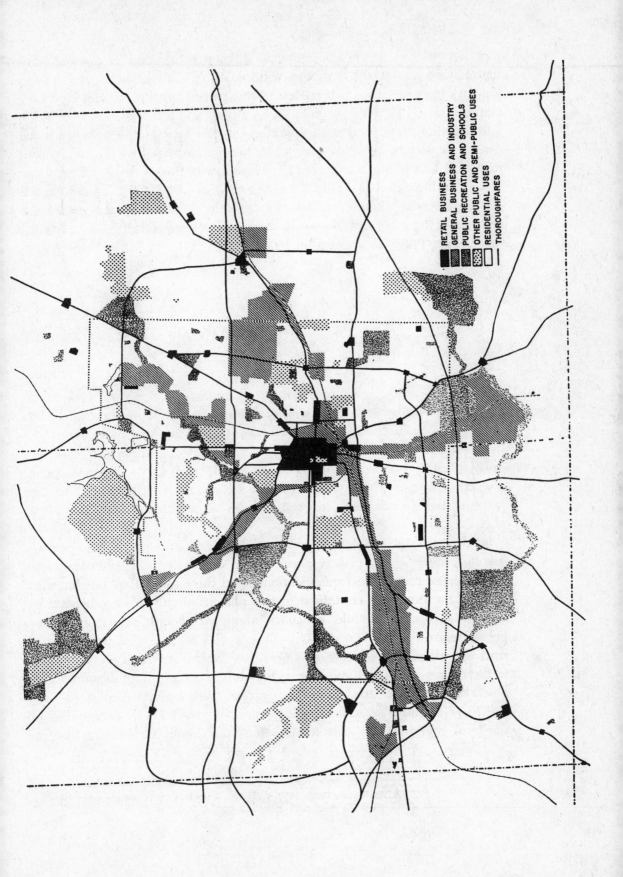

RETAIL BUSINESS
GENERAL BUSINESS AND INDUSTRY
PUBLIC RECREATION AND SCHOOLS
OTHER PUBLIC AND SEMI-PUBLIC USES
RESIDENTIAL USES
THOROUGHFARES

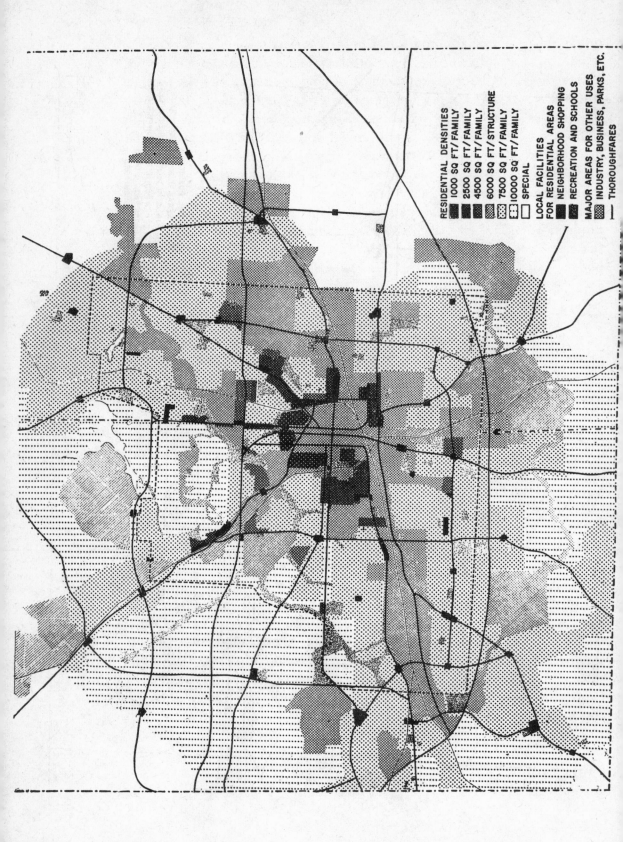

RESIDENTIAL DENSITIES
1000 SQ FT/ FAMILY
2500 SQ FT/ FAMILY
4500 SQ FT/ FAMILY
6000 SQ FT/ STRUCTURE
7500 SQ FT/ FAMILY
10000 SQ FT/ FAMILY
SPECIAL

LOCAL FACILITIES
FOR RESIDENTIAL AREAS
NEIGHBORHOOD SHOPPING
RECREATION AND SCHOOLS

MAJOR AREAS FOR OTHER USES
INDUSTRY, BUSINESS, PARKS, ETC.
THOROUGHFARES

quires special information on the debt structure and the revenue and expenditure trends in municipal finance. Although a local finance study is not normally within the purview of the planning agency's activities, such a study is an essential reference in determining how realistic the "price tags" are which go with public improvement proposals in the plan.

The comparison of public improvement costs with long-range financial capabilities may well necessitate adjustments in the preliminary land use plan. These investigations and adjustments are an essential part of the next steps in the review, refinement, and revision of the preliminary land use plan. As the comprehensive plan takes shape, one of the important end products is a financial program for the public improvements proposed in the plan. Such a program, of course, becomes the basis for the capital budget, a well-recognized means for effectuating the comprehensive plan.

PERSPECTIVES OF LAND USE PLANNING

We have been viewing the land use planning process in a technical perspective. Although excluded from the scope of this book, there are other important perspectives which warrant at least passing mention as they relate to the technical aspects of the process. These final observations concern citizen and official perspectives of land use planning.

Citizen Perspectives

It may be observed that the citizen view of land use planning traditionally has been vague, if indeed, he has recognized it as a process at all. Generally, it touches him either in a *fait accompli* situation such as "that new subdivision down the street" or "the slum clearance project on the northside," or in connection with some zoning issue that affects him or a friend. He is thus aware of land use planning in an effectuation context, either in connection with a developmental or a regulatory measure, and usually only

FIGURE 35. Illustrative Presentation of the Pattern of Proposed Residential Densities in the Preliminary Land Use Plan. (*Source:* Greensboro, N.C., Department of Planning, *Land Use Plan, Greensboro Metropolitan Area,* 1948.)

in an isolated segment of the whole and in one section of the city. It might be noted too that other aspects of city planning are frequently viewed by the citizen in this same kind of fuzzy perspective.

Partly because of the lack of understanding of the nature and purposes of city planning and the consequent public apathy to planning proposals, and partly because of a genuine interest in bringing planning decisions closer to the ultimate consumers of planning, city planners today are devoting increasing attention to civic relations. While older approaches were based largely on promotion through eye-catching reports and newspaper articles, much more positive and broadly conceived civic relations programs are being undertaken today. The objectives of these programs are generally threefold:

1. To develop an *understanding* among citizens and the organized private interests in the community of the principal physical problems and needs of the area and the role of urban planning in dealing with them and generally bringing about a more livable environment.
2. To cultivate the practice among civic leaders and civic organizations of *sharing in the planning* from the earliest study stages through the later review stages.
3. To provide media for *reporting* on planning studies and recommendations so that civic action programs have the benefit of studied analysis of the community's problems and needs.

In some of the more advanced approaches, the civic relations program is as carefully scheduled and timed as the technical program, with very specific civic relations activities keyed into particular stages of the technical program.

Much can be gained by tying the land use planning process into the civic relations program. General citizen advisory committees have been extremely effective in goal-definition assignments and in exercising review functions at strategic points in the course of land use planning studies, and special advisory committees composed of technical people have provided invaluable guidance on special technical problems. The value of these types of groups are attested to in the Detroit Metropolitan Area Regional Planning Commission's successful civic relations program. In a number of communities such groups as the Jaycee's and various women's service organizations have proved to be of valuable assistance in carrying out some types of surveys. These ways of bringing people into the land use planning process not only facilitate the work but broaden the base of participation and assist in achieving more widespread understanding of the full scope and purpose of land use planning.

Thus, under such a civic relations program, by the time the preliminary land use plan is developed, more widespread response and more intelligent reactions can be anticipated. As the detailed comprehensive planning studies are initiated and carried forward, an intensive review of the preliminary plan can be scheduled as a logical extension of earlier review activities. Review is accomplished through study committees of chamber of commerce, merchant association, real estate, homebuilder, and other special interest groups as well as through orientation meetings with civic clubs, neighborhood organizations, and similar general interest groups. Thus, element by element of the plan can be given careful review, the cumulative result of which is a picture of both the workable and unworkable features of the plan as viewed by these participating groups. The results of these review sessions become important reference sources in the work ahead in the refinement and revision of the preliminary land use plan.

Official Perspectives

What are the perspectives of the official groups in the urban area—the city council and the administrative officials of the one or more municipalities that may be involved? Obviously, they have a direct stake in the product of the land use planning process. If features of the plan are carried out as proposed, not only are many of the community facilities built and maintained by the city, but the whole pattern of development as effectuated through zoning, subdivision, urban renewal, and other public measures affects the cost-revenue balance that develops and thus the basic long-run municipal finance outlook as we have noted. Yet the way the planning process is viewed by the council, the mayor, or city manager and the various department heads is dependent upon the confidence these officials have in the planning agency which, in turn, is largely a function of human relations.

The perspectives of city officials thus can vary from one urban center to another. Some city councils are well versed in the basic purposes and principles of land use planning and have confidence in the land use plan as a guide to many of the decisions they must make, and some city councils have never heard of the land use plan or, if they have, it is vaguely recalled as a bit of "legal fluff" in the wording of planning and zoning enabling legislation. While mayors and city managers have more opportunity to become conversant with the general elements of the process, their confidence in land use planning tends to be a function of the extent to which the process gives attention to cost considerations, local developmental policies and similar factors and the extent to which it supplies answers to present-day problems they are facing. While department heads are less apt to take a broad view of land use planning and will generally be concerned with proposals that directly affect their primary functions, astute relations with these officials can contribute immeasurably to the effective implementation of the land use plan.

While coverage of the many complex elements of political behavior involved in keeping the land use planning process attuned to the broader governmental processes is beyond the scope of this discussion, it is evident that in the conduct, scheduling, and timing of land use planning studies, the city planner must be both sensitive to the necessities of maintaining effective rapport with all segments of the city hall family and appreciative of the contributions that each of these segments can make to the process. At the same time he must recognize and make use of the opportunities the land use planning process affords for bringing public officials into more studied contact with some of the most fundamental and critical problems of local government today.

With this glimpse of some of the nontechnical factors that impinge on land use planning, in conclusion we return to the underlying rationale of the approach followed in Part III. Land use planning has been viewed in the framework of a process embodied in the progressive planning concept. While the coverage of the process given here would appear to give it a straight-line sequence, in reality it follows a circular progression, with the preliminary land use planning studies constituting the initial cycle. The preliminary plan discussed in this chapter provides a generalized but studied view of future land development requirements. It offers a sufficient basis for the preparation and adoption of a zoning ordinance, for carrying forward public urban renewal programs, and for making a variety of day-to-day planning decisions. At the same time the culmination of this cycle furnishes the beginning point for the next more detailed round of planning studies eventually culminating in the adoption of a comprehensive plan. Beyond this are other cycles involving the reëxamination of economic and population trends, the restudy of land development requirements in the light of changing conditions, and as necessary, the revision of the comprehensive plan. Thus conceived, the process supplies the thread of continuity to land use planning and the basic framework for an orderly organization of the land use planning task.

index

391

974